INDO-PACIFIC

Emerging Powers, Evolving Regions and Global Governance

INDO-PACIFIC

Emerging Powers, Evolving Regions and Global Governance

Edited by
D. Gopal
Dalbir Ahlawat

INDO-PACIFIC
Emerging Powers, Evolving Regions and Global Governance
Edited by D. Gopal and Dalbir Ahlawat

First Published 2016

ISBN 978-93-5002-401-0

Published by
AAKAR BOOKS
28 E Pocket IV, Mayur Vihar Phase I, Delhi 110 091
Phone: 011 2279 5505 Telefax: 011 2279 5641
aakarbooks@gmail.com; www.aakarbooks.com

Laser Typeset at
Arpit Printographers, Delhi 110 032

Printed at
Mudrak, 30 A Patparganj, Delhi 110 091

To

Our Guru

Prof. R. Narayanan

Contents

Preface 9

Abbreviations 12

1. Towards a Strategic Triangle in the Indo-Pacific: India's Initiatives with China and the United States 15
   D. Gopal
2. Indo-Pacific Region: Evolving Strategic Contours 33
   Dalbir Ahlawat and Fred C. Smith
3. Multilateralism in the Indo-Pacific: Change or Continuity 60
   Pankaj K. Jha
4. Unpacking India-China Strategic Futures Using Causal Layered Analysis 75
   Jeanne Hoffman
5. Russia's Pivot to Asia: Constructing a Eurasian State in a Multipolar World 116
   Glenn Diesen
6. Indo-Pacific as an Emerging Geopolitical Construct: US Policy and Ramifications 142
   Chintamani Mahapatra and Vivek Mishra
7. Understanding Trade Competitiveness of the Indian Ocean Countries: A Statistical Appraisal 158
   Faisal Ahmed and M. Absar Alam
8. Governance in Federations: Agendas for Change in India and Australia 204
   RFI Smith

9. Maritime Security in the Indo-Pacific Region: String of Pearls and Maritime Silk Road — 230
Wang Dehua

10. India's Role in the Emerging Indo-Pacific Security Architecture — 244
Arvind Kumar

11. Indonesia-Australia Relations and the Indo-Pacific Developments — 255
Munmun Majumdar

12. Australia's Uranium Deal with India: Strategic, Economic or Simply *Ad Hoc*? — 272
Aakash Tolani

Bibliography — 294

Contributors — 305

Index — 311

Preface

The present global order is changing. By most accounts it is changing more rapidly than ever before, with a palpable shift in power from West to East—captured more graphically—from Atlantic to Indian and Pacific Oceans. In the ultimate analysis, what final shape the fast-changing global order will take is a subject of intense debate, contestation and speculation.

While some tendencies are seen in sharp relief, others are hazy and indistinct. For instance, what appears clear is the Western Europe—a traditional ally of the United States (NATO alliance partner) has departed its ways apparently forcing the latter in search of alternate stable partnerships if possible, alliance framework in the Indo-Pacific region.

The 'rise' of China in the Pacific Ocean and India in the Indian Ocean together are perceived by the US as an opportunity as much as a challenge to its hegemony. So, a better strategy for the US, it is believed, at least for the time being, appears to be 'India-in-and-China-out' while at the same time bolster up existing alliances and forge where necessary new partnerships in Asia and elsewhere. This is by no means an easy task given the economic inter-dependency of the US on China that makes the task not only complex but even daunting.

After centuries of humiliation, China for its part has found an opportune time to take its 'rightful' place in global affairs, mainly when the US after its harrowing fatigue of wars in Iraq and Afghanistan and attendant economic downturn is unintentionally creating a power vacuum, if not, anywhere else, at least in Asia.

Russia, the inheritor of power from the erstwhile Soviet Union, instead of considering itself as a European state after a rebuff from the Western world and threatened by a series of economic sanctions, is more inclined to project itself as a Eurasian power.

In all these, India is apprehensive of China's 'rise', attendant military build-up and renewed claims over territories in the East China Sea, South China Sea and border areas of India. No less is India apprehensive if not, reticent of the US with military networking initiative which India considers as a threat to peace in the region. In the short-run, riding on both the powers through robust economic relations with China on the one hand and technology imports from the US on the other, India seeks in the long-run to retain its so-called 'non-aligned' credentials by maintaining strategic autonomy while at the same time developing its own deterrence.

In the backdrop of these layers of strategic and related developments, this compendium—comprising twelve chapters very richly and well documented—is based on research and analysis by young scholars from both sides of the Indian Ocean who are in a sense a direct witness to the developments delineated above. Some of them have attempted an assessment of the role performance of the emerging powers, evolving regions, and the changes they are likely to usher in the global governance with specific focus on the Indo-Pacific region.

Based on an in-depth study, the compendium brings to fore the implications of the shift in power to the Indo-Pacific region—the vast and single geo-strategic arc and geo-economic realm spanning the eastern Pacific Ocean to the western Indian Ocean along the eastern coast of Africa. Encompassing half of the world's population and repository of vast natural resources with most important commercial water-ways criss-crossing the two-ocean region, the geo-strategic significance of the Indo-Pacific is undoubted. As a new constellation of economic and political power, the Indo-Pacific is undoubtedly influenced by the rise of both China and India rapidly dwarfing all other regional constructs and centres of trade, investment, security, competition and cooperation across the world.

Be that as it may, the Indo-Pacific power narrative is not about China and India alone. The book therefore devotes attention to the stakes of erstwhile super powers as well as middle powers of the region such as Australia, Indonesia and Japan who by all means are no less the stakeholders in the evolving regional construct.

In accomplishing the task of giving a final shape to this book project we, the Editors, were quite fortunate for the cooperation and support we received at each stage from different sources—to all of whom we owe our deep sense of gratitude.

First and foremost, we record our grateful and sincere thanks to Professor (Dr.) R. Narayanan, former Dean, School of International Studies, Jawaharlal Nehru University, and currently the Academic Advisor to the Australian Studies Programme of Indira Gandhi National Open University (IGNOU) for motivating us to undertake this joint research project. His purposive initiative has no doubt paved the way and has already facilitated forging bi-national collaboration between the Australian Studies Programme of IGNOU and the Department of Policing, Intelligence and Counter Terrorism, Macquarie University.

The book publication project has further contributed to organising a joint international conference supported by the two Universities. We thank the authorities of both the Universities for extending material support to hold a conference scheduled for November.

Needless to say the collaborative project would not have seen the light of day but for the ready and generous cooperation we received from the co-contributors to this compendium. We record our sincere thanks to all the authors. Also, we take this opportunity to thank the reviewers for their blind review and providing us with very constructive feedback. We are beholden to them.

As Editors, we are launching the publication in the hope that it proffers useful new insights as well as a rich bibliography for further in-depth research and study for graduate and postgraduate students engaged in studies and analyses on contemporary international relations.

Finally, we owe our thanks to our publisher Aakar Books for bringing out the publication in the time frame we had desired.

New Delhi
25 October 2015

D. Gopal
Dalbir Ahlawat

Abbreviations

ACIJK	:	ASEAN, China, India Japan, and Korea
ADIZ	:	Air Defence Identification Zone
ADMM	:	ASEAN Defence Ministers' Meeting
AEC	:	Asian Economic Community
AIIB	:	Asian Infrastructure Investment Bank
ALP	:	Australian Labour Party
ANZUS	:	Australia, New Zealand and United States
APEC	:	Asia-Pacific Economic Cooperation
ASEAN	:	Association of Southeast Asian Nations
BCIM	:	Bangladesh-China-India-Myanmar
BIMSTEC	:	Bay of Bengal Initiative for Multi-Sectoral Technical and Economic Cooperation
BJP	:	Bharatiya Janata Party
BRICS	:	Brazil, Russia, India, China and South Africa
CAF	:	Council for the Australian Federation
CCP	:	Chinese Communist Party
CEC	:	Changi Exhibition Centre
CECA	:	Comprehensive Economic Cooperation Agreement
CEPA	:	Comprehensive Economic Partnership Agreement
CICA	:	Conference on Interaction and Confidence-Building
CICIR	:	China Institute of Contemporary International Relations
CIPS	:	China International Payment System
CLA	:	Causal Layered Analysis
CNECA	:	Civil Nuclear Energy Cooperation Agreement
CNP	:	Comprehensive National Power
CNPC	:	China National Petroleum Corporation
COAG	:	Council of Australian Governments
DCL	:	Direct Communications Link
DIME	:	Diplomacy, Informational, Military and Economic

EAS : East Asia Summit
ECS : East China Sea
EEZ : Exclusive Economic Zone
EIO : Eastern Indian Ocean
ESPO : East Siberia-Pacific Ocean
GCC : Gulf Cooperation Council
GDP : Gross Domestic Product
GFC : Global Financial Crisis
GST : Goods and Services Tax
IIT : Intra-Industry Trade
IMF : International Monetary Fund
IONS : Indian Ocean Naval Symposium
IORA : Indian Ocean Rim Association
IORARC : Indian Ocean Rim Association for Regional Cooperation
IPEC : Indo-Pacific Economic Corridor
KK : Kundankulam
LMI : Lower Mekong Initiative
MSF : Military Support Facility
NATO : North Atlantic Treaty Organisation
NFSC : New Framework for Security Cooperation
LNG : Liquid Natural Gas
NPT : Nuclear Non-proliferation Treaty
NSG : Nuclear Suppliers Group
OECD : Organisation for Economic Cooperation and Development
PACOM : Pacific Command
PDI-P : Indonesian Democratic Party-Struggle
PIF : Pacific Island Forum
PLA : People's Liberation Army
PLAN : People's Liberation Army Navy
PPP : Purchasing Power Parity
PRC : People's Republic of China
RCA : Revealed Comparative Advantage
RCEP : Regional Comprehensive Economic Partnership
RFE : Russian Far East
ROO : Rules of Origin
RTA : Regional Trade Agreement

SAARC	:	South Asian Association for Regional Cooperation
SADC	:	South African Development Community
SCS	:	South China Sea
SEATO	:	Southeast Asia Treaty Organisation
SKV	:	Sakhalin–Khabarovsk–Vladivostok
SLOC	:	Sea Lines of Communication
SWIFT	:	Society for Worldwide Interbank Financial Telecommunication
TAPS	:	Tarapur Atomic Power Station
TCI	:	Trade Complementarity Index
TNI	:	Indonesian Armed Forces
TPP	:	Trans Pacific Partnership
TKR	:	Trans-Korean-Railway
TSR	:	Trans-Siberian Railway
UNCLOS	:	UN Convention on the Law of the Seas
UNHRC	:	United Nations Human Rights Committee
UPA	:	United Progressive Alliance
WPNS	:	West Pacific Naval Symposium

1

Towards a Strategic Triangle in the Indo-Pacific: India's Initiatives with China and the United States

D. Gopal

ABSTRACT

The evolving world order following the disintegration of the Soviet Union has resulted in new power dynamics which has not only diluted the NATO alliance networking but at the same time has enhanced Russia's belligerence. Even more, it has led to the rapid "rise" of China. What seems to be shaping today's world order is the hegemonic presumption of the US and the multiple challenges posed by a rising China. Perceptions of these developments vary from those who consider that China will pose a security and strategic challenge to US dominance to others who are of the view that both countries in the final analysis will accommodate each other's strategic interests that would contribute towards better global governance. Against these developments, India is thrust into uncharted waters where the choice for New Delhi appears to range from aligning to partnering or hedging or band-wagoning with one or the other powers.

The end of the Cold War gave rise to new strategic dynamics. The Western European states that worked under the strategic umbrella of the United States reoriented their policy postures and in the process strengthened the European Union framework. Moreover, disenchantment from the wars in Iraq and Afghanistan and later the so-called "Arab Spring" put heavy economic pressure as well as adverse domestic public opinion in the Western countries that ultimately gave rise to a fracture in the North Atlantic Treaty

Organisation (NATO). Even though the United States emerged as the only super power, with the advent of the 21st century, it witnessed the first-ever attack on its soil. This resulted in the United States getting embroiled in the wars in Afghanistan and Iraq and currently recuperating from the war fatigue. At the same time, Russia that was lured by the European Union (EU) and NATO membership could not pass the test to assimilate and forgo its own identity, became a rebel and ultimately faced sanctions and castigation. This further deepened the chasm between the US and EU mainly on account of EU's dependence on Russian energy supplies. China that had been re-orienting its strategic and economic policies reached to a point to establish unipolar order in the Asia-Pacific region and challenge the international order and institutions. Certainly, this posed serious multiple challenges to China's neighbours in the Asia-Pacific region and no less to the United States which since the end of the Second World War had acted as a guarantor of peace in the Asia-Pacific region.

Based on the above developments, new strategic calculations and dynamics have emerged not only to challenge US hegemony, but also to contain a rising China through building new alliances and partnerships. A major objective of this paper is to monitor these developments and assess the strategic challenges and options for a traditionally "non-aligned" India in the evolving geopolitical construct of the Indo-Pacific.

Strategic Challenges in the Indo-Pacific Region

The United States in its 2015 *National Military Strategy* document while discussing the global strategic environment, without mentioning China by name, states: "[S]ome states...are attempting to revise key aspects of the international order and are acting in a manner that threatens our national security interests". These actions "are adding tensions to the Asia-Pacific region". Specifically, in contravention of international law, China claims "nearly the entire South China Sea". Much against public opinion seekingto resolve this issue amicably, China "has responded with aggressive land reclamation efforts that will allow it to position military forces astride vital international sea lanes". For this, the US intends to pursue an "integrated approach composed of three National

Military Objectives: to deter, deny, and defeat state adversaries" and strengthen the global network of allies and partners. Further, it proposes that "[if] deterrence fails… the military will be capable of defeating a regional adversary in a large-scale, multi-phased campaign while denying the objectives… or imposing unacceptable costs". Therefore, the US appears to have developed phased strategic contours as to what is permissible and what may constitute crossing red lines and may be subject to "imposing unacceptable cost".[1]

In May 2015, China released its ninth Defence White Paper entitled *China's Military Strategy* which outlined a new military strategy that underlines a more "active defence posture". In this regard, the Paper highlights challenges at two levels, one at regional level referred to as "some of its offshore neighbours take provocative actions and reinforce their military presence on China's reefs and islands that they have illegally occupied" and the other of "external countries…busy meddling in South China Sea affairs". Considering the evolving strategic challenges, China envisages winning the "local wars under informatised conditions" and the external wars by expanding "offshore waters defence" with "open seas protection".[2]

In response to the US sketched red lines, China has demonstrated a firm but conciliatory approach to pursue its strategic goals not only in its sphere of influence but also out of the region. To counterbalance both these fronts, China responded by stating: "In line with the evolving form of war and national security situation, the basic point for PMS [Preparation for Military Strategy] will be placed on winning informationised local wars, highlighting maritime military struggle and maritime PMS".

Against this backdrop, the bilateral trade between the US and China reaching US$590 billion in 2014 also supports interdependency based on China's holding of US$ 1.2 trillion in US Treasury bonds. Furthermore, in the post-Cold War period, no doubt, China has become the number two country in the world, it shares UN Security Council membership with the US, G20 and East Asian Summit. However, in other global institutions such as the International Monetary Fund and World Bank where the US has an advantage, China having been disenchanted with the activities of these institutions has initiated alternative global institutions such as Shanghai Cooperation Organisation and Asian Infrastructure Investment Bank (AIIB).The popularity of the AIIB has been unprecedented, not only because major Asian countries including Australia have responded positively. In March 2015, the United Kingdom decided to apply to join the AIIB, becoming thereby the first major Western country to do so. However, this action of the UK attracted sharp reaction from the US. A US government official expressing anguish stated: "We are wary about a trend towards constant accommodation of China, which is not the best way to engage a rising power".[3] In addition, transcontinental initiatives such as BRICS (Brazil, Russia, India, China and South Africa) and extending financial support to developing countries without the addendum of Western style strings such as promotion of democracy or respect for human rights have certainly placed China at the centre stage in the evolving world order.

Although the US still enjoys supremacy over China in the defence sector—in its alliance system, defence manufacturing, force deployment, strategic presence and experience in fighting wars in multi-theatres—no doubt indicates US strategic depth, but in the changing strategic and security environment, the focus seems to be shifting towards the high technological wars. In this regard, over a period of a decade or so, China has demonstrated unprecedented progress in this sector, mainly with the public display in September 2015 of the Dongfeng DF-21D, an anti-ship ballistic missile, while commemorating the 70th anniversary of Japan's surrender during the Second World War.[4] The uniqueness of this missile is that it has a target range of over 1,450 kilometres and the projected speed of ten times faster than the speed of sound. After its launch in the orbit and re-entry in the atmosphere, it is non-traceable mainly because of its hypersonic speed that is why it is popularly called "carrier killer". According to military experts: "This is the missile that really does potentially encroach on US capability to deploy military power close to Chinese shores".[5] In a sense, the strategic advantage that the US had with its possession of multi-aircraft carriers has now been neutralised thanks to China's development of advanced missile system.[6] Moreover, China's quiet pursuit of war machinery adds weight to its publicly stated strategic contours such as Anti-Access Area Denial (A2/AD), second island chain of defence, creation of Air Defence Identification Zone (ADIZ) and its claims over the South China Sea islands.

Yet another new dynamics that is mentioned in the 2015 Defence White Paper is in regard to Russia. Perhaps to outweigh the US alliance system and partnerships in the Indo-Pacific region, the document emphasises that "China's armed forces will further their exchanges and cooperation with the Russian military within the framework of the comprehensive strategic partnership of coordination between China and Russia, and foster a comprehensive, diverse and sustainable framework to promote military relations in more fields and at more levels".[7] There appears to be a convergence of convenience in the backdrop of Russia being rebuffed by the West and the US in the recent past. Moreover, at the recently held UN General Assembly session in September 2015, Chinese President Xi Jinping in his address while critically commenting on the existing inequality among the states, expressed solidarity with the developing countries. He stated that "the law of the jungle leaves the weak at the mercy of the strong" and to come out of this perplexity "new type of international relations based on win-win cooperation" is required.[8]

This poses a dilemma to the US as to when responding to a rising China, should it counter, or accommodate China. Currently, opinions diverge among the US strategists. A section opines that before China reaches a high point, "the United States might need to demonstrate its capabilities early and often as a way of undermining China's confidence in its perceived superiority".[9]

To counter any US initiative, China's response could possibly be the twenty-four character strategy coined by Deng Xiaoping which is to "watch and observe calmly, secure our own position, behave with confidence and patience, hide our capacities and bide our time, be good at keeping a low profile, never play the leader".[10] This calculated orientation has its genesis in the works of Chinese strategist Sun Tzu who stated centuries back: "All warfare is based on deception".[11] This consideration is particularly important as the Chinese leadership often makes references to the "century of humiliation", the People's Liberation Army (PLA) as heir to the ancient Chinese legacy and frequent references to battles fought in the past. Therefore, the historic strategic treatise such as *The Art of War* and the *Seven Military Classics of Ancient China* are still considered as reference points. This is further underlined in the People's Liberation Army's publication: *Analysis of China's Strategic Culture* which goes at length to contrast Chinese strategic culture with the Western strategic culture.[12]

Strategic Calculations Between US and China

While underlining the security and strategic challenges arising from China, the United States in its 2015 *National Military Strategy* document nevertheless mentions its reconciliatory approach and postures towards China by stating: "We support China's rise and encourage it to become a partner for greater international security". Similarly, China too in its 2015 *Defence White Paper* highlights its "active defence posture" through engagement:

> China's armed forces will continue to foster a new model of military relationship with the US armed forces that conforms to the new model of major-country relations..., strengthen defence dialogues, exchanges and cooperation, and improve the CBM mechanism for the notification of major military activities as well as the rules of behavior for safety of air and maritime encounters, so as to strengthen mutual trust, prevent risks and manage crises.[13]

Even though they emphasise the apparent strategic competition between them, nevertheless they do underscore on the basis of the mutually growing economic interdependency that they are on a convergence continuum.

No doubt, China's 'rise' has been misconstrued by both the US and the other Indo-Pacific states based on the exaggerated fear that China would pull the regional states into its orbit in a dependent relationship. However, during the Asian Financial Crisis of 1997-98 as well as in the Global Financial Crisis of 2008-09 China's track record proved otherwise as China instead of exploiting the crises to its advantages offered very purposive regional bail out packages devoid of conditionality elevating thereby its status as a 'good global citizen'. No less than the president of the US gave credence to the term G2 coined by C. Fred Bergsten paving the way for both countries to work together to set the terms of the regional order, and towards this objective the United States should provide for the demands of a rising China.[14] However, because of the concerns expressed by alliance partners like Japan and other major states like India in the region the US retracted somewhat from its position.

No doubt, China draws its lineage from the Middle Kingdom and tributary system and did not "accept the need to Westernise itself completely, but sought to find a stable and workable blend of modernising reforms and 'Chinese characteristics'".[15] Notwithstanding these reservations, Beijing participated in most of the international institutions and accepted international rules and norms at operational and functional levels, however at the ideational level maintained some reservations and supported a 'progressive status quo'. At the ideational level, while differing with the US and other Western values, China supported the Asian values such as traditional view of sovereignty, non-intervention, strong government structure, communitarian system with limited individual rights, along with many of its neighbours. In a sense, China supports the Confucian approach that has its genesis in "hierarchy and band-wagoning than to balance of power".[16] Given its historical legacy some even argue that alienating China could prove disastrously counterproductive. As Zbigniew Brzezinski states: "We cannot have that relationship if we only dictate or threaten and condemn those who disagree".[17]

Stretching this line of argument further, others are of the view that China's rise over the last thirty years, "certainly looks peaceful compared to that of most other recent great power arrivistes"—countries such as Germany, Japan and Russia challenged the status quo by first building up military might and then "invaded and occupied their neighbours" as a demonstration of 'big power' status, whereas China without serious threat to its neighbours or the world order only supports 'progressive status quo'.[18] Towards such an objective, Chinese leadership has time and again been making public statements underlining that it is neither a contestant nor even an aspirant for world leadership; instead it supports a democratic, multi-polar world system with multiple leadership focused on peace and development.[19] On its own volition China has indicated that it is neither in an arms race nor in military build-up with the US rather its major focus is on economic development. The most tangible example of this being that notwithstanding the US and its NATO alliance partners passing through serious GFC, instead of cashing in on the weakness, China served as a saviour of the Western world as well as Japan, its arch rival. In this case, if China emerges as a world leader by default, it is more in a positive sense than as achallenger to the US hegemony or a 'fellow competitor' rather than an 'enemy competitor'. This means that "it would like to keep US leadership in place at least for the time being as a prop for its ongoing domestic development".[20]

According to most of the prognoses, even if in the future China intends to challenge the US or disrupt the global order, it is unlikely that it will be on a collision course or on a confrontational approach towards the US. Rather China would prefer to build a group of countries who share its vision of a multi-polar world, which among others would include influential countries like Russia, India, Brazil, France and Germany. If such polarisation does not accrue, it is more likely that China will continue with the current arrangements in the foreseeable future.

Current US posturing suggests that it would prefer strengthening its alliance system, and find new partners or even, if need be, adopt a conciliatory approach to engage instead of confronting China militarily. As Zbigniew Brzezinski comments: "Engaging with China in a dialogue regarding regional stability would not only help reduce the possibility of US-Chinese conflicts but also diminish the probability of miscalculation".[21] It appears in the near future, instead of challenging China, the US could be limited to probing China such as on the issue of Taiwan, supporting Japan's anti-China overtures as an alliance partner or as currently the US undertaking the Malabar exercise with Japan and India, and its intention to enter in the territorial waters of the islands claimed by China in the South China Sea. To such probes, it appears, Beijing will have a calculated response, along the lines outlined by the Chinese leader Fan Changlong, the Vice-Chairman of China's Central Military Commission (CMC) which includes scaling down its rhetoric, not use force "recklessly" for resolving disputes and propose joint defence drills with ASEAN countries to brace for unplanned and accidental military encounters at sea.[22] These conflicting policy pronouncements together with unpredictable foreign policy postures in recent times, critics indicate an apparent lack of "clear and coherent long-term fundamental national objectives, diplomatic philosophy and long-term or secular grand strategy" of China.[23]

Given these uncertainties in terms of policy objectives as well as policy options on the part of both the US and China, a large number of the countries of the Indo-Pacific region themselves are at a loss in evolving an appropriate strategy to face their security challenges in their immediate neighbourhood. No wonder their options range from alliance with the US, bilateral and trilateral security arrangements among themselves and with the US and hedging, band-wagoning to reconciliation with the People's Republic of China.

India-China Strategic Challenges

Against these uncertainties arising out of the shifting power dynamics, what opportunities and dilemmas obtain for India to craft and chart out its mid- to long-term strategic framework that would enable New Delhi to address its anxieties and aspirations effectively is a question that is analysed in this concluding section and alongside some prognoses are proffered. There is no gainsaying that the challenges faced by India are both real and daunting. Yet India's Ministry of Defence in its Annual Report of 2014-15 emphatically stated: "Guided by the principle of building strength through the principles of strategic autonomy and self-reliance, India seeks to enhance her own capabilities and also to pursue a constructive engagement with neighbours and partner countries in the regional and global community to promote peace and stability".[24] Crafting a coherent policy against the stated objective is by no means an easy task because it has to take into consideration a variety of factors including importantly the policy orientations and strategic equations of other big, middle and small powers vying for strategic advantage as well as competition in the shifting power dynamics.

True, China and India have existed side by side since time immemorial but mostly remained immune from each other. It was only after India's independence in 1947 and revolution in China in

1949, that the two countries came closer and supported peaceful co-existence and committed to the ideal of 'Hindi-Chini-Bhai-Bhai' (Indian and Chinese are brothers). But the 1962 Chinese incursion in Indian soil led to trust-deficit and show of force on the border. Since then both countries have remained circumspect and suspicious of each other and have been engaged in counter-balancing each other.

If Samuel P. Huntington was alive, he would have certainly cited the Indo-Chinese conflict as an instance of 'clash of civilisations'.[25] In reality however it is more a clash of similar aspirations, interests and geo-strategic calculations and how these clashes impact on bilateral and regional issues. Since 1948, China has formally resolved territorial and border disputes with its twelve neighbouring states through a concessionary diplomatic approach.[26] But India remains the only exception, mainly because India is considered as the competitor 'next door' that could pose a challenge to China's 'big power' ambition. India hedges its relationship with China by engaging with East Asian powers and the US to check China's rise and maintain a strategic balance. In a sense, the security dilemma "stems from the impossibility of gauging with certainty the intentions of another state".[27]

After eighteen rounds of talks, the most recently held in March 2015, between the Special Representatives of India and China on the boundary question, the issue remains unresolved and the usual rhetoric of maintaining "peace and tranquillity in the border areas" is being ceremonially repeated in press statements.[28] Strategists have also noticed a shift in China's postures on other geo-strategic issues. This was evident with China's claim over the area south of Tawang-Arunachal Pradesh. Beijing appears to have purposely kept the boundary issue alive to deter India from joining the US and to discourage India from challenging China's influence in the region. Additionally, China has shifted its policy on Kashmir to give legitimacy to the Pakistan Occupied Kashmir, with its intentions to link Gwadar Port facility in Pakistan to its western states through road and railway networks.[29] Moreover, to give credence to Pakistan's stance on Indian Kashmir as a 'disputed territory', China continues to fund projects in the region, including upgrading the Karakoram Highway, the Bunji and Bash dams, and the Kohala and Neelam-Jhelam hydroelectric projects, all actions that "undermine China's neutrality in the India-Pakistan dispute over Kashmir".[30]

A more basic issue that bedevils relations between the two countries is China's "all weather" friendship with Pakistan. Beijing continues to bolster Islamabad's military capabilities and assists in supplying nuclear reactors. Some geo-strategists argue that China's policy initiatives vis-à-vis the Indian Ocean have also exacerbated India's apprehensions. China's so-called 'string of pearls' strategy of developing sea ports such as Gwadar in Pakistan, Hambantota in Sri Lanka, Sittwe in Myanmar, Chittagong in Bangladesh and entering into strategic relations with India's neighbours in the Indian Ocean are construed as deliberate and calculated moves.[31]

China's response, however, is that its ambition is that of a "peaceful rise" and asserts that the "string of pearls" and "21st century maritime silk road" are merely intended to facilitate further trade with India, which, in recent years, has exceeded a substantial US$70 billion. Notwithstanding this, China's overall rise and 'muscling up' in its bilateral relations with India serve as a challenge to New Delhi, a challenge of just how it is to respond to China's rising power.

Taking note of increasing Chinese hawkish posturing as well as the tightening of relationship between China and Pakistan, Indian military strategic doctrines are evolving to a "two-front war" and "cold start" against a collective threat posed by both China and Pakistan. Moreover, to counter China's motorised high altitude divisions and missiles positioned towards India, the Indian Ministry of Defence took some tangible initiatives, such as approval of a five-year plan with a budget to the tune of US$13 billion. To overcome infrastructural deficiencies and to establish a more credible deterrence, India decided in November 2011 to deploy a regiment of *BrahMos* surface-to-surface supersonic cruise missiles in Arunachal Pradesh, "making it India's first offensive tactical missile development against China".[32]

Even if only to demonstrate its 'big power' credentials, India enhanced its deterrence capabilities by test-firing the *Agni*-V and VI intercontinental ballistic missiles, which, with a range of over

5,000 kilometres, have capability to reach major Chinese cities. These actions demonstrate a definite shift in India's traditional approach of 'dissuasion' to one of credible deterrence. India has also taken tangible steps to modernise its navy, by budgeting for the acquisition of new submarines and aircraft carriers and becoming a net security provider in the Indian Ocean region.

Overall, what is emerging in the Asian region is a "China threat" perception, mainly due to China's own claims and actions over land and maritime jurisdictions. These trends also indicate that Asia-Pacific countries are more likely to "balance China instead of accepting Chinese primacy in a hierarchical tributary state system".[33] This opens an opportunity for India to further strengthen its 'Act East' strategic relations with 'China-wary' countries.[34] Considering India's overall development and increasing strategic posturing, Asia's small and medium powers identify leverage in India to counter balance a rising China. In this regard, most ASEAN countries view India's naval growth as a promising development. This posturing makes India's engagement with Southeast Asia somewhat easier than that experienced by China.

In response to China's hegemonic perceptions in the Pacific region, countries like Australia, Japan, Vietnam and the US have recognised the importance of India's growing influence in the South Asian and Indian Ocean regions, while India has recognised its potential to work more closely with these countries, forging a convergence of interests giving rise to bilateral strategic relationships. Security agreements between India and major Pacific countries are not only linked to address issues of terrorism, piracy and safeguarding sea lines of communication, but also to help shape the shifting balance of power in the region. Just as China established the so-called "string of pearls", in a sense, India has developed its own parallel strategy: the so-called "necklace of diamonds".[35]

Commenting on India's signing of security agreements and its inclination towards the US presence in the region, a Chinese expert, Dai Bing, asserts: "For the foreseeable future ... a 'cold war' between the two countries is increasingly likely...".[36] In the process, "New Delhi's perspective of China's strategic encirclement of India, and Beijing's fears of Indian attempts to limit China's influence in South and Southeast Asia, as well as its power projection into the Indian

Ocean, override their formulaic statements of shared interests as partners in strengthening a multipolar world".[37]

India's Strategic Balancing Role

After the disintegration of the Soviet Union, India taking cognisance of the new geo-strategic landscape followed a pragmatic approach by diluting its non-aligned policy to build a new partnership with the US. However, it was only after its 1998 nuclear tests that India justified its detonation as an act to deter the 'China threat', as well as to show displeasure with China's assistance to Pakistan's nuclear programme, that a broader regional strategic framework with the US was sought.[38] The US, in its efforts to counter a rising China and finding limited advantage in supporting Pakistan after withdrawal from Afghanistan, found it appropriate to claim India as an ally and avail opportunities that an emerging India offered. This started with the US government's shift on its stance on Kashmir and "advised Islamabad to forget about history and see ahead".[39]

India reciprocated the US gestures by extending strong support for its fight against international terrorism, particularly after the 9/11 attacks. The changing perceptions of each country towards the other reflected a substantial positive shift in relations, taking down barriers that had previously existed. As against China's rise, the US appreciated India's role in the region, acting as a buffer and Indian Ocean chokepoint for China's ambitions, further prescribed an elevated role for India in the Indo-Pacific region. Increasing proximity further resulted in signing a Defence Framework Agreement in 2005 and Civil Nuclear Cooperation Agreement in 2008. These two landmark agreements aimed to provide assistance to India's civilian nuclear programme, notwithstanding resistance from China, changed the regional power dynamics.[40] A 10-year defence accord further strengthened the relationship and opened new vistas that included technology transfer, weapons production, and missile defence cooperation, ultimately resulting in India being awarded status of "a responsible state with advanced nuclear technology", providing India *de facto* recognition as a nuclear weapons state.[41]

The election of US President Barack Obama provided further impetus to the bilateral relationship, couched in phrases that portrayed India as an "indispensable power" and a "leader in Asia".[42] This development triggered the first round of the India-US strategic dialogue in 2009, in a sense "institutionalising" formal bilateral consultations on China. Obama also made two visits to India, unprecedented for a US president, and assured US support to India's membership of the UN Security Council, non-proliferation regimes, export of advanced military technology and weapons to India. Underlining the strengthening partnership with India, Obama stated that: "We support India's role as a regional provider of security and its expanded participation in critical regional institutions. We see a strategic convergence with India's "Act East" policy and our continued implementation of the rebalance to Asia and the Pacific".[43]

Although the 1998 nuclear tests by India and Pakistan attracted international criticism and sanctions, China categorically criticised only India, stating that it was "infuriated and deeply hurt, not as much by the tests themselves" but by the justification that India construed China as a "threat".[44] The *People's Daily* noted that the US "needs to rely on India to restrict China. India needs to show its value to the United States by flexing its muscle towards China so that it could gain US military support and help raise its international status".[45] According to these Chinese sources, in the past China "tended to dismiss India as a peer competitor...Beijing is now paying increasing attention to India's drive for a great power status through diplomatic initiatives and a military buildup".[46]

India's development of credible deterrence, strengthening relations with the US, and hedging towards the Asia-Pacific region has resulted in China moderating its tone and recognising New Delhi's elevated status. Beijing now apparently sees that its diplomatic campaign to isolate New Delhi is only pushing India into the US camp. Realising this, Chinese strategists then adopted a reconciliatory approach by engaging India directly and dissuading it from joining the US, Japan, Vietnam or any other 'China-wary' country. Moreover, while expressing rapprochement with India, China forewarned India to be cautious of the ill-conceived US rhetoric of the US-India relationship, as democratic and natural allies, to "foil Western conspiracies aimed at dividing China and India".[47] To avoid such division, Chinese strategists coaxed India to be a partner architect in sculpting of the 21st century as the Asian century.

Concluding Observations

Considering the predicament in which India is placed, as one observer says: "New Delhi will persist with its policy of engaging with both China and the US, without antagonising either side".[48] From a positive perspective for India, in the short-term, it finds this to be an opportune time, when it can ride both tides (China and the US) while navigating the channels—extracting the most from both big powers while still playing the role of a regional balancer. However, in the medium-to-long-term, India will need to come out with its own security and strategic doctrine, so that through this transparency, it will be possible to pursue its interests with like-minded countries.

NOTES

1. *The National Military Strategy of the United States of America 2015*.<http://www.jcs.mil/Portals/36/Documents/Publications/2015_National_Military_Strategy.pdf> accessed 1 October 2015.
2. *China's Military Strategy* (Beijing: Ministry of National Defence, The People's Republic of China, 26 May 2015). <http://eng.mod.gov.cn/Press/2015-05/26/content_4586805_6.htm> accessed 5 October 2015.
3. Tyler Durden, "US Attacks 'Closest Ally' UK for 'Constant Accommodation' With China", *Global Research*, 29 March 2015. <http://www.globalresearch.ca/us-attacks-closest-ally-uk-for-constant-accommodation-with-china/5439249> accessed 15 October 2015.
4. James Hardy and Richard D. Fisher Jr, "China previews new ballistic missiles in practices for 3 September parade", *Jane's Defence Weekly (IHS)*, 30 August 2015. <http://www.janes.com/article/53896/china-previews-new-ballistic-missiles-in-practices-for-3-september-parade> accessed 15 October 2015.
5. "An Eastern Wind China's Carrier-Killer Ready for Its Close-Up", *The American Interest*, 2 September 2015. <http://www.the-american-interest.com/2015/09/02/chinas-carrier-killer-ready-for-its-close-up/> accessed 5 October 2015.
6. Jonah Bennett, Did China's New Assassin Mace Missile Just Make Aircraft Carriers as Obsolete as Battleships? *The Daily Caller*, 9 April 2015. <http://dailycaller.com/2015/09/04/did-chinas-new-assassin-mace-missile-just-make-aircraft-carriers-as-obsolete-as-battleships/#ixzz3obVliSrc> accessed on 4 October 2015.

7. *China's Military Strategy* (Beijing: Ministry of National Defence, The People's Republic of China, 26 May 2015). <http://eng.mod.gov.cn/Press/2015-05/26/content_4586805_6.htm> accessed 5 October 2015.
8. China engages with the world, Spaceship China, 1 October 2015. <http://spaceshipchina.com/2015/10/01/china-engages-with-the-world/> accessed 5 October 2015.
9. Thomas G. Mahnken, *Secrecy and Stratagem: Understanding Chinese Strategic Culture* (Sydney: Lowy Institute for International Policy, February 2011), p. 10.
10. Cited in Ross Terrill, *The New Chinese Empire* (New York: Basic Books, 2003), p. 256.
11. Sun Tzu, Samuel B. Griffith, *The Art of War*, trans. (Oxford: Oxford University Press, 1980), p. 66.
12. Gong Yuzhen, *Analysis of China's Strategic Culture* (Beijing: Military Science Press, 2002).
13. *China's Military Strategy (Beijing: Ministry of National Defence: The People's Republic of China, May 2015.* <http://eng.mod.gov.cn/Database/WhitePapers/> accessed 2 October 2015.
14. David Kampf, "Moving the G-2 Forward", *Foreign Policy Association*, 14 May 2009.<http://www.fpa.org/topics_info2414/topics_info_show.htm?doc_id=912530> accessed 5 October 2015.
15. Barry Buzan, "China in International Society: Is 'Peaceful Rise' Possible?", *The Chinese Journal of International Politics*, Vol. 3, 2010, p. 13.
16. David Kang, "Hierarchy, Balancing and Empirical Puzzles in Asian International Relations", *International Security*, Vol. 28, No. 3, 2003-4, pp. 165-80.
17. *Congressional Record, Proceedings and Debates of the 108th Congress*, Volume 149, Part 2325 (Washington, DC: United States Government Printing Office, 2003, p. 31866.
18. Buzan, n. 15, p. 15.
19. Read the full text of Xi Jinping's first UN address, *Quartz*, 29 September 2015. <http://qz.com/512886/read-the-full-text-of-xi-jinpings-first-un-address/> accessed 2 October 2015; Hu Jintao, "Build Towards a Harmonious World of Lasting Peace and Common Prosperity", 15 September 2005. <http://www.un.org/webcast/summit2005/statements15/china050915eng.pdf> accessed 2 October 2015.
20. Buzan, n. 15, p. 21.
21. Zbigniew Brzezinski, "As China Rises, A New US Strategy: We Should Embrace Russia, japan and South Korea as We Seek to Manage the Rise of China", *The Wall Street Journal*, 14 December 2011. <http://www.wsj.com/articles/SB10001424052970203413304577088813 49304486> accessed 30 September 2015.
22. "Won't use force 'recklessly' in South China Sea, says top Chinese

official", *The Times of India*, 17 October 2015. <http://timesofindia.indiatimes.com/world/china/Wont-use-force-recklessly-in-South-China-Sea-says-top-Chinese-official/articleshow/49431459.cms> accessed 18 October 2015.

23. Shi Yinhong, *The Rising China: Essential Disposition, Secular Grand Strategy, and Current Prime Problems* (Washington, DC: Sasakawa Peace Foundation USA, 12 February 2002). <https://www.spf.org/publication/upload/178474a17de.pdf> accessed 1 October 2015.
24. *Annual Report 2014-2015* (New Delhi: Ministry of Defence, Government of India), p. 2. <http://www.mod.nic.in/writereaddata/AR1415.pdf> accessed 15 September 2015.
25. Samuel P. Huntington, "The Clash of Civilisations?", *Foreign Affairs*, Vol. 72, No. 3, 1993, pp. 22-49.
26. Hongi Hongyi, "Explaining Chinese Solutions to Territorial Disputes with Neighbour States", *Chinese Journal of International Politics*, Vol. 2, No. 4, 2009, pp. 487-523. China signed border agreements with Kazakhstan (April 1994), Kyrgyzstan (July 1996), Tajikistan (August 1999), Vietnam (December 1999), Russia (May 1991), Myanmar (October 1960), Nepal (October 1961), North Korea (October 1962), Mongolia (December 1962), Pakistan (March 1963), Afghanistan (November 1963), Lao PDR (October 1991).
27. Robert Jervis, "Cooperation Under the Security Dilemma", *World Politics*, Vol. 30, No. 2, 1978, pp. 167-214.
28. *18th Round of Talks Between the Special Representatives of India and China on the Boundary Question* (New Delhi: Ministry of External Affairs, 24 March 2015). <http://mea.gov.in/press- releases.htm?dtl/25002/18th+Round+of+Talks+between+the+ Special+ Representatives+of+India+and+China+on+the+Boundary + Question>accessed 6 May 2015.
29. Salman Masood and Declan Walsh, "Xi Jinping Plans to Fund Pakistan", *The New York Times*, 21 April 2015. <http://www.nytimes.com/2015/04/22/world/asia/xi-jinping-plans-to-fund-pakistan.html?_r=0> accessed 5 June 2015.
30. Cited in Chietigj Bajpaee, "China-India Relations: Regional Rivalry Takes the World Stage", *China Security*, Vol. 6, No. 2, 2010, p. 5.
31. David Brewster, *India's Ocean: The Story of India's Bid for Regional Leadership* (London: Routledge, 2014), p. 32.
32. "India to Deploy Brahmos Cruise Missiles to Counter China", *Asian Defence News*, <http://www.asian-defence.net/2012/02/india-to-deploy-brahmos-cruise-missiles.html> accessed 2 May 2015.
33. Mohan Malik, "India Balances China", *Asian Politics and Policy*, Vol. 4, No. 3, 2012, p. 346.
34. Danielle Rajendram, *India's New Asia-Pacific Strategy: Modi Acts East* (Sydney: Lowy Institute for International Policy, December 2014.

35. "Why India is pursuing military strength?", *People's Daily Online*, 20 August 2009.
36. Dai Bing, "India building a security barrier against China", *China.org.cn*, 8 February 2010. <http://www.china.org.cn/opinion/2010-02/08/content_19387164.htm> accessed 28 March 2015.
37. Francine R. Frankel, "The breakout of China-India strategic rivalry in Asia and the Indian Ocean", *Journal of International Affairs*, Vol. 64, No. 2, 2011, pp. 1-2.
38. George Fernandes, "China is enemy no 1: George", *The Indian Express*, 4 May 1998. <http://expressindia.indianexpress.com/ie/daily/19980504/12450024.html> accessed 20 June 2015.
39. Shabana Fayyaz, "Kashmir Conflict: US Post-Cold War Perspective", *Pakistan Journal of American Studies*, No. 15, Spring/Fall 1997, p. 76.
40. Condoleezza Rice, "Promoting the National Interest", *Foreign Affairs*, Vol. 79, No. 1, January-February 2000, p. 56.
41. *Jane's Sentinel: Country Risk Assessments, South Asia* (Surrey: HIS Global Limited), Issue 27, 2011, p. 285.
42. Merle David Kellerhals Jr, "India an indispensable partner, US officials say", 1 June 2010. www.america.gov/st/peacesec-english/2010/June/20100601090431dmslahrellek0.7037622.html accessed 20 November 2014.
43. Barack Obama, *National Security Strategy* (Washington), February 2015, p. i. <https://www.whitehouse.gov/sites/default/files/docs/2015_national_security_strategy.pdf>accessed 14 May 2015; *Obama's speech a statement of intent.*<http://www.abc.net.au/news/2011-11-17/brack-obama27s-speech-to-parliament/3678058> accessed 11 April 2015; Barak Obama, *US-India Strategic Dialogue: A Defining Partnership in the 21st Century* (Bureau of South and Central Asian Affairs), 17 June 2011. <http://www.state.gov/documents/organization/168999.pdf> accessed 28 December 2014.
44. Jing-dong Yuan, "The Dragon and the Elephant: Chinese-Indian Relations in the 21st Century", *The Washington Quarterly*, Vol. 30, No. 3, 2007, p. 132.
45. He Zude and Wei Fang, "India's increasing troop may go nowhere", *People's Daily*, 15 November 2011. <http://english.people daily.com.cn/90777/7644825.html> accessed 30 November 2014.
46. Yuan, n. 44.
47. John W. Garver, "The China-India-US Triangle: Strategic Relations in the Post-Cold War Era", *NBR Analysis*, Vol. 13, No. 5, 2002, pp. 1-2.
48. Ranjan Mathai, "India's foreign secretary", quoted in Hu Yinan, China, India resume military dialogue, *China Daily*, 8 December 2011, <http://usa.chinadaily.com.cn/china/2011-12/08/content_14230300.htm> accessed 17 May 2014.

2

Indo-Pacific Region: Evolving Strategic Contours

Dalbir Ahlawat and Fred C. Smith

ABSTRACT

China's rise since the end of the Cold War and particularly after the 9/11 terrorist attacks has created a shift in the balance of power in the Indo-Pacific region. This shift has called into question the dominant position of the US in the region, as China challenges the US both economically and militarily. India's role in southwest Asia, sharing a disputed border with China and now more engaged in Southeast and East Asian affairs has added to the complexity of security relationships. More recently, maritime territorial disputes in the South China Sea, impacting both ownership of resources and freedom of navigation of critical sea lines of communication, have increased volatility in the region, as China's so-called 'peaceful rise' is no longer viewed as being all-benign. As a result, Indo-Pacific countries are reformulating their individual strategic contours by entering into bilateral, and in some cases multilateral, security and geo-strategic arrangements. The United States has also reacted to this changing strategic landscape, announcing in 2011 a 'pivot' or 'rebalance' to Asia to ensure it remains engaged and relevant in the region. This paper will discuss the trajectory of Indo-Pacific security relationships, analysing the evolving strategic construct, cooperation, friction and challenges.

Geo-strategic Construct

Adjoining two separate Oceans, the Indian and the Pacific, an Indo-Pacific strategic construct is a logical consequence of developing geo-strategic realities emerging in the region. If history is any witness, geo-strategic terminologies have been crafted and coined with specific purposes or objectives in mind, ranging from short, to medium, to long-term strategic interests. Within the Indo-Pacific geo-strategic construct, three countries, the United States, China and India, act as key players in the developing new power equation, surrounded by many other interested parties, some allied and others opposed to each key player. The US aims at 'pivoting' or 'rebalancing' to the region to remain relevant and competitive. China intends to assert its increasing power, not only in the South China Sea (SCS), but also in the Indian Ocean and beyond, while India in strategic competition with China, aims to exert pressure on China for border dispute resolution and strategic balancing, using its improving strategic relationship with the US as a hedge against China, without entering into any close strategic or security alliance.

To serve respective national interests, each state computes its strategic framework in a way that enhances its own strategic power equations. Digging below the strategic surface, it is assessed that the United States envisages a unipolar world with a multipolar Asia, including an ambition to contain an increasingly militarily aggressive and territorially expansive China, while retaining its status, as the only superpower, acquired after disintegration of the Soviet Union. China, on the other hand, envisages a multipolar world with a unipolar Asia, elevating its status as a major power with a powerful say in the international arena, while taking back its rightful place at the centre of the Asian region by exerting hegemonic control over Asia in a modern tributary system. As attested by retired US Marine Corps General James Mattis, China intends to construct a "tribute model," with the intention to exert a "veto authority in each of the countries around their periphery".[1] Finally, India envisages a multipolar world with a multipolar Asia, the objective being to match power with a militarily (and not so peacefully) rising China, while supporting a global order conducive to its aspirations of maintaining strategic autonomy in international affairs.

The evolving power and strategic matrix in both the Asia-Pacific and Indo-Pacific regions, one that includes a rising China—rising not only economically but also in the full spectrum of Diplomacy, Informational, Military and Economic (DIME)[2] aspects of national power, particularly its rising military capabilities—is tilting the balance of power that has worked well to provide security and stability since the end of the Second World War. If 'this' China continues to exert its power into the region, Asia-Pacific nations most likely will band together to contain and constrain Beijing's increasing influence and power, in order to ensure their own influence is not diminished in this zero-sum game. China has already expressed its resentment over the new Indo-Pacific strategic construct in that it believes this effort is being orchestrated, not only to deny China its rightful place in the international system, but to create multi-polarity, multilateralism and a so-called rules-based international order, all interfering with China's one-on-one relations with its neighbours.[3]

Moreover, Beijing protests the new Indo-Pacific paradigm because it portends a predominant role for the US in Asia, and also creates a triumvirate of regional powers by adding India, giving rise to multi-polarity in what Beijing sees as its sole region or sphere of influence.[4] This Chinese perception is very well reflected by Andrew Phillips and Nick Bisley, that "[v]iewed from Beijing, the idea of the Indo-Pacific...appears to be to keep the United States in, lift India up and keep China out".[5] To include the Indian Ocean region in this calculus only raises China's apprehension that it is being bracketed and isolated by a wider-ranging containment strategy, one where India is considered a threat to China's ambitions in the medium-to-long term.

Against this backdrop, the major objectives of this paper are to discuss the evolving strategic complexities occurring in the region, provide analysis of the evolving strategic configurations, and consider evolving potential future scenarios for the Indo-Pacific region.

Evolving Strategic Complexity

After the defeat of Japan in the Second World War, the US emerged as the guarantor of peace and security in the Pacific region. Despite the Cold War, many countries in the region took advantage of this relative peace by focusing on their respective economic development. Specifically in the case of China, with Deng Xiaoping's ascendancy to leadership of the Communist Party of

China (CPC) in the 1980s, boosted its upward economic trajectory, resultantly developing interdependency in business and trade relations with major economies such as the US, Japan, India, Australia and many others, based on its claimed policy of peaceful development.[6] As stated by Dujarric: "Indeed, not only have the United States and its allies not tried to hinder China's growth, they have actually helped provide the CCP a stable regional environment free of charge".[7]However, after 9/11 when the US was attacked on its own soil and its focus shifted significantly to Iraq and Afghanistan, further solidified by the economic distractions of the Global Financial Crisis of 2008, in the CCP leadership's mind, a power vacuum was created in the Pacific region.

Since then, China sensing at a minimum a relative decline in US power, and based on China's own enhanced economic and growing military power, filled the power vacuum by projecting its intent to create a Chinese sphere of influence in Asia. As Babayan states: "In many ways, it was China's economic development that made Beijing's desire to extend its influence far beyond its borders inevitable".[8] At least to some extent to counter China, the US expressed its intentions to 'pivot' or 'rebalance' in Asia by strengthening existing alliances and converging its strategic interests with new partners in the region.[9] India, the champion of non-alignment since its independence in 1947 and throughout the Cold War, mellowed over the years on this idealism but retained remnants of the policy in the form of strategic autonomy. As such, India supports a multipolar world with a multipolar Asia. So the question arises, how will these three powers manoeuvre, challenge, or accommodate each other? As stated by one author: "The emerging power equations marked by an assertive China, a rising India, a resurgent Japan, together with a rebalancing United States make for a potentially turbulent region".[10]

China: Multipolar World with a Unipolar Asia

China, motivated by its desire to return to its rightful place as a central decisional power in the international order after suffering its 'Century of Humiliation' and disastrous policies of Mao,[11] has skilfully used its growing economic power to exert influence over other Asian states that first suffered under the 1997 Asian Financial Crisis and then the 2008 Global Financial Crisis. Acting as a port in the storm, China has taken a central economic role in the region. Meanwhile, China's military modernisation, coupled with a 'relative' decline in US military power vis-à-vis China's military build-up and US preoccupation with the Middle East and Afghanistan, has given China the impression that it can fill any power vacuum created in the region by a distracted US. Beijing's economic and infrastructure initiatives with ASEAN nations now mean that China is their largest and most influential trading partner. In a sense, "China lobbied for the exclusion of not only the United States but also India, Australia and New Zealand...from the East Asia Summit...".[12]

However, possessing a large economy by no means assures China of a long-lasting big power status. Accordingly, China not only accelerated the process of military modernisation by consistently increasing defence budgets over a period of two decades, currently reaching to around US$145 billion[13], but also cast a shadow in the Asia-Pacific region by its expansive territorial claims in both the South and East China Seas, as well as against India through border incursions and an increased naval military presence in the Indian Ocean. Beijing's territorial claims expressed through its UN-submitted '9-dashed line' map, its 2014-2015 building expedition, dredging-and-filling to create man-made islands in disputed areas of the South China Sea, as well as claims against the Japanese Senkaku Islands and the establishment of an Air Defence Identification Zone (ADIZ) in the East China Sea (ECS), backed up by aggressive military, maritime security and coast guard actions in both the South and East China Seas, have not only jolted Japan, Vietnam and Philippines but also have clearly signalled China's aggressive intentions to the US. To further assert its dominance in the region, China is developing an anti-access/ area denial naval[14], air and missile strategy, through the first island chain (the Ryukyu, Philippines and Malaysia/Indonesia islands and archipelagos) out to the second island chain, stretching from Japanese-held Bonin Islands and the US-held Northern Marianas, Guam, Palau and the Carolines to Guam with a motive to "subtract the US factor from the East Asian regional equation".[15] In a sense,

China's submission of the '9-dashed line map', its declaration of an ADIZ in the East China Sea, while threatening to declare an ADIZ in the South China Sea, potentially presents itself as a direct challenge to freedom of navigation in these regions.

Against this backdrop, Beijing's strategic intent and framework becomes clearer, a desire to establish a unipolar Asia with the People's Republic of China at the centre. In November 2014, President Xi Jinping in his address to a Central Foreign Affairs Work Conference affirmed that "a proactive, balanced, and where necessary, muscular foreign policy approach is likely to be a hallmark of his rule". At the same time assuaging the concerns of its neighbours, Xi beseeched that "China's rise can only be accomplished by peaceful means and will only be pursued with an eye towards achieving 'win-win' outcomes for all concerned".[16]

Despite Xi's 'good cop, bad cop' rhetoric, China's actions portend a much more belligerent rise and a much less certain peaceful future. As China considers the US insistence on resolving the SCS and other regional conflicts in accordance with the existing international law as a subterfuge to lessen its big power status and place it on par with other disputants. Placed on the defensive and lacking reliable allies other than North Korea, Pakistan and potentially Russia, China is somewhat isolated in its own region of influence, as its aspirations of a China-centric, unipolar Asia appear to be threatened by US military presence, interference and particularly military alliances.[17]

Economically, China seeks to exert financial leverage against US economic strength by launching parallel banking institutions, such as the BRICS Bank, Shanghai Cooperation Organisation, aimed at "re-writing of the international financial architecture and a gradual de-coupling from American dollar hegemony".[18] The establishment of the Asian Infrastructure Investment Bank (AIIB) can be seen as a continuation and expansion of this policy aimed to marginalise US banking and economic dominance at least in the developing countries.[19]

Diplomatically, against the evolving US strategy to rebalance Asia, China has comparatively improved relations with India and initiated several confidence-building measures to ensure India remains non-aligned rather than joining the US camp. However, despite China's championing of the concept of a multi-polar world order, India remains concerned that, "alignment between Washington and its rival [China] would place it in a very difficult strategic situation".[20] From an Indian perspective, China not only maintains cooperative relations with the United States but also has developed economic interdependency based on two-way trade. China may assess India's increasing role in the Pacific region, strengthening security agreements and deepening relations with the US, as a zero-sum game, despite some hopeful thinking that it does not.[21,22] Beijing understands that to establish a unipolar Asia and a multipolar world, it cannot afford insecurity in the Indo-Pacific region and that India could act as a counter-balance or rival to China's strategic ambitions there.

United States: Unipolar World with a Multipolar Asia

The US perspective and its continued military presence in both the Asia-Pacific and Indo-Pacific regions are framed by its sacrifice of blood and treasure during the Second World War in the Pacific, fighting along with its allies to defeat the Imperial Japanese military. Having learned a valuable lesson in what happens when space is ceded to a territorially expansive nation, as occurred with Imperial Japan in the early-to-mid 20th century, and faced with a similar challenge from the Soviet Union in the post-Second World War; the US chose to remain engaged in these regions rather than to retreat.

Witnessing China's rise at an unprecedented rate and its demonstration of military power in the region, President Barack Obama emphatically stated: "The question is never whether America should lead, but how we lead". Further outlining the central role for the US and importance of its alliance partners, he emphasised: "In an interconnected world, there are no global problems that can be solved without the United States, and few that can be solved by the United States alone".[23] In response to the PRC's regional hegemonic postures, the US announced a pivot or rebalance to Asia. In his address to the Australian Parliament in 2011, Obama reinforced that the United States is a "Pacific power 'here to stay'" and that he had instructed his national security team to make "America's presence in the region a top priority". Further, he reiterated that "let there be no doubt, in Asia-Pacific in the 21st century, the United States of America is all in".[24] In addition to these overtures, Obama also offered that, "we'll seek more opportunities for cooperation with Beijing, including greater communication between our militaries to promote understanding and avoid miscalculation". However, China expressed its displeasure about Obama's announcement of an increased US presence in Australia and other regions in Asia. The visit and subsequent developments in a sense appeared to be aimed at subduing China's ambition to dominate the region by: initiating rotational stationing of US forces in Australia, the Philippines, Japan and South Korea; promoting the Trans-Pacific Partnership regulatory and investment trade deal (that excludes China); and attempting to resolve South China Sea disputes in multilateral forums, as against China's insistence on bilateral discussions.

With the US announcement of its pivot or rebalancing, a new strategic dynamics emerged, new in the sense that India was the only country mentioned by name as a vital US partner. This was construed by Beijing as a ploy to curtail its role in the international fora and to diminish its influence in the region. This perception was further reinforced in the new US defence strategy launched in January 2012, when the US Chairman of the Joint Chiefs of Staff, General Martin Dempsey, without mentioning China by name outlined that: "All trends are shifting to the Pacific.... Our strategic challenges will largely emanate out of the Pacific region".[25] Commenting on these developments, a Chinese Major General Luo Yuan retorted that the US' intent to return and stay in Asia was aimed at positioning "forces on China's periphery" and "contain China". Further he underlined that "China has not provoked US interests, so what are you doing running to Asia to encircle China?".[26]

Notwithstanding their differences in the region, China and the US agree on a number of issues, including trade interdependency and the need to combat international terrorism. However, concerning other international security-related issues, China has reservations on the imposition of sanctions against Iran, Afghanistan policy and the role of Pakistan. What has changed more recently is the US giving credence to India in the context of the Indo-Pacific region. What the US envisages from both China and India is that they play significant roles in the Indo-Pacific and Asia-Pacific regions without becoming territorially expansive and abiding by existing international agreements and norms, while deferring to the US global leadership.

India: Multipolar World with a Multipolar Asia

President Obama during his visits to India in November 2010 and January 2015 assured India of its due place in international organisations and forums, perhaps intended to endorse India's equivalent status to China. However, China expressed its resentment over a potential elevation of India's status. To give further credence to the tightening US-India relationship, Obama in his address to the Indian Parliament stated, "the relationship between India and America will be one of the defining partnerships of the 21st century, rooted in common values and interests".[27] With the US rebalance to Asia, India has been coaxed that "it is not enough to 'Look East'" but also "engage East" and "act East".[28]India considers an understanding with the US on core issues such as freedom of navigation, multilateral framework, and applicability of international law as essential to counter Chinese hegemonic postures. To give credence to its convergence with US policy postures in the region, New Delhi signed the US-India Joint Strategic Vision for the Asia-Pacific and Indian Ocean Region.[29]

Rooted in its non-alignment policy postures of the Cold War years, Indian public and policymaker opinion is divided on the US 'rebalance' to Asia. This is mainly based on apprehension that US strategic priorities in relation to China and India could shift as per its strategic interests; whereas India, geographically located next to China, must maintain a constant and consistent geo-strategic perspective on China to serve its national interests best.[30] Even India's relations with Iran, Afghanistan, Pakistan and other neighbouring states create potential points of friction with corresponding US policy. At the same time, a rising China poses at least three challenges to India. These include increased Chinese military pressure on disputed border areas, increased People's Liberation Army Navy (PLAN) naval presence in the Indian Ocean,[31] a tightening of China's geo-strategic relationship with

Pakistan, and growing Chinese influence with other South Asian countries through its 'One Belt, One Road' initiative.[32,33] To counter a rising China, over the years India has turned itself into a major weapons importer in order to build a credible military deterrence force in the region. No doubt, cooperation between India and China has increased multi-fold in various economic endeavours but so has competition, if not rivalry, particularly focused on border disputes such as over Arunachal Pradesh and China's support to Pakistan.

India, instead of aligning with China or the US, continues its Cold War legacy of strategic autonomy, if not in real terms, at least in rhetoric. Under Prime Minister Narendra Modi, India seeks a more visible and leading role in Asia by achieving a broader understanding with China about its due place in the regional order, a closer security relationship with the US, Australia, Japan and other ASEAN nations, and a more prominent role in regional institutions and security architectures.[34] India understands its geo-strategic importance that Kaplan has rightly underlined, "the direction India tilts could determine the course of geopolitics in Eurasia in the 21st century. India, in other words, looms as the ultimate pivot state".[35]

In a nutshell, there is a trust deficit between the three powers and at the same time all three are dependent on each other. How these powers interact and how they work with other states in the region, channelising their interests, will be discussed in the next section.

US-China: Counterbalance Through Strategic Engagement

The issue of a rising China is hotly debated both in the US and in the Asian strategic circles. Mainly two opinions come to fore, that a rising China poses an unabated threat to its neighbours and therefore needs to be checked and contained in its rise, while others believe that China's rise is inevitable and it should be accommodated in the evolving world order.[36] The first concern attracts more attention, not only because of China's military modernisation and territorial expansion as witnessed in the SCS, but because of its direct challenge to a US-dominated regional and global status quo.

China's rise is viewed with suspicion by many regional states, fearing it will eventually pull these states into a dependent, tribute-state relationship. However, based on the goodwill China gained by bailing-out countries of the region during the Asian financial crisis and subsequently smoothing out the economic impact of the GFC, coupled with US preoccupation in Afghanistan and Iraq and a slimming US defence budget, at least some Chinese strategists reached the conclusion that US power was in decline.[37] Against this backdrop, China indicated to the US and other regional countries that the South China Sea was "an area of 'core interest' that is ...non-negotiable".[38] Further testing the premise of US decline, China firmed up its maritime claims in the East and South China Seas, while projecting military power through naval presence in the Indian Ocean.[39]

In an evolving China-centric Asia, ASEAN meanwhile preferred the use of ASEAN-centric, multilateral institutions, based on "strategies that promote economic interdependence, commitment to ASEAN norms, and soft balancing".[40] Considering the smaller size of ASEAN states, they generally prefer to be part of larger multilateral arrangements, rather than entering into unequal bilateral relations with a much larger and more powerful China. These developments posed a serious security dilemma for regional states. To counter a rising China, states were left with three alternatives: increase their respective national defence budgets; unite into alliance arrangements; or bandwagon against a rising China; or making overtures to the US, the traditional regional peacekeeper, to seek assurance about its continued engagement in the region.

Witnessing increasingly assertive military power projection in the region, the US in response to these overtures in turn gave impetus to its strategy of 'rebalancing', as Secretary of State, Hillary Clinton underlined in her article in the journal *Foreign Policy*, the US' "strategic turn" to the Indo-Pacific region. These strategies among others included: strengthening bilateral security alliances; deepening working relationship with emerging powers including China; engaging with regional multilateral institutions; and forging a broad-based military presence. In order to enforce a rebalance, a major focus of the US has been to modernise existing alliances with treaty allies such as Japan, Korea, Australia, the Philippines and

Thailand, while expanding and deepening partnerships with Singapore, Vietnam, India, Indonesia and others.[41]

After evaluating these policy postures, Beijing firmed up its assessment that US naval presence and the alliance system emboldened countries of the region to challenge China. In the minds of China's CCP leadership, these countries would have accommodated China's rise without US presence and support; therefore, the US alliance system was considered by Chinese strategists as a destabilising, rather than a stabilising factor. Polling numbers indicate that 77 per cent Chinese commentators oppose US presence and its rebalance to Asia, while 80 per cent non-Chinese regional experts support the rebalance.[42]

China believes that the US alliance system encourages the Asian states to initiate provocative actions against China. Faced with these perceived provocations by US alliance partners, "Chinese foreign policy experts are now increasingly questioning the effectiveness of China's economic diplomacy".[43] It is believed that economic leverage alone is not sufficient to counter the increasing US security presence in the region. Therefore, China's only other option left is to use hard power against these regional provocateurs, without bringing Chinese forces into direct conflict with US forces in the region.

China also continues to blame others for "the many injustices of the past 30 years.... China has been standing on the sidelines pursuing a diplomatic course while others in Southeast Asia have been advancing and consolidating their claims".[44] The state-controlled news media *People's Daily* justified China's position by stating that, "the reason why some countries are so unbridled may be related with the adjusted geo-strategy of the United States",[45] quite clearly implying that it is all the fault of the US. Regardless of these PRC perceptions, real or imagined, the US continues to build on and reinforce its Indo-Pacific partnerships with India, Japan, Australia, South Korea and Taiwan because it cannot defend vital national interests in Asia without them.[46]

Evolving Scenarios

Regional States Clash with China

Based on the current trajectory of territorial disputes in both the ECS and SCS, there is a strong probability that countries like Japan, the Philippines and Vietnam will continue to find themselves in direct conflict with China's interests over disputed maritime territories. As a result, nations that have firm alliances with the US, particularly those with mutual defence treaty obligations such as Japan and the Philippines, will be better placed to resist expansive Chinese claims, particularly those that cross-over into national maritime Exclusive Economic Zones (EEZs). Other regional ASEAN nations affected by China's expansive claims that do not have a close US military alliance relationship will most likely consider attempting to establish one, as well as seeking increased US military presence in the region as a hedge against an increasingly aggressive China. Summed-up by Weitz: "Despite their growing economic cooperation with the PRC, ASEAN nations now acknowledge that improved security ties with the United States offer the safest and most effective way—and a far better one than they could achieve alone—for them to hedge against China's growing power and to exercise influence on Chinese policy".[47]

As tensions rise, it is envisaged that the US alliance partners will clash with China, both because these weaker nations feel more empowered to push-back against China, knowing the US will support them militarily, as well as because China, feeling more and more isolated, may lash-out by even more rapidly and aggressively staking their claims, using military force more readily as they realise that time is no longer on their side. The end result could be a direct confrontation between China and the US. This scenario could become what's known as a 'Thucydides Trap', where a rising power threatens the established power, causing fear and eventually war.[48] However, there are factors that will dissuade war, such as economic interdependency, the existence of both conventional military and nuclear deterrence on both sides, as well as open lines of diplomatic communication. Furthermore, while the US may believe that there is need to develop a "bilateral relationship...building strategic trust between Washington and Beijing" that could prove a panacea to "mitigate insecurity and risk of conflict", China does not interpret tensions with the US as a "bilateral dispute but...conflict between allies", in that it is US-encouraged allies who are creating tensions, not China. In this case, it may be the actions of the smaller states that spring the

'Thucydides Trap' rather than actions of the main, large-state actors, effectively dragging the US "into an unnecessary confrontation with China".[49]

An example of this potential scenario playing out occurred when Japan nationalised three of the five Senkaku/Diaoyu islands in September 2012. China objected vehemently, considered nationalisation as a violation of its sovereignty, responded aggressively with maritime air and surface patrols around the islands and even within the islands' 12 nautical mile territorial waters zone, and clearly expressed its intent to 'protect' sovereignty.[50] The confrontation escalated by December 2012, when China stated that flights by Japanese aircraft over the islands were a violation of PRC's airspace and in retaliation, dispatched fighter jets to intercept Japanese aircraft. Referring to these aggressive military actions, Japan in its '2012 Defence White Paper' accused China of changing the status quo by using "force based on its own assertion, which is incompatible with the existing order of international law".[51] If escalation of military actions were to occur over the Senkakus, this potentially would have invoked the US-Japan Security Treaty obligations, an obligation that Obama unequivocally declared in April 2014 is covered under the bilateral Treaty of Mutual Cooperation and Security.[52]

Along similar vein, China's occupation of Scarborough Shoals using maritime security forces in 2012 is another example of the potential for 'cascading effects' and 'unintended consequences' pulling the US into a conflict between the Philippines and China.[53] At Scarborough Shoals, after a confrontation broke out between the Philippines and PRC maritime naval and security forces earlier that year over an attempt to arrest Chinese fishermen illegally fishing within the Philippines EEZ, both sides agreed to pull back, with US diplomatic support and encouragement. After both nations pulled back and deescalated tensions, the PRC then sent its maritime security units back to the reef, occupied it in contravention of their agreement, even constructed 'a chain barrier across the mouth of the shoal to block Philippines access to it', then later in the year diplomatically threatened the Philippines against its actions to get the reef back during talks to settle the dispute peacefully.[54] Specifically, during October 2012 diplomatic discussions in Manila, Chinese Foreign Minister Fu Ying warned the Philippines against its course of actions that include, "appeal to the UN, internationalisation of the issue in forums such as the ASEAN, coordination with other states such as the US, and issuance of press release regarding the negotiations".[55] Exactly this type of action, if the Philippines had retaliated and based on the US-Philippines Mutual Defence Treaty, could have caused direct military conflict between the US and China.

China has periodically harassed Vietnamese ships involved in fishing and oil exploration in the South China Sea near the Paracel Islands in 2007, 2012, 2013 and 2014, the Paracel Islands occupied by South Vietnamese forces prior to 1974 when taken over by China but still claimed by Vietnam as its territory under Chinese occupation.[56] Beijing's aggressive actions, even on several occasions clearly ramming Vietnamese vessels intentionally,[57] could instigate an aggressive Vietnamese reaction, eventually pulling the US military forces into the conflict. Witnessing Chinese hegemonic postures, former US Defence Secretary, Chuck Hagel warned that "China has undertaken destabilising, unilateral actions asserting its claims in the South China Sea".[58] More recently, in relation to PRC's construction of artificial islands on submerged reefs in the SCS and subsequent PRC complaints against US naval air reconnaissance flights in the vicinity of these artificial islands, current US Secretary of Defence Ashton Carter asserted in May 2015 that: "We want a peaceful resolution of all disputes, and an immediate and lasting halt to land reclamation by any claimant.... We also oppose any further militarisation of disputed features" but that: "There should be no mistake: the United States will fly, sail, and operate wherever international law allows, as we do all around the world".[59]

Similarly, China's unilateral declaration of an ADIZ in the East China Sea in November 2013, without prior consultation with regional neighbours, international commercial air carriers or commercial air authorities, created additional tensions by requiring all aircrafts entering the ADIZ to announce flight plans to Chinese authorities, maintain radio contact and reply promptly to identification inquiries. The PRC ADIZ not only overlaps Japan's ADIZ in the ECS, but unlike any other declared ADIZ in the world, requires both military and civilian aircrafts to check-in (not just civilian aircrafts), further excessively applying not only to aircrafts entering China's territorial airspace, but to all aircrafts entering the ADIZ.[60] Yang Yujun, a PRC defence ministry spokesman, justified setting up of the zone to safeguard China's sovereignty, territory and security while maintaining flight order.[61] However, this action received a prompt retaliatory response in the form of a US B-52 military bomber aircraft purposefully flying through the newly declared ADIZ without checking in with Chinese air controllers; shortly thereafter Japan and South Korea followed suit.[62] Such declarations and follow-on events can lead to miscalculations on either side, eventually escalating into conflict.

China's aggressive security posture and extensive claims over disputed territories in the ECS and SCS escalated to the point of confrontation at the Shangri-la Dialogue held in May-June 2014, in which Japanese Prime Minister Shinzo Abe in his speech forewarned China to follow the "rule of law at sea" that includes "making claims that are faithful in light of international law, not resorting to force or coercion, and resolving all disputes through peaceful means".[63] China responded by emphasising on international norms, rather than international law, that include "respecting sovereignty, independence and territorial integrity; non-interference in internal affairs; respect[ing] social systems and chosen development paths".[64] The US Secretary of Defence at the time, Chuck Hagel, taking cognisance of the evolving conflicts warned that "the United States will not look the other way when fundamental principles of the international order are being challenged".[65]

Deterrence Through Alliance

As China rises, the CCP leadership rather than working within the perceived US-led regional or international institutions and processes, is building its own alternative regional, multilateral forums and institutions (such as Asia Infrastructure Investment Bank, BRICS Development Bank, Xiangsham Forum, Shanghai Cooperation Organisation). These initiatives appear to be part of a conscious effort to bind regional countries into a China-centric economic and trade sphere, thereby limiting the role of the US in the region.

Chinese leadership is also sensitive to a growing number of bilateral and particularly multilateral security alliance formations in the region and considers these as encouraged by the US to contain China. This was reflected by President Xi Jinping in his address to the Conference on Interaction and Confidence Building Measures in Asia (CICA), without naming the US specifically, that to "beef up and entrench a military alliance targeted at a third party is not conducive to maintaining common security". He went on to say, "it is for the people of Asia to run the affairs of Asia, solve the problems of Asia and uphold the security of Asia".[66]

However, these alliances are growing, spurred not so much by the US-announced 2011 pivot or rebalance to the region, as suggested at times by China[67], but by China's own actions. In actual fact, the US has never left the region rather has maintained a significant security presence since the end of Cold War, while China's declaration of the '9 Dash Line' map in 2009 and subsequent military and security force actions within those lines have created serious regional apprehensions.[68] There have been China's own aggressive initiatives, initiatives that include territorial expansion into the SCS and ECS and its own military modernisation programme, building-up naval, air and missile combat capabilities in the region that has caused apprehension and disquiet[69] as against its obligations under the 2002 SCS Declaration of Conduct which it signed and promised to uphold.[70]

In the meantime, to deter China's expansionist initiatives, the US has focused on capacity building of vulnerable and militarily weaker alliance partners, further ensuring regional allies of its long-term commitment while holding out an olive branch of military cooperation to China to encourage good behaviour and cooperation. Quite paradoxically, the US is the "primary security partner for many Southeast Asian nations, while China is the primary economic partner". The US pivot or rebalance to the Asia-Pacific region potentially disrupts this balance since "a key feature of the rebalance is a US move to strengthen its alliance relationships in the region".[71] As such, it is important to the US that the rebalance strategy be well supported in the region, not just from countries most clearly in China's crosshairs, but also by other ASEAN nations who although concerned of China's intent, are fearful of stirring the dragon. For the time being at least, Malaysia falls into this category, while Thailand, currently estranged from the US due to its 2014 military coup d'état, seems to be quietly acquiescing to China's manoeuvres, although one must wonder how heartfelt and committed this marriage of convenience really is.

The Centre for Strategic and International Studies has categorised regional countries by their perceptions of the rebalance. It classifies Australia, Japan, the Philippines and South Korea as strong supporters; New Zealand, Singapore and Taiwan as supporters; India, Indonesia, Malaysia, Thailand and Vietnam as cautious supporters; Brunei, Cambodia, Laos and Myanmar as cautious observers; China as opponent and North Korea as a strong opponent.[72] No doubt, the *strong supporters* will unequivocally support the US security framework, but countries in the category of *supporters* and *cautious supporters* cannot necessarily be counted on to side with the US, preferring 'not to choose' while maintaining strategic ambiguity, alienating neither side.

The PLA's intent to create an anti-access, area denial military force and its territorial ambitions, as well as the high value attached to alliance arrangements in US strategy, is well documented.[73] For its part, the US has initiated tangible measures to not only build deterrence, but also achieve a cutting edge advantage over Chinese strategies and weapon systems. US Secretary of Defence, Ash Carter, emphasises that, "it's human nature for some in the region to take security for granted. But we cannot...afford to – and will not – make that mistake".[74]

Against this backdrop, the rise of China is not considered a zero-sum-game. Rather, what is desired is a cooperative and positive approach to engage China. In this regard Obama asserts that, "The United States welcomes the rise of a stable, peaceful, and prosperous China. We seek to develop a constructive relationship with China...[that] promotes security and prosperity in Asia and around the world.....While there will be competition, we reject the inevitability of confrontation... while seeking ways to reduce the risk of misunderstanding or miscalculation".[75] Some progress has been made in this regard, including two historic confidence-building agreements announced by Presidents Obama and Xi.[76]

Middle Powers: Riding the Tides and Navigating the Channels

Yet another scenario could be that countries like Malaysia, Indonesia, India, Thailand and others would like to continue to have trade relations with China while maintaining a loose security understanding with the US. These countries hesitate to consider the rise of China and shifting power equations in the Indo-Pacific region as a zero-sum game, rather they are still optimistic that there is sufficient space to accommodate a rising China. Yet at the same time, though apprehensive of China's secretive strategic underpinnings, support the US' traditional role in the region as a peace keeper. In a sense, these states wish to exploit the best of the two worlds.

The position of these countries can be labelled from different perspectives that range from 'peace lovers', 'neutral', 'maintaining strategic autonomy' to the notion 'Asia for Asians'. However, considering the power polarisation in the Indo-Pacific region, the US enriching its existing alliances, opening vistas for new partners and friendly countries and China instituting new structural frameworks for economic inclusion pose challenges as to how to posit themselves between the vagaries of the economic development and strategic balance.

In this case, if these countries come on a shared platform with common minimum understanding, it appears they may have a say in shaping the Indo-Pacific strategic contours otherwise they will be part of history rather than architects of history. As discussed in Chapter 1, India has taken lead in developing its minimum but credible strategic deterrence against China, maintaining strategic autonomy in its relations with the US and developing its naval power to have strategic influence in the Indian Ocean. How other countries will respond, it is too early to envisage.

Conclusion

Despite the many good reasons for cooperation and collaboration in the Indo-Pacific region, great security challenges loom ahead. Maintaining peace and security will be no easy task. A 'not so peacefully' rising China is emerging, one that intends to take its rightful place as a dominant power in the Indo-Pacific region, a position it enjoyed in past centuries. In this new world order, China sees Asia as falling clearly under its domination, a unipolar region with China at the centre. Farther afield, on a global scale, China believes that multiple nations must have a say in how global economic and security matters are carried out, not just the US. The US-dominant position enjoyed since the end of the Second World War Two will be challenged by China's new assertiveness in both regional and international affairs. Tensions will not lessen but accelerate as China becomes both economically and militarily stronger. China will continue to aggressively use its newfound economic leverage and military strength to influence regional nations to comply with its new vision for the region and the world.

The US on the other hand understands the reality of a rising China and its economic benefits but will not sit back and allow China to dominate Asia without checks-and-balances. Mutual defence treaties and alliances, particularly with Australia (straddling both the Asia-Pacific and Indo-Pacific regions), Japan (in the East China Sea) and the Philippines (in the South China Sea) will ensure that the US maintains a key and critical presence in the Asia-Pacific and Indo-Pacific regions, a presence needed in its mind to ensure economically-critical sea lines of communication are kept open and free and that China does not take territory outside of established international legal processes. This will continue to place the US and China in a militarily confrontational relationship, one that will have to be carefully managed. The US realises that China's rise is inevitable but it will push for a multipolar Asia, not the China-dominated sphere of influence that Beijing desires. Using alliances, military presence and the international legal system, the US will not leave the Indo-Pacific region to China's supremacy or hegemony and it will not easily acquiesce to China's desire to change existing global 'status-quo' organisations, systems and processes to meet China's self-vision.

India's desire to maintain at least on paper, a 'non-aligned' status will restrict just how close its relationship with the US becomes. India's reality of a shared, disputed border with a rising and more assertive China—one that is making no effort to negotiate, compromise or smooth-over existing border claims with India—balanced against the shared economic benefit of close trade relations with China, means that India must walk a tightrope, balancing aspirations with reality. Although India desires a multipolar Asia, with India, China and the US playing key roles, it clearly sees that this is not what China desires in the longer-term. This reality will drive India into a closer relationship with the US, as both economically and militarily India lags China and needs a hedge to China's border machinations and ever-tightening relationship with Pakistan. From a worldview, India shares China's desire for a multipolar global order, rather than one dominated by the US, but not to the extent that it should weaken the US if India needed its help in a contingency crisis with China.

This back-and-forth balancing act, balancing national interests, aspirations and capabilities, as well as those of allied nations in the region, will continue to dominate the Indo-Pacific security environment. There are no easy answers or solutions for this one, so hang on for the ride.

NOTES

1. John Gandy, "Mattis: US Suffering 'Strategic Atrophy'", *US Naval Institute (USNI)*, 14 May 2015.<http://news.usni.org/2015/05/14/mattis-u-s-suffering-strategic-atrophy?utm_source=USNI +News&utm _campaign= 8d7 f 618f02-USNI_NEWS_DAILY&utm_ medium =email&utm_term= 0_0dd4a1450b-8d7f618f02-230372749 &mc_cid= 8d7f618f02&mc_eid=7d9cd8bf7d>accessed 22 May 2015.
2. For details see Robert David Steele, "Information Operations: Putting the 'I' Back to DIME" (Carlisle: Strategic Studies Institute, February 2006), pp.117-18. <http://www.strategicstudiesinstitute.army.mil/pdffiles/PUB642.pdf>accessed 1 March 2015.
3. Martin Stuart-Fox, "Southeast Asia and China: The Role of History and Culture in Shaping Future Relations", *Contemporary Southeast Asia*, Vol. 26, No. 1, April 2004, pp. 117-18.
4. Martin Sieff, *Shifting Superpowers: The New and Emerging Relationship Between the United States, China and India* (Washington DC: Cato Institute, 2009), p. 125.
5. Andrew Phillips and Nick Bisley, "The Indo-Pacific: What Does it Actually Mean?", *East Asia Forum: Economics, Politics and Public Policy in East Asia and the Pacific*, 6 October 2012. <http://www.eastasiaforum.org/2012/10/06/the-indo-pacific-what-does-it-actually-mean/>accessed 18 March 2015.
6. For details see Ezra Vogel, *Deng Xiaoping and the Transformation of China* (Cambridge: Belken, 2011), p. 193.

7. Robert Dujarric, "China's Zero-Sum Game: Comparative quiet in China's neighbourhood has given it the chance to rise peacefully. Will it keep flexing its muscles?" *The Diplomat, 26* July 2011. <http://thediplomat.com/2011/07/chinas-zero-sum-game/> accessed 2 May 2015.
8. David Babayan, "China Will Inevitably Extend Its Sphere of Influence: The failure of isolationism", *Oriental Review.org,* 21 May 2010. <http://orientalreview.org/2010/05/21/china-will-inevitably-extend-its-sphere-of-influence/> accessed 12 January 2015.
9. Hillary Clinton, "America's Pacific Century: The future of politics will be decided in Asia, not Afghanistan or Iraq, and the United States will be right at the center of the action", *Foreign Policy,* 11 October 2011. <http://foreignpolicy.com/2011/10/11/americas-pacific-century/> accessed 23 February 2015.
10. Udai Bhanu Singh, "Maritime Strategies of China and Southeast Asia", *Strategic Analysis,* Vol. 39, No. 1, 2015, p. 88.
11. Arthur Waldron, "The Asia Mess: How Things Did Not Turn Out as Planned", *FPRI- Foreign Policy Research Institute,* 17 February 2015, p. 9.
12. Yves-Heng Lim, *China's Naval Power: An Offensive Realist Approach* (Surrey: Ashgate Publishing, 2014), p. 50.
13. *China's Defence Budget* (Global Security Organisation) <http://www.globalsecurity.org/military/world/china/budget.htm> accessed 22 May 2015.
14. Michael McDevitt, "The PLA Navy's Anti-access Role in a Taiwan Contingency", in Phillip C. Saunders, Christopher Yung, Michael Swaine and Andrew Nien-Dzu Yang, eds., *The Chinese Navy: Expanding Capabilities, Evolving Roles* (Washington DC: National Defence University, 2011), pp. 191-92.
15. Lim, n. 12, p. 158.
16. Christopher K. Johnson, *Xi Jinping Unveils His Foreign Policy Vision: Peace Through Strength* (Washington DC: Centre for Strategic and International Studies), Issue 15, December 2014, p. 1.
17. "Military alliances no longer relevant: diplomat", *Xinhua,*4 December 2013.<http://eng.chinamil.com.cn/news-channels/pla-daily-commentary/2013-12/04/content_5676635.htm>accessed 22 February 2015.
18. Johannes Dragsbaek Schmidt, "The Asia-Pacific Strategic Triangle: Unentangling the India, China, US Relations on Conflict and Security in South Asia", *Journal of Asian Security and International Affairs,* Vol. 1, No. 2, 2014, p. 204.
19. C. Huang, "China-led Asian bank challenges US dominance of global economy: America's 70-year dominance of the global economy faces

challenge from Chinese-led Asian bank", *South China Morning Post,* 11 April 2015. <http://www.scmp.com/news/china/economy/article/1763525/china-led-asian-bank-challenges-us-dominance-global-economy>accessed 28 April 2015.

20. Thomas Ambrosio, "The Third Side? The multipolar strategic triangle and the Sino-Indian rapprochement", *Comparative Strategy,* Vol. 24, No. 5, 2005, p. 404.
21. "Not a zero-sum game", *The Hindu,* 28 March 2015. <http://www.thehindu.com/opinion/editorial/not-a-zerosum-game/article7040792.ece>accessed 14 April 2015.
22. A Gupta, *The US-India Relationship: Strategic Partnership or Complementary Interests?* (Carlisle Barracks, PA: Strategic Studies Institute, US Army War College, February 2005), p. 36.
23. Barack Obama, *National Security Strategy* (Washington), February 2015, p. i. <https://www.whitehouse.gov/sites/default/files/docs/2015_national_security_strategy.pdf>accessed 14 May 2015.
24. *Obama's speech a statement of intent.*<http://www.abc.net.au/news/2011-11-17/brack-obama27s-speech-to-parliament/3678058> accessed 11 April 2015.
25. Cited in *Ed Pilkington,* "Barack Obama sets out plans for leaner military in historic strategy shift", *The Guardian,* 5 January 2012.*<http://www.theguardian.com/world/2012/jan/05/barack-obama-plans-leaner-military*>accessed 30 April 2015.
26. "PLA researcher says US aims to encircle China", *Reuters,* 28 November 2011. <http://www.reuters.com/article/2011/11/28/us-china-usa-pla-idUSTRE7AR07Q20111128> accessed 27 January 2015.
27. Barack Obama, *US-India Strategic Dialogue: A Defining Partnership in the 21st Century* (Bureau of South and Central Asian Affairs), 17 June 2011. <http://www.state.gov/documents/organization/168999.pdf> accessed 28 December 2014.
28. White House, Hillary Rodham Clinton, *Remarks on India and the United States: A Vision for the 21st Century* (Chennai: Anna Centenary Library, 20 July 2011). <http://www.state.gov/secretary/20092013clinton/rm/2011/07/168840.htm> accessed 2 May 2015.
29. The White House, *US-India Joint Strategic Vision for the Asia-Pacific and Indian Ocean Region,* 25 January 2015. <https://www.whitehouse.gov/the-press-office/2015/01/25/us-india-joint-strategic-vision-asia-pacific-and-indian-ocean-region>accessed 18 February 2015.
30. Tanvi Madan, "The US-India Relationship and China", *Brookings, India-U.S. Policy Memo,* 20 January 2015. <http://www.brookings.edu/research/opinions/2015/01/20-us-india-

relationship-and-china-madan> accessed 27 May 2015.

31. "China's Navy Extends its Combat Reach to the Indian Ocean", *US-China Economic and Security Review Commission - Staff Report*, 14 March 2014. <http://www.uscc.gov/Research/china%E2%80%99s-navy-extends-its-combat-reach-indian-ocean#sthash.JanuoBQ7.dpuf >accessed 3 April 2015.
32. "China maps out 'One Belt, One Road' with action plan", *Global Times*, 31 March 2015. <http://www.globaltimes.cn/content/914743.shtml> accessed on 23 April 2015.
33. T. Durden, "'New Silk Road' Could Change Global Economics Forever, Part 1", *Zero Hedge*, 23 May 2015. <http://www.zerohedge.com/news/2015-05-23/new-silk-road-could-change-global-economics-forever-part-1> accessed 26 May 2015.
34. P. Cronin and D.M. Baruah, "The Modi Doctrine for the Indo-Pacific Maritime Region", *The Diplomat*, 2 December 2014.<http://thediplomat.com/2014/12/the-modi-doctrine-for-the-indo-pacific-maritime-region/> accessed 10 May 2015.
35. Robert Kaplan, *South Asia's Geography of Conflict* (Washington DC: Centre for New American Security, August 2010), p. 3.
36. Barry Buzan, "China in International Society: Is 'Peaceful Rise' Possible?", *The Chinese Journal of International Politics*, No. 3, 2010, pp. 5-36.
37. Bonnie S. Glaser, "A Shifting Balance: Chinese Assessments of US Power" (Washington DC: Centre for Strategic & International Studies, 17 June 2011), pp. 5-7. <http://csis.org/publication/shifting-balance-chinese-assessments-us-power> accessed 12 May 2015.
38. Caitlin Campbell, Ethan Meick, Kimberly Hsu and Craig Murray, *China's 'Core Interests' and the East China Sea* (US-China Economic and Security Review Commission Staff Research Backgrounder), 10 May 2013. <http://www.uscc.gov/sites/default/files/Research/China's%20Core%20Interests%20and%20the%20East%20China%20Sea.pdf>accessed 18 May 2015.
39. Alastair Iain Johnston, "How New and Assertive Is China's New Assertiveness?", *International Security*, Vol. 37, No. 4, 2013, p. 45.
40. Carlyle A. Thayer, *The Rise of China and Maritime Security in Southeast Asia*, 8 February 2012. <http://www.ide.go.jp/Japanese/Publish/Download/Seisaku/120208.html>accessed 8 December 2014.
41. For details see David J. Berteau, Michael J. Green and Zack Cooper, *Assessing the Asia-Pacific Rebalance* (Washington DC: Centre for Strategic and International Studies, December 2014), p. 44.
42. For details see, Michael J Green and Nicholas Szechenyi, *Power and Order in Asia: A Survey of Regional Expectations* (Washington: Centre for Strategic and International Studies, 2014), p. 10.

43. Zha Wen, "Managing Provocative Reactions to the US Asia-Pacific Pivot", in Melanie Hart, ed., *Exploring the Frontiers of US-China Strategic Cooperation: Visions for Asia-Pacific Security Architecture* (Washington: Centre for American Progress, November 2014), p. 20. <https://cdn.americanprogress.org/wp-content/uploads/2014/11/China Report-Security-FINAL.pdf> accessed 18 May 2015.
44. Ely Ratner, "Can China make peace in the South China Sea?", in *Hart*, n. 43, p. 27.
45. "A neutral US helpful to stability in South China Sea", *China Daily*, 5 July 2012.<http://usa.chinadaily.com.cn/opinion/2012-05/07/content_15226749.htm> accessed 1April 2015.
46. Robert D. Blackwill and Ashley J. Tellis, "Revising US Grand Strategy Towards China", *Council on Foreign Relations, Council Special Report No. 72,* March 2015, pp. 27-33.<http://www.cfr.org/china/revising-us-grand-strategy-toward-china/p36371>accessed 19 May 2015.
47. Richard Weitz, "Nervous Neighbors: China Finds a Sphere of Influence", *World Affairs Journal,* March/April 2011. <http://www.worldaffairsjournal.org/article/nervous-neighbors-china-finds-sphere-influence>accessed on 12 May 2015.
48. G. Allison, "Thucydides's trap has been sprung in the Pacific", *Financial Times,* 21 August 2012. <http://www.ft.com/intl/cms/s/0/5d695b5a-ead3-11e1-984b-00144feab49a.html?siteedition=intl#axzz3alQPwsIK> accessed 24 March 2015.
49. Sheena Chestnut Greitens, "Lost in Translation: Problematic Metaphors in Contemporary US-China Relations", in *Hart*, n. 43, p. 4-5.
50. Andrew S. Erickson, "New US Maritime Strategy: Initial Chinese Responses", *China Security*, Vol. 3, No. 4, Autumn 2007, p. 53; Richard Katz, "Mutual Assured Production Why Trade will Limit Conflict Between China and Japan", *Foreign Affairs*, Vol. 92, No. 4, 2013, p. 18; Linda Jackobson, "China's Foreign Policy Dilemma", *Lowy Institute for International Policy*, February 2013, p. 9.
51. *Defence of Japan 2013* (Ministry of Defence), p. 30. <http://www.mod.go.jp/e/publ/w_paper/2013.html>accessed 1June 2015.
52. Ankit Panda, "Obama: Senkakus Covered Under US-Japan Security Treaty", *The Diplomat,* 24 April 2014. <http://thediplomat.com/2014/04/obama-senkakus-covered-under-us-japan-security-treaty/>accessed 30 March 2015.
53. R. Cruz De Castro, "The Philippines in the South China Sea Dispute", *Australian National University, National Security College,* pp. 30-33. <http://nsc.anu.edu.au/documents/occasional-5-brief-6.pdf accessed>accessed 28 May 2015.
54. R. Cruz De Castro, *Abstract of 'China's Realpolitik Approach in the South China Sea Dispute: The Case of the 2012 Scarborough Shoal Stand-Off*

(Washington DC: Centre for Strategic and International Studies, 2013).<http://csis.org/files/attachments/130606_DeCastro_ConferencePaper.pdf> accessed 20 April 2015.

55. Ibid., p. 11.
56. Mark J. Valencia, Jon M. Van Dyke and Noel A. Ludwig, *Sharing the Resources of the South China Sea* (Honolulu: University of Hawaii Press, 1999), pp. 39-59.
57. Scott Bentley, "Vietnam and China: A Dangerous Incident - A new Chinese documentary offers startling revelations from a 2007 confrontation in the South China Sea", *The Diplomat, 12* February 2014. <http://thediplomat.com/2014/02/vietnam-and-china-a-dangerous-incident/> accessed 19 March 2015.
58. Cited in *Sangri-la Dialogue in Singapore,* 1 June 2014. <http://www.abc.net.au/news/2014-05-31/an-us-china-concerns/5491730> accessed 17 June 2014.
59. Cited in David J. Lynch, "Carter Warns China That US Will Go Wherever Global Law Permits", *Bloomberg News,* 27 May 2015. <http://finance.yahoo.com/news/carter-warns-china-u-wherever-220207597.html> accessed 28 May 2015.
60. Lowell Bautista and Julio Amador III, "Complicating the Complex: China's ADIZ", *PacNet - Pacific Forum CSIS, Honolulu, Hawaii - Number 87A,*4 December 2013. <http://csis.org/files/publication/Pac1387A.pdf>accessed 20 May 2015.
61. Zhou Wa, "China maps out its first air defence ID zone", *China Daily,* 24 November 2013. <http://europe.chinadaily.com.cn/china/2013-11/24/content_17127102.htm>accessed 15 April 2015.
62. "Japan, South Korea and China step up provocative aircraft patrols over disputed Senkaku/Diaoyu islands", *news.com.au,* 29 November 2013.<http://www.news.com.au/world/japan-south-korea-and-china-step-up-provocative-aircraft-patrols-over-disputed-senkaku-diaoyu-islands/story-fndir2ev-1226770944006>accessed 27 April 2015.
63. Cited in Shannon Tiezzi, "Shangri-La Dialogue Highlights Regional Tensions", *The Diplomat,* 31 May 2014. <http://thediplomat.com/2014/05/shangri-la-dialogue-highlights-regional-tensions/> accessed 14 December 2014.
64. *Conference on Interaction and Confidence Building Measures in Asia* (CICA), 2014.<http://www.s-cica.org/page.php?lang=1> accessed 30 December 2014.
65. "China is destabilising Southeast Asia, US defence secretary says", *The Guardian,* 1 June 2014. <http://www.theguardian.com/world/2014/may/31/china-is-destabilising-south-east-asia-us-defence-secretary-warns> accessed 5 October 2015.
66. Statement by Xi Jinping.<http://www.s-cica.org/page.php?page_

id=711&lang=1>accessed 30 December 2014.

67. Michael D. Swaine, "Chinese Leadership and Elite Responses to the US Pacific Pivot", *Hoover Institute, China Leadership Monitor,* Issue 38, Summer 2012, 6 August 2012, p. 5. <http://www.hoover.org/sites/default/files/uploads/documents/CLM38MS.pdf>accessed 31 May 2015.
68. *Communication from China to the United Nations,* 7 May 2009, English version. <http://www.un.org/Depts/los/clcs_new/submissions_files/submission_vnm_37_2009.htm>accessed 30 August 2012.
69. Bonnie S. Glaser, "Armed Clash in the South China Sea", *Council on Foreign Relations – Contingency Planning Memorandum No. 14,* April 2012. <http://www.cfr.org/world/armed-clash-south-china-sea/p27883>accessed 29 May 2015.
70. For details see Ronald O'Rourke, *Maritime Territorial and Exclusive Economic Zone (EEZ) Disputes Involving China: Issues for Congress* (Washington DC: Congressional Research Service, 22 April 2015), p. 85. <https://www.fas.org/sgp/crs/row/R42784.pdf>accessed 28 May 2015.
71. Zha Wen, "Managing Provocative Reactions to the US Asia-Pacific Pivot", in *Hart*, n. 43, p. 20.
72. David J. Berteau, Michael J. Green, Zack Cooper, *Assessing the Asia-Pacific Rebalance* (Washington DC: Centre for Strategic & International Studies, December 2014), p. 20.
73. A. Cordesman, *Chinese Military Modernization and Force Development: Chinese and Outside Perspectives* (Washington DC: Centre for Strategic and International Studies), 2 July 2014, pp. 52-52; *PLA anti-access/area denial and territorial disputes*, pp. 32-35. <http://csis.org/files/publication/140702_Chinese_MilBalance.pdf>accessed 12 May 2015.
74. Ash Carter, *Next Phase of the US Rebalance to the Asia-Pacific* (McCain Institute: Arizona State University, 6 April 2015). <http://www.defence.gov/Speeches/Speech.aspx?SpeechID=1929> accessed on 28 May 2015.
75. Obama, n. 23.
76. The White House, *Remarks by President Obama and President Xi Jinping in Joint Press Conference,* 12 November 2014. <https://www.whitehouse.gov/the-press-office/2014/11/12/remarks-president-obama-and-president-xi-jinping-joint-press-conference>accessed 25 May 2015.

3

Multilateralism in the Indo-Pacific: Change or Continuity

Pankaj K. Jha

The understanding and the debate about the formation of a region is contested. In 1973, Thomson identified 21 different features that were regularly included in the definition of an international subsystem. Despite the resurgence of interest in regions and regional processes in the early 1990s, there is relatively scarcity of literature about what a region really is and if there is even such a thing as a precise definition of a region. Yet despite this predicament, most of the available literature remains concentrated in one of the three ontologically and epistemologically differentiable strands of thought; 'outside-in' or geopolitical approaches; 'inside-out' or cultural behavioural approaches; and 'region building' or constructivist approaches. This discourse gives salience to the concepts of the regional powers and the theories supporting the emergence of regional powers.[1]

In the context of geopolitical understanding of regions, the geopolitical approach defines regions in relation to their external environment. Geography and natural strategic landmarks such as mountain ranges and sea borders define the parameters. This way of thinking is in confluence to the realism in International Relations. According to which a region's only significance lies in its relevance and role in conjunction with the great power strategies for meeting their objectives and long-term goals.[2] This clearly has repercussions for theorising and conceptualising of regional powers, as most realist approaches categorise states from a global perspective as great, middle or small powers. This to a certain extent ignores the regional perspective, where the middle and even small powers might have significant influence within their respective neighbourhoods.[3] Over the past two decades spatial concepts have come to play an important role in formation of multilateral institutions as well as security communities. The growing recognition of the role of uneven development and regional transformation in the dynamics of modern capitalism has spurred thinking about spatial constructs as well; regional differences assume importance while devising such constructs.[4]

Along with these regional and trans-regional institutions, the increasing challenges from the piracy, natural calamities and other hazards forced nations to upgrade their naval capabilities, not only for their traditional security role but also to provide security against non-traditional threats. However, this competition to secure resources and energy supplies has led to the conceptualisation of new coalitions and alignments such as Asia-Pacific Security, East Asian Security and Indo-Pacific security complexes. The latest construct 'Indo-Pacific' has created a larger debate about the outcome and viability of such security complexes which has geopolitical and geo-strategic implications. In contemporary times, the multilateral institutions are also becoming more inclusive and strive for building common consensus on regional security and developmental issues. As a result, a debate has started on whether multilateralism would define security constructs or vice versa. In a seminal article in *Foreign Policy* journal in November 2011, Secretary of State Hillary Clinton referred to the Indian and Pacific Oceans as being "increasingly linked by shipping and strategy" and constituting the "key driver of global geopolitics." The idea of an Indo-Pacific axis is gaining much currency among Asia's main powers and maritime security experts.[5] In the more contemporary times, a few strategic thinkers and countries such as Australia, Indonesia have subscribed to the new concept of Indo-Pacific. The then Indian Prime Minister Manmohan Singh had outlined the preferred strategic choices for India that highlighted the 'Indo-Pacific' as a new paradigm for enhancing cooperation in the region. Giving preference to the "quest for stability and peace in the vast region in Asia that is washed by the Pacific and Indian Oceans" the Indian leader enlisted Japan as the preferred partner. Earlier also, during the India-ASEAN Commemorative Summit in 2012, the Indian PM had alluded to the term Indo-Pacific.

Michael Auslin in his report 'Security in the Indo-Pacific Commons' states that the Indo-Pacific's unique physical outline makes the balance of regional security most vulnerable in its "commons": the open seas, air lanes, and cyber networks that link the region together and to the world.[6] Given the importance of the Indo-Pacific commons to the continued prosperity and stability of the region, the policy objectives of the United States and its Indo-Pacific allies and partners have been to:

- Ensure accessibility for all nations to the Indo-Pacific commons.
- Dissuade or manage conflict in the commons.
- Preserve credible military capabilities that can act as deterrent and even overcome the most likely regional threats.
- Support the liberal-democratic norms that will assist in propagating freedom and promoting cooperative behaviour.[7]

The overarching goal of this approach is to supplant a security environment that augments stability and development without the use of US or allied military power. The interests of the United States and its allies and partners is primarily aimed to pre-empt any disorder that would trigger political strain or conflict, negatively affecting global economic activity, or hamper the access of any nation to the rest of the region and globe for political or military reasons. However, as a result of China's military modernisation in particular, the United States and its allies are apprehensive of maintaining their regional superiority of forces numerically or, eventually, qualitatively.[8] In this regard there are new trilateral formulations which are taking shape. These include regular interactions through strategic dialogues, maritime exercises and carefully calibrating institutions to meet certain agenda and objectives.

Multilateralism in the Indo-Pacific

Multilateralism has become a preferred *modus operandi* of nation states in contemporary world politics, primarily defining new strategic, environmental and economic configurations as well as global environmental politics. Over the past few years, nations have acknowledged that among other things, a number of challenges, pandemics, peacekeeping, piracy, climate change and environmental pollution, are too complicated to manage for any nation on its own. Multilateralism has helped in bringing consensus on a number of economic issues within a region. It has led to the development of Regional Trade Agreements (RTAs) and Regional Economic Zones. It has also facilitated expansion of mandate and membership of organisations such as the Indian Ocean Rim Association (IORA, previously known as IOR-ARC) while at the same time led to formation of informal mechanisms like the East Asia Summit (EAS).[9]

There are two distinct trends which are shaping the new multilateralism. A distinct preference is given to multi-polarity by a rising number of states. With the new developments at the global stage, several countries have become major global or regional actors. The collective clout of BRICS nations (Brazil, Russia, India, China and South Africa) in the regional and international bodies like UN, IMF and the G-20 illustrates this development.[10]

Secondly, the participation of new types of actors is redefining the interplay in the multilateral field. Political institutions like the European Union (EU) are getting speaking rights in institutions like the UN. These two important trends highlight that multilateralism is no longer the prerogative of states but state centrality in multilateral arrangements is essential. As a sign of changing multilateral dynamics, there are new templates which are emerging like Trans Pacific Partnership (TPP), East Asia Economic Community, Developing Eight (D-8), etc.[11]

Multilateralism, however, poses a risk to developing countries insofar as multilateral agreements call upon them to implement regulatory measures beyond their reasonable capacity to do so. Developing countries do not have the financial and technological resource base readily available to industrialised nations. Consequently, internationally determined policy changes are often both more difficult for developing countries to comply with and less of a priority for them to implement than more fundamental policies, for example, to reduce poverty and improve access to basic services. The requirements of multilateral agreements can also hinder further development in developing countries, by demanding the reduction or termination of activities that would facilitate more rapid economic development. This is particularly true with regard to environmental issues. Natural resources are the foundation of many developing economies.[12]

The more democratic processes generally involved in arriving at multilateral arrangements can be used by developing countries to avoid the aforementioned risks. Rather than establishing regulatory levels or criteria that are applied equally to countries at all levels of development, agreements can be negotiated in such a way as to maximise long-term benefits for all parties involved. In exchange for concessions on resource regulation, for example, developed countries can provide less developed countries with aid, in one form or another.[13] Within the larger Asia-Pacific region, the multilateralism has been undergoing changes in terms of membership and larger agenda. Non-traditional security threats and economic issues have increasingly defined the new parameters of discussion. Almost all multilateral institutions have given birth to new regional and trans-regional economic grouping.

In terms of expansion of membership there are different conceptual understandings which are being discussed. This can be seen in the case of APEC, EAS and even ASEAN. As Robert Keohane observes, regional organisations differ in goals and intent from universal membership organisations by the very fact of their restricted membership; the restrictions they place on membership are a crucial part of the goods they offer their members: 'Restricted membership institutions...seek to achieve gains vis-a-vis outsiders (a function for which there must be outsiders to exploit) or to build strong bonds of community'.[14] The criteria establishing eligibility for membership are determined by and are crucial to selecting the combination of states thought best to deliver the desired objectives of the regional organisation.[15]

The other major set of considerations concerning membership criteria are those associated with group effectiveness. Olson's concept led him to the conclusion that the larger a group, the smaller the fraction of the total group to benefit that accrues to each participant; the lower the incentive of each individual to contribute to the collective benefit; and the greater the organisation costs. Consequently, "the larger the group, the farther it could fall short of providing an optimal supply of the collective good and very large groups normally will not, in the absence of coercion or separate, outside incentives, provide themselves with even minimal amounts of a collective good". There are organisational disincentives to each expansion in group size, depending on whether the group is providing exclusive or inclusive goods to its members. The second effectiveness consideration is that of decision-making effectiveness[16]. Buchanan and Tullock's model of group size and decision-making costs leads them to the conclusion that the 'costs that the member expects to incur as a result of his own participation in collective decision-making vary directly with the size of the deciding group in a given sized total population'.[17] In other words, the larger the group, the longer it would be and the more diplomatic resources it will absorb to generate a collective decision. For Buchanan and Tullock, there are also disincentives to increasing membership: 'One means of reducing these costs is to organise collective activity in the smallest units consistent with the extent of the externality that collectivisation is designed to eliminate'.[18] Within the existing multilateral institutions a phase of transition is being witnessed which might give way to larger superregional organisations. It would be rational to scrutinise the existing institution and its evolving mandate.

IORA

The adoption of IORA name for the Indian Ocean organisation, known formerly as the Indian Ocean Rim Association for Regional Cooperation (IORARC) is seen as an important step signifying the resolve to strengthen the Association and focus on its developmental work. It was proposed during the Perth Communiqué that IORA should work towards bolstering maritime security and safety, particularly in light of continued threats to maritime commerce, and freedom of the high seas, consistent with the UN Convention on the Law of the Seas (UNCLOS); as well as on the safety of seafarers. The Indian Ocean Dialogue which was held in Kochi in India in 2014 was meant to explore, *inter-alia*, concrete options to enhance counter-piracy cooperation, including through improved maritime information-sharing arrangements and stronger national legal capacity and laws.[19] Within IORA more mandate is given to dialogue partners so as to bring more participation and investment to the forum. The cooperative security module and the core areas that are being recalibrated within the institution signify the larger geopolitical and economic footprints.

The Bay of Bengal Initiative for Multi-Sectoral Technical and Economic Cooperation (BIMSTEC) is the only association that includes Eastern Indian Ocean (EIO) countries at present. It has addressed terrorism, natural disaster mitigation and drug trafficking, but its main focus is economic and social development, as well as the management of climate change and natural hazards. The inclusion of Malaysia and Indonesia as members would enhance BIMSTEC, and Australia might seek observer status.[20] Further, there has been discussion with regard to the Bay of Bengal Community. India has also tried to get maximum attention through the Mekong Ganga Economic Corridor which would encapsulate large parts of the Bay of Bengal.

ASEAN-centred Institutions

The Direct Communications Link (DCL) mechanism is a model worth looking at if an Indo-Pacific wide framework is to be considered in the future. However, this multilateral mechanism must first demonstrate its workability; only then will it be possible to consider expanding it into a wider arrangement. The ideal platform in this regard is the ADMM-Plus which was established in 2010, four years after ADMM, to include the eight extra-regional powers: Australia, China, India, Japan, New Zealand, the Russian Federation, South Korea and the US. The ASEAN Maritime Forum was also subsequently enlarged to become the Expanded ASEAN Maritime Forum, which includes the Plus-Eight partners. This "building block" approach is thus not unusual.[21]

This wider arrangement couched within the Indo-Pacific geo-strategic construct fits neatly within ASEAN's objective of sustaining its centrality in an inclusive regional architecture.

ASEAN can serve as an honest broker in an Indo-Pacific crisis management framework, encouraging mutual understanding amongst regional militaries and coastguards via a common regional platform. An Indo-Pacific air-maritime crisis management framework could naturally stem from this ASEAN DCL initiative, using ADMM-Plus as the avenue.[22]

APEC, RCEP and TPP-Blurred Lines

India has applied for membership of the Asia-Pacific Economic Cooperation (APEC) Forum but has not been admitted as yet. Many APEC members support India's membership believing that India's military and maritime strength, and its network of strong relations among the region's major players, can be used to counterbalance China's economic and military power.[23] The debate over India's membership to APEC has been gaining ground since the moratorium on new membership expired in 2010. Within India, the arguments supporting APEC membership are primarily based on India's growing 'strategic clout and economic power'. However, within the global discourse, there is a group of scholars such as Selig Harrison and Paul Kennedy, who advocate that given the gap which exists between India's strategic perceptions and its 'actual' role in the international order, this claim for membership would need further examination. In terms of economic liberalisation, it has still to sign bilateral free trade agreements with a number of countries in Asia-Pacific including Australia, US and many other members of APEC. India has a relatively high tariff regime and is yet to formalise services and investment agreement with ASEAN. According to analysts, India still needs to undertake a slew of economic reforms, trade and tariff liberalisation policies in order to gain APEC membership. India, particularly, needs to work on regional value chains, promotion of Indian investments abroad and ease its customs procedures as well as rules of origin (ROOs).These issues have frequently cropped up during India's negotiations for CECA/CEPA with other countries. In 2014 when the Modi government took charge, a new policy innovation memorandum of the Council on Foreign Relations (CFR), recommended that the Obama administration has an opportunity to revitalise its economic ties with India by the latter's inclusion in the Asia-Pacific Economic Cooperation (APEC) Forum.[24] In January 2015 when President Obama visited Delhi, it was expressed that the US would support India's membership in APEC.[25]

Incremental Shift or a Connecting Link

Within multilateral institutions in the Indo-Pacific region, Indian Ocean institutions are finding the necessary traction under the chairmanship of India, Australia and followed by Indonesia. Indonesia which has also subscribed to the Indo-Pacific concept would maintain the continuum as Chair of IORA in 2015. Indonesia has also proposed an Indo-Pacific treaty. Indonesia's then foreign minister Marty Natalegawa proposed the signing of an Indo-Pacific Treaty of Friendship and Cooperation.[26] Moreover, Indonesia wants to be the connecting bridge between ASEAN and Indo-Pacific construct. Joko Widodo, Indonesian president in his sea-centric speech placed his country instantly on the same wavelength as the US rebalancing, China's Silk Road initiative and India's Act East policy, as he has also sought greater engagement with multilateral maritime groupings like the Indian Ocean Rim Association (IORA).[27]

During the election campaign, Joko and his running mate Jusuf Kalla had released a Vision Mission (Visi Misi), a policy platform that indicated expanding engagement in the Indo-Pacific, viewing the region as a single geopolitical and strategic entity. Also, it articulated the concept of "dynamic equilibrium" that envisaged cooperation with major powers for inclusive regional development and, as some analysts say, the development of a counterweight to China's assertiveness in the South China Sea.[28] Joko's strategic plan to place Indonesia as the global maritime axis is expected to promote connectivity between the Indian Ocean and the Pacific and thereby stability in the region.[29]

While Australia espouses the Eastern Indian Ocean (EIO) as the fulcrum of the Indo-Pacific region, a focus on common interests of EIO countries should provide a potential 'building block' for addressing concerns of the wider IOR without the diversions of the strategic troubles of East Asia and the Northwest Indian Ocean.[30] India's perception is to include the whole of the Indian Ocean into the construct. India's perception is that the predominance of the

Indian Ocean in its strategic calculations would serve its immediate strategic interests while at the same time subscribing to the Indo-Pacific would serve its future strategy.

India and the Indo-Pacific Multilateral Institutions

While the United States is facilitating the development of India's relationships in the Asia-Pacific, it might also act as an implicit inhibitor of India's role in the region. The United States may see some benefit in Sino-Indian strategic rivalry, and may even at times encourage that rivalry, at least in the Indian Ocean. However, there may be circumstances in which the United States may come to regard India as a destabilising factor in the regional security dynamics (for example, in case of conflict in the South China Sea). It is different to imagine India being able to take a substantial direct security role in the Asia-Pacific in the face of strong opposition from the United States.[31] Over the past few years, the term "Indo-Pacific" has gained currency in strategic discourse in India. From a geopolitical perspective it represents the inclusion of the Western Pacific within the range of India's security interests, thus stretching beyond the traditional focus on the Indian Ocean theatre.[32]

The geo-strategic and geo-economic compulsions have left India out of a few groupings and which has acted both to the disadvantage of the nation as well as the divergence of attention of India to other regional groupings. Questions are being raised now that whether there should have been increased strategic interaction between India and the Asia-Pacific, and China and the Indian Ocean be seen as part of a long run strategic convergence between the Asia-Pacific and Indian Ocean regions? Should their Pacific and Indian Ocean regions be seen as a strategic whole? This view is gaining adherence among strategic analysts.[33] Commentators with a geopolitical perspective see common strategic outlooks of an arc of maritime or 'rimland' states around the periphery of the Asian continent, particularly in their interaction with the 'continental' state of China. Robert Kaplan claims that the maritime world from Africa eastward to Indonesia and north to Korea and Japan will become one sweeping continuum—a process that will be hastened by the various canal and land-bridge projects that will provide links between the two oceans in addition to the existing straits.[34]

India has the potential to become a positive force in the Asia-Pacific strategic order. But a major strategic role in the Asia-Pacific will not come automatically with its growing economic power. To fulfil its self-described 'destiny', including aspirations to become an Asia-Pacific power, India will need to go beyond its rhetoric and demonstrate a significant commitment to provide security to the region.[35]

India in the South Pacific: Natural Extension of 'Act East'

One of the major achievements of Prime Minister Narendra Modi as an international leader has been to reach out to the maximum number of countries while visiting any particular region or continent. This was apparent when he visited Latin America during the BRICS Summit meeting where he tried to reach out to the maximum number of heads of governments/states. The same feat was repeated during his visit to the South Pacific islands including the visit to Fiji. He showed and it also reflected in his speech that developing nations are the close partners for India and island nations which are facing challenges related to global warming, climate change, transnational crime and paucity of natural resources. These constraints and limited connectivity to the outside world add to their woes. These island nations need support for sustainable development and growth. He clearly articulated that India wanted to be a close partner in the development priorities and growth opportunities for the small islands. Offering a financial support of special adaptation fund of US$1 million might be perceived as a small aid but given the fact that India is adept at providing low cost solutions along with its expertise and personnel training as a capacity building initiative. This fund might open a new phase of engagement with these Pacific Island nations. The other proposals which he listed on the table were the Pan Pacific Island Project, visa on arrival for all fourteen Pacific Island nations. The South Pacific region has increasingly become an important theatre in the emerging great power contestation in the Indo-Pacific. As elsewhere, the rapid rise of China and its intensive outreach to the islands in the last few years has stirred other major powers into action. What began initially as a competition with Taiwan for diplomatic recognition among the island states has now acquired an intensive strategic dimension.[36] In meeting all the leaders of the Pacific Islands, promising to make the joint forum a regular affair, enhancing India's economic assistance programmes and unveiling defence cooperation with Fiji, Modi has demonstrated that India is ready to turn its historic links with the South Pacific into a strategic partnership.[37] Further India's greater involvement through the Pacific Island Forum (PIF) as a dialogue partner would give a transcontinental touch to its initiative to integrate various multilateral institutions under the Indo-Pacific construct.

Conclusion

Multilateralism in the Indo-Pacific has been gaining momentum while at the same time institutions have been expanding the role of dialogue partners as well as members; there is still lack of interconnectivity between different organisations. ASEAN has steadfastly maintained its centrality which to a certain extent has stalled progress on the elevation of the East Asia Summit forum, an informal mechanism to an East Asian security forum. The geographic and geo-strategic construct has been followed by a multilateral institution supporting the cause. It has been seen in the case of APEC and East Asian Summit; this has been missing from the Indo-Pacific discourse. Secondly, India has been missing from important forums such as APEC which has been detrimental to the scope of the Indo-Pacific. As a result, India is still circumspect about Indo-Pacific and has also not given a serious thought to Trans Pacific Partnership which is a connection between Southeast Asia, Oceania and Pacific Rim. India's major concentration remains in Southeast Asia; however, its strategic partnership with Japan, Korea and Australia shows that the structural edifice is there to build the Indo-Pacific. In case strategic partners such as ASEAN, Australia, Japan, Korea and Indonesia start subscribing more to the Indo-Pacific then India might also play the card. The merger of IONS and the West Pacific Naval Symposium (WPNS) would be a good beginning. Thirdly, the reasons for the Indo-Pacific to prosper would either mean security or economic. In both cases, the resolve of the participating countries is missing. In terms of multilateral agenda there is a need for maxima–minima subscription which might give a lease of life as well as decide the future of the concept.

Multilateral institutions need to be supported and expanded in the Indo-Pacific region. However, whether China should be included in such structures is not very clear. Therefore, the future would primarily depend on the bigger question of exclusiveness or inclusiveness. As for the contemporary discourse, the concept has a future but the advocates need to be clearer about the objectives.

NOTES

1. Miriam Pyres, *Redefining Regional Power in International Relations: Indian and South African Perspectives* (London: Routledge, 2012), p. 14.
2. Ibid, p. 15.
3. Ibid.
4. Ibid.
5. Luis Simón, "Reaching Beyond the Indo-Pacific", *Comparative Strategy*, Vol. 32, No. 4, 2013, p. 331.
6. Michael Auslin, "Security in the Indo-Pacific Commons: Towards a Regional Strategy", *American Enterprise Institute for Public Policy Research*, December 2010. <http://www.aei.org/wp-content/uploads/2011/10/AuslinReportWedDec152010.pdf> accessed 21 November 2014.
7. Ibid.
8. Ibid.
9. Lindsey Powell, "In Defence of Multilateralism", Paper Prepared for *Global Environmental Governance: The Post-Johannesburg Agenda*, 23-25 October 2003 (New Haven, CT: Yale Center for Environmental Law and Policy) <http://www.yale.edu/gegdialogue/docs/dialogue/oct03/papers/Powell.pdf> accessed 21 November 2014; Pankaj Jha, *India Pacific Construct and India*. <http://www.carstudies.in/pdfs/commantries/Indopacific.pdf> accessed 21 November 2014.
10. Jha, n. 9.
11. Ibid.
12. Powell, n. 9.
13. Powell, n. 9.
14. Robert O. Keohane, "Multilateralism: An Agenda for Research", *International Journal*, Vol. 45, No. 4, Autumn, 1990, pp. 731–764.
15. Michael Wesley, *Regional Organisations of the Asia-Pacific: Exploring Institutional Change* (Basingstoke: Palgrave Macmillan, 2003), p. 98.
16. M. Olson, *The Logic of Collective Action: Public Goods and the Theory of Groups* (Cambridge MA: Harvard University Press, 1965).
17. Milton Z. Kafoglis and Richard J. Cebula, "The Buchanan-Tullock

Model: Some Extensions", *Public Choice*, Vol. 36, Issue 1, 1981, pp 179–186. Also see Wesley, n. 15, pp. 98–99.

18. Wesley, n. 15, pp. 98–99.
19. *Perth Communiqué, 13th Meeting of the Council of Ministers of the Indian Ocean Rim Association*, (Perth, Australia), 1 November 2013.
20. Sam Bateman, *Background Paper-The Second Trilateral Dialogue on Indian Ocean (2nd TDIO)* (Canberra), 9–10 September 2014. <https://www.aspi.org.au/__data/assets/pdf_file/0016/23821/2nd-TDIO-Background-Paper-Dr-Bateman.pdf> accessed 21 November 2014.
21. Koh Swee Lean Collin and Darshana M. Baruah, "Managing Indo-Pacific Crises", *The Diplomat*, 19 November 2014. <http://thediplomat.com/2014/11/managing-indo-pacific-crises/>accessed 21 November 2014.
22. Ibid.
23. Bateman, n. 20.
24. *US urged to back India's APEC entry.* <http://www.thehindu.com/news/national/us-urged-to-back-indias-apec-entry/article6150405.ece/> accessed 30 May 2015.
25. *India ready to join APEC, US to help.* <http://timesofindia.indiatimes.com/business/india-business/India-ready-to-join-Apec-US-to-help/articleshow/46024577.cms/> accessed 23 May 2015.
26. Joseph Chinyong Liow, *What to Make of Indonesia's Indo-Pacific Treaty.* <http://www.straitstimes.com/news/opinion/more-opinion-stories/story/what-make-indonesias-indo-pacific-treaty-20141016#sthash.K6vl644l.dpuf> accessed 21 November 2014.
27. "India needs to act with Indonesia for Indo-Pacific security", *IANS*, 3 November 2014. <http://www.business-standard.com/article/news-ians/india-needs-to-act-with-indonesia-for-indo-pacific-security-comment-114110300134_1.html> accessed 21 November 2014.
28. Ibid.
29. Ibid.
30. Bateman, n. 20.
31. David Brewster, *India as an Asia-Pacific Power* (London: Routledge, 2013), p. 160.
32. Shyam Saran, *Mapping the Indo-Pacific.* <http://www.cprindia.org/blog/borders/3574-mapping-indo-pacific> accessed 21 November 2014.
33. Brewster, n. 31, p. 157.
34. Robert D. Kaplan, *Monsoon: The Indian Ocean and the Future of American Power* (New York: Random House, 2010), p. 283. Also quoted in Brewster, n. 31, p. 157.
35. Brewster, n. 31, p. 163.

36. C. Raja Mohan, *Chinese Takeaway: Modi's Indo-Pacific.* <http://indianexpress.com/article/opinion/columns/chinese-takeaway-modis-indo-pacific/#sthash.GfKJLPjE.dpuf> accessed 21 November 2014.
37. Ibid.

4

Unpacking India-China Strategic Futures Using Causal Layered Analysis

Jeanne Hoffman

ABSTRACT

India and China have a complex and uneasy relationship marked by their different political, and socio-economic paths since establishing modern statehood, their recent roles as emerging regional powers and lingering unresolved territorial dispute. This paper uses Causal Layered Analysis (CLA) to map the International Relations (IR) paradigms of 'China threat' and 'Chindia' used to construct their strategic relationship and to move deeper into the worldviews and myths that drive these epistemologies. The futures offered by both IR theories are problematic in that they offer futures that are closed with no alternatives for a better world. The goal here is to problematise and deconstruct the dominant discourses and offer an alternative more desirable futures asking "What visions for alternative futures for India and China are imaginable, desirable, and achievable"? rather than accepting well-rehearsed patterns of the future to emerge.

Introduction

> *When it comes to predicting the nature and location of our next military engagements, since Vietnam, our record has been perfect. We have never once got it right.*[1]

The global balance of power is shifting from West to East and with it focus has moved to the relationship between the two major powers of the region: India and China. These countries are home to two of the world's largest and oldest civilisations and, perhaps owing to the moderating influence of the Himalaya mountain range for most of their history, have lived side by side in peace.[2] This quiet and mostly cooperative relationship developed over the millennia via the material and spiritual cultural exchange of the Silk Road. Between Indian and Chinese independence, in 1947 and 1949 respectively, and 1957 this relationship enjoyed a period of cooperation based on a kind of respect and peaceful coexistence between the two post-colonial countries known, in Hindi, as '*Hindi Chini Bhai Bhai*' (India and China are brothers), despite China's military takeover of Tibet in 1950 and the Dalai Lama seeking refuge in India in 1959.[3]

This relationship began to change in 1962 after a full scale war erupted between the two countries, provoked by a territorial dispute in the Aksai Chin and Arunachal Pradesh border regions, and the relationship has since been known as 'Hindi Chini Bye Bye'. One of the lingering narratives of the war was a statement by Chinese Premier Zhou Enlai that the war was meant to "teach India a lesson" because "India was moving too close to the United States".[4] The Indian narrative is to blame the Chinese, or at least Prime Minister Jawaharlal Nehru's naïve understanding of international politics of the time.[56] The Chinese, for their part, mainly blame Nehru, claiming that he was using "China's Tibet region as an Indian sphere of influence".[7] Indeed this border remains a military hot spot and continues to vex the two countries' relations, which have not been fully normalised.[8]

India and China have recently seen their economic and political prominence rise after centuries of stagnation. This is not a completely new phenomenon: for over 1,500 years, from the early 1st century to 1500, India was the world's largest economy. China's economy jumped ahead of India's and held the mantle of the world's largest from about 1500 to the mid-1800s till its economy collapsed between the 1840s and 1940s.[9] In 1700 India and China combined may have accounted for 60-70 per cent of world GDP before their economic and political collapses after their experiences with Western colonialism and war. Goldman Sachs' 2003 BRIC (Brazil, Russia, India and China) study estimated that by 2032 India's economy, in terms of Purchasing Power Parity[10] (PPP), could be larger than world number two Japan's, and that by 2041 China's economy would be larger than that of the United States, the current leader. India's economy beat Goldman Sachs' prediction by 20 years, surpassing Japan's in 2011.[11,12] Goldman Sachs (2003) also predicted that the BRIC economies, taken together, could be larger than the G6 (the US, Japan, Germany, the United Kingdom, France and Italy) by 2039. The National Intelligence Council's *Global Trends 2030* predicts that by 2030 Asia will have more global power than the US and Europe combined, in terms of population, gross domestic product (GDP), military spending and investment in technology.[13] The IMF declared in 2014 that China had overtaken the US as the world's largest economy, signalling the end of the "American Century" and the start of the "Chinese Century".[14]

The IMF reports that "India will be the fastest growing major economy in 2016, with projected GDP growth of 6.5 per cent against China's 6.3 per cent".[15] There are a number of favourable factors for India: its younger population, vigorous democracy, easy movement of people and goods, its use of the English language, large, sophisticated companies, such as Tata Group, that can compete globally, the Reserve Bank of India's relative independence from government influence and the country's free press.[16] In response to India's overtaking of China, the *Global Times* reported that "[if] India could give up its Cold War mindset, China-India cooperation will be promising. Even if India does outrun China some day in the future, Beijing will give New Delhi its warmest congratulations".[17]

But India, too, will vie for this title as a "superpower" in its own "Indian Century".[18] Whether it is China or India that is 'victorious' in struggle for the naming rights the next century, what is known is that the Indian Ocean is emerging as the nexus of 21st century geopolitics.[19] Who will lead? How will they lead? And under what circumstances will they lead? This changing power dynamic within Asia, particularly between the seemingly endless dyads of India-China, India-Pakistan, China-Pakistan, China-Japan, Japan-India; the triangular relationships between India, China and Pakistan, India, China and Japan, and India, China and the US, as well as their relationships with smaller countries in the region, all stretch the Western body of knowledge about international relations (IR); this is a multipolar, chaotic and uncertain world.[20]

The methodology used in this paper is causal layered analysis (CLA), a narrative-based approach. The body of knowledge that

IR provides for the futures of Sino-Indian relations, as well as the impact their relationship will have on the region, is used at the expense of alternative discourses: "Virtually all theories of IR seek replicable truths and are deeply ill-at-ease with results that are unclear or open-ended or with projects that reveal ambiguity and ambivalence".[21] Stephen Walt (1998) defended the use of IR theory to explain the future actions of a country, saying that it is important to have a "diverse array of competing ideas rather than a single theoretical orthodoxy".[22] However, the truths offered by the primary IR schools of thought, realism and liberalism, used by India and China are based on assumptions and evidence is needed to support their positions. But future facts do not exist. "Evidence" can be found to support any theory based on the assumptions of these schools of thought, because the underlying assumptions themselves are not questioned, only the evidence to support the facts. The result is then used to conflate or deflate any particular action by a state to fit with the chosen theory. Walt also acknowledges that a theory that is internally incoherent generates illogical hypotheses, creating a false view of the world.[23]

Within security studies, changes in the global distribution of power affect states' propensity to go to war. This article argues that no matter the IR theory used, seeing the future of India-China relations through the lens of IR theory is problematic in that "the level of debate can be argued to be shallow, suffering from motivated belief and unable to provide deeper understandings".[24] In security studies, as in futures studies, it is important to understand and interpret the past, to situate the present and to use this understanding, interpretation and situating to influence the future.[25] To civilisations such as India and China, whose histories go back almost 6,000 and 3,000 years respectively, Western international relations theories can be seen as colonising, resting on the dominant ways of thinking of Western power structures and not as relevant to their own futures as they are to those of Europe and the United States. This article will deepen the discussion on the geo-strategic and geo-economic futures of India-China relations by mapping the two most commonly discussed futures of India in China and of China in India as seen through the IR theories of realism and liberalism using CLA. The article will also offer two alternative futures: (1) eco-spiritual and (2) a new beginning.

Theoretical Framework of Causal Layered Analysis

The providing of insight and the understanding of change should not rely solely on the IR episteme—the particular historical era of a society as reflected by its knowledge practices—as this limits what we can do and what we can think.[26] The future is an empty space, but by understanding the forces of change we are able to influence the course of events in order to avoid tragedy.[27] This paper relies on the futures studies method of CLA used by Hoffman.[28] CLA, developed by Inayatullah,[29] allows the most common images of the India-China strategic relationship to be mapped and, in doing so, allows a deconstruction of the present and past to create alternative futures rather than simply predicting a particular future based on a narrow empiricist or IR viewpoint alone. I argue that the perspective and language of IR policy-makers, researchers and academics have precluded other ways of thinking and knowing, thus limiting their understanding. In the changing world system, with all its ambiguity, uncertainty, complexity, dynamism and chaos, new approaches are needed.

CLA requires the user to travel through vertical and horizontal layers which ultimately question or 'un-define' the future and make the units of analysis problematic. CLA's unique layered approach allows the user to unpack the unconscious stories used to make sense of the way reality is formed. Importantly, CLA explores not just the noise of the litany and the systems, but the deeper worldviews and myths that support these layers of data.[30] CLA does not claim or argue for any particular 'truth', but aims to explore how a discourse becomes privileged—that is, who gains and who loses when a particular discourse becomes dominant. For this reason it is useful for examining the conclusions reached in popular images of the future of India-China relations and their impact on Indo-Pacific futures.

CLA has four overlapping layers: (1) litany, (2) systemic causes, (3) discourse/worldview, and (4) myth/metaphor. The litany level identifies the trends, events and issues that make up the "official unquestioned view of reality".[31] The facts presented at this level are not value-free, and they are hard to challenge because they are presented as the 'truth' or are 'self-fulfilling prophecies' on which the system, worldview or myth rests. The systemic causes level interprets this data through the lens of systemic and social causes and their effects. The data can be questioned, but not the paradigms within which the question is framed.[32] At this level, the government, experts from academia, or simply 'someone else', are expected to solve the problem. These two levels, the litany and systemic causes, are considered 'shallow' and short-term in their focus. In order to move into deeper and more complex analysis, the next two levels must be uncovered.

The worldview layer examines the interests and perspectives of multiple stakeholders. The key here is to recognise what deeper positions are legitimising the assumptions behind the systemic causes and the litany views. Whether to include or exclude a particular discourse can ultimately privilege the issue and the scenarios which emerge. This level allows other perspectives to place claims on how the scenarios are framed, so whether one has a realist versus idealist worldview, an Indian versus a Chinese worldview, or even a Nationalist versus a Communist worldview will have consequences for how scenarios are constituted.[33]

The myths and metaphors create an unconscious archetype within which a person's or group's experiences, perceptions and worldviews are framed. This makes these images difficult to change because they are highly valued and, in a sense, held sacred by the person or group. Most importantly the ability to open up or transform the future can require unlearning particular myths or worldviews held dear so as to learn new ways of thinking about the future.[34]

International Relations Constructs

The narrative on the rise of China and the concurrent rise of India is embedded in how these nations will revise or integrate themselves into the current world order and with US interests and is often discussed through two competing IR frameworks: realism and liberalism. A common narrative posits India and China as natural competitors "whose proximity and zero-sum interests are creating tensions that will make it extremely difficult to avoid sustained strategic rivalry".[35] China's ascent has been the primary focus of discussion in IR circles.[36,37,38,39] Relatively less scholarship has been devoted to India's rise[40] and even less to how the two nations perceive each other's ascendancy.[41]

Realism is grounded in fear and anarchy and in "selfish human appetites for power, or the need to accumulate the wherewithal to be secure in a self-help world".[42] Its central premises include balance-of-power politics, great power alliances, deterrence, and containment.[43] War is considered the 'normal' state of affairs when the hegemonic balance becomes disrupted, as in this current time of change.

Defensive realism holds that states want to maintain stability and that the only way to do this is to pursue ambitious economic, military and diplomatic strategies.[44,45] These defensive responses, including acquiring nuclear weapons and forming balancing alliances, only seek to maintain a self-defence posture without threatening others; although other nations can misconstrue this behaviour as threatening, thus decreasing collective security.[46,47]

Offensive realists, such as Mearsheimer, believe that states are "power maximisers" vis-à-vis other states. This notion rests on five assumptions: (1) that the international system is anarchic with no central authority, (2) that states possess offensive military capacity, (3) that states can never be certain of other states' intentions, (4) that survival is the primary goal of a state, and (5) that great powers are rational actors.[48] Many offensive realists consider that China's regional strategy will be a zero sum game between itself and the United States.[49,50]

In China, realists dominate this discourse about China's futures, and they sit in "offensive" and "defensive" camps.[51] One added component of the realist worldview in China is a layer of historical discontentment over China's "century of humiliation" at the hands of the West and Japan; a series of events starting with the Opium Wars (1839-1842 and 1856-1860) progressing through various military defeats, "unequal" treaties and foreign occupation which culminated in the 1937-1945 Japanese War.[52,53]

According to the Indian writers, such as Joshi, "Indian perceptions of China range from implacably hostile to unchangeably warm".[54] Ollapally and Rajagopalan call India an "ambiguous power" because of its lack of a well-articulated grand strategy or national doctrine,[55] but there are signs that India is moving from a defensive to an offensive perspective, particularly with regard to its relationship with China.[56,57] As one Indian analyst asserts: "China and India are natural rivals in Asia for geo-strategic, economic, and ideological (democracy vs autocracy) reasons. In every aspect, we are contrasts... Such rivalry is not easily reconcilable".[58]

Liberal theory (liberalism) focuses on two streams of explanation for peace, one focusing on the forms and practices of government, the other on free markets and private property.[59] The first stream is concerned with individual rights, constitutionalism, democracy and limitation on the power of the state as seen through the spread of democracy and globalisation.[60] Immanuel Kant, the enlightenment philosopher, rejected the concept of the 'balance of power', believing that perpetual peace was only possible by the conquest of the whole world by one country, a view shared by offensive realists.[61,62] The followers of the second stream of liberal theory are those who believe economic interdependence as the pathway to peaceful relations. Liberalists claim that the incentive to initiate war is lowered when the value of trade is increased. This viewpoint is empirically supported by the results of a study by Gartzke,[63] who found economic freedom to be about 50 times more effective as a predictor of reduced violent conflict between nations than what sort of political regime controls the country.

The future is unpredictable, but by deconstructing the dominant ways of thinking and allowing preferred images of the future to emerge, transformation, rather than just 'more of the same', can occur. The shape of the future for India and China is sure to become more complicated with their increasing wealth and confidence. The way this future unfolds will be about the establishing of a 'new normal' unrestrained by old beliefs, policies and processes so as to create and re-create preferred futures.

Narrative 1: "China Threat" as India Sees It

Litany Level

The primary concern of Indian offensive realists at the litany level is their distrust and fear of a rising China. Fear is a powerful political tool that can bias political beliefs and support for certain governmental policies, including war.[64,65] The message at this level is superficial, appealing to a mass readership, and fails "to probe beneath the surface of social and cultural life".[66] From an offensive realist's perspective, the economic growth of China is leading to desire for political and military gains, and in doing so will necessitate military conflict. China will have 'no choice' but to push for hegemony, as attempted by Germany (1900-1918, 1933-1945) and Japan (1931-1945) and as achieved by the United States.[67] Realist and neo-classical international relations frameworks hold that the rapid rises of India and China and their unresolved territorial disputes will see a Sino-Indian 'rivalry' take shape.[68]

Mutual distrust is growing. A recent Lowy Institute poll (2013) found that a large majority of Indians (83 per cent) consider China a security threat. There were four main reasons for this mistrust: China's possession of nuclear weapons, competition for resources in third countries, China's efforts to strengthen its relations with other countries in the Indian Ocean region, and the China-India border dispute.[69] Approximately 72 per cent of the population in India held strong concerns about territorial disputes with China.[70] Among the Chinese, 62 per cent had an unfavourable view of India, although 44 per cent viewed economic growth in India as positive for China.[71]

India was once a leading initiator of the 'China threat' theory: that the Chinese cannot be trusted is almost a mantra in India, and relations between the two countries are almost always coloured through this lens that has its origin in the border dispute and the 1962 war.[72] In 2009, Bharat Verma, an army captain and editor of the reputable *Indian Defence Review*, made the dramatic claim that "China will launch an attack on India before 2012... to teach India the final lesson, thereby ensuring Chinese supremacy in Asia in this century".[73] This did not happen, but it hasn't stopped negative and aggressive images of China being widely reported in credulous terms by mainstream Indian media outlets. Vikram Sood, the former head of India's external intelligence service, wrote that "China is determined to keep us... psychologically and strategically handicapped".[74] Deng explains that China threat theories held by offensive realists underscore how China's political and economic rise engenders a hostile "other" status, which in the words of Alexander Wendt could "turn a no-holds-barred power politics behind it" resulting in an established image of the enemy.[75]

Systemic level

The border between China and India has never been officially delineated and is central in understanding the tensions in the Indian psyche with regard to China. When the Communist Party of China assumed power, they renounced all prior foreign agreements as unequal treaties imposed upon China during the "century of humiliation" and demanded renegotiation of all borders, including the McMahon Line, moving the border of British-controlled India northwards.[76] India's loss in the Sino-Indian border war of 1962 bred a deep distrust of China. Territorial disputes are particularly war-prone because they become infused with "transcendental" qualities that make them intangible, creating a zero-sum paradigm to which the data of the litany must be made to fit. This in turn gives such disputes great symbolic value, because they represent other perceived hurts.[77]

Prime Minister Narendra Modi's Bharatiya Janata Party (BJP) has long called for a militarily-strong India to counter potential threats from both China and Pakistan. India has been the world's top arms buyer for the last three years (2012-15), although still spent less than a third of China's $145 billion expenditure in 2014.[78]India has embarked on the deployment in the air, and on sea and land of nuclear weapons creating by 2016 what military planners call a 'nuclear theatre' in South Asia between India, China and Pakistan.[79] Old antagonistic upsets are being repurposed for new overlapping claims to the East and South China Seas. China has faced disputes with Japan, Vietnam, and the Philippines over its claims on the Senkaku/Diaoyu Islands in the East China Sea, and to the long archipelagos in the South China Sea that comprise hundreds of islets, all areas rich in fish, petroleum and gas.[80] China's development of an economic and diplomatic "maritime silk road" in ports such as Colombo, Sri Lanka, and Gwadar, Pakistan have many, especially in India, suspicious of China's motives. India seeks to strengthen relations with the United States, Vietnam, Myanmar (Burma), Taiwan, Japan, South Korea and the ASEAN states to balance the rise of China.[81]

Worldview/Discourse Level

"China cannot rise peacefully" because "it is likely to lead to an intense security competition between China and the United States" according to Mearsheimer.[82] Mearsheimer goes on to say that "most of China's neighbours, *including* India, Japan, Singapore, South Korea, Russia, Vietnam—and Australia—will join with the United States to contain China's power".[83] In fact, if India does continue to rise, this would further increase the potential for great power conflict and the world would remain a "dangerous place".[84] This worldview assumes that China will strive to become so militarily powerful that it dominates all the other states in the region, including the United States and India, because that would be the only way to ensure its survival.

India's first "peaceful" detonation of a nuclear weapon in 1974 was a reaction to the Sino-Indian War of 1962 and India's need to achieve a balance of power with China. Waltz calls this the 'military logic for self-help' and that India becoming a nuclear power was inevitable.[85] Even Mahatma Gandhi, the great apostle of non-violence, believed that the atomic bomb had tremendous power to achieve political goals.[86] Later, in 1998, Indian Prime Minister Atal Bihari Vajpayee explained to US President Bill Clinton that:

> We have an overt nuclear weapon state on our borders, a state which committed armed aggression against India in 1962. Although our relations with that country have improved in the last decade or so, an atmosphere of distrust persists mainly due to the unresolved border problem. To add to the distrust that country has materially helped another neighbour of ours to become a covert nuclear weapons state. At the hands of this bitter neighbour we have suffered three aggressions in the last 50 years. And for the last ten years we have been the victim of unremitting terrorism and militancy sponsored by it in several parts of our country, especially Punjab and Jammu & Kashmir.[87]

The nuclearisation of India rests on this worldview of the currency of power and on the idea that "there are no better means of self-protection than nuclear weapons". Mearsheimer believes that the US should support India's nuclear ambitions to help it contain China as it "would be foolish to allow China to gain a nuclear advantage over it".[88]

The realist worldview symbolises "the Lockean paradigm of rivalry at its best and the Hobbesian paradigm of conflict at its worst".[89] The structure of anarchy and states' unstoppable pursuit of power ensure that rivalry and conflict are the only options and that no matter what action a state takes, it will be seen as a threat. Whether India's posturing can be seen as defensive rather than offensive is a moot point as defensive actions have often triggered an offensive nuclear arms race. Any policies that promote engagement, or even military coöperation, are doomed to fail because the ultimate goal is to gain hegemony and, in the case of China and India, each will do whatever it can to prevent the other from achieving regional hegemony.[90]

Myth/Metaphor

China is a Bully

The metaphor for China from an Indian realist point of view is that China is a bully guilty of "relentless border violations" and that "India must be willing to respond to Chinese incursions by sending troops into strategic Chinese-held territory".[91] There is a prevailing myth that "China and Pakistan will coordinate an invasion of India, and balkanise the nation, or at least destroy [India's] economy".[92] Numerous examples of China's bullying are given: its military relationship and involvement in Pakistan's nuclear weapons development, used to gang-up on India; China's bullying of Vietnam and the Philippines over the Paracel Islands and Spratly Islands respectively; China's bullying Japan over the Senkaku Islands, and most importantly; China's bullying of India over the territorial borders of Arunachal Pradesh. The India-China relationship is naturally assumed to be antagonistic. Karnad goes so far as to suggest that India should help Japan and Vietnam in defence and Taiwan in the nuclear sector as payback for Chinese assistance to Pakistan's strategic programmes.[93] Headlines from around the world support this 'fact' that China is a bully: "The Bullies of Beijing: China's Image Problem",[94] "Why does China bully India?";[95] and statements such as "China is behaving exactly as one would expect a great power to behave".[96] Harsh Pant, an academic based at King's College in London, insists that "India cannot have a foreign policy shaped by the assumed kindness of its neighbours", implying the need for "a more robust official reaction than has hitherto been forthcoming".[97] This discourse is bounded by its own definitions and cannot see China as anything other than a bully. At all of these levels, China must be contained, diminished and stood up to through balancing, and eventually, inevitably, war.

Good vs evil

Prime Minister Vajpayee ventured into the mythology of the power of nuclear weapons, expressing that they gave India *Shakti* (energy and will), strength and self-confidence.[98] *The Bhagavad Gita* (Gita) tells of a mythic narrative of Arjuna who represents 'good' and his dialogue with Krishna about when to use powerful weapons against the 'evil' Kauravas. Arjuna possesses a powerful weapon the *brahmastra* that has the power to restore the balance of power in the world by ridding the planet of evil as well as the potential of destroying the universe. Vajpayee and his party, BJP, used this rhetorical device of Arjuna's struggle to 'situate India as the origin of nuclear technology', and also to moderate the morality of nuclear weapons policies.[99] This political connection to the myth of Arjuna has had the effect of building a narrative around India being able to conquer evil and affirming China (and Pakistan) as the evil 'other'.

Narrative 2: "China Threat" as the Chinese See It

Litany

The litany for realists in China is that the United States and Japan are its primary enemies, with India serving as these countries' "tool".[100] India is portrayed as a dysfunctional democracy with the dubious distinction of having extreme and persistent levels of poverty, while China has achieved a steady rise in people's living standards since 'opening' itself to the world in 1978. Zhang Weiwei, a former Chinese diplomat, characterises India as the land of slums and terrorist attacks in his book *China Shock: The Rise of a Civilisation-State.*[101] Zhang then traces the foundation for all of India's problems —poverty, corruption, communal violence, terrorism—to its parliamentary system of government.[102] This dysfunctional democracy is coupled with a media that promotes antagonistic attitudes toward China, including hyping the 'China threat theory', which conspire to threaten China's borders. The media "have long been so accustomed to calibrating to curry favour with the Western anti-China forces that they invariably present their readers with biased information and fabricated stories about China". This gravely hampers "the normal development of the bilateral relations".[103] The 'China threat', therefore, is merely an inferiority complex suffered by India, which harbours a mix of "awe, vexation, envy and jealousy—in the face of its giant neighbour".[104]

There is also a racial element in the portrayal of India as the 'other'. According to Yu Longyu, director of the Centre for Indian Studies at Shenzhen University, Chinese ignorance of India is alarming. This lack of knowledge expresses itself in the most extreme perceptions about India as a place of "rape, Buddhism (despite the fact that less than 1 per cent of Indians are Buddhists), and yoga".[105] Chinese netizens frequently summarise India as the "yellow sick man" and a troublemaker for China, using racist stereotypes such as "curry", "dirty" and "poor".[106]

Systemic level

China has a deep distrust of India. The 'China threat' theory is seen as a way for both the US and India to justify India's security role in Southeast Asia as a means of balancing China.[107] Under threat are the core interests and related national security of China. A 2014 study by three researchers at the Beijing Naval Research Centre explained that "India's 'Look East' strategy will have a huge impact on our country's geopolitical security" and that India may "join the confluence" of Japan's "Down South Strategy" (WSN & beu, *Nanka Senryaku*) and America's "Rebalance to the Asia-Pacific"; "[If these three strategies] were coordinated, in effect encircling China's maritime geopolitical environment, this would constitute even greater harm to our country's maritime security and its development of sea power".[108]

The mass feelings of frustration around domestic social issues, such as the expanding income gap, corruption, environmental pollution and social injustice, are able to be vented through nationalism with concepts like 'peaceful coexistence' deemed harmful to China's interests.[109] This effect of nationalism forces all strategic choices in reclaiming China's lost international status to be hard options, the result being that China and the Chinese people will be dissatisfied until they "reclaim their superpower status".[110]

Worldview

The offensive realist paradigm fits neatly with Classical Chinese statecraft, based on Chinese strategic tradition:

> The Chinese not only want to restore China's dominant role at the centre of Asia, but seek to establish their country as one of the major poles – second to none – in a multipolar world... This conceptualisation of interstate relations based upon a hierarchical system with China at the top is ingrained in their cultural worldview. Today, this sense of hierarchy is expressed in notions of comprehensive national power and military power.[111]

As a means to forecast the future status hierarchy of power rivals, China uses a "comprehensive national power" (CNP) numerical assessment of its security which purports to measure the relative military, economic and cultural (soft) powers of a nation-state over time.[112] Colonel Huang Shuofeng explains that its role is to quantitatively measure the rise and fall of nations.[113] India's CNP rank is "somewhere above Brazil but below Germany" according to Ye Hailing, the deputy director of South Asia at the Chinese Academy of Social Sciences.[114] So while India sees China as its greatest threat, India is not as great a strategic concern to China. Despite China holding an image of India's desire to be a "great power" as unrealistic and unachievable, in the 1990s China insisted on India adhering to the "five Nos":

1. Don't peddle "the China threat theory"
2. Don't support Tibet's or Taiwan's independence
3. Don't oppose the Sino-Pakistani "all weather relationship"
4. Don't align with the United States to contain China
5. Don't seek to be, or to project India as, an equal to China[115]

An article published in *Wenweipo*, a CCP-sponsored newspaper, on 8 July 2013 entitled "The Six Wars to be fought by China in the coming 50 years" is an offensive realist's propaganda dream, explaining that:

> China is not yet a unified great power. This is a humiliation to the Chinese people, a shame to the children of the Yellow Emperor. For the sake of national unification and dignity, China has to fight six wars in the coming fifty years. Some are regional wars; the others may be total wars. No matter what is the nature, each one of them is inevitable for Chinese unification.[116]

The six wars to be fought include: 1) Taiwan (2020-25), 2) Spratly Islands (2025-30), 3) Southern Tibet (India, 2040), 4) Diaoyu and Ryukyu Islands (Japan, 2045), 5) Mongolia (2050), and 6) Tuva and Vladivostok (Russia, 2060). With respect to India, the *Wenweipo* article states that: "Of course, such a plan may fail. But China should at least try its best to incite Assam province and, once conquered, Sikkim to gain independence, in order to weaken the power of India. This is the best strategy".[117] And so the existing hierarchy must be maintained.

Myth/metaphor

Culturally the Chinese do not see others as equal, and the phrase "*Tian-xia*", or "all under heaven", captures this belief in cultural superiority and greatness. Traditional Chinese statecraft dictates that "states are either hostile or subordinate".[118]

India is a Cow

The image of India as a failed country that cannot compete on equal terms with China is well exemplified by a 1974 poem by Mao Zedong which "described the US as the tiger, Britain as the lion, the Soviet Union as the bear, the Islamic countries as the moon, the rich West as the sun and India as a cow". And a cow is "only food or for people to ride and for pulling carts; it has no particular talents. The cow would starve to death if its master did not give it grass to eat.... Even though this cow may have great ambitions, they are futile".[119]

As a 'cow', India is safe for China to isolate and ignore. India has a desire to be a permanent member of the UN Security Council, but has been snubbed by China due to India siding with the United States against Beijing, "its Armed Forces activities on the border areas with China, its tacit support [of the] Dalai Lama on his Arunachal Pradesh visit and its track record of [declared] and undeclared nuclear reactors' radioactive leaks".[120] It may not be possible to maintain this position, as the US has announced its support for India's quest to become a permanent member of the United Nations' Security Council. Perhaps, like Mao's wrong assessment of the US as a 'paper tiger' in 1956, regarding India as 'less than' has prompted India to "look East" for greater influence with the region's democracies (stretching from Mongolia to Taiwan, and from Japan and South Korea to Indonesia, Thailand, Singapore and Australia), and, like a cow, to bide its time.

Encirclement

The 'China threat' card is seen as a way for India to assert its designs on Chinese territory. China's growing interest in the Indian Ocean region represents the myth that if China does not take action, India will try to encircle it; "The US wants India to encircle China in China's west; Japan wants India to join it in confronting China, Russia wants to have a Russia-China-India alliance while China wants to solve border disputes to improve ties with India".[121] That the China threat theory is being used to contain China is a prevalent view. Yan Xuetong of the China Institute of Contemporary International Relations (CICIR) says:

> For a long time India has repeatedly pushed forward its expansionist policy, threatening its neighbouring countries in various ways. In 1962 it even started a large-scale border war against China; it also provided bases in Indian territory for the Dalai clique and encouraged them to engage in activities splitting China. People should wait and see whether the current Indian Government will create new trouble that may lead to a regional danger, to prove to the world a 'China Threat' really exists.[122]

People's Liberation Army Navy Rear Admiral Wang Ling, the second in command of the North Sea Fleet, simply says, "I believe Japan and the US are trying to contain and encircle China".[123]

Indeed, it is believed that this need to encircle China must be due to India's colonial past. A report written by the late Premier Zhou Enlai described India's 'blood relationship' (interbreeding) with the British, and explained that the Indian middle classes "took over from British imperialism this concept of India as the centre of Asia"; the Indian middle classes want to have "a great Indian empire that dominates Asia".[124] China must align itself with Pakistan to contain a common enemy. For China to restore itself to its "Middle Kingdom" status and for Pakistan to dream of restoring the Mughal Empire—both utopic desires—a compact against secular India, with all its pluralism and democracy, must be created before China and Pakistan both become victims once again.[125]

Narrative 3: Chindia

The counter argument to the realist assumption of inevitable war is the liberal theory of economic interdependence. This theory posits that if the civil society of China and India see the benefits of trade and cross investment this will place natural constraints on state aggression. A prosperous and stable Asia will ensure that the major emerging powers do not come into conflict.[126]

Litany

The view here is that India and China have complementary economies. China is the world's workshop and India the back office with its focus on IT and outsourcing. They can "make beautiful music together".[127] This concept of mutual prosperity resting on China and India as 'stakeholders' in US global dominance is appealing for its promise of stability. This linear economic and political view is still grounded in positivism, with the extrapolation of trends forward dependent on China and India working together within the current world system to lead themselves, and the world, to a new kind of prosperity based on Asian values.[128] China is expected to overtake the US as the world's largest economy by 2032, and by 2050 China's economy is expected to be 20 per cent larger than that of the United States in real dollar terms.[129] India is predicted to post the most rapid growth of all G20 countries, 5.9 per cent annually. India is expected to surpass China to become the world's most populous nation in 2031.[130] In this scenario, although a diminished US will still retain its first-among-equals status, China and India will emerge as two of the world's largest economies, representing the two largest populations.

Systemic

For China and India to prosper their systems will need innovation and reform. Better control of inflation, lower deficits, increasing productivity, richer social programmes and greater political stability have given the emerging giants greater room for error at a time when the macro-economic environment in rich countries has been deteriorating.[131]

In the short term, China's 13th Five Year Plan, the development of blueprint for the period from 2016 to 2020, is being drawn up now. This document creates a set of targets and guidelines spanning a range of social, economic and environmental issues and informs China's economic and political success. By 2021, the 100th anniversary of the founding of the CCP, China has a grand objective of achieving a more enabling international environment for China's peaceful development. By 2020, Xi Jinping has called for "two centenary goals" of CCP rule to be achieved: a doubling of its 2010 GDP and the subjectively assessed achievement of a "moderately well-off society"–meaning, in hard terms, that the per capita income in China will be double the 2010 figure.[132]

There are certainly differences between the two countries that make this concept difficult: per capita income and general quality of life in India is significantly lower, and class divisions China are also more progressive. Internally both countries have their own problems with inequality, particularly the rural-urban divide; land acquisition and the provision of other basic human rights are also contentious issues.[133]

A simultaneous economic and political rise of India and China is a challenging civilisational concept for both countries to accept. Austin Coates argues that the concept of centrality—the unassailable civilisational concept of surveying the world and everything in it in terms of its own centrality—is "responsible for the blindness China and India exhibit in regard to each other's nature".[134]

Worldview

China regards the liberal economic order and political system as an existential threat. It is working to build a parallel order through the establishment of a wide range of international institutions covering a broad spectrum of policy areas, including financial and monetary policy, trade and investment, trans-regional infrastructure projects, security policy, technology, in particular

ICT, and diplomatic forums.[135] The Asian Infrastructure Investment Bank (AIIB) intends to mirror the Asian Development Bank, the Shanghai Cooperation Organisation to mirror NATO in Central Asia, and the proposed "BRICS Development Bank" to mirror the World Bank, to name a few. These competitive and complementary institutions seek to shape the international order beyond Western claims to leadership.[136]

India has committed to greater integration into the world economy. As it straddles "all important global fault lines", the choices through which it can now engage are, thanks to China's efforts, doubled.[137]

Myth

Chindia

The myth/metaphor of Chindia rests on India and China being able to overcome their mutual distrust. Alternative futures can only be achieved if India and China are both able to decolonise their minds and move beyond the "irreducible problem of the Other".[138,139] Both countries face enormous internal challenges, including the need for "maximising human and material resources for development, balancing growth with equity, distribution of resources and monies between its rich and poor,... access to education, health and other social services, rural-urban disparities, migration, unevenness of standards of governance and systems of laws, and, above all, keeping rates of economic growth above the rates of growth of populations and inflow into the labour market".[140] Chindia cannot exist until the worldviews and myths of its shadow, the 'China threat' or 'India as a dismissive submissive junior' found in historical antipathy, and the power politics of maintaining the dominant future and cultural one-upmanship of who first achieves rejuvenation, can be overcome. Both countries will need to take bold steps. China will need to support India for permanent membership on the UN Security Council, and India will need to make certain its developing relationships with Japan and the United States are not just strategic partnerships developed to contain China. They will need to come to an agreement on Aksai Chin and on the Arunachal Pradesh border regions.

An alternative view of the Chindia myth is that it is *really* a myth. Mohan Malik says: "I know that these two are fierce competitors determined to outdo each other, not collaborators with common agendas. Both are uncomfortable with each other's rise and harbour intense suspicion and hostility. Beijing, in particular, shows no desire to accommodate India as an equal partner".[141]

Peaceful Rise

For Chindia to become a reality there needs to be an acceptance of China's peaceful rise. The peaceful rise of China will make other contributions for the good of humanity as well: "Many Indians continue to have dreams of forging India-China solidarity in the name of third-world unity, developing-world unity, anti-American unity and myriad other causes for which Indians have been fighting for decades".[142] Malik remarks that there are those in the Indian strategic community who believe that "China's 'peaceful rise' diplomacy has long sought to prevent Asian countries from banding together and/or entering into alignment with the United States in order to countervail China's power".[143]

The concept of a peaceful rise of China has some challenges. Ross Terrill believes that "Peace and development are means rather than ends for Beijing's foreign policy", and that China's long-term strategy is to establish a regional hegemony, including 'regaining lost territories' that Beijing feels rightfully belong within the PRC.[144] Hoffman notes that "as a non-democratic, authoritarian state in a region with democratic societies [whose] regional security relies on the large liberal democracy of the United States, China faces challenges in its capacity to establish the legitimacy of its discourse".[145]

4. Alternative Futures

Can India and China as well as the rest of the Indo-Pacific region overcome their recent legacy of conflict and colonialism and build futures that include more than just reflections of IR strategic power dynamics and economic growth models? Two alternatives can be offered.

4.1 Eco-Spiritual

> *Ojibwe prophecies speak of a time during the seventh fire when our people will have a choice between two paths. The first path is well-worn and scorched.*

> *The second path is new and green. It is our choice as communities and as individuals how we will proceed.*[146]

Litany

In this future, a shift to an eco-spiritual awakening, supported by a kind of emancipation from the dynamics of the current material world culture, is the way forward. The litany of environmental abuse and degradation is regularly reported in the media; the polluted skies, dead rivers, disappearing forests, and "incidents of poisoned milk, adulterated pork, and even exploding watermelons" in both China and India make this ecological and spiritual shift imperative.[147]

China is getting old. According to a RAND study, the proportion of the population at working age peaked and started to decline in 2012. By 2025 the share of the population that is elderly (65 or older) is expected to be around 14.3 per cent. Political and economic marginalisation has the potential to increase tensions between the people and the government. Economic inequality is increasing. The term *yizu* ("ant tribe") is now used to describe a struggling, disillusioned middle class who, although university educated, cannot return to their home towns for lack of jobs, nor settle in big cities because housing prices are out of their reach. The government is pushing ahead with plans to relocate 250 million rural residents by 2025 into newly constructed cities in order to create a new class of urban consumers. The Chinese are becoming increasingly dissatisfied with the "growth first" model of development and are demanding greater social justice and equity.[148]

India, too, is struggling with rising inequality and social justice issues. Income inequality has doubled in India since the early 1990s, according to a 2011 report published by the Organisation for Economic Cooperation and Development (OECD). India's top one per cent now holds close to half of the country's total wealth, while with about 42 per cent of its population is still living on less than US$1.25 per day.[149,150] There is a growing belief that crimes such as thefts, attempted murders, and assaults on women, children and the elderly are on the rise across Indian cities, and that this rising criminality is a product of the widening gap between the rich and the poor.[151] Ajai Sahni, executive director of the Delhi-based Institute for Conflict Management, believes that this increasing criminality "is led by a corrupt elite, many of whom have themselves resorted to crime to secure or sustain their power".[152]

China is the world's largest emitter of greenhouse gases and will produce 50 per cent more than the United States by 2015.[153] Not only is New Delhi the world's most polluted city, India is home to 13 of the 20 cities with the most polluted air.[154] India and China have 2.7 billion people between them, 37.5 per cent of the world's population.

An alternative model of human progress rests on the "inseparable spiritual connection of every person to nature and community".[155] In the last thirty years, China has seen a rise in spirituality, particularly in Christian beliefs. In 1949, China had just four million Christians and today the number is estimated to be as high as 130 million, with China home to the world's seventh largest Christian population, mostly comprising followers of Protestant and Catholic faiths.[156,157] By 2040 the proportion of Christians is expected to reach 30 per cent of the population.[158] Although Confucianism is still considered to be the primary tradition of Chinese society, the spiritual awakenings of Buddhism and Taoism have played a significant role in disrupting the dominant view in order to meet the demands of society during times of turmoil. Today, Christianity is fulfilling a number of roles, from its theological notions of salvation to its sociological links with modernity, as well as meeting a mass desire for social and spiritual healing through ritual congregationalism.[159] Yan Xuetong, a noted and influential academic, warns that "the Party leaders realise they don't have a dominant ideology they can use to run the country. For them there is no core social value. At this moment, the sole dominant ideology shared by this government and its people is money worship".[160] As one convert explains: "Our life has become so hectic, there is so much pressure. When my husband left me, I was devastated. But one of my friends took me to one of their gatherings and I realised that someone loves me. I want my daughter to grow up knowing that there is more in life than just money. I want her to care more about other people".[161]

Similarly, Kapoor believes that "the underlying mindset of the ordinary Indian is of ambiguity, uncertainty and seeking godly benevolence".[162] The number of eco-spiritual groups is growing. The Swadhyaya movement arose in the mid-20th century in the

Western states of Gujarat and Maharashtra in India. The main goal of Swadhyaya is to transform human society on the basis of the Upanishad's concept of "In dwelling God"; a sense of spiritual self-respect irrespective of materialistic prestige or possession, with the result being an Indian cultural renaissance through a reverence for natural resources such as the earth, the water, the trees, and cattle.[163] India will become the world's largest Muslim-majority country by 2050[164]; their growing numbers could be influential in setting the course for India, be that in international relations with neighbours such as Pakistan, or in demands for greater social inclusion. Batra believes that India's problems today can only be solved with practical spirituality that embodies universalistic philosophy, selflessness and a dynamic way of life, and that there needs to be a social revolution to achieve this.[165,166]

Systemic

Whoever owns the images of the future holds a vital element of modern state power.[167] The image of an endlessly growing, materialist India and China is based on the twin promises of technological progress and growth in aggregate consumption as measured by GDP. Within this narrative the consciousness that economic growth can provide sustainable outcomes, including social justice and happiness and technology to clean up the contamination, is being challenged. Gross Domestic Product is being replaced by Gross National Happiness, as used by Bhutan, which aims to improve the lives of those 'not yet happy'. Bhutan's 1729 legal code declared that "if the Government cannot create happiness (*dekid*) for its people, there is no purpose for the Government to exist".[168] This notion of happiness is multidimensional and declares that "the beneficial development of human society takes place when material and spiritual development occur side by side to complement and reinforce each other".[169] As part of the Millennium Development Goals, the UN General Assembly passed a resolution in 2011 to give "more importance to happiness and well-being in determining how to achieve and measure social and economic development".[170]

Worldview

The focus here is on how to create a new system, one where spiritual practice and community replace striving for material abundance and endless economic growth. With the increasing spiritual and ecological awareness in the face of rising inequity, what is being discovered is a "holistic approach to socio-economic development which fully provides for our physical needs while, at the same time, [nurturing] the development of our subtler capacities—and that does this in a manner that promotes the welfare of all, and that is not destructive towards nature".[171]

At the 2015 International Buddha Purnima Diwas celebrations in Delhi, Indian Prime Minister Modi spoke as follows: "It is said that the 21st century will be Asia's century. There is no disagreement on that. Without Buddha this century cannot be Asia's century". Modi further stressed that "if the humanity wanted freedom from war, it was only possible through peace, the Marg of Buddha. It required great courage and conviction to leave everything; money, power and work towards Manav Kalyan".[172]

Myth

The metaphor is of a spiritual awakening being a unifying force; an awakening of self, an awakening of community, an awakening of global civil society; "Spirituality, community and a bonding to place or habitat are central values that have unified the Asian cultures over centuries".[173]

4.2 Common Future: Mutual Benefit

Litany

2014 was the year of friendly exchanges between India and China, with political, economic and cultural ties increasing. Chinese language, with an accompanying 22 Chinese teachers, has been introduced into middle schools in India.[174] Xi Jinping visited India from 17 to 19 September 2014 and "Where the Chinese President goes, so goes the Chinese world".[175] Narendra Modi will visit China from 14 to 16 May 2015. Indian Foreign Minister Sushma Swaraj preceded Modi to hold discussions with both President Xi Jinping and Foreign Minister Wang Yi to lay the groundwork for an agreement over China and India's disputed border, this being "the next big diplomatic target for the government".[176]

Bilateral trade expanded 67-fold from 1998 to 2012. The Chinese and Indian armies held their first-ever joint military exercise in

2007, followed by two more in 2008 and 2013. The two countries are finding common agendas on global issues of mutual interest like world trade, climate-change negotiations, the primacy of state sovereignty, and the need to reform global-governance institutions".[177]

Systemic

Engagement between high level officials and the development of avenues for direct communication and cultural exchange are key to this scenario. This also includes improving the relationship with Pakistan. "Dialogue is the only way forward," says Indian analyst Kanti Bajpai, because "everything else India has tried", including the threat of war following the 2001 Indian Parliament attack, has failed to change the dynamic".[178]

India's economic relations with China are booming and there is an emerging alphabet of multi-faceted engagement between the two Asian powers—the ABCD of India-China relations: A for Asia, B for Business, C for Culture, and D for Diplomacy and Development. This new semantic of a growing pragmatic relationship allows new pathways for cooperation and for the reconfiguring of the evolving world order.[179] High level meetings are happening like never before. The Indian Vice-President Hamid Ansari met with his counterpart Li Yuanchao in China in June 2014 to mark the 60th anniversary of the Panchsheel Treaty, or Five Principles of Peaceful Coexistence; Ansari and Li signed several agreements on manufacturing and flood monitoring. Bilateral trade has increased 230 per cent since 1990, reaching $66 billion in 2012. China and India's militaries have begun conducting joint exercises with India's Army Chief, General Bikram Singh, visiting China, the second such official to do so.[180]

Bilateral ties are not yet developed enough to jointly address the regional and global security issues.[181] Work is continuing on a Regional Trade Agreement (RTA), the Regional Comprehensive Economic Partnership (RCEP), setting up industrial zones and aligning the Bangladesh-China-India-Myanmar (BCIM) Economic Corridor to improve connectivity and infrastructure, the sharing of energy resources, agriculture, and trade and investment.[182] India has implemented the Mausam and Spice Route projects with the aim of "re-connecting and re-establishing communications between countries of the Indian Ocean Region enhancing understanding of cultural values and concerns".[183] The Spice Route project meanwhile focuses on an India-centred linkup of historic sea routes in Asia, Europe and Africa".[184] China has expressed its desire to be involved. Even the border dispute has been given focused attention. Seriousness reflects from appointing National Security Adviser, Ajit Doval, as the contact person for India-China border negotiations. In India there is widespread expectation that "if the border issue gets resolved then we can return to the days of '*Hindi Chini Bhai Bhai*'".[185]

Worldview

This new model is not a reworking of Chindia, but a new story on the need for mutual sensitivity and recognition of the shared aspirations of India and China. The worldview will need to change from one of competition and self-interest, or even comparative advantage, to one of cooperation and shared knowledge similar to a Kantian peace ethic. Both countries need to move away from ontological insecurity concepts of "civilisational exceptionalism"[186] and "Middle Kingdom Syndrome"[187] to one in which a "special relationship" can be constructed similar to that between the US and Britain and the one being constructed for the US and India.[188]

The worldviews of Indian and Chinese leaders are important here. Xi Jinping holds near-absolute power in China. He is the General Secretary of the Communist Party of China, the president of the state and chairman of the Central Military Commission. Narendra Modi holds a clear parliamentary majority, the first Prime Minister to do so since Rajiv Gandhi in 1984. With such large, unencumbered amounts of power, both leaders "have the power to walk the talk" to achieve peace and grow out of the old rivalries.[189,190]

Myth/Metaphor

Inter-Connected Dreams

At the sixth BRICS summit of emerging powers in Fortaleza, Brazil in 2014, PM Modi and President Xi spoke of India and China's "inter-connected dreams" and of "a new and ambitious agenda" needed to fulfil the dreams of the Asian century. Xi shared Modi's view of the need for "building a high degree of engagement and familiarity between the two countries, to harness the full potential of their relationship".[191]

This message was reinforced when Indian Vice President Ansari, speaking to the Chinese Academy of Social Sciences, said that: "Our destinies are linked by geography and history. We welcome China's peaceful development and regard it as a mutually reinforcing process. There is enough space in the world for the development of India and China, and the world needs the common development of both countries".[192]

As with the 'China threat theory' for India or 'encirclement' for China, there needs to be recognition that these myths and metaphors are based on the power of the need for existential threat. Indian Ambassador to the US Shivshankar Menon told a group of students in April 2015 at Harvard University that: "Our goal is to transform India. China, like the US, or the world economy for that matter, is a fact of life. We must learn to use it to achieve our goals. Where it is a hindrance, deal with it—prevent it, eliminate it, work around it, divert it, and so on".[193]

For civilisational resurgence to be realised, the 21st century needs not only a meeting of the minds but of the shared cultural experiences of India and China.

Conclusion

Which future for India and China? The leaders and citizens of both countries need to engage in creating transformative futures. It has long been noted that there exists a dialectical relationship between strategic culture and operational behaviour. Decision-makers are "socialised in the strategic culture they produce, and thus can be constrained by the symbolic myths which their predecessors created" and "cannot escape the symbolic discourses they manipulate".[194] The reference point for talking about the India-China strategic relationship, either as the next great power rivalry or as a new global order, is based on mainstream Western IR or economics ontologies concerned with physical survival and material gain. This is a mistake.

The future is not certain. It is impossible to know which scenario will happen. The future that emerges does so because of three intersecting forces: the image of the future, the pushes of the present and the weights of history—those mindsets that can conspire to ensure the status quo remains.[195] If India and China believe and follow the views of either realism or liberalism without reflection or critical thinking, their futures will be compromised. They will be copying a used future that rests on an alien set of values left over from political systems and theories imported from the West. Alternatives are needed.

The IR futures are seen to be the 'disowned self' of the other pushing away its opposite, and as long as no alternatives are allowed, stories that sit outside our discursive frames cannot be developed. Each of the IR futures presented in this article is seen to be a used and disowned future. The structuralist and positivist nature that dominates the IR theories used by both Indian and Chinese policy-makers and pundits assumes that these countries, and individuals in these countries, lack the agency to shape politics and must fall into their neat Eurocentric categories of behaviour.

If India and China do indeed follow an offensive realist or liberalist path and no alternative futures are considered, they are doing nothing more than copying a linear, Western path of development and a material viewpoint based on a capitalist-technological worldview. Dialogue about alternative futures is an important step in understanding the various framings of China-India political theory and their limitations. Opening up to new ways of thinking allows us to identify the challenges to China-India futures and in so doing to increase cultural resilience and adaptive capacity, allowing new stories of transformation to be told.

NOTES

1. Robert M Gates, "Secretary of Defence Speech", 2011. <http://www.defence.gov/speeches/speech.aspx?speechid=1539> accessed 9 February 2015.
2. Atul Singh, "China and India: Relations Between the Two Asian Giants", *Fair Observer*, 14 February 2013. <http://www.fairobserver.com/region/central_south_asia/china-and-india-relations-between-two-asian-giants/> accessed 9 February 2015.
3. Arif Sheikh Mohd, "A History of Sino-Indian Relations: From Conflict to Cooperation", *International Journal of Political Science and*

Development, Vol. 1, No. 4, 2013, pp. 129-37.

4. Jasjit Singh, "Indian Air Power", in John Andreas Olsen, ed., *Global Air Power* (Washington, DC: Potomac Books, 2011), p. 210.
5. S. Kalyanaraman, "India and China: 50 years after 1962", *Institute for Defence Studies Analyses*, 2012. <http://www.idsa.in/IndiaChina1962war.html> accessed 19 February 2015.
6. Dibyesh Anand, "Remembering 1962 Sino-Indian Border War: Politics of Memory", *Journal of Defence Studies*, Vol. 6, No. 4, 2012, pp. 229-48.
7. Jagannath Panda, "The 1962 War: Will China speak about it?", *Institute for Defence Studies Analyses*, 2012. <http://www.idsa.in/idsacomments/The1962WarWillChinaspeakaboutit_ jppanda_161012.html#footnote1_q5t1tsa> accessed 19 February 2015.
8. Ivan Lidarev, "History's Hostage: China, India and the War of 1962", *The Diplomat*, 21 August 2012. <http://thediplomat.com/2012/08/historys-hostage-china-india-and-the-war-of-1962/>accessed 9 February 2015.
9. Angus Maddison, *Chinese Economic Performance in the Long Run*, 4th edn. (Paris: OECD Development Centre Studies, 2007).
10. Purchasing power parity is an economic estimate of the real cost of living; useful when measuring improvement in the standard of living.
11. Dominic Wilson and Roopa Purushothaman, "Dreaming with BRICs: The Path to 2050", *Goldman Sachs*, 1 October 2003. <http://www.goldmansachs.com/our-thinking/archive/archive-pdfs/brics-dream.pdf> accessed 9 February 2015.
12. "India's Rise to World's Third Largest Economy Puts More Pressure on China to Perform", *China Briefing*, 4 May 2014.<http://www.china-briefing.com/news/2014/05/04/indias-rise-worlds-third-largest-economy-puts-pressure-china-perform.html#sthash.AlLnx7Kp.dpuf> accessed 9 February 2015.
13. National Intelligence Council, "Global Trends 2030: Alternative Worlds", *Office of the Director of National Intelligence*, 2012, p. 15. <http://www.dni.gov/files/documents/GlobalTrends_2030.pdf> accessed 9 February 2015.
14. Hugo Duncan and David Martosoko, "America Usurped: China Becomes World's Largest Economy – Putting USA in Second Place for the First Time in 142 Years", *Daily Mail*, 8 October 2014. <http://www.dailymail.co.uk/news/article-2785905/China-overtakes-U-S-world-s-largest-economy-IMF-says-economy-worth-17-6trillion-America-falls-second-place-time-1872.html> accessed 10 April 2015.
15. R. Jagannathan, "IMF's Global Growth Forecast: It's Advantage India Over China by 2016", *First Post*, 21 January 2015. <http://

www.firstpost.com/business/imfs-global-growth-forecast-its-advantage-india-over-china-by-2016-2055075.html> accessed 19 March 2015.

16. A. Gary Shilling, "Why India Will Displace China as Global Growth Engine", *Bloomberg*, 16 December 2012. <http://www.bloombergview.com/articles/2012-12-16/why-india-will-displace-china-as-global-growth-engine> accessed 19 March 2015.
17. Anonymous, "India faces tests before it can overtake China", *Global Times*, 19 January 2015. <http://www.globaltimes.cn/content/902646.shtml> accessed 19 March 2015.
18. Sanjay Sanghoee, "India: The Next Superpower", *Fortune*, 25 January 2015. <http://fortune.com/2015/01/25/india-the-next-superpower/> accessed 20 February 2015.
19. Assad Homayoun, "The Indian Ocean Emerging as Central Nexus of 21st Century Geopolitics", *World Tribune*, 18 February 2015. <http://www.worldtribune.com/2015/02/18/indian-ocean-emerging-central-nexus-21st-century-geopolitics/> accessed 20 February 2015.
20. Amitav Acharya and Barry Buzan, "An Introduction", in Amitav Acharya and Barry Buzan, eds., *Non-Western International Relations Theory* (London: Routledge, 2010), p. 1.
21. Elizabeth Dauphinee, "Critical Methodological and Narrative Developments in IR: A Forum", *The Disorder of Things*, 12 March 2013. <http://thedisorderofthings.com/2013/03/12/critical-methodological-and-narrative-developments-in-ir-a-forum/> accessed 27 April 2015.
22. Stephen M. Walt, "Rigor or Rigor Mortis?: Rational Choice and Security Studies", *International Security*, Vol. 23, No. 4, 1999, pp. 5-48.
23. Ibid., p. 12.
24. Jeanne Hoffman, "Unpacking Images of China Using Causal Layered Analysis", *Journal of Futures Studies*, Vol. 16, No. 3, 2012, pp. 1-24.
25. Paul D. Williams, "Security Studies: An introduction", in Paul D. Williams, ed., *Security Studies: An Introduction*, 2nd edn. (London and New York: Routledge, 2013), pp. 1-12.
26. Sohail Inayatullah, "Six Pillars: Futures Thinking for Transforming", *Foresight*, Vol. 10, No. 1, 2008, pp. 4-21.
27. Noni D. Kenny, "Meta-level Terrorism Futures: Constructing and Deconstructing Using Causal Layered Analysis", PhD Thesis (Brisbane: Queensland University of Technology, 2013).
28. Hoffman, n. 24.
29. Sohail Inayatullah, "Causal Layered Analysis: Theory, Historical Context, and Case Studies", in Sohail Inayatullah, ed., *The Causal Layered Analysis (CLA) Reader* (Tamsui: Tamkang University, 2004),

p. 8.
30. Hoffman, n. 24.
31. Inayatullah, n. 29.
32. Patricia Kelly, "Engineering, A Civilising Influence?", *Futures*, Vol. 42, No. 10, 2010, pp. 1110-18.
33. SohailInayatullah, "Deconstructing and Reconstructing the Global Financial Crisis", in Jorgen Johansen and John Jones, eds., *Experiments with Peace*, (Oxford and Cape Town: Pambazuka Press, 2010), pp. 89–102.
34. Hoffman, n. 24.
35. Rory Medcalf and Ashley Townshend, "India and China: Competitive Coexistence in the Asian Century", in Amitendu Palit and Gloria Spittel, eds., *South Asia in the New Decade Challenges and Prospects* (Singapore: World Scientific, 2013), pp. 1-2.
36. Richard Bernstein and Ross Munro, *The Coming Conflict with China* (New York: First Vintage Press, 1997).
37. Alastair Iain Johnston, "Is China a Status Quo Power?", *International Security*, Vol. 27, No. 4, 2003, pp. 5-56.
38. John J. Mearsheimer, *The Tragedy of Great Power Politics* (New York & London: WW Norton, 2001).
39. Samuel P. Huntington, "The Clash of Civilisations?", *Foreign Affairs*, Vol. 72, No. 3, 1993. <https://www.foreignaffairs.com/articles/united-states/1993-06-01/clash-civilizations> accessed 10 May 2015.
40. An important source is Rakesh Kapoor, "Plural Dreams: India in the 21st Century", *Futures*, Vol. 36, 2004, pp. 637-53.
41. Vincent Wei-cheng Wang, "'Chindia' or Rivalry? Rising China, Rising India, and Contending Perspectives on India-China Relations", *Asian Perspectives*, Vol. 35, 2011, pp. 437-69.
42. Colin Elman and Michael A. Jensen, "Realisms", in Paul D. Williams, ed., *Security Studies: An Introduction*, 2nd edn., (Abingdon, Oxon, New York: Routledge, 2013), p. 16.
43. Tom Barry, "The US Power Complex: What's New", *Foreign Policy in Focus*, November 2002, pp. 1-11. <http://www.igadi.org/arquivo/pdf/te_se07/te19_7_005tom_barry_srpower_us.pdf> accessed 12 March 2015.
44. K.N. Waltz, *Theory of International Politics* (New York: McGraw Hill Inc. 1979).
45. Jason J. Blazevic, "Defensive Realism in the Indian Ocean: Oil, Sea Lanes and the Security Dilemma", *China Security*, Vol. 5, No. 3, 2009, pp. 59-71.
46. Walt, n. 44.
47. Blazevic, n. 45.
48. Mearsheimer, n. 38, pp. 29-30.
49. Denny Roy, "Southeast Asia and China: Balancing or

Bandwagoning?", *Contemporary Southeast Asia*, Vol. 27, No. 2, 2005, pp. 305-22.
50. Mearsheimer, n. 38, pp. 29-30.
51. Hoffman, n. 24.
52. David Shambaugh, "Coping with a Conflicted China", *The Washington Quarterly*, Vol. 34, No. 1, 2011, p. 12.
53. David Blair, "The Clash of Historical Memory: The 'Century of Humiliation' vs. the 'Post-WWII Liberal World Order'", *China Currents*, Vol. 12, No. 2, 2013, pp. 10-22.
54. Shashank Joshi, "Why India is Becoming Warier of China", *Current History*, April 2011, p. 156.
55. Deepa Ollapally and Rajesh Rajagopalan, "India: Foreign Policy Perspectives of an Ambiguous Power", in Henry R. Nau and Deepa M. Ollapally, eds., *Worldview of Aspiring Powers* (Oxford: Oxford University Press, 2012), pp. 73-113.
56. Frank Jack Daniel, "India Won, China Nil as Sri Lanka Turfs out Rajapaksa", *Sydney Morning Herald*, 22 January 2015. <http://www.smh.com.au/world/india-won—china-nil-as-sri-lanka—turfs-out—rajapaksa-20150122-12vnto.html> accessed 15 February 2015.
57. George J. Gilboy and Eric Heginbotham, "Double Trouble: A Realist View of Chinese and Indian Power", *The Washington Quarterly*, Vol. 36, No. 3, 2013, pp. 125-42.
58. Wang, n. 41, p. 455.
59. Erik Gartzke, "Economic Freedom and Peace", in Robert Lawson, Erik Gartzke and James Gwartney, eds., *Economic Freedom of the World: 2005 Annual Report* (Vancouver: Fraser Institute, 2005), pp. 29-44.
60. Scott Burchill, "Liberalism", in Scott Burchill, et al., eds., *Theories of International Relations*, 4th edn., (Basingstoke: Palgrave Macmillan, 2009), pp. 57-84.
61. Mearsheimer, n. 38.
62. Cornelia Navari, "Liberalisms", in Paul D. Williams, ed., *Security Studies: An Introduction* (London: Routledge, 2013), p. 33.
63. Gartzke, n. 59, pp. 34-35.
64. Florette Cohen and Sheldon Solomon, "The Politics of Mortal Terror", *Current Directions in Psychological Science*, Vol. 20, No. 5, 2011, pp. 316-20.
65. Daniel Antonius and Justin Sinclair, "How the Fear of Terrorism Drives Corporate and National Culture", *Security Magazine*, November 2013. <http://www.securitymagazine.com/articles/84902-84902-how-the-fear-of-terrorism-drives-corporate-and-national-culture> accessed 18 March 2015.
66. Richard Slaughter, ed., *The Knowledge Base of Futures Studies:*

Directions and Outlooks, Vol. 3 (Hawthorne: DDM Media Group, 1996), p. 318.

67. John J. Mearsheimer, "China's Unpeaceful Rise", *Current History*, Vol. 105, No. 690, 2006, pp. 160-62.
68. Renaud Egreteau, "The China–India Rivalry Reconceptualized", *Asian Journal of Political Science*, Vol. 20, No. 1, pp. 1-22.
69. Rory Medcalf, *India Poll 2013: Facing the Future, Indian Views of the World Ahead* (Sydney: Lowy Institute for International Policy, 2013).
70. Pew Research Centre, "Global Attitudes and Trends" 2012. <http://www.pewglobal.org/2012/10/16/how-the-chinese-view-other-countries/> accessed 12 February 2015.
71. Ibid.
72. Anand, n. 6, pp. 229-48.
73. Joshi, n. 54, p. 159.
74. Ibid.
75. Yong Deng, *China's Struggle for Status: The Realignment of International Relations* (Cambridge: Cambridge University Press, 2008).
76. "India-China Border Dispute", *GlobalSecurity.org*, September 2014. <http://www.globalsecurity.org/military/world/war/india-china_conflicts.htm> accessed 12 February 2015.
77. Gautam Wahi, "The Common Futures of India and Pakistan: A New Approach", *Journal of Futures Studies*, Vol. 18, No. 2, 2013, pp. 83-102.
78. Sanjeev Miglani, "India Raises Military Spending, Eases Foreign Investment Limit in Arms Industry", *Reuters*, 10 July 2014. <http://in.reuters.com/article/2014/07/10/india-budget-defence-idINKBN0FF0WQ20140710> accessed 18 March 2015.
79. Tom Hussain, "India's Weapons Plans Raise Spectre of Nuclear Arms Race in Asia", *McClatchy*, December 2014. <http://www.mcclatchydc.com/2014/12/08/249370/indias-weapons-plans-raise-spectre.html> accessed 18 March 2015.
80. "China's Maritime Disputes: A CFR InfoGuide Presentation", *Council on Foreign Relations*, 2013. <http://www.cfr.org/asia-and-pacific/chinas-maritime-disputes/p31345#!/?cid=otr-marketing_use-china_sea_InfoGuide> accessed 13 February 2015.
81. Namrata Goswami, "Power Shifts in East Asia: Balance of Power vs. Liberal Institutionalism", *Perceptions*, Vol. 18, No. 1, 2013, p. 12.
82. John J. Mearsheimer, "The Gathering Storm: China's Challenge to US Power in Asia", *The Chinese Journal of International Politics*, Vol. 3, No. 4, 2010, p. 382.
83. Ibid.
84. John J. Mearsheimer, "Structural Realism", in Milja Kurki, Tim Dunne and Steve Smith, eds., *International Relations Theories: Discipline and Diversity*, 3rd edn. (Oxford: Oxford University Press,

2013), pp. 77-93.

85. Bharat Karnad, *India's Nuclear Policy* (Westport, CT: Praeger Security International, 2008), p. 6.
86. Singh, n. 4.
87. Atal Bihari Vajpayee, "Nuclear Anxiety: Indian's Letter to Clinton on the Nuclear Testing", *The New York Times*, 13 May 1998. <http://www.nytimes.com/1998/05/13/world/nuclear-anxiety-indian-s-letter-to-clinton-on-the-nuclear-testing.html> accessed 19 March 2015.
88. John J. Mearsheimer, "India Needs the Bomb", *The New York Times*, 24 March 2000. <http://www.nytimes.com/2000/03/24/opinion/india-needs-the-bomb.html> accessed 12 March 2015.
89. Wahi, n. 77, p. 87.
90. Mearsheimer, n. 84.
91. Brahma Chellaney, "China's Borderline Belligerence", *Project Syndicate*, September 2014. <http://www.project-syndicate.org/commentary/brahma-chellaney-criticizes-india-for-allowing-china-to-dominate-the-bilateral-relationship#oJ2bpmCctIahwsz 3.99> accessed 18 March 2015.
92. Subramanian Swamy, "Myth and Reality in India-China Relations", *The Hindu*, 18 September 2009. <http://www.thehindu.com/opinion/lead/myth-and-reality-in-indiachina-relations/article21762.ece> accessed 17 March 2015.
93. Karnad, n. 85, p. 36
94. Minxin Pei, "The Bullies of Beijing: China's Image Problem", *The Diplomat*, 15 December 2012. <http://thediplomat.com/2012/12/the-bullies-of-beijing-chinas-image-problem/> accessed 20 March 2015.
95. Kanwal Sibal, "Arunachal Border Issue: Modi should not let China Bully India", *Daily O*, 26 February 2015. <http://www.dailyo.in/politics/arunachal-border-issue-modi-should-not-let-china-bully-india-xi-jinping-/story/1/2272.html> accessed 20 March 2015.
96. Robert Kagan and Dan Blumenthal, "China's Zero Sum Game", *The Washington Post*, 9 November 2009. <http://www.washington post.com/wp-dyn/content/article/2009/11/09/AR2009110902 793.html> accessed 5 May 2015.
97. Joshi, n. 54, p. 159.
98. Prabhu Chawla, "Interview with Atal Bihari Vajpayee", *India Today*, May 1998. <http://fas.org/news/india/1998/05/980518-interview.htm> accessed 19 March 2015.
99. Brian L. Delong, "The Nuclear Arjuna: A Narrative Criticism of Vajpayee's Lok Sabha Address", *Wake Forest University*, August 2010, p. 7. <https://wakespace.lib.wfu.edu/bitstream/handle/10339/30395/DeLong_wfu_0248M_10021.pdf> accessed 5 May 2015.

100. Simon Shen, "Exploring the Neglected Constraints on Chindia: Analysing the Online Chinese Perception of India and its Interaction with China's Indian Policy", *The China Quarterly*, Vol. 207, 2011, pp. 541-60.
101. William Callahan, "China vs India: A Democracy Battle", *Open Democracy*, 19 October 2012. <https://www.opendemocracy.net/william-callahan/china-vs-india-democracy-battle> accessed 23 March 2015.
102. Ibid.
103. Hongmei Li, "Veiled Threat or Good Neighbor?", *People's Daily Online*, 19 June 2009. <http://en.people.cn/90002/96417/6682302.html> accessed 25 March 2015.
104. Ibid.
105. Xin Li, "India Through Chinese Eyes", *World Policy*, Winter 2013/2014. <http://www.worldpolicy.org/journal/winter2013/india-through-chinese-eyes> accessed 23 March 2015.
106. Shen, n. 100, p. 547-8.
107. Amitav Acharya, "Seeking Security in the Dragon's Shadow: China and Southeast Asia in the Emerging Asian Order", *Asian Security Conference, 2003* (New Delhi: Institute of Defence and Strategic Studies, 2003).
108. Lyle J Goldstein, "China's Biggest Fear: US-Indian Encirclement", *National Interest*, 11 February 2015. <http://nationalinterest.org/feature/chinas-biggest-fear-us-indian-encirclement-12225> accessed 20 March 2015.
109. GongqinXiao, "Superficial, Arrogant Nationalism", *China Security*, Vol. 5, 2009, pp. 53-58.
110. Xuetong Yan, "The Rise of China in Chinese Eyes", *Journal of Contemporary China*, Vol. 10, No. 26, 2001, pp. 33-39.
111. M. Weisenbloom and R. Spotswood, cited in Mohan Malik, *China and India: Great Power Rivals* (Boulder: First Forum Press, 2011), p. 27.
112. J. S. Bajwa, "Defining Elements of Comprehensive National Power", *Centre for Land Warfare Studies*,Summer 2008, pp. 151-62. <http://www.claws.in/images/journals_doc/1302263399_JS Bajwa.pdf> accessed 13 March 2015.
113. Michael Pillsbury, "Geopolitical Power Calculations", in Michael Pillsbury, ed., *China Debates the Future Security Environment* (Washington, DC: National Defence University Press, 2000).
114. Cited in Jeff M. Smith, *Cold Peace: China–India Rivalry in the Twenty-First Century* (Lanham, MD: Lexington Books, 2014), p. 7.
115. Malik, n. 111, p. 87.
116. "The Six Wars to be Fought by China in the Coming 50 Years", *Midnight Express 2046*, 16 September 2013. <https://midnightexpress2046.wordpress.com/2013/09/16/the-six-wars-to-

be-fought-by-china-in-the-coming-50-years/> accessed 5 May 2015.
117. Ibid.
118. Coates cited in Malik, n. 111, p. 26.
119. Garver cited in Malik, n. 111, p. 74.
120. "China Snubs India on Security Council Seat", *Associated Press of Pakistan*, 2010. <http://app.com.pk/en_/index.php?option=com_ content &task=view&id=100154> accessed 20 March 2015.
121. Kai Yee Chan, "India Being Hotly Courted Internationally; Difficult for China to Woo", *China Daily Mail*, 15 September 2014. <http:// chinadailymail.com/2014/09/15/india-being-hotly-courted-internationally-difficult-for-china-to-woo/> accessed 20 March 2015.
122. Pillsbury, n. 113.
123. Charu Sudan Katsuri, "China Sees 'Encircle' Ploy in India Ties", *The Telegraph*, 22 July 2013. <http://www.telegraphindia.com/ 1130722/jsp/nation/story_17142889.jsp#.VRJH_DuUePU> accessed 25 March 2015.
124. Pillsbury, n. 113.
125. Malik, n. 115.
126. Goswami, n. 81, pp. 3-31.
127. "The Myth of Chindia", *The Economist*, 22 November 2006. <http:/ /www.economist.com/node/8311987> accessed 22 April 2015.
128. Sohail Inayatullah, "World Futures and the Global Financial Crisis: Narratives that Define and Scenarios that Create", *Ekonomiaz*, Vol. 76, No. 1, 2011, pp. 64-86.
129. Uri Dadush and Bennett Stancil, *The World Order in 2050* (Washington, DC: Carnegie Endowment for International Peace, 2010).
130. Ibid.
131. Rana Foroohar, "BRICs Overtake G7 by 2027", *Newsweek*, 20 March 2009. <http://www.newsweek.com/brics-overtake-g7-2027-76001> accessed 14 April 2015.
132. Shannon Tiezzi, "Why 2020 Is a Make-or-Break Year for China", *The Diplomat*, 13 February 2015. <http://thediplomat.com/2015/ 02/why-2020-is-a-make-or-break-year-for-china/> accessed 14 April 2015.
133. Louise Merrington, "Debunking 'Chindia': Chinese and Indian Strategic Interests, Foreign Policy and the Myth of the 'Mutual Rise'", *Biennial Conference of the Asian Studies Association of Australia* (Adelaide: Australian National University, 2010), p. 2.
134. Austin Coates, *China, India and the Ruins of Washington* (New York: The John Day Company, 1972), p. 53.
135. Sebastian Heilmann, Moritz Rudolf, Mikko Huotari and Johannes Buckow, "China's Shadow Foreign Policy: Parallel Structures Challenge the Established International Order", *China Monitor*,

No. 15, 28 October 2014. <http://www.merics.org/fileadmin/templates/download/china-monitor/China_Monitor_No_18_en.pdf> accessed 16 April 2015.

136. Ibid.
137. "The Future of Liberal Internationalism: Global Governance in a Post–American Hegemonic Era", *Council on Foreign Relations, 2012* (Princeton: Council on Foreign Relations, 2012).
138. Ashis Nandy, *Traditions, Tyranny, and Utopias: Essays in the Politics of Awareness* (Oxford: Oxford University Press, 1987).
139. Ziauddin Sardar, "Coming Home: Sex, Lies and all the 'I's in India', *Futures*, Vol. 29, No. 10, 1997, p. 899.
140. Tirumalai Cunnavakum Anandan Pillai Rangachari, "India's Security Calculus in Balancing Regional and Global Geopolitical Agendas", in A Francis and Narnia Bohler-Muller Kornegay, eds., *Laying the BRICS of a New Global Order: From Yekaterinburg 2009 to Ethekwini* (Pretoria: The Africa Institute of South Africa, 2013), p. 239.
141. Luke Hunt, "China and India: Great Power Rivals", *The Diplomat*, 21 November 2011. <http://thediplomat.com/2011/11/china-and-india-great-power-rivals/> accessed 16 April 2015.
142. Ravi Mishra, "What the 'Peaceful Rise of China' Means for India, Part 1", *IBNLive.com*, 15 September 2014. <http://www.ibnlive.com/news/india/what-the-peaceful-rise-of-china-means-for-india-714007.html> accessed 5 May 2015.
143. Malik, n. 115, p. 92.
144. Ross Terrill, "What Does China Want?", *Wilson Quarterly*, Vol. 29, No. 4, 2005.
145. Hoffman, n. 24, p. 16.
146. Winona La Duke, *Launching a Green Economy for Brown People: Minnesota Tribal Energy and Food Sovereignty Handbook* (Minnesota: Honor the Earth, 2008), p. 2.
147. Dexter Roberts, "China: For Many Expats, It's Not Worth It: Council on Foreign Relations", *Businessweek*, 20 September 2012.
148. "The Dragon's New Teeth", *The Economist*, 7 April 2012, pp. 23-26.
149. S. Rukmini, "India's Staggering Wealth Gap in Five Charts", *The Hindu*, 8 December 2014. <http://www.thehindu.com/data/indias-staggering-wealth-gap-in-five-charts/article6672115.ece> accessed 20 April 2015.
150. "Special Focus: Inequality in Emerging Economies (EEs)", *OECD*, 2011. <http://www.oecd.org/els/soc/49170475.pdf> accessed 20 April 2015.
151. AarefaJohari, "Battlelines Drawn in Urban India: Is Economic Inequality Creating Anger?", *Hindustan Times*, 15 September 2013. <http://www.hindustantimes.com/newdelhi/battlelines-drawn-in-urban-india-is-economic-inequality-creating-anger/article1-

1122214.aspx> accessed 20 April 2015.

152. Ibid.
153. Lisa Friedman and Climatewire, "China Greenhouse Gas Emissions Set to Rise Well Past US", *Scientific American*, 3 February 2012. <http://www.scientificamerican.com/article/china-greenhouse-gas-emissions-rise-past-us/> accessed 30 April 2015.
154. Madison Park, "Top 20 Most Polluted Cities in the World", *CNN*, 8 May 2014. <http://edition.cnn.com/2014/05/08/world/asia/india-pollution-who/> accessed 30 April 2015.
155. David Korten, "Economy, Ecology and Spirituality: A Theory and Practice of Sustainability", 1992. <http://livingeconomies forum.org/economy-ecology-spirituality accessed 30 April 2015> accessed 30 April 2015.
156. Rodney Stark, Byron Johnson and Carson Mencken, "Counting China's Christians", *China Aid*, 4 May 2011. <http://www.chinaaid.org/2011/05/counting-chinas-christians.html> accessed 5 July 2013.
157. Conrad Hackett and Brian J. Grim, *Global Christianity: A Report on the Size and Distribution of the World's Christian Population* (Washington, DC: Pew Research Centre's Forum on Religion and Public Life, 2011), p. 58.
158. Donata Hardenberg, "Christianity: China's Best Bet?",*Al Jazeera*, 5 July 2013. <http://www.aljazeera.com/programmes/101east/2011/06/2011629646319175.html> accessed 1 July 2011.
159. Fengang Yang, *Why Christianity is Thriving in China Today* (Georgetown: Georgetown University, Berkley Centre for Religion, Peace and World Affairs, 2011).
160. Gerard Lemos, *The End of the Chinese Dream: Why the Chinese People Fear the Future* (New York and London: Yale University Press, 2012), p. 261.
161. Hardenberg, n. 158.
162. Rakesh Kapoor, "Plural Dreams: India in the 21st Century", *Futures*, Vol. 36, 2004, p. 638.
163. Pankaj Jain, "Dharmic Ecology: Perspectives from the Swadhyaya Practitioners", *Worldviews*, Vol. 13, 2009, pp. 305-20.
164. Conrad Hackett, "By 2050, India to Have World's Largest Populations of Hindus and Muslims", *Pew Research Centre*, 2015. <http://www.pewresearch.org/fact-tank/2015/04/21/by-2050-india-to-have-worlds-largest-populations-of-hindus-and-muslims/> accessed 5 May 2015.
165. Ravi Batra, *Proutist Economy and India's Brilliant Future* (Bombay: Jaico Publishing House, 1990).
166. Ravi Batra, *The New Golden Age: A Revolution Against Political Corruption and Economic Chaos* (New York: Palgrave Macmillan,

2008).

167. Jeanne Hoffman, "China's Search for the Futures: A Genealogical Approach", *Futures*, Vol. 54, 2013, pp. 53-67.
168. Karma Ura, Sabina Alkire, Tshoki Zangmo and Karma Wangdi, *A Short Guide to Gross National Happiness Index* (Thimpu: The Centre for Bhutan Studies, 2012), p. 6.
169. Ibid., p. 7.
170. "Happiness should have greater role in development policy – UN Member States", *UN News Centre*, 19 July 2011. <http://www.un.org/apps/news/story.asp?NewsID=39084#.VVmL3fmqpBc> accessed 5 May 2015.
171. Ravi Logan, "The Rise of Spiritual-Centred Social Philosophy", *Prout Globe*, undated <http://proutglobe.org/2012/11/the-rise-of-spiritual-centered-social-philosophy/> accessed 1 May 2015.
172. Narendra Modi, "Asia Century Not Possible Without Buddha", *Indiawrites*, 5 September 2015. <http://www.indiawrites.org/culture/asian-century-not-possible-without-buddha-modi/> accessed 1 May 2015.
173. Korten, n. 155.
174. Hamid Ansari, "Speech by Vice-President of India on 'Calibrated Futurology: India, China and the World'" (Beijing: Chinese Academy of Social Sciences, 30 June 2014).
175. Jagannath P. Panda, *India-China Ties: Between Personalities and Principles* (New Delhi: Institute for Defence Studies and Analysis, 2014). <http://pib.nic.in/newsite/PrintRelease.aspx?relid=105953> accessed 4 May 2015.
176. Shannon Tiezzi, "China and India Want a Breakthrough on Their Border Dispute", *The Diplomat*, 5 February 2015. <http://thediplomat.com/2015/02/china-and-india-want-a-breakthrough-on-their-border-dispute/> accessed 4 May 2015.
177. Jeff M. Smith, "India and China: The End of Cold Peace?", *The National Interest*, 10 February 2014. <http://nationalinterest.org/commentary/india-china-the-end-cold-peace-9853> accessed 1 May 2015.
178. Mustafa Qadri, "Can India and Pakistan Find Friendship?", *The Guardian*, 25 March 2010. <http://www.theguardian.com/commentisfree/2010/mar/25/india-pakistan-government-peace> accessed 1 May 2015.
179. Manish Chand, "The Long View: ABCD of India-China Relations", 17 September 2014. <http://mea.gov.in/in-focus-article.htm?24009/The+Long+View+ABCD+of+IndiaChina+relations> accessed 1 May 2015.
180. Stanley Weiss, "Could China Become India's New Best Friend", *The Huffington Post*, 10 July 2014. <http://www.huffingtonpost.com/

stanley-weiss/could-china-become-indias_b_5570553.html> accessed 1 May 2015.

181. Panda, n. 175.
182. Pravakar Sahoo and Abhirup Bhunia, "BCIM Corridor a Game Changer for South Asian Trade", *East Asia Forum*, 24 July 2014. <http://asiapacific.anu.edu.au/blogs/southasiamasala/2014/07/24/5554/> accessed 5 May 2015.
183. "Project 'Mausam' Research Programme 2014 to 2019". <http://ignca.nic.in/mausam.htm> accessed 1 May 2015.
184. Arushi Gupta, "The China-India defence dialogue", *The Diplomat*, 19 April 2015. <http://thediplomat.com/2015/04/the-china-india-defense-dialogue/> accessed 4 May 2015.
185. Anil A. Athale, "Can India and China ever be Friends?", *Rediff News*, 4 December 2014. <http://www.rediff.com/news/column/anil-a-athale-can-india-and-china-ever-be-friends/20141204.htm> accessed 4 May 2015.
186. Priya Chacko, "A New 'Special Relationship'? Power Transitions, Ontological Security, and India-US Relations", *International Studies Perspectives*, Vol. 15, 2014, pp. 329-46.
187. Malik, n. 115.
188. Chacko, n. 186.
189. Manish Chand, "Modi-Xi Meeting: Mapping Ambitious Agenda for India-China Relations", *Indiawrites*, 4 September 2014. <http://www.indiawrites.org/diplomacy/modi-xi-meeting-mapping-ambitious-agenda-for-strategic-ties/> accessed 3 May 2015.
190. Qadri, n. 178.
191. Chand, n. 189.
192. Ansari, n. 174.
193. Shivshankar Menon, "China is an Opportunity and a Challenge", *Rediff News*, 5 May 2015. <http://www.rediff.com/news/special/rise-in-communal-violence-is-worrying/20150312.htm> accessed 6 May 2015.
194. Alastair Iain Johnston, "Thinking about Strategic Culture", *International Security*, Vol. 19, No. 4, 1995, p. 32.
195. Inayatullah, n. 128.

5

Russia's Pivot to Asia: Constructing a Eurasian State in a Multipolar World

Glenn Diesen

ABSTRACT

Russia's pivot to Asia is motivated by the conviction that its survival relies on cementing itself as a Eurasian state in a multipolar world. The primary objective is to eliminate the political, economic and military foundations sustaining the US unipolar moment, while the secondary aim is to prevent the emergence of a bipolar dynamic between the US and China that would empower Russia's main challengers in the East and the West. A two-tiered balance-of-power is thus pursued as China is Russia's key ally as a bridgehead to Asia and an indispensable balance to the US. Albeit, concurrently developing a regional balance-of-power in the Indo-Pacific region as to prevent China from emerging as an unconstrained hegemon. These ambitious and the somewhat conflicting objectives are formidable, but achievable due to the favourable geopolitical climate. While the balance-of-power logic in Europe creates incentives for excluding Russia from the main institutions and the security architecture, in the Indo-Pacific region there are systemic pressures for accommodating Russia. China shares the objective of integrating Eurasia and needs Russia for energy supply, as a physical land-bridge to Europe, and to balance the US. The failure of the rest of the region to accommodate Russia would result in excessive reliance on China, thus augmenting Beijing's power further, something even the US should be careful to avoid. Russia appears to replace geopolitics with geo-economics as a balance of power is sought primarily by controlling markets rather than territory. Trade and monetary policies, and the physical energy and transport infrastructure, spearheads Russia's geo-strategic project of bolstering itself as an indispensable power in an integrated Eurasia.

Introduction

For long, Moscow has recognised the economic opportunities that could be availed of by hinging its wagon to the rapidly rising Indo-Pacific region. Political momentum to act upon the incentives has however lacked due to the underdevelopment of the Russian Far East (RFE), fears of excessive dependency on China, a predominantly European identity, and because Russia is deeply embedded in the US/Western-centric international system. Over the last decade, Russia has nonetheless incrementally developed closer links with the Indo-Pacific region to develop a multipolar world. An official 'pivot to Asia' was announced symbolically when Russia hosted the Asia-Pacific Economic Cooperation (APEC) summit in Vladivostok in 2012. In preparation for the summit, Russia spent $20 billion to upgrade the infrastructure of Vladivostok as the main entry point to Asia. The capacity to follow through on this immense geopolitical manoeuvre has been the source of much scepticism due to the deteriorating conditions of the RFE, a dwindling population, outdated technology, crumbling infrastructure, and lack of a business-friendly environment. The cynicism is not limited to the states in the Indo-Pacific region and the West, but it is also widespread within Russia. However, the political impetus for seeking more attractive markets grew as a result of the global financial crisis that has caused a prolonged stagnation in Europe. The momentum for a rapid geopolitical reconfiguration increased drastically as a result of the war in Ukraine, which was perceived to be caused by the West's ongoing attempts to marginalise Russia in Europe. Furthermore, the ensuing sanctions by the West demonstrated the vulnerability from excessive dependency on Europe and the US. It is argued here that Russia's pivot to Asia has not received the attention it merits, considering the possible momentous impact it can have on the region and the broader world.

The primary motivation for Russia's pivot to Asia is to balance the dominant global power of the US, which is consistently recognised as the main threat since hegemony can only be sustained by marginalising Russia in Europe. The secondary motivation is to support a balance-of-power in the Indo-Pacific region in order to preclude China from challenging Russia's sovereignty over the

RFE and influence in Central Asia. In this two-tiered balance-of-power, China is Russia's key partner to de-construct the unipolar moment, while simultaneously Russia must diversify its relations in the region to prevent excessive reliance on China. Replacing the unipolar moment with a US-Chinese bipolar system where states must bandwagon behind one to balance the other would only empower the main two states that challenge Russian security.

Due to its exclusion from the post-Cold War security architecture in Europe and its weakening power in the rising East, Russia envisions its security and existence to be dependent on a successful 'pivot to Asia'. As a Eurasian state that can integrate the vast Eurasian landmass with infrastructure, trade, financial institutions and security cooperation, other states would become more dependent on Russia while Russia could diversify its reliance on others. In other words, Russian power would derive from becoming an independent power pole that facilitates the development of a balanced and constrained multipolar world. Its future as a Eurasian state is largely dependent on developing the RFE, which must be integrated with both the Indo-Pacific region and European Russia. Energy and transport infrastructure projects are therefore essential for this 'dual integration', which can bring together the vast regions of Russia and the enormous Eurasian landmass. As a 'medium power' in the Indo-Pacific region that can contribute to develop a multipolar world, though without capacity for hegemony, Russia presents itself an attractive partner to a region that is desperately seeking to diversify away from excessive reliance on the US and China. A shared interest in Russia not becoming China's 'junior partner' that further augments Beijing's power, serves as a further incentive for South Korea, Japan, India, Vietnam, and other states in the region to accommodate Russia.

Motivation: The Dual Threat to Russia's Survival

Moscow consistently identifies the US as its primary threat due to its promotion of NATO as the dominant European security institution. Instead of harmonising security interests by accommodating Russia in broader European security architecture as a post-Cold War settlement, the rise of a NATO-centric Europe is perceived as a policy aimed to cement US hegemony. This development is believed to be the result of Russian weakness, which enables the West to develop European security without and against the largest state on the continent. The Yeltsin administration had idealistically believed that Russia's commitment to democracy and capitalism would make Gorbachev's 'Common European Home' more feasible. However, the West is perceived to have exploited Russia's weakness and seeking to perpetuate it by embracing an exclusive conception of 'Europe' that is predominantly represented by NATO and the EU. The expansion of NATO in 1999, without Russia, was interpreted as the confirmation that a 'Greater Europe' had been abandoned.[1] The severely skewed balance-of-power also reduced NATO's constraints, evidenced by the abandonment of its status as a 'defensive alliance' by bombing Yugoslavia without a UN mandate. The development of missile defence as a NATO asset that could negate Russia's nuclear retaliatory capabilities brought further credence to the idea that an unconstrained and unilateral NATO is unravelling the foundations of European security and thus posing an existential threat to Russia. The Russian Foreign Policy Concept of 2013 portrays several conflicts to be the product of Western preference for a "bloc-based approach to addressing international issues" that relies on "unilateral sanctions and other coercive measures".[2]

The EU was initially seen as more benevolent and believed to become an independent pole in a multipolar world that could constrain the US. Moscow has however become incrementally resentful of the EU due to its expansion of membership and 'external governance' without consideration for Russian security interests. Furthermore, the convergence with NATO implied that the EU tends to supplement rather than constrain US power. The asymmetrical power relations vis-à-vis Russia are seen to have had detrimental effects on diplomacy, as the EU and NATO have replaced negotiation and compromise with ultimatums and coercion. Both the EU and NATO conceptualise cooperation with Russia in terms of a 'teacher-student' or 'subject-object' relationship, implying that Russia make unilateral concessions and policy adjustments. Proposals for international treaties and arrangements that impose mutual constraints are regularly dismissed since Russia should not be allowed to have a 'veto' over the security of member states. Since the EU and NATO subscribe to an exclusive conception of 'Europe', 'European integration' becomes a zero-sum geopolitical project where states in the 'shared neighbourhood' must make a 'civilisational choice' between the West and Russia. The EU's proposed Association Agreement with Ukraine, an ultimatum of integrating with 'Europe' or Russia, is seen to have led to the coup that installed an anti-Russian government and resulted in war. Besides demonstrating the need for Russia to gain greater leverage, the sanctions on Russia exposed the risk of excessive reliance on the West as trade dependency is used as a 'weapon'.

The secondary threat to the existing borders of Russia is the crumbling condition of the RFE, plagued by a shrinking population, outdated technology, weak infrastructure and an uncompetitive economy. This decline has further accelerated the increasingly unfavourable asymmetrical power relations with the rising China on the other side of the border. Trenin argues that "nothing concentrates minds in Moscow as much as the thought of Russia becoming a raw materials appendage to China".[3] A neighbour in the East that is becoming stronger than Russia is causing an 'earthquake' in geopolitical considerations.[4] Beijing's influence over the RFE gradually increases as the region becomes more reliant on Chinese investments and migrant workers, with fears that Russia's sovereignty would over time erode. Furthermore, as China increases its influence in Central Asia, Russia risks also becoming isolated on its southern borders. In 2009, China, Kazakhstan, Uzbekistan and Turkmenistan inaugurated the Central Asian-China gas pipeline running 2000 km through all these states. China also launched a land-bridge project or a 'Silk Road' project to Europe through Central Asia by harmonising the railway infrastructure. The route is already in use, which goes from China to Germany, through Kazakhstan, Russia, Belarus and Poland. While including European Russia, the project skirts the RFE, which Russia would prefer to develop and anchor into the transport infrastructure.[5] Without infrastructure projects connecting the RFE with European Russia, Moscow fears that Russia is fragmenting into two separate power poles.[6] As former President Medvedev suggested: "The more often we refer to the Russian Far East as a separate entity, the more likely we are to have problems".[7] While Russia enjoys its position as an arms exporter to China, this relationship may not be sustainable in its current format. China counterfeits or reverse-engineers imported Russian weaponry and incrementally replaces them with its own production. Russia has therefore been apprehensive to sell its most advanced weaponry to China as a potential future threat and to prevent its most recent technology from being copied. However, the economic incentives for fomenting a strategic partnership with China compels Russia to disregard these concerns, as demonstrated by its decision in 2015 to sell its most advanced S-400 surface-to-air missile system to China.

The Influence of a Eurasian State in a Constrained Multipolar World

Russian statements and policies reflect a realist understanding of the world, which implies that a balance-of-power is required for peace since states do not constrain themselves. Realist theory predicts that the unipolar moment is a temporary condition since it depends on containing and weakening rising powers, thus creating incentives for the other great power to unite in order to balance the hegemon. In an increasingly interdependent world, US hegemonic power derives from its capacity to increase the dependency of others on the US through its central role in security, political and economic arrangements. The geopolitical strategy of the US in Eurasia is defined by Zbigniew Brzezinski as "to prevent collusion and maintain security dependence among the vassals, to keep tributaries pliant and protected, and to keep the barbarians from coming together".[8] The geo-economic equivalency suggests that Eurasian integration would undermine US hegemony by developing infrastructure projects, trade agreements and routes, and financial institutions and arrangements independent of the US.

State power is enhanced by maximising both autonomy and influence. For Moscow, the accumulation of power translates into specialising or monopolising on certain political, economic or military capabilities in order to increase other states dependency on Russia, while Russia diversifies its partnership to eliminate the vulnerability of excessive reliance. This reflects a realist understanding of globalisation. Interdependence does not 'transcend realism' in terms of states prioritising absolute gain from cooperation. Instead the basic assumption remains that survival is enhanced by seeking relative gain to constrain and balance other great powers. Diversification of relationships allows for states to manage the balance-of-power more smoothly as the power of various states will expand and contract. The formidable task in a multipolar system is to develop a system where the great power can both cooperate and compete, as peace is dependent on collaborating for mutual security and simultaneously constraining each other through balancing.

Russia's capacity to integrate its own territory will determine its ability to act as an independent pole of power in a multipolar world. The concept of Russia as a 'Eurasian' state suggests that its territory is used to integrate the vast landmass from Europe and Asia. The enormous territory of Russia provides it with opportunities to reduce dependency on individual states, while concurrently developing reliance of others on Russia through transportation and energy infrastructure. Russia can diversify away from its dependence on Europe for energy exports, and as the only source of technology and investments for Russia's modernisation efforts. On a broader geopolitical scale, Russia can contribute to weaken the overall Western-centric international system. Sakwa defines Russia as "neo-revisionist" since it does not repudiate the existing international order, but being unable to join the Western constellation, it seeks to facilitate the development of a more equal and multipolar system.[9]

Russia's development of the Eurasian Union provides a strong foundation for its Eurasian strategy. The Eurasian Union focuses mainly on economic integration between its members, which are the former Soviet Republics that include Russia, Belarus, Kazakhstan and Armenia, while Kyrgyzstan joined in May 2015. The Eurasian Union reveals a higher level of integration of trade, laws and convergence of infrastructure than previous Russian-led integration efforts. Putin envisages that the Eurasian Union will become "one of the poles of the contemporary world and would play the role of an effective 'bridge' between Europe and the dynamic Asia-Pacific region".[10] The Union creates an external barrier to cement a privileged position for Russia as the 'first among equals' in the region. Russia's 'spheres of interests' concept suggests that Russia's voice in its immediate neighbourhood must be dominant, or at least be accommodated and respected, since what occurs on its borders is integral to its security. This is distinguishable from 'spheres of influence' as it denotes exclusive influence. In other words, Russia seeks to obstruct its neighbours from joining integration projects such as the EU and NATO that are closed off to Russia, while concurrently being open to inclusive integration projects as Moscow does not demand exclusive influence. The benefit of the Eurasian Union to its member states is that it enables collective negotiation from a position of strength for the terms of integration with both Europe and the Indo-Pacific region. This presents a favourable alternative to NATO's and the EU's zero-sum approach to 'European integration' where states must choose between the East and West. Non-members can also benefit from a single transit system (shared custom zone, technical and legal standards) through the territory of the Eurasian Union that physically connects some of the world's largest markets from Asia to Europa.[11]

An important and challenging aspect of Russian efforts to decentralise power in the international system, is to prevent the unipolar system to be replaced by a bipolar regional dynamic between the US and China. In such a construct, states in the region seeking to balance either the US or China would be required to bandwagon behind the other. This would effectively empower both the US and China as the two key challengers to Russian security. While Russia relies mostly on 'soft-balancing' China, efforts are also made to rapidly modernise its Pacific fleet. Rather than confronting China with 'hard-balancing' that would undo the partnership and undermine Eurasian integration, Russia seeks to constrain Chinese influence by diversifying its partnerships in the region. The Russian Foreign Minister, Sergei Lavrov, defined Russia's interest in the Indo-Pacific region as being a "truly stable balance of power", in which Russia can act as an "important stabilising factor".[12] The Indo-Pacific region represents a diametrically opposite geopolitical situation for Russia compared to the exclusive environment in Europe. Europe is economically in relative decline compared to the rest of the world, and Russia is feared as a large military power that seeks to challenge the main institutions. In contrast, the Indo-Pacific region is perceived as the "fastest-developing geopolitical zone, towards which the centre of the world economy and politics is gradually shifting".[13] Furthermore, the region is mostly concerned with the excessive influence of the US and China, while Russia is not feared or sought to be balanced by any of the major powers.[14] The failure by the other states in the Indo-Pacific region to accommodate Russia would make Russia become excessively reliant on China, which would further increase Beijing's power in the region.

The transportation infrastructure is envisaged to attract much interest due to the ability to physically connect the Eurasian landmass that could be supplemented by Arctic sea-lanes. In an op-ed in the *Wall Street Journal*, Putin presented Russia's contribution to 'diversify trade routes':

> We are already building modern ports in the Russian Far East, modernising the transportation and shipment infrastructure, and improving national customs and administrative procedures. According to assessments by experts of the APEC Business Advisory Council, the implementation of these projects will increase traffic flow between Europe and the Asian-Pacific region via Russia's territory no less than fivefold by 2020. Such shipments are cost-competitive with the traditional routes through the Strait of Malacca and the Suez Canal, and offer advantages in terms of speed and safety.[15]

The RFE is also to be developed as an energy-hub for the region. Putin ordered the RFE to be established as a special economic zone and for the federal government to fund the development of infrastructure for the industry.[16] This has entailed the hasty construction of a new LNG plant in Vladivostok to catch up with this growing section of the market and thus reach beyond China. In 2011, Russia completed the Sakhalin–Khabarovsk–Vladivostok (SKV) pipeline that transports gas from the energy rich Sakhalin region to Vladivostok. Incentives for relocation to the RFE is developed with initiatives such as the 'Homestead Act', which offers free land for Russians seeking to start a business or a farm. Russia is also pursuing deep reforms to improve the business climate as a widely recognised deterrent for investors. In 2012, Putin announced that Russia would become one of the top 20 business friendly states in the world by 2018, which was an ambitious goal since Russia at the time ranked as the 112th economy in the world according to the World Bank's annual "Doing Business" report.[17] However, in 2013, Russia jumped to 93rd place and in 2014 to 63rd place. Russia's overall population decline has also reversed due to a steadily growing fertility rate that is currently 0.3 higher than the EU average, immigration levels second only to the US, a rapid decline in alcohol abuse, and a sharply rising life expectancy.[18]

The Chinese Bridgehead: Balancing the US and the EU

Russia and China are in similar geopolitical situations as rising powers seeking to diminish the global hegemonic position of the US, and face the threat of military containment. After Moscow accepted painful concessions in order to settle its border disputes with China in 2009, the shared Chinese-Russian border is one of the longest in the world and a source of much desired stability. This has enabled a peaceful back-to-back position as both states face threats on their other borders. Russia perceives the US and NATO to destabilise its Western borders by militarising a division of Europe and supporting anti-Russian political groups and governments in its neighbourhood, while its southern borders are vulnerable due to Islamic fundamentalism. China perceives a similar containment on its Eastern and Southern borders by the US, and fears Islamic fundamentalism to exacerbate terrorism and secessionist sentiments in the predominantly Muslim Uyghur population in the Western Xinjiang province. With the possible threat of the US to Chinese maritime trade routes and energy supply, China welcomes diversification of energy and trade through landlines.

Both Russia and China are apprehensive of the capacity of the US to use its dominant administrator role of the networked global society as a foreign policy tool. The international system that evolved after the Second World War cemented a central role of the US through the Bretton Woods system. The US took leadership in the IMF and the World Bank, and the US dollar became the global reserve currency and international trading currency. Furthermore, as virtually all international payments go through the US-based

SWIFT system, the US claims jurisdiction by applying its domestic laws to international trade. For example, a French bank was fined $9 billion dollars by the US government for trading with Cuba, as the US applied its own laws since the use of US dollars through the SWIFT payment system is cleared through US-based computer.[19] The huge benefits from the global demand for dollars, control over global financing, trade, development and banking has set a powerful foundation for the dominant role the US plays in the international system.

China and Russia as large holders of US dollar reserves express unease as the US can 'tax' them by printing money/inflating the money supply at the expense of diluting the value of their reserves. Besides enabling the US to accumulate huge deficits, it also implies that China and Russia to some extent fund the military containment that they fear. While China can be argued to have benefited by accumulating large foreign currency reserves, the debt levels suggests it is improbable that the US will be able to repay without printing the money and thus debasing the value of the US dollar.[20] When the crisis in Ukraine erupted, the US demonstrated its control over the international financial system with the sanctions against Russia. Russia was restricted from some of the financial markets in the West, Mastercard and Visa that handle approximately 90 per cent of Russian card transactions suspended their service in Crimea, and the threat to exclude Russia from the international SWIFT system would be devastating if realised as it would prevent Russian companies from making bank transfers.[21]

China is Russia's key partner in spearheading the de-construction of the US-centric international financial system by creating alternative institutions and de-dollarising their economies. The percentage of US dollar holdings in both China's and Russia's foreign-exchange reserves has been severely reduced. The use of the US dollar in international trade has gradually declined over the past decade from 70 per cent to 61 per cent, while China and Russia are pursuing initiatives to intensify this process. Russia as a major energy exporter has the capacity to undermine the petrodollar by facilitating payments in domestic currencies, while China has even more leverage as it is becoming the world's largest economy. An incremental expansion of currency-swaps with trading partners and reduction of US dollars in reserves diminishes the US position. While only three per cent of China's international trade was denominated in its own currency in 2010, this figure increased to 18 per cent by 2014. Russia has escalated its process of de-dollarising by selling dollars to buy gold and trading in local currencies.[22] Former Russian President, Dimitri Medvedev, proposed to develop a basket of currencies to serve as a new reserve currency, possibly backed by gold. China has greater capacity to lead this effort, and has initiated currency swaps with key trading partners such as Brazil, Argentina, UK, Switzerland, Singapore, South Korea, Malaysia and India. For countries such as Kazakhstan that has Russia and China as its main trading partners, the complete de-dollarisation of the economy has been announced to be achieved by 2016. The Deputy Managing Director of the IMF, Naoyuki Shinohara, encouraged emerging Asian economies to de-dollarise.[23] Russia's major banks have begun issuing Chinese Union Pay cards to replace Visa and Mastercard, while concurrently developing a national card system. Russia has also begun developing its own SWIFT system that is already being implemented for domestic transactions, which has great potential for international partners as well since it would skirt US jurisdiction and open up for more trade with Cuba and Iran. These efforts are concurrently pursued by China with the development of its own alternative to SWIFT, the China International Payment System (CIPS), which is expected to be launched in 2015.

Reluctance by the US to reform the voting power of the IMF created the incentives to develop alternatives. The BRICS countries (Brazil, Russia, China, India and South Africa) are establishing their own BRICS Development Bank with a $100 billion in reserve. China has also challenged the primacy of a second Bretton Woods institution, the World Bank, with the establishment of the Chinese-led Asian Infrastructure Investment Bank (AIIB). To the great discontent of the US, key European powers such as the UK, Germany, France and Italy have expressed their aspiration to become founding members of AIIB. Besides financial convergence, the BRICS format enables Russia and China to harmonise their political positions with the other emerging powers. For example, during the G20 meeting in 2014, the BRICS countries met on the sidelines and released a joint statement that condemned the West's sanctions on Russia. For Russia this was crucial to demonstrate that when the West claims that "there is a kind of world community, which condemns us, they mean 28 NATO member states and the EU".[24] While China took an even more active role in supporting Russia with the announcement in December 2014 that it would 'bail-out' the Russian economy if required due to problems from sanctions and falling oil prices. Furthermore, in February 2015 the Chinese Ambassador to Belgium demonstrated China's convergence with Russia's view of the EU and NATO dividing Europe, by encouraging the West to "abandon its zero-sum mentality" over Russia and instead take "the real security concerns of Russia into consideration".[25] Additional institutional convergence is facilitated by the Russian and Chinese-led Shanghai Cooperation Organisation, which has an unofficial objective of preventing US and NATO incursion into Asia.

The Sino-Russian strategic partnership is increasingly supported with trade that has been growing at a rapid rate over the last decade. Trade reached $20 billion in 2005, $56 billion in 2008, $90 billion in 2014, and by 2020 aims $200 billion. Energy cooperation laid the foundation for this partnership and was strengthened when the East Siberia-Pacific Ocean (ESPO) oil pipeline was completed in 2012, which enables Russia to export more than an additional million barrels of oil a day. In 2013, Rosneft and China National Petroleum Corporation (CNPC) signed a major agreement of a joint venture to collectively develop fields in Eastern Siberia.[26] The foundation for future trade expansion rapidly intensified in 2014. Long-term multi-billion dollar trade agreements were concluded at the top-political level, including an historic $400 billion gas deal. Yuan-ruble trade increased more than ten-fold since these transactions were not denominated in dollars, and large-scale infrastructure projects were agreed to connect Russia and China. Redirecting Russian gas infrastructure towards China had long been negotiated, though Russia struck a deal quickly after the West imposed sanctions. Besides diversifying gas consumers, it also includes China as a partner for jointly developing the Eastern Siberian fields and financing the construction of the pipeline. In 2014, trade between Russia and the border region of Xinjiang increased by 374 per cent.

China has also become a key partner for realising Russia's 'Iron Silk Road' aspirations of becoming a physical bridge between Europe and Asia. Russia has unveiled its 'Trans-Eurasian Belt Development' plan that will connect the Atlantic Ocean with the Pacific Ocean with infrastructure alongside the Trans-Siberian Railway, which includes a new high-speed railway, major roads, and pipelines for oil and gas. Joint railway ventures with China to diversify away from maritime trade will also link East Asia to Russia. In 2008, a memorandum was signed for the use of existing railways to establish a Eurasian land-bridge through China-Mongolia-Russia-Belarus-Poland-Germany. This signified an opening salvo for further developing Russian territory as the key link between Asia and Europe. With Germany's share of export to EU countries being in decline, such infrastructure projects could accelerate the trend of making the German economy more reliant on the Eurasian economic space. With the understanding that the US is the main power that marginalises Russia in Europe, the economic de-coupling of Europe from the US could facilitate the development of a Greater Europe. In late 2014, China and Russia announced another large-scale infrastructure project with the joint development of a high-speed train from Moscow to Beijing that would limit the travel time to two days, a vast reduction from the current six days with the trans-Siberian train. For an approximate cost of $242 billion, the high-speed rail would be built over a period of ten years. The first section of the rail will connect Moscow with Russia's third largest city, Kazan, 800km to the east.

Regional Balance-of-Power: Diversification of Asian Partners

President Putin has sought to dispel the fears of China as an obstruction to its Asian pivot. However, besides diplomatic sensitivities Moscow is seeking to minimise lack of symmetry in relations by reaching out to other powers in the region. At its immediate periphery is South Korea and Japan as modern economies that can provide technology and investments to develop the RFE and modernise the Russian economy. Russian Foreign Minister, Sergei Lavrov, argued that the notion that "the West, and only the West" has the technology and know-how to help modernise Russia and the Russian Far East should be rejected.[27]

The close proximity implies that Russia has some leverage in terms of providing energy and transportation infrastructure. With more partners and investors, Russia could use the leverage and can negotiate more technology transfer and investments in RFE, in addition to reducing its dependency on China. Further from its periphery are India and Vietnam as historical time-tested partnerships with a strong foundation that are underutilised, but immensely significant in terms of preventing the emergence of a Chinese hegemony in the region. While scholars such as Klein posit that the US is an "indispensable" partner for Russia in order to be successful in its diversification strategy in East Asia,[28] this argument misses the point that the US is deemed to be the primary threat to Russia and main challenger to multi-polarity.

Koreas: Developing an Exclusive Land-bridge?

With apprehensions of an increasingly powerful China, an antagonistic relationship with North Korea, and historical tensions with Japan, South Korea has become overly reliant on the US. South Korea's ambition for diversifying relations across Eurasia corresponds impeccably with Moscow's geopolitical project of becoming a key facilitator of Eurasian integration. In October 2013, Seoul announced its 'Eurasian Initiative', which recognised vast opportunities associated with integrating the Eurasian landmass. It envisions the emergence of a 'Eurasian economic bloc' spearheaded by energy and transportation infrastructure. Russia is central in this strategy by relying on the Russian territory for both a land-route and an Arctic Sea lane to connect South Korea with Europe.[29] South Korean President, Park Guen-hye, argues that "if trade barriers are gradually taken down and Eurasia becomes a free trade zone, Eurasia could be made into a gigantic market like the European Union".[30]

South Korea is an ideal economic partner to Russia, as the second largest liquid natural gas (LNG) importer in the world, a source for investment and technology, and its market links to Europe. In 2005, South Korea and Russia signed an agreement to develop LNG terminals in order for Russia to enhance its share of the Korean demand for LNG, which was also linked to foreign investment and development of the RFE. Russia currently provides only six per cent of South Korea's gas imports, but has the potential to increase the market share to 30 per cent.[31] Transportation infrastructure for goods between South Korea and Europe can also be made more efficient by further developing the container port in Vladivostok, which is linked to the Siberian railway. In 2014, the port was announced to become a 'free port' due to benefits in terms of reformed and easier customs regulations, duty-free, tax benefits and reduced costs for ships.[32] The 'Eurasian cargo infrastructure' would be further enhanced as China and Russia announced in late 2014 the decision to collectively construct the largest deep-water port in Northeast Asia. The port in Zarubino, is located south of Vladivostok, next to the North Korean border.

The real potential for integrating South Korea into the Eurasian landmass entails opening up North Korea. While a formidable undertaking, the momentous prize for Russia would be to monopolise on the only land-link to South Korea. Moscow has already negotiated with North Korea the construction of railroads and energy pipelines through its territory, though the reliability and sustainability is vulnerable to the antagonistic relations between North and South Korea. Gas pipelines would provide a competitive alternative to the LNG market, while railways would dramatically reduce the time and cost of cargo transportation. Already in 2001, Moscow indicated that it desired to construct an 'Iron Silk Road' by connecting its Trans-Siberian Railway to a Trans-Korean railway. The President of South Korea promoted the integration of these railroads as a source for peace on the peninsula.[33] The CEO of Russian Railways, Vladimir Bakunin, argued that shipping goods between South Korea and Europe is almost three times faster than via the Suez Canal.[34] This could provide transit revenue and infrastructure development.[35]The Korean railroad Research Institute reiterated that the completion of the trans-Korean Rail, linked to the Siberian railway, could "lead to the development of a strategic international multimodal transport route connecting to Northeast Asia and Europe".[36]

The main challenge is to open up North Korea to Russia, the most closed and isolated regime in the world. Russia and North Korea already agreed in 2002 to move forward on the process of linking the Trans-Korean-Railway (TKR) to Trans-Siberian Railway

(TSR).[37] However, expectations for the partnership did not harmonise as North Korea desired a similar protection and support as the Soviet Union provided, while Russia was dissuaded by the lack of influence it had over North Korea's nuclear posturing. Subsequently, relations and cooperation stagnated. Obstructions were however overcome when Kim Jong Il died in December 2011, as Russia was able to engage North Korea with more pragmatism in terms of developing a limited mutually beneficial relationship.[38] Moscow agreed to write off 90 per cent of North Korea's debt, while the remaining ten per cent of the debt would be converted into equity in North Korean investments. Concurrently, Moscow and Pyongyang also agreed to construct a pipeline from Sakhalin through North Korea to South Korea, and open a rail link between Khasan in Russia and Rajin in North Korea. The joint venture also included the development of the port in Rajin that include coal and container terminals, an ice-free port that could receive cargo from South Korea. Five years and $340 million have been spent on renovating the double-track rail link between Rajin and Khasan, which reopened in September 2013. The fundamentals of the infrastructure is thus in place as South Korean businesses can already ship products to Rajin and then transport to the West via Russian railways.[39]

Russia is seeking to increase its role significantly on the Korean peninsula to develop mutually beneficial and stable relations. Russia has announced its desires to develop trilateral energy, railway and electricity infrastructure projects with both Koreas.[40] The North Korean economy is sought to be transformed as Russia is entering the Joint-Korean Kaesong Industrial Complex, the trade with North Korea is increasingly denominated in Russian roubles, Russia has obtained favourable visa conditions, and enhanced business climate for Russian companies that are for example granted better internet access. Russia also considers the potential of Korean unification a desirable objective to create more stable and predictable relations.[41]

Japan Energy Export in Return for Technology and Investments

Japan shares the concern that Russia can become excessively dependent on China, especially since Tokyo desires a more independent and neutral position from Moscow in the territorial disputes between China and Japan.[42] Japan is also the largest importer of natural gas in the world and is interested in diversifying its energy supplies, which has become even more acute since the Fukushima accident. Russia has thus not taken a side in its disputes with China, and sought to attract Japanese investments and technology to develop and modernise the RFE and the broader Russian economy. Japan becomes possibly the most interesting partner for Russia's modernisation programme, in order to diversify away from the stagnated modernisation partnership with the EU.With a capacity to pay a higher price for energy, a comprehensive agreement with Japan could set a benchmark for the region. Russia is seeking for joint energy extraction in the RFE and the Arctic with Japan. Furthermore, Japan is sought to finance the expansion of Sakhalin-2, development of Sakhalin-3, and a second LNG plant in Vladivostok due to the increased capacity from the SKV pipeline.[43]

The main obstruction to further enhancing relations is the contested ownership of the Kirill Islands that were seized by the Soviet Union during the Second World War, and Tokyo's strategic partnership with the US. The prospect of compromising and resolving the issue of the Kirill Islands could unlock much potential in Russian-Japanese relations, and Putin has called for a compromise that could be linked to further economic convergence. Putin enjoys an immense popularity rate domestically for reunifying Crimea with Russia, and could subsequently use this political leverage to accept a compromise on a territorial settlement similar to what Moscow accepted with China and Norway. Japan's dependency on the US has made its relations with Russia susceptible to conflict, as Japan will host a more important part of the US missile defence system and as Japan also sanctioned Russia over Ukraine in the US efforts to isolate Russia. While the sentiment in Japan is that relations could resume and be enhanced once the crisis in Ukraine is over, the bilateral relationship will nonetheless be vulnerable to US-Russian relations in the future.

Beyond Japan and South Korea in North-East Asia, Russia looks to the advanced economies of Singapore and Taiwan as sources of technology, investment, and best practices. Since these four states are close allies of the US, their partnerships with Russia can be constrained by Washington. However, the US is faced with a dilemma as the containment of Russia in the Indo-Pacific could further strengthen the China-Russia partnership further, and augment the power of Beijing as the only possible future hegemon in the region.[44]

India: An Underutilised Time-tested Partnership

While the Indo-Russo partnership is less attractive since the geographical distance results in less trade, the relationship has a sound foundation that is underutilised. India and Russia have a long history of a mutually beneficial partnership and shared interests in terms of diversifying relations and constraining both the US and China. The relationship between Moscow and New Delhi stretches back to the Soviet-era, with India being the largest partner within the non-alignment movement. For India, Russia is a "time-tested and respected friend".[45] During the height of tensions with the West over Ukraine, accompanied by difficult sanctions, India eliminated any possible ambiguity concerning its position. The sanctions on Russia were condemned and Prime Minister Modi wrote in Russian: "Times have changed, but our friendship has not... We stick together through thick and thin".[46]

The primary political objective of Russia is also a shared interest by India, the development of a multipolar world to constrain and replace the current US global hegemony. In this shared objective, both India and Russia recognise the important role of China and thus pursue common projects within BRICS. The secondary political objective of Russia is to maintain a balance in the Indo-Pacific region, which could be destabilised by the rise of China and result in lack of constraints. India is apprehensive concerning a future threat from China if the power disparity continues to grow. However, alignment with the US in an anti-Chinese bloc would be counter-productive as it would alienate Russia and push China closer to Pakistan.

Central Asia, the main area of potential disputes between Russia and China, is a region where both India and Russia see a common interest in enhancing cooperation to limit Chinese influence. India's 'Connect Central Asia' policy initiated in 2012 underscored its interest in developing trade and infrastructure to facilitate trade with the Central Asian states, and by extension with Russia. With no current ambition or ability to become the dominant power in Central Asia, India is likely to respect Russia's desire to remain the 'first among equals' in the region.[47] The main infrastructure/trade route to be established is the North-South Corridor Agreement. This route would reduce the time of the maritime route for trade with Russia by almost 50 per cent, and eliminate Europe as a transit point between Russia and India. Albeit initially signed by India, Russia and Iran in 2000 and stalling for more than a decade, India revamped its efforts in 2012 and tested the route for the first time in 2014. India's engagement in Central Asia is also aimed to influence and constrain Islamic fundamentalism, which has a dangerous contagion effect on the Muslim regions of India and Russia's southern regions.

In terms of trade, a key industry for Russia has been weapons sale to India. Russia has always been willing to sell more advanced weaponry and accepted certain technology transfer.[48] While being the largest supplier of arms during the Soviet era, this declined during the 1990s. This negative trend was reversed with Russia establishing itself again as India's main supplier of arms. India accounts for 31 per cent of Russian arms exports, while 75 per cent of India's arms imports derive from Russia.[49]Prime Minister Modi announced: "Even as India's options have increased today, Russia will remain our most important defence partner".[50] In 2013, Russia bolstered its position as an arms supplier to India by delivering an aircraft carrier. In December 2014, a major expansion in military cooperation was agreed as Russia and India agreed to cooperate on the construction of 400 advanced twin-engine Ka-226T military helicopters, with assembly in India. In 2015, it was announced that Russia may replace a French contract for fighter jets, as Moscow and New Delhi are ironing out an agreement for Russia to develop and construct fifth-generation stealth fighter jets. In February 2015, India announced it would enter negotiations for establishing a Free-Trade Agreement with the Russian-led Customs Union.

Russia is also seeking to further increase its supply of energy in terms of oil, gas, uranium and nuclear power. After announcing the large pipeline deals with China in 2014, Moscow moved on to

India to explore the prospect of a $30 billion oil pipeline to India, passing through the Xinjiang province in China. During one meeting in 2014, Moscow and New Delhi signed commercial contracts worth more than $100 billion. This included $50 billion oil and gas agreement, and a $40 billion civilian nuclear power agreement to build 12 nuclear reactors. Russia would gain greater access to India's huge diamond cutting and polishing industry, introduce the Russian GLONASS satellite system in the Indian market, and develop various factories and assembly plants.[51] These agreements coincided with the ongoing arrangements to settle trade in domestic currencies rather than the US dollar.

Vietnam: Gateway to Southeast Asia and a Check on Chinese Power

Much like Russia's relationship with India, the partnership with Vietnam has strong time-tested foundation that has not been sufficiently utilised. The ties with the ruling Communist Party in Vietnam reaches back to the Soviet-era, when Moscow provided indispensable military assistance to repel the US invasion. Vietnam has an antagonistic relationship with China that is further exacerbated by the disputed maritime borders in the South China Sea. For Moscow, this means that Vietnam is an eager consumer of Russian military hardware that is used to balance Chinese power in Southeast Asia.Vietnam also represents a gateway to Southeast Asia that links Moscow closer with Malaysia, Indonesia and Myanmar, which are also interested to open up to Russia in order to construct a multipolar world.[52] These ties have withstood Chinese pressure on Russia to abandon its increasing ties with Vietnam, and US pressure on Vietnam to end its military cooperation with Russia.

Russian arms sales have increased in the recent years, which included the sale of six kilo-class attack submarines.[53]Russia again uses the Cam Ranh Bay naval base, which had been suspended in the 1990s. Russia is also establishing itself as a major energy provider with recent agreements to construct Vietnam's first eight nuclear reactors, and is also considering selling LNG.[54] Russia is also partnering with Vietnam for joint hydrocarbon extraction off the coast of Vietnam, which other states have been more cautious to pursue due to the maritime border disputes.The aspirations to develop trade in other areas are also being pursued, and in 2015, Vietnam signed a Free Trade Agreement with the Russian-led Customs Union.

Conclusion

The political impetus in Moscow for its pivot to Asia increased as the European economies stagnated after the financial crisis, and has dramatically escalated since the crisis in Ukraine erupted that exposed the vulnerabilities of excessive reliance on the EU. Russia's strategic objective is to develop itself as a Eurasian state that can facilitate the emergence of a constrained multipolar world. The vast territory of Russia enables it to enhance its autonomy and influence as it can monopolise much of the energy and transport infrastructure, while concurrently enhancing its capacity to diversify relations and become less reliant on individual states. Russia's primary objective is to eliminate the foundations for a unipolar world under US leadership and its secondary objective is to prevent a US-Chinese bipolar world to replace US global hegemony. Without any ambition or capacity for hegemony in the Indo-Pacific region, Russia appears as an attractive partner to a region wary of the dominant influence of the US and China. It is argued here that while the Russian aims to transform the Indo-Pacific region are daunting and may be even overly ambitious, its progress is accelerating and rapidly producing results.

The greatest challenge in a multipolar system is for the great powers to develop a functioning system where they can act both as partners and competitors, in order to collaborate for mutual security gain while concurrently balancing each other to ensure constraints. Russia's ability to achieve its objectives relies on its capacity to find a functional approach to China that allows both to cooperate and balance each other. If cooperation with China results in Russia becoming overly dependent on China, relations could deteriorate as Moscow would refute becoming a 'junior partner' in an increasingly unfavourable asymmetrical power relationship. In contrast, excessive balancing to create more symmetry in relations could lead to confrontation and thus undermine the mutually beneficial integration of Eurasia. If Russia and China are successful in their endeavour to weaken the global dominance of the US, Russia must adjust to the emerging challenges associated with multi-polarity as China could be expected to become less accepting of Russian balancing.

NOTES

1. Glenn Diesen and Steve Wood, "Russia's proposal for a new security system: confirming diverse perspectives", *Australian Journal of International Affairs*, Vol. 66, No. 4, 2012, pp. 450-467.
2. *Concept of the Foreign Policy of the Russian Federation* (Moscow: Russian Ministry of Foreign Affairs), 12 February 2013.
3. Dimitri Trenin, "Russia Can Pivot to the Pacific, Too", *The Globalist*, 7 September 2012.
4. Dmitri Trenin, "Challenges and Opportunities: Russia and the Rise of China and India", in Ashley J. Tellis, Travis Tanner and Jessica Keough, eds., *Strategic Asia 2011–12: Asia Responds to Its Rising Powers – China and India* (Seattle and Washington, DC: National Bureau of Asian Research, 2011), p. 227.
5. Richard Weitz, "Massive East-West Transit Corridor Nears Crucial Phase", *CACI Analyst*, 11 December 2013.
6. Dmitri Trenin, "Russia's Asia Policy Under Vladimir Putin, 2000-2005", in Gilbert Rozman, Kazuhiko Togo and Joseph P. Ferguson, eds., *Russian Strategic Thought Towards Asia* (New York: Palgrave Macmillan, 2006), p. 131.
7. Natasha Kuhrt, "The Russian Far East in Russia's Asia Policy: Dual Integration or Double Periphery?", *Europe-Asia Studies*, Vol. 64, No. 3, 2012, p. 478.
8. Zbigniew Brzezinski, *The Grand Chessboard* (New York: Basic Books, 1997), p. 40.
9. Richard Sakwa, "The Problem of 'the International' in Russian Identity Formation', *International Politics*, Vol. 49, No. 4, 2012, pp. 449-465.
10. Interview with Vladimir Putin, "A new integration project for Eurasia: The future in the making", *Izvestiya*, 4 October 2011.
11. Cordula Rastogi and Jean-Francois Arvis, *The Eurasian connection: Supply-chain efficiency along the modern silk route through Central Asia* (Washington DC: The World Bank, 2014), p. 4.
12. Sergei Lavrov, *Towards Peace, Stability and Sustainable Economic Development in the Asia-Pacific Region* (Moscow: Ministry of Foreign Affairs of the Russian Federation), 5 October 2013.
13. *Concept of the Foreign Policy of the Russian Federation* (Moscow: Russian Ministry of Foreign Affairs), 12 February 2013.

14. Elena Martynova, "Strengthening of Cooperation between Russia and ASEAN: Rhetoric or Reality", *Asian Politics & Policy*, Vol. 6, No. 3, 2014, pp. 397-412; Anna Kireeva, "Russia's East Asia Policy: New Opportunities and Challenges", *Perceptions*, Vol. 17, No. 4, 2012, p. 71.
15. Vladimir Putin, "An Asia-Pacific Growth Agenda", *The Wall Street Journal*, 6 September 2012.
16. Zachary Keck, "Russia Accelerates Asia Pivot", *The Diplomat*, 18 April 2014.
17. "#62: Russia jumps record 30 places in 'Doing Business' ranking", *RT*, 29 October 2014.
18. *World Bank Indicator Report* (Washington DC), 2014.
19. Society for Worldwide Interbank Financial Telecommunication (SWIFT) provides a network for secure payment orders between financial institutions and currently manages the majority of interbank messages. US government institutions, including the NSA and CIA, have access to the SWIFT transaction database. In 2012, the US expelled Iran from the use of SWIFT due to US sanctions.
20. In 2009, the US presented China with the ultimatum of either buying more US debt or else the Federal Reserve would buy the debt. This effectively blackmailed China to either accept more US debt or to have their existing investments devalued. The near zero interest rather over several years also raises questions whether the US would be able to service its debts if interest rates were increased.
21. SWIFT is already blocking bank transactions from Crimea.
22. Gold hedges against decline in the dollar and can also be used to support a new reserve currency or basket of currencies.
23. Nyshka Chandran, "Is the dollar losing its clout among Ems?", *CNBC*, 9 March 2015.
24. "BRICS condemn sanctions against Russia", *The BRICS Post*, 16 July 2014.
25. Zachary Boren, "Ukraine crisis: Top Chinese diplomat backs Putin and says West should 'abandon zero-sum mentality'", *The Independent*, 27 February 2015.
26. Andrew Kuchins, "Russia and the CIS in 2013: Russia's Pivot to Asia", *Asian Survey*, Vol. 54, No. 1, January/February 2014, pp. 129-137.
27. Viktor Sumsky, 'ModernizatsiyaRossii, geopolitikaVostochnojAzii I factor ASEAN' (Modernisation of Russia, geopolitics of East Asia and the ASEANfactor), *Mezhdunarodnayazhizn*, No. 10, 2010.
28. Margarete Klein, "Russia: A Euro-Pacific Power?", *SWP Research Paper* (Berlin), September 2014, p. 20.
29. Seung HoJoo, "Russia's Policy on Nuclear Proliferation and National

Unification on the Korean Peninsula", *Pacific Focus*, Vol. 29, No. 2, 2014, pp. 167-187.

30. Alicia Campi, "How expanding trans-border transportation networks will impact South Korean-Mongolian energy cooperation, Using the Greater Tumen river initiative to realise the Eurasia initiative", *KEI*, 22 January 2014.
31. Gal Luft, "Can America Stop Russia's Energy 'Pivot' to Asia?", *The National Interest*, 13 May 2014.
32. "Vladivostok chosen as Russia's first 'free port' to help bolster economy", *The Siberian Times*, 7 December 2014.
33. Park Geun-Hye, "New Kind of Korea: Building Trust Between Seoul and Pyongyang", *Foreign Affairs*, Vol. 90, No. 5, 2011, pp. 13-18.
34. "Russia to extend Trans-Eurasian rail project to Korea", *RT*, 6 June 2014.
35. Joseph Ferguson, "Russia's role on the Korean Peninsula and great power relations in Northeast Asia", *NBR Analysis*, Vol. 14, No. 1, 2003, pp. 33-50; Jae-Young Lee, "Iron Silkroad: Prospects for a Land-bridge through Russia from Korea to Europe", *Post-Soviet Affairs*, Vol. 20, No. 1, 2004, pp. 83-105.
36. Campi, n. 30, p. 5.
37. Joo, n. 29.
38. Ibid.
39. Campi, n. 30.
40. Stephen Blank, "Russia's Game in North Korea", *Eurasia Daily Monitor*, 7 May 2014.
41. Kuchins, n. 26.
42. Klein, n. 28.
43. Kuchins, n. 26, p.134.
44. Dimitri Trenin, "Russia: Pivoting to Asia or Just to China?", *Carnegie Moscow Centre*, 24 March 2014.
45. Lavina Lee, "Russia's Engagement with India: Securing the Longevity of a 'Special and Privileged' Strategic Partnership", in Ian Hall, ed., *The Engagement of India* (Washington: Georgetown University Press, 2014) p. 62.
46. Liam Halligan, "India's star rises out of QE taper tantrum", *The Telegraph*, 13 December 2014.
47. Lavina Lee and Graeme Gill, "India, Central Asia and the Eurasian Union: A New Ballgame?", *India Quarterly*, Vol. 71, No. 2, 2015, p. 2.
48. Ibid.
49. Jeffrey Mankoff, "Russia's Asia Pivot: Confrontation or Cooperation?", *Asia Policy*, Vol. 19, No. 1, 2015, p. 80.
50. "Vladimir Putin's visit: Russia offers to fully 'Make in India' one of its most advanced helicopters", *The Economic Times*, 11 December 2014.

51. Dipanjan Roy Chaudhury, "Russia and India have a huge potential of bilateral trade and economic cooperation: Vladimir Putin", *The Economic Times*, 10 December 2014.
52. Paradorn Rangsimaporn, "Russia's Search for Influence in Southeast Asia", *Asian Survey*, Vol. 49, No. 5, 2009, pp. 786–808.
53. Mankoff, n. 49, p. 81.
54. Kuchins, n. 26, p. 136.

6

Indo-Pacific as an Emerging Geopolitical Construct: US Policy and Ramifications

Chintamani Mahapatra and Vivek Mishra

ABSTRACT

The Indo-Pacific region might have been the latest kid on the global bloc, but it has shown a rare combination of economic and strategic worth to move the geopolitical focus of the United States to this region. From a term of occasional reference in American politics, "Indo-Pacific" has gained currency as a more appropriate strategic reference point than the "Asia-Pacific". At the political level, the importance of the term has been emphasised at the highest levels; after former Secretary of State Hillary Clinton and her Assistant Secretary for East Asia Kurt Campbell used the term on more than a few occasions. It got further institutionalised under references from John Biden, John Kerry and Samuel J. Locklear.

Over the years, particularly since 2010, the maintenance of safe and secure sea lanes in the Indo-Pacific has become a priority for the Obama Administration and the same has been reflected in different policy decisions. The Indo-Pacific has a dual significance for American interests in the region; economic and strategic. Within the economic dimension, securing the Sea Lines of Communication (SLOC) passing through this region and the economic interests of its partners seems to be the core concerns of the US in the Indo-Pacific. At the strategic level, the region forms a new strategic ground for the US to build new partnerships to manage the rising power and assertiveness of China. The emphasis by the US to add India in the regional politics of the Indo-Pacific is a pointer towards the same.

Through the Indo-Pacific, the US finds a quasi-justification in extending its Pacific Rebalance up to the Indian Ocean, thereby creating a single geo-

strategic construct from the Western Pacific to the Western Indian Ocean. Together with Japan and India, the US policies in this region will seek to create a strategic bulwark in the wake of fast changing balance of power in this region. What will be the major geopolitical and economic ramifications of Washington's evolving policy towards the Indo-Pacific"?

Changing US Conception: Why the Indo-Pacific?

The American strategic psyche was already toying with the idea of finding a new theatre to reposition the future of its geopolitics in Asia, even as it was deciding to wind up its engagement in Iraq and drawdown troops from Afghanistan. Both these commitments forced unapologetic depletion of resources from the US, thereby prolonging the recovery of its recuperating economy. In such circumstances the US was dealing with very few options in so far as areas, to relocate its resources into a new region, were concerned. The need for a reformulation of US priorities was intensely felt, and strategic reassessment in the Asia-Pacific came to be seen as a deft option for the US. Campbell and Ratner argue that by the year 2014, reorienting its foreign policy to commit greater attention and resources to the Asia-Pacific region had attained the importance of a 'substantial national project'[1] for the US. For these and a host of other reasons, the Indo-Pacific came out as a region that was perfectly placed to suit US' interests in seeking a redefined engagement in Asian geopolitics.

First, the Indo-Pacific came to fit the US' envisaged conception of a reengagement in Asia which sought a balance between its economic needs and military commitments, with the former subtly mitigating the need of the latter. The Indo-Pacific with its maritime trade dominance and as a region that hardly needed combat military commitments (as opposed to maritime security patrols), precisely suited the US' interests. A renewed engagement of the US in the Indo-Pacific offered a dual possibility; one that stood to gain from trade engagements in an economically resurgent Asia as well as maintain a strong regional presence without having to commit militarily in the region. Second, the Indo-Pacific seemed to be the US' best bet in getting its presence closest to Beijing, comprising a new geo-strategic calculation. China's phenomenal economic rise and military modernisation compelled the US to think about a repositioning in the Asian maritime theatre apropos

China. The Indo-Pacific appeared to be Washington's foremost choice as, while it placed the US in the thick of a dominant regional role, the Indo-Pacific also strategically located the US as peripheral to Beijing, thereby according a post-facto justification to US' "managing China" rhetoric, as opposed to containing it. Third, through an engagement in the Indo-Pacific the US saw a possibility to strengthen its presence in Southeast Asia. Southeast Asia has not been a traditional US stronghold in the same vein as, for instance, Northeast Asia. Involvement of the US in projects such as Indo-Pacific Economic Corridor (IPEC) and the Lower Mekong Initiative (LMI) points towards such US interests in the Southeast Asian region. Fourth, the US factored its engagement in the Indo-Pacific to find maritime conduit to extend its Pacific Rebalance up to the Indian Ocean. In doing so, the US would be creating ample net-security-provider role for itself, in a region that would form a single geopolitical expanse from the western Pacific to the Indian Ocean Region (IOR). Washington's growing closeness with New Delhi has only emboldened any such proposition.

Beside all the important reasons mentioned above, the US has moved its focus to the Indo-Pacific as it coincides geographically with Southeast Asia, a region of increasing geo-economic significance in the US conception. Southeast Asia (and hence also the Indo-Pacific) returned under US foreign policy focus, particularly under the second term of the Obama Administration, because of several factors; a more grounded presence of the US in this region is likely to make it more involved in the activities of ASEAN which now represents a massive $2 trillion economy representing more than 600 million people. The amount of investments made in Southeast Asia is likely to cross that made in China soon. The US presence in the Southeast Asian region will place it in the heart of the region that is witnessing arguably the greatest maritime trade traffics in the world. Apart from these, through its presence in Southeast Asia, the US will seek to concretise its IPEC project, simultaneously gaining access to the Indian Ocean; a region that recent American discourses have held as having high strategic worth.[2]

Emergence and Institutionalisation of "Indo-Pacific" in US Strategy

For all the above reasons and more, from a term of occasional reference in American politics, "Indo-Pacific" has gained currency as a more appropriate strategic reference point than the "Asia-Pacific". At the political level, the importance of the term has been emphasised at the highest levels; after former Secretary of State Hillary Clinton[3] and her Assistant Secretary for East Asia Kurt Campbell used the term on more than a few occasions. It got further institutionalised under references from John Biden, John Kerry and Samuel J. Locklear. In an era that witnessed the relative decline of the American power globally, as in Asia, Hillary Clinton in her "America's Pacific Century"[4] speech tried to project the Asia-Pacific in a new light on three key concerns; sustaining leadership in the region, securing interests and advancing values. While she held US' treaty alliances with Japan, South Korea, Australia, the Philippines, and Thailand as the fulcrum for the US' 'strategic turn' to the Asia-Pacific, she cautioned the US against just sustaining these alliances, as opposed to making modifications in these alliances and building new ones in a changing world. In that context she mentioned about the need to change America's Pacific alliance with Australia into an "Indo-Pacific" one. Assistant Secretary of State for East Asian and Pacific Affairs (2009-13), widely credited as being a key architect of the "pivot to Asia",[5] has probably played one of the most important roles in etching the concept of "Indo-Pacific" in American strategic circles. During his tenure, his leadership undertook some of US' efforts to strengthen security alliances and partnerships in the Indo-Pacific region.

On July 19, 2013, just days ahead of his India visit, Vice-President Joe Biden hinted that India should be incorporated in the Asia-Pacific strategy of the US. He pointed out that the new focus in the Obama administration was on improving US relations in Southeast Asia and in that region there was possible meeting ground for both India and the US, as he said, "India is increasingly looking east as a force for security and growth in Southeast Asia and beyond".[6] The meeting ground between India and the US in Southeast Asia, for convergences in trade and strategic concerns, is undoubtedly the Indo-Pacific region. Biden, in his speech, made it clear that the reassessment in the American strategic thinking has moved Washington's focus to Southeast Asia. To quote from his speech,[7] the Obama administration has moved its 'particular focus' to Southeast Asia, a region overlapping the Indo-Pacific. In one of the most important references vis-à-vis the Indo-Pacific region, Biden laid out the policy intention of the US; "our goal is to help tie Asia-Pacific nations together—from India to the Americas—through strong alliances, institutions and partnerships". Biden through his various references to the "Indo-Pacific" emphasised India's centrality to the US role in the Indo-Pacific, by an implicit proposal that the Indian Ocean should be seen as the western leg of the Pacific Rebalance with the Indo-Pacific being the geo-strategic maritime corridor connecting the two.

US Secretary of State John Kerry has also talked about the Indo-Pacific on several occasions. Apart from invoking the newly opened Burma as part of an "Indo-Pacific economic corridor,"[8] Secretary John Kerry has held the Indo-Pacific as being of high value to the Indo-US relationship. During his January 2015 visit to the Vibrant Gujarat Summit he joined leading US business executives and innovators at the Summit to highlight the critical role that US technology plays in supporting sustainable economic growth across India and the Indo-Pacific region.[9] After both Vice-President Biden and Secretary Kerry referred to India as being a lynchpin in the US Indo-Pacific strategy, US Pacific Command (PACOM) commander, Admiral Samuel Locklear went a step further and called the Asia-Pacific region the "Indo-Asia-Pacific".[10] Commander Locklear's use of the term, as the top US grounds-man in the region, conclusively signalled the US desire to connect the two oceans separated by the IPEC.

The documentary evolution of a serious maritime strategy of the US in the Indo-Pacific can be traced to at least two documents; October 2007 document called, "A Cooperative Strategy for 21st Century Sea Power (CS21)",[11] and the 2010 release, Naval Operations Concept (NOC10). The first document has laid out the common principles for US maritime strategy. Two quotes from CS21 lays out the US maritime intention in the larger region that incorporates the Indo-Pacific, "Credible combat power will be continuously postured in the Western Pacific and the Arabian Gulf/

Indian Ocean to protect our vital interests, assure our friends and allies of our continuing commitment to regional security, and deter and dissuade potential adversaries and peer competitors", and, "We will not permit conditions under which our maritime forces would be impeded from freedom of manoeuvre and freedom of access, nor will we permit an adversary to disrupt the global supply chain by attempting to block vital sea-lines of communication and commerce". Both these quotes from recent document coming out of the US Navy's stable depict that maintaining a credible combat power and freedom of navigation in the maritime domain are among its core interests.

US Policy Objectives in the Indo-Pacific

Over time, several references to the "Indo-Pacific" from US strategic circles have come to establish, publicise and institutionalise the term, first as a concept and then as a serious policy objective. The primary goal of the US in the Indo-Pacific is shaping the future of trade pattern, rules and dimensions, and promoting suitable connectivity to suit its interests. To achieve that goal and as a dominant extra-regional power in the region, the US intends to perpetuate its role as the net-security-provider, including providing maritime security for safety of the Sea Lines of Communication (SLOC) passing though the region. Thus broadly, the US policy in the Indo-Pacific region is hinged on triple purpose emanating from a fairly common assessment: one that caters to securing economic interests, second, albeit related concern, is that of maintaining security in the Indo-Pacific maritime domain and the third policy purpose is tethered to a plethora of strategic concerns, together clubbed under what this paper intends to call the 'Grand Strategy' of the US.

Trade and Connectivity

On the economic front, one of the most important factors guiding US policy objectives is the issue of preserving and promoting trade interests. As the Indo-Pacific region is sandwiched between the Pacific and the Indian Oceans and is contiguous to littorals of Southeast Asia, the issue of regional connectivity impinges to a significant degree on how trade in this region is carried out. Hence, 'trade and connectivity'[12] forms one of the core concerns of the US in the Indo-Pacific.

The Indo-Pacific falls in a region where trade has thrived for centuries. Today the daily trade transiting the Indo-Pacific corridor is worth trillions of dollars and is more than ever. This region, moreover, straddles three of Asia's biggest economies—India, Japan and China. India and China are also the world's two largest markets and two fastest growing economies. The appetite for energy in this region is increasing by the day and by 2030, eighty-five per cent of global energy consumption will come from the Indo-Pacific region,[13] clearly depicting the region's future needs and stakes for all stakeholders in this region. A well connected and safe Asian maritime trade environment, the fulcrum of which rests in the Indo-Pacific region, will accrue not just trade benefits for the US and others but also secure stability in Asia.

The primary strategy of the US in the Indo-Pacific will rivet around the Indo-Pacific Economic Corridor. Pushing for freedom of navigation in the IPEC for a safe trade transit route is and will continue to be among US top priorities in the region. The Indo-Pacific is an inherent part in the US effort to push for building regional linkages all the way from Central Asia to Southeast Asia, via South Asia. The Indo-Pacific region also happens to be suitably placed to help the US realise its dream of placing in the wider Asia-Pacific region, a range of connectivity; physical infrastructure, regulatory trade architecture, and human and digital connectivity.[14]

The US also aspires to use the Indo-Pacific as a handy strategic tool to promote its agenda of 'greater regional economic cooperation'[15] in Asia. The larger Asian region in US estimations has been held to be a weakly linked region with an even more fragile economic integration. While ASEAN stands out as a good example of regional economic cooperation, it has failed to solidly promote intra-regional trade and investment regimes. Moreover, it consists of only Southeast Asian countries. South Asia, East Asia and Central Asia are yet to experience robust regionalism. The Asian trade network thus is probably the worst connected in the world with less than five percent of intra-regional trade flows and less than one per cent of intra-regional investment flows.[16] In a fair assessment, the US understands that in the coming years China's dream of building a Maritime Silk Route is likely to fructify putting the IPEC in the heart of this mega Chinese initiative. Since China has already pledged a commitment[17] of a whopping $40 billion to set up a Silk Road infrastructure fund to boost connectivity across Asia, Washington's apprehensions are conspicuous.

Washington's 'India Preference' Strategy

India's status as a regional heavyweight and the only credible future counter-weight to China in this region presents sufficient reasons as to why the US should prefer India as a regional frontrunner in the Indo-Pacific. The US defence strategy in the Indo-Pacific basically borders on a duality of purpose; one that seeks to support its combat power in the western Pacific through the Indian Ocean up to the Persian Gulf and the other that looks to maintain a well-knit web of defence-related connectivity for logistical advantages in the vast waters encompassing this geopolitical construct. Both these imperatives in the region are and will continue to be bolstered by a strong naval presence of the US in the Indo-Pacific. But the accomplishment of both these imperatives in totality by the US is being stonewalled by the rapid rise of China's naval capabilities and its intent to develop a blue water naval capability to protect its growing interest in the Indian Ocean region.

China is perceived to be blocking US' successful realisation of its imperatives involving military needs, logistics, trade and freedom of navigation because of its revisionist approach to the issues of maritime security in the Indo-Pacific region. Militarily, China has shown clear intent by emphasising its sovereignty over vast stretches of the South China Sea by drawing the nine-dotted-line. While there are five other countries that dispute China's claim, the United States has begun to counter China's claim by asserting the doctrine of freedom of navigation. As far as China's growing presence in the Indian Ocean is concerned, both New Delhi and Washington have found valid reasons to be anxious about. For instance, the unprecedented forays of the Chinese ship Changbaishan, a Yuzhao-class amphibious transport dock during early 2014 in the Indian Ocean, not only caused deep concern in New Delhi but in Washington also. Besides, the Chinese Surface Action Group conducted a sophisticated maritime exercise in 2014 which showed that China's combat reach extended to the eastern Indian Ocean.[18]

The US maintains muscular military presences in Hawaii (US Pacific Command), Yokosuka, Japan (US Seventh Fleet) and Bahrain (US Fifth Fleet). Moreover, it has a Military Support Facility (MSF) in Diego Garcia in the Indian Ocean region, but that serves only half its purpose, that of logistics and disaster management. However, expansion of the Chinese naval capability and demonstration of Beijing's rebellious approach to maritime issues require more forthcoming role from the US and more active participation by the littoral countries to prevent a radical change in the status quo. This is where the US perhaps needs a regional country like India to pivot its presence around the Indo-Pacific corridor. It is here that India becomes very important for the US strategy in the Indo-Pacific.

In India, the US finds a country of converging interests in the region and probably the only country capable of 'managing China' along with the US in the Indo-Pacific region, if only it is assisted to enhance its military capabilities. Both the countries have core interests in preventing any disruption in the vital sea lines of communications (SLOCs) passing through this region. The US has shown keenness to work with India in this region, particularly during the second Obama administration. Emerging challenges to freedom of navigation have brought India and the US closer than ever before to cooperate in the Indo-Pacific region. While stimulus for the two countries to enhance their naval cooperation has been there for over a decade now, it has been shrouded by a reluctance to forcefully articulate them. Washington to some extent and New Delhi in particular appear apprehensive about China's reaction. Beijing, while refraining from making declaratory statements, is apparently concerned that Indo-US naval cooperation would be directed against China. However, for the first time Indian and American governments have put out a comprehensive document, at the highest level, projecting their common strategic outlook, by signing on to a "Joint Strategic Vision for the Asia-Pacific and Indian Ocean Region" during President Obama's India visit in January 2015.[19] In the joint vision statement the two countries have pledged to work together 'from Africa to East Asia' and to accelerate 'infrastructure connectivity and economic development' in a manner that links South, Southeast and Central Asia.

Besides, the US has found a new vigour in India's refashioned "Act East Policy." It clearly has sensed a more forthcoming Indian engagement with the countries to its east and has quite justifiably supported India's expanding ties with ASEAN and initiatives like "The Mekong-India Economic Corridor". Together with India, the US has expressed its desire to cooperate in energy, infrastructure and technology sectors in the Indo-Pacific region. Indeed, the strong US commitment to "realising the potential of the Indo-Pacific Economic Corridor"[20] cannot be accomplished without a strong preference for cooperating with India in the region. Also implicit in the US aspiration to involve India as a frontrunner in the Indo-Pacific is its grand strategy to marry India's Act East Policy with US Rebalance in the Pacific. The merger of these two policies, it has been argued, will create opportunities for mutual benefit through interoperability and joint maritime efforts. Interoperability, nonetheless, remains a desired goal and this cannot be achieved without raising the threshold of the current level of defence cooperation The commonality of interests between India and the US in the Indo-Pacific region was recently emphasised in an address[21] by Puneet Talwar, Assistant Secretary, Bureau of Political-Military Affairs, who said: "Prime Minister Modi's "Act East" policy—just like President Obama's rebalance to Asia—is rooted in the leading economic role that the Asia-Pacific is already playing in this century and beyond. Our interests in the region, and our policies towards the region, have never been more complementary". Emphasising the importance of cooperation with India in the Indo-Pacific region he further said, "This is a time of great possibility; of great excitement; and of great importance for the United States and India. We're seeing a natural convergence not only of our values... not only of our interests... but also of our vision for the way forward... in the Indo-Pacific and the world at large".[22]

Converting Challenges into Opportunities

The US has adopted a balanced approach in its engagement with the countries of the Indo-Pacific region as against involving an outright military dimension. In fact, one of the primary reasons why the US pivot-to-Asia climbed down to being its Rebalance strategy in the Pacific can be attributed to the scope of opportunities created by the Indo-Pacific region. The dominance of trade and transit activities in the Indo-Pacific, its geographical position of being a gateway to both the Pacific and the Indian Oceans and the lack of any continuous continental stretch makes the Indo-Pacific region a maritime domain where any rivalry, combat and military showdown will have equally grave consequences for the economies of the players involved in the region. In the Indo-Pacific region, the countries find their roots of cooperation primarily in economic activities and therefore have more reasons to cooperate than clash with one another. Yet, competitiveness seems to have made its way with the US and India keeping close in the wake of China preferring to go it alone and assert its views and positions on critical issues, including on maritime disputes. China has voiced its interests in the Indian Ocean and Southeast Asia, but its massive investment in port construction in troubled countries like Pakistan, use of its money power to buy influence in other littoral countries and muscle flexing in South China Sea have caused concern. Both India and the US appear to be searching for ways and means of engaging China and making it a stakeholder.

Many analysts have talked about a remote possibility of a strategic triangle between India, the US and China in the Indian Ocean. This possibility still looks remote as any Chinese presence in the Indian Ocean would be too close to India causing strategic uncertainties. However, the Indo-Pacific provides the most ideal geographical domain to test the possibility of a tripartite cooperation between India, the US and China. This region is vast enough to accommodate their interests, prevent any immediate strategic concerns, and hold hopes for genuine cooperation in both the security and economic domains in this region, such as the safety of trade routes and prevention of weapons proliferation and piracy. More than half of India's trade passes through the Malacca Strait falling in the Indo-Pacific. For China, even as it has become one of the largest energy importers, the Indo-Pacific region accounts for the maximum trade transit for China. The Indo-Pacific, thus, provides grounds for converting challenges into opportunities for all the three countries; India, US and China, as it does for other bickering nations in the contiguous region.

Multilateral Approach

The United States always shied away from taking a lead role in Asian regionalism. While it was the brain behind the creation of NATO, it took no steps to establish a similar collective defence arrangement in Asia in the immediate post-Second World War era. China's emergence as a Communist country and three years of war in Korean Peninsula did not provoke the US to create an Asian NATO. It is only when the Eisenhower administration was compelled to step into Indochina after the humiliating French defeat at Dien Bien Phu that it took active interest in regional defence and established the Southeast Asia Treaty Organisation or SEATO. However, the American experiment with SEATO was a grand failure and it then played an indirect role in the birth of ASEAN. While ASEAN slowly moved towards regional cooperation, the US remained outside it.

In the post-Cold War era, Canberra's temerity to propose Asia-Pacific Economic Cooperation Forum and keeping the US out of it, enraged the US and in due course it pushed itself into this forum. However, China also became a part of it and APEC could not move beyond an informal grouping to seek trade liberalisation. There was another attempt to keep the US out in regional cooperation mechanism when East Asia Summit (EAS) came into being. The US again flexed its diplomatic muscle and became part of it.

Now in the emerging strategic goal of the US, being part and parcel of Asian multilateralism is an important aspect. Washington plays an active role and maintains a closer look at all the Asian multilaterals. The US priority of cooperating with the countries of Southeast Asia assumed a top position, as the Indo-Pacific rose in prominence with its geopolitical and geo-strategic stakes. A latest approach from the US towards the countries of Southeast Asia has taken multilateralism into its stride and is improving relations with the countries of this region. The US has placed emphasis in improving its ties with ASEAN as an organisation. Since 2005, gradually the US has come to accord more importance to its participation in the East Asia Summit, another important organisation of the region. The United States has significantly improved relations with important emerging powers like Indonesia and Vietnam while tightening its partnerships with New Zealand and Singapore, in addition to broadening and deepening relations with China.[23] In strategic considerations, the US has shown a keenness to work closely on a multilateral basis with India and Japan in the Malabar Exercises, despite hackles being raised in China.

Economic Cooperation

But the most significant development in this regard is the Obama administration's desire to create a new trade promotion mechanism in this region with active US participation. As a result, it joined the TPP or Trans-Pacific Partnership grouping and began to push for its early conclusion.Recognising the Indo-Pacific as a region that will hold the key to economic growth in Asia and even in the US, the Obama Administration has, more recently revamped its economic cooperation with the countries of this region. The Indo-Pacific is also being seen by the US as the most lucrative opportunity for an involvement in trade in Asia, and probably the US' best bet to accelerate or speed up the pace of its economic recovery back home. The US also seeks to forge greater economic ties with important economies of this region like Japan, Singapore, Indonesia and Myanmar, besides others. Alternatively, the US has also taken steps to facilitate the investment in countries contiguous to the Indo-Pacific region. The US government has taken steps to create a political and international regulatory environment to facilitate closer commercial ties across the Pacific and promote shared economic growth. During its host year in 2011, the United States refocused APEC on its core mission of facilitating Asia-Pacific economic integration, its larger goal in the Indo-Pacific region.[24]

China and the US are certainly part of APEC Forum and several other multilaterals. But China is not part of the US-led TPP and the US is not part of China-led Regional Comprehensive Economic Partnership (RCEP). The two economic giants seem to be trying to shape the regional economy under their respective leadership and this is not a good sign. India interestingly is part of the RCEP and TPP. Japan is part of TPP and RCEP. When Sino-Japanese tension rises, Japan goes slow in its participation in RCEP. It now actively backs the US-led TPP. While India is part of the RCEP process, China is increasingly becoming apprehensive of Indo-US defence cooperation in the Indo-Pacific region. The best way to move forward in the multilateral diplomacy at least in the field of trade and investment is to find the US, China, India and Japan along with other regional countries together in the same forum.

Conclusion

What the Indo-Pacific has done is that it has created a single strategic system imparting maritime access to regional countries from the Gulf of Aden in the IOR to Northeast Asia, up to Australia and New Zealand. However, China's presence in this region as a resident assertive power with an increasingly powerful navy and a desire to enter the Indian Ocean, India as a regional heavyweight with its reset strategic regional priority for the region enunciated through its Act East Policy, and the US as the most dominant extra regional power in the region are likely to create an interesting mix of geopolitics that will naturally belly up to a regional contestation among at least these three countries, if not more. The US will seek to prioritise maritime security, freedom of navigation and most of all to maintain a balance of power in the region through its push-India strategy. For the US, one of the primary concerns in the Indo-Pacific region will be to prevent the violation of freedom of navigation in the region and hence forestall China from replicating its South China Sea strategy in the Indo-Pacific. China has already shown its keenness to cross its traditional nine-dotted-line and make its naval presence in Southeast Asia the new-normal for the Indo-Pacific region through frequent exercises and dockings. The US, thus far, has avoided a direct confrontational posture vis-à-vis China in the Indo-Pacific and is likely to continue with that strategy for at least three reasons; first, as a resident power in the Indo-Pacific the US understands that China's rise needs to be accommodated. Second, the *numerouno* priority for the US through its involvement in the Indo-Pacific is to benefit from rising Asian trade activity in this region and any confrontation with China will only subvert that possibility. Third, the US finds a willing partner in India whose interests in the Indo-Pacific converge. To that extent, the strategy to convince India for a pre-emptive role in the region is going to be the likely strategy of the US, apart from jointly monitoring the area.

For particularly the third reason, the US is likely to rely more on its India-preference strategy in the Indo-Pacific. The US effort to back an enhanced role for India in the Indo-Pacific, much as its own, also stems from both these countries' exclusion from regional economic organisations such as APEC and ASEAN which in turn prevented these countries from integrating fully with the Asia-Pacific. In that sense, the Indo-Pacific could be opening a new window of opportunity of economic integration by merging the Asia-Pacific through Southeast Asia up to South Asia in the Indian Ocean as a single-stretch maritime economic corridor.

However, the real challenge for the US in the region will be to strike the right balance between the need for its involvement in trade thereby benefiting from it and the undesirability of flaring up of tensions due to intense geopolitical contestation in the Indo-Pacific. This can better be done by creating a multilateral trade negotiation forum that would go beyond the narrow membership size of RCEP or TPP and be more inclusive.

NOTES

1. Kurt M. Campbell and Ely Ratner, "Far Eastern Promises: Why Washington Should Focus on Asia?", *Foreign Affairs*, May/June 2014. <http://www.foreignaffairs.com/articles/141241/kurt-m-campbell-and-ely-ratner/far-eastern-promises> accessed 20 March 2015.
2. Robert D. Kaplan, *Monsoon: the Indian Ocean and the Future of American Power* (New York: Random House, 2010), Preface.
3. Hillary Clinton, "America's Pacific Century", *Foreign Policy*, Issue 189, November 2011, pp. 56-63.
4. Ibid.
5. Kurt M. Campbell, *People* (Washington: Centre for a New American Security). <http://www.cnas.org/CampbellKurt> accessed 20 April 2015.
6. Joe Biden, "Asia-Pacific Policy", (George Washington University), 19 July 2013. <https://www.whitehouse.gov/the-press-office/2013/07/19/remarks-vice-president-joe-biden-asia-pacific-policy> accessed 19 April 2015.
7. Ibid.

8. Rory Medcalf, "The Indo-Pacific: What's in a Name?", *The American Interest*, 10 October 2013. <http://www.the-american-interest.com/2013/10/10/the-indo-pacific-whats-in-a-name/> accessed 19 April 2015.
9. *The Economic Times*, 7 January 2015.
10. Medcalf, n. 8.
11. A joint document on maritime strategy of the US by the US Navy, Marine Corps and Coast Guard.
12. Fatema Z. Sumar, "Shaping the Future of Trade and Connectivity in the Indo-Pacific", *Remarks* (Kolkata), 8 May 2014. <http://www.state.gov/p/sca/rls/rmks/2014/226364.htm> accessed 14 April 2015.
13. Iskander Rehman, *Indo-Pacific Geopolitics* (Centre for Strategic and Business Assessment), 2014. <http://www.csbaonline.org/2014/04/12/indo-pacific-geopolitics/> accessed 15 April 2015.
14. Sumar, n. 12.
15. Ibid.
16. Ibid.
17. "China to establish $40 billion Silk Road infrastructure fund", *Reuters*, 8 November 2014. <http://www.reuters.com/article/2014/11/08/us-china-diplomacy-idUSKBN0IS0BQ20141108> accessed 20 April 2015.
18. V. Mishra, "Chinese bases in IOR: A new maritime awakening for India?", *South Asia Monitor*, 28 April 2015. <http://southasiamonitor.org/detail.php?type=pacific&nid=11561> accessed 8 May 2015.
19. P. Jha, "India, US articulate joint Asia-Pacific vision; China not happy", 27 January 2015. <http://www.hindustantimes.com/india-news/where-india-publicly-articulates-joint-asia-vision-with-us-china-not-happy/article1-1310898.aspx> accessed 28 April 2015.
20. Voiced by US Secretary of State, John Kerry when he visited India in 2013.
21. Puneet Talwar, "Remarks at the Institute for Defence and Strategic Analyses" (New Delhi), 3 December 2014. <http://www.state.gov/t/pm/rls/rm/2014/234643.htm> accessed 29 April 2015.
22. Ibid.
23. K. Campbell and B. Andrews, *Explaining the US 'Pivot' to Asia* (London: Chatham House) August 2013. <http://www.chathamhouse.org/sites/files/chathamhouse/public/Research/Americas/0813pp_pivottoasia.pdf> assessed 20 April 2015.
24. Ibid.

7

Understanding Trade Competitiveness of the Indian Ocean Countries: A Statistical Appraisal

Faisal Ahmed and M. Absar Alam

ABSTRACT

The Indian Ocean Rim Association for Regional Cooperation (IOR-ARC or IORA) that comprises twenty countries represents eight per cent of the global output and hosts around one-third of the world population. It includes countries from Southeast Asia, South Asia, West Asia and Australia. This chapter studies the economic profile of the region and the level of the trade participation of the constituent countries of the region. Based largely on statistical analyses this chapter purports to ascertain the level of trade competitiveness of the countries of the region and helps to understand the potentials and prospects of regional integration better.

Introduction

The historical prominence of the Indian Ocean in shaping the world economic and geo-economic order may be traced to the ancient period like those in the era of Sumerian prominence.[1] The same role was played during the colonial period when major economic powers tried to control the Ocean in order to gain influence in countries/regions like India, Australia and Africa.[2] The economic rise of countries of the Indian Ocean further helped them evolve a structured economic development. The Indian Ocean Rim is the initiative in the same direction. The idea was not only the promotion of regional cooperation but *prima facie* was to promote North-South dialogue on various issues relating to multilateral negotiations through the representation of this forum.[3]

Indian Ocean Rim initiative has now been formally shaped as an international organisation known as Indian Ocean Rim Association (IORA) or IOR-ARC (Indian Ocean Rim Association for Regional Cooperation). Various studies on the Indian Ocean rim and its cooperation initiatives[4] have pointed out to a huge potential for regional cooperation. The organisational structure seems to be tripartite in nature which aims at working in close cooperation with three major stakeholder, viz. governments, business and academia. IOR-ARC has a vast region and also has a vast geographical coverage. It includes countries of Africa, Middle East, South Asia, Southeast Asia and the Pacific. It comprises of twenty countries encompassing those from Southeast Asia, Indian subcontinent, Southern and Eastern Africa, Arabian peninsula and Australia. These countries include Australia, Bangladesh, Comoros, India, Indonesia, Iran, Kenya, Madagascar, Malaysia, Mauritius, Mozambique, Oman, Seychelles, Singapore, South Africa, Sri Lanka, Tanzania, Thailand, United Arab Emirates (UAE) and Yemen. The IOR-ARC also creates possibilities of an efficient value chain being developed in the region. It is therefore imperative to assess the emerging directions of trade and economic cooperation within the region. Having 20 member states, the organisation covers almost one-third of the world population and 8 per cent of the global output.

Indian Ocean has its own natural and geographical features. It is the largest ocean in the world with second largest populated country in the world situated along the Ocean and has in its bed the emerging markets in the world. The Indian Ocean is one of the main areas of trade-related activities. Almost 30 per cent of the world's trade happens through this Ocean. Major sailing points like the Suez Canal and Malacca Strait are situated in the Indian Ocean. Notably, Malacca Strait handles one-quarter of world trade (25 per cent). Major oil producing countries are situated along this Ocean. In this context, the regional cooperation among countries along the Indian Ocean will have both economic and geopolitical impacts on the international community. On the one hand, it underpins international trade by supporting adequate infrastructure, security and safety to trade-related activities. Member countries have agreed upon the IOR-ARC charter. The charter presents fundamental principles and objectives of IOR-

ARC. It outlines the institutional set up of the organisation. The charter also points out that the member countries will endeavour to promote economic cooperation among member countries.

The progress of regional cooperation among member countries of IOR-ARC has been geopolitically complicated. Therefore, geo-economic cooperation has been an important area to explore new paradigms to strengthen this initiative. The region has already several regional organisations such as ASEAN, GCC, SAARC, BIMSTEC and SADC. On the other hand, there have been several other attempts for regional cooperation which include Trans-Pacific Partnership (TPP) and Regional Comprehensive Economic Partnership (RCEP). In this context, the importance of IOR-ARC needs to be recognised. There is a growing trend of regional cooperation in the world. With this growing trend, it becomes imperative to explore the economic basis for regional cooperation among IOR-ARC countries. A PTA is necessary to promote trade and investment opportunities within the region. This can be rendered possible by ensuring enhanced preferential market access and removing the non-tariff barriers by the countries of the region.[5] However, it is important to investigate the nature of economic integration in IOR-ARC. In fact, it is argued that IOR-ARC would require following the WTO timeline of trade liberalisation in order to gain from regional integration.[6] Furthermore, trade openness and growth are closely related with each other in the countries of the region.[7]

The present paper examines the trends of intra-regional trade in the Indian Ocean Rim. Also, it employs two statistical methods namely the Revealed Comparative Advantage (RCA) index and the Intra-Industry Trade (IIT) index to assess the level and direction of economic cooperation in the region. The economic integration would be largely beneficial to the vast population. Intra-regional trade within IORA is 24 per cent of its global trade. The increase in intra-regional trade would require close cooperation in certain areas including fisheries which have also been discussed in this paper.

Trading Position

As pointed out earlier, IOR-ARC has been a basket of regional economic institutions.[8] It has a few successful regional institutions like ASEAN, GCC and SADC. The countries of these institutions are part of their respective regional free trade agreements. These agreements automatically provide an important route for regional trade among IOR-ARC. Some of the institutions such as SAARC and BIMSTEC are likely to be an important part of this initiative. Any trade agreements among IOR-ARC countries will get preferential treatments and routes among countries under their respective sub-regional initiatives. Moreover, the trade routes under free trade agreements under the aegis of IOR-ARC will therefore, need to be comprehensive and exclusive in its sectors and areas.

The pattern of trade in the IOR-ARC, the region has experienced evolving level of intra-regional trade. Table 1 and Figure 1 present the recent trade patterns of IOR-ARC at both regional and global levels. Regional trade has more than 25 per cent share in IOR-ARC's global trade. The present analysis does not include statistics for Seychelles and Comoros.

Table 1: IOR-ARC Regional and Global Trade, US$ Billion

Trade	*Regional*				*Global*			
Direction	2010	2011	2012	2013	2010	2011	2012	2013
Exports	500.9	623.6	617.7	616.2	1744.2	2205.5	2111.6	2141.7
Imports	485.3	608.0	588.1	586.6	1734.5	2161.4	2253.3	2240.8

Source: International Trade Centre, Geneva, 2015 data

Figure 1: IOR-ARC Regional and Global Trade, US$ Billion

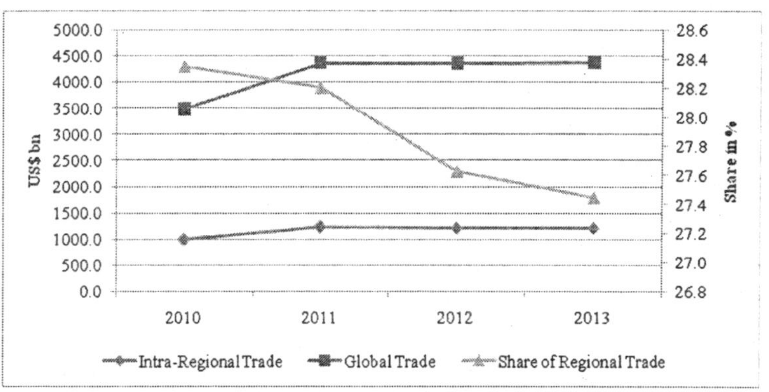

Source: Based on International Trade Data Centre, Geneva, 2015 data

The present trend also suggests some important aspects of the trade potential of IOR-ARC countries. Major countries of exports are Thailand, UAE, Malaysia, Singapore, Indonesia and India. In the year 2013, Singapore, India, Australia, Thailand, Indonesia, Malaysia, South Africa and UAE accounted for more than 90 per cent of IOR-ARC global exports. On the other hand, these countries also accounted for more than 95 per cent of its regional trade. Thus, countries which have a higher share in the region's global exports also have a higher share in regional exports. Table 2 presents this situation. Countries like Australia, Singapore, Thailand, India, UAE and South Africa are expected to play a vital role in shaping regional trade under the IOR-ARC region. It becomes very difficult to negotiate on account of regional free trade negotiations by countries like Bangladesh, Tanzania, Mozambique and Kenya. Other countries like Oman, Yemen, Mauritius and Iran will also play a pivotal role in shaping regional energy requirements. Trade pattern of the region further indicates that IOR-ARC regional economic integration will further be derived by sub-regional cooperation. Countries like Singapore, Thailand, Malaysia and Indonesia are also active suppliers in ASEAN countries.

Table 2: Country-wise Global and Regional Exports of IOR-ARC (per cent)

Country	*Global Exports*			
	2010	*2011*	*2012*	*2013*
Singapore	20.174	18.567	19.341	19.155
India	12.637	13.669	13.713	15.717
Australia	11.851	12.216	12.135	11.773
Thailand	11.198	10.375	10.871	10.670
Malaysia	11.397	10.292	10.772	10.670
United Arab Emirates	9.261	10.001	10.097	10.388
Indonesia	9.046	9.227	9.000	8.524
South Africa	4.737	4.897	4.698	4.446
Iran	4.804	5.919	3.973	2.953
Oman	2.098	2.135	2.469	2.591
Bangladesh	1.103	1.102	1.291	1.447
Sri Lanka	0.476	0.454	0.444	0.467
Yemen	0.369	0.315	0.334	0.333
Kenya	0.296	0.265	0.247	0.247

Tanzania	0.232	0.215	0.263	0.206
Mozambique	0.129	0.163	0.164	0.188
Mauritius	0.106	0.102	0.107	0.109
Madagascar	0.062	0.067	0.058	0.086
Seychelles	0.023	0.018	0.023	0.029
		Regional Exports		
	2010	*2011*	*2012*	*2013*
Singapore	24.59	23.71	24.06	23.68
India	13.31	14.49	14.90	16.68
United Arab Emirates	15.41	16.32	14.56	15.31
Malaysia	12.94	11.91	13.03	13.30
Thailand	9.66	9.00	9.51	9.67
Indonesia	9.32	9.79	9.53	9.20
Australia	7.42	7.36	6.71	5.08
South Africa	2.20	1.99	2.12	2.04
Iran	1.30	1.58	3.01	1.76
Oman	2.00	2.21	0.88	1.49
Yemen	0.71	0.40	0.43	0.43
Tanzania	0.23	0.24	0.34	0.33
Mozambique	0.11	0.17	0.15	0.30
Sri Lanka	0.30	0.31	0.27	0.25
Bangladesh	0.20	0.23	0.22	0.24
Kenya	0.20	0.17	0.14	0.11
Mauritius	0.06	0.07	0.08	0.08
Madagascar	0.04	0.05	0.04	0.04
Seychelles	0.02	0.01	0.01	0.01

Source: Authors' compilations from International Trade Centre database, Geneva, 2015

At the global level, IOR-ARC total exports are concentrated to seven major commodity groups at two-digit level classification. The commodities are mineral fuels, electrical and electronic equipment, machinery, pearls and stones, etc., ores, vehicles and plastics and its products. These products accounted for more than 63 per cent of total exports from IOR-ARC in 2013. In 2012, these products accounted for more than 64 per cent of total exports from the IOR-ARC region. Other potential exports are chemicals, textiles and iron and steel. Commodity-wise exports from IOR-ARC region are presented in Table 3. In case of imports, the listed top commodities of exports are also the listed top commodities in imports in the

IOR-ARC region from the world. Table 4 presents commodity-wise imports in the IOR-ARC region.

Table 3: Commodity-wise Exports from the IOR-ARC Region, US$ Billion

Code	Product Label	2010	2011	2012	2013
'27	Mineral fuels, oils, distillation products, etc	434.7	627.8	596.8	588.4
'85	Electrical, electronic equipment	232.3	245.8	237.8	244.4
'84	Machinery, nuclear reactors, boilers, etc	150.1	155.7	154.4	153.1
'71	Pearls, precious stones, metals, coins, etc	111.0	147.9	140.1	133.3
'26	Ores, slag and ash	83.4	111.6	98.8	109.3
'87	Vehicles other than railway, tramway	53.4	55.9	66.1	68.0
'39	Plastics and articles thereof	41.7	52.8	51.0	53.7
'29	Organic chemicals	40.1	55.2	55.9	52.2
'99	Commodities not elsewhere specified	41.0	57.5	46.2	45.9
'40	Rubber and articles thereof	37.0	53.7	43.6	41.0
'15	Animal, vegetable fats and oils, cleavage products, etc	36.3	50.0	44.8	39.3
'90	Optical, photo, technical, medical, apparatus, etc	24.8	28.4	32.1	33.4
'62	Articles of apparel, accessories, not knit or crochet	21.2	26.4	27.2	30.7
'61	Articles of apparel, accessories, knit or crochet	21.7	26.5	27.2	30.7
'72	Iron and steel	29.0	33.5	27.3	27.8
'10	Cereals	14.9	22.5	23.2	25.5
	Others*	371.6	454.2	439.2	464.9

Source: Authors' compilations of International Trade Centre database, Geneva, 2015
*others include commodities not mentioned in this table.

Table 4: Commodity-wise Imports by IOR-ARC Region, US$ Billion

Code	Product Label	2010	2011	2012	2013
'27	Mineral fuels, oils, distillation products, etc	340.0	495.2	530.6	542.2
'85	Electrical, electronic equipment	268.4	291.8	296.7	298.5
'84	Machinery, nuclear reactors, boilers, etc	222.9	259.6	275.1	256.5
'71	Pearls, precious stones, metals, coins, etc	127.5	175.1	167.1	153.7

'87	Vehicles other than railway, tramway	84.5	95.6	112.0	108.4
'39	Plastics and articles thereof	45.8	54.6	56.1	58.8
'72	Iron and steel	55.3	66.8	64.4	58.1
'29	Organic chemicals	39.6	46.8	47.3	49.6
'90	Optical, photo, technical, medical, etc apparatus	37.8	42.7	47.7	48.6
'73	Articles of iron or steel	31.5	38.0	44.6	43.5
'88	Aircraft, spacecraft, and parts thereof	22.7	27.3	33.5	34.6
'99	Commodities not elsewhere specified	35.8	36.7	36.3	32.6
'30	Pharmaceutical products	20.7	25.1	25.3	25.8
'40	Rubber and articles thereof	18.8	24.8	26.4	23.7
'38	Miscellaneous chemical products	17.4	20.6	21.0	22.2
'10	Cereals	13.1	18.9	19.0	19.5
	Others*	352.8	441.9	450.0	464.6

Source: Authors' compilations of International Trade Centre database, Geneva, 2015
*Others include commodities not mentioned in table.

Economic Profile of the Region

Countries in the IOR-ARC region are in different stages of economic progress. Therefore, the region comprises a heterogeneous group of countries. These countries not only vary in its economic quantum but also in its geographical sizes, resource availability and relative competitive factors of production. There economic policies are at different stages of economic openness and liberalisation. With such varying characteristics of the economies in the region, IOR-ARC has potential for regional cooperation. The main reason is the different economic structure which also determines the levels of complementarities between countries. There are some countries which have surplus natural resources and also have potential to supplement growth prospects of other member countries which have a resource deficit but high demand. For instance, the demand for crude oil in India and other emerging countries may be sourced from countries in the western part of the Indian Ocean like Iran.

Considering this, it becomes important to examine macroeconomic developments in member countries of IOR-ARC with a view to present levels of economic progress with reference to their respective economic structure. The average growth of IOR-ARC countries has been impressive during 2004-07 with more than 6 per cent growth in GDP yearly. This growth is also seen in the year 2010. However, after 2010 the level of economic progress has slowed down in IOR-ARC countries. The average GDP growth during 2011-14 has been hovering around 4.1 per cent. The main constituent of such a low growth is the economic performance of India, Singapore and Iran. A quick slow down at global level caused deceleration in economic growth in these countries leading to slowdown in overall IOR-ARC region. The country-wise GDP growth on a yearly basis has been presented in Table 4. Relatively better performance can be witnessed in countries like Bangladesh, Indonesia, Malaysia, Mozambique, Sri Lanka, Tanzania and UAE. Deceleration in economic progress is witnessed in countries like India, Iran, Kenya, Singapore, Thailand and Yamen. On the other hand countries like Australia, Comoro, Mauritius, South Africa and Madagascar seem to be experiencing lower GDP growth stagnated during the recent years.

Table 4: GDP Growth Rate (per cent)

Country	*2010*	*2011*	*2012*	*2013**	*2014**
Australia	2.2	2.6	3.6	2.3	2.8
Bangladesh	6.0	6.5	6.3	6.1	6.2
Comoros	2.2	2.5	3.0	3.5	3.9
India	10.3	6.6	4.7	5.0	5.6
Indonesia	6.2	6.5	6.3	5.8	5.2
Iran	6.6	3.9	-6.6	-1.9	1.5
Kenya	8.6	7.6	4.6	4.6	5.3
Madagascar	0.1	1.5	2.5	2.4	3.0
Malaysia	7.4	5.2	5.6	4.7	5.9
Mauritius	4.1	3.9	3.2	3.2	3.3
Mozambique	7.1	7.3	7.2	7.1	8.3
Oman	4.8	4.1	5.8	4.8	3.4
Seychelles	5.9	7.9	2.8	3.5	3.7
Singapore	15.2	6.1	2.5	3.9	3.0
South Africa	3.1	3.6	2.5	1.9	1.4
Sri Lanka	8.0	8.2	6.3	7.3	7.0
Tanzania	7.0	6.4	6.9	7.0	7.2
Thailand	7.8	0.1	6.5	2.9	1.0
UAE	1.6	4.9	4.7	5.2	4.3
Yemen*	7.7	-12.7	2.4	4.8	1.9

Source: *World Economic Outlook*, IMF
*Estimated Growth rates

The level of economic growth in terms of GDP is one aspect to judge the economic progress of a country. Other economic indicators will further assist in order to understand the structure of an economy. Table 5 brings out other macroeconomic indicators of IOR-ARC countries for the year 2012. The indicators cover overall investment, savings and BoP as a percent of GDP. In addition, it also brings out GDP growth for the year 2012 over 2011. The same is presented for exports and imports. The data reflects that investments are higher as a percent of GDP in both larger and smaller countries in terms of area as well as population. In case of developed countries like Australia, Singapore and South Africa investment was estimated to be 29 per cent, 30 per cent and 19 per cent of GDP respectively in 2012. In case of emerging countries like India, Indonesia, Sri Lanka, Tanzania and Thailand over 30 per cent of GDP was the total investment in 2012. These countries also having higher savings in their economy reflecting both investment levels fuelling economic progress for future as well as total savings in order to finance investment requirement. Trade performance has been mixed for the member countries in 2012. Some countries are performing well, whereas some are experiencing downturn or negative growth in exports and imports. For example, Iran experiences negative growth in both exports and imports.

The countries are also experiencing severe current account deficit reflecting high import level compared with exports. Countries like Mozambique, Seychelles and Tanzania have a higher level of current account deficit. The level of current account deficit is low in emerging and relatively developed countries like India, Indonesia, Kenya, South Africa, Sri Lanka, Thailand, etc. Countries with higher natural resources and technological advantages have a positive current account balance like Iran, UAE, Malaysia and Singapore.

Overall taking average of all the member countries, investment was 28 per cent of GDP in IOR ARC region. Similarly, savings recorded to be 24 per cent of GDP with average of 4 per cent current account deficit. The region has been experiencing higher growth in imports registering 9 per cent growth in imports in 2012. Growth in exports on the other hand is slower in 2012 with average growth of 1.5 per cent. Such trend is essential to understand the structure of the economies of the IOR-ARC region. It is apparent that major countries like, Australia, South Africa, UAE, Singapore, Thailand, India, Malaysia, Indonesia and Tanzania are dominating the region.

Table 5: Macroeconomic Indicators, 2012

S. No.	*Countries*	*Per Cent Change in GDP*	*Total Invest-ment Per Cent of GDP*	*Gross National Savings Per Cent of GDP*	*Per Cent Change in Import of Goods*	*Per Cent Change in Exports of Goods*	*Current Account Balance Per Cent of GDP*
1	Australia	3.60	29.11	24.75	6.73	6.91	-4.36
2	Bangladesh	6.26	28.30	30.06	6.77	8.93	0.69
3	Comoros	3.00	16.77	8.48	12.21	-28.07	-8.28
4	India	4.74	34.70	29.96	2.07	2.23	-4.74
5	Indonesia	6.26	34.74	31.97	15.70	2.97	-2.78
6	Iran	-6.57	41.93	48.53	-13.12	-25.67	6.60
7	Kenya	4.604	19.138	10.69	12.753	9.557	-8.443
8	Madagascar	2.505	17.63	10.872	14.005	3.884	-6.758
9	Malaysia	5.644	25.925	31.71	0.257	-3.844	5.784
10	Mauritius	3.2	24.766	17.478	1.635	4.475	-7.287
11	Mozambique	7.246	53.595	8.233	52.954	36.261	-45.363
12	Oman	5.764	25.295	38.639	21.777	10.756	13.343
13	Seychelles	2.806	37.574	12.367	5.111	3.852	-24.675
14	Singapore	2.504	30.372	47.851	1.505	0.03	17.48
15	South Africa	2.467	19.404	14.162	5.995	0.386	-5.242
16	Sri Lanka	6.336	30.649	23.941	-18.903	-8.308	-6.707
17	Tanzania	6.933	34.463	18.166	11.351	3.285	-15.862
18	Thailand	6.49	29.741	29.339	7.064	2.459	-0.402
19	UAE	4.678	19.06	37.582	11.352	15.267	18.522
20	Yemen	2.393	8.704	6.996	22.837	-15.455	-1.708

Source: World Economic Outlook, IMF

The trade-GDP ratio is given in Table 6. It shows that the overall trade openness is found higher except for Bangladesh, India and Tanzania. In fact, Malaysia, Singapore, Thailand and UAE could be considered as highly export-oriented economies in the region (see Table 6).[9]

Table 6: Trade as a Per Cent of GDP

S. No.	*Country's Name*	*2010*	*2011*	*2012*	*2013*
1	Australia	39.9	41.3	42.8	41.0
2	Bangladesh	37.8	47.4	48.1	46.3
3	Comoros	69.9	71.6	74.6	78.2
4	India	48.3	54.1	54.7	53.2
5	Indonesia	47.5	51.3	50.1	49.5
6	Iran	N.A	N.A	N.A	N.A
7	Kenya	54.2	60.4	55.3	50.9
8	Madagascar	68.0	69.1	73.0	73.1
9	Malaysia	169.7	166.6	158.9	154.1
10	Mauritius	116.3	119.8	121.3	120.8
11	Mozambique	69.0	71.7	68.9	70.5
12	Oman	89.8	100.8	98.6	-
13	Seychelles	194.1	201.5	205.5	164.0
14	Singapore	372.1	374.0	367.7	358.0
15	South Africa	56.1	60.8	61.8	65.1
16	Sri Lanka	53.1	60.7	59.3	54.5
17	Tanzania	66.4	81.3	74.9	67.4
18	Thailand	135.1	149.4	148.8	143.8
19	UAE	151.0	163.1	173.3	176.1
20	Yemen	N.A	N.A	N.A	N.A

Source: WDI, World Bank

Trade Competitiveness of the Region

In this section a discussion on the competitive advantages of IOR-ARC countries are discussed. To carry out this analysis we used revealed comparative advantage (RCA) index. This index helps us identify sectors in which countries have relative cost advantages as well as comparative competitiveness. Higher the RCA index, higher is the competitiveness in the sector for the country.[10] RCA index was developed to analyse the trade comparative advantage based on the Ricardian hypothesis[11] and has been used by several researchers to study trade patterns of different countries and regions across various sectors.[12] In this study, we have used the traditional RCA index developed by Balassa.

A country-wise examination of RCA index for the year 2013 suggests that Australia has competitive advantages in sectors like ores, slag, wool, lead and its products, meat, cereals, zinc, inorganic chemicals and milling products, etc. Bangladesh has advantages in the sectors like textiles, raw hides, fish, textile fibers, etc. India has competitive advantage in sectors like fruits and vegetables, cotton, carpets and flooring-related products, foodgrains and cereals, paper yarn, vegetable fabrics, woven yarn, textile items, precious metals, tea and spices, pharmaceuticals and petroleum products, etc. In crude oils and fertiliser products, Iran has been higher competitive advantages. Kenya has advantages in the sectors like coffee and vegetables. In the sectors like rubbers, tin, cleavage products, cocoa, etc. both Indonesia and Malaysia are major suppliers. Manufacturing sectors in the area of electronic and electrical equipment and heavy machinery, Singapore, Thailand and South Africa have a competitive advantage. These countries are also complementing in various sectors. For detailed identification of the sectors where RCA is higher for the member countries of IOR-ARC, sector and country-wise RCA index is placed in Annexure I.

This analysis is further supplemented by Trade Complementarity Index (TCI) between countries to evaluate the viability of regional integration.[13] A comparative picture of the index suggests that as exporters, complementarity between member countries of IOR-ARC has been increasing. In some cases, this index has also decreased depicting lower complementarity. Table 7 presents country-wise average complementarity index (average of indices with other counties in the region) as exporter and importers. The detailed indices are presented in Annexure II. Countries like Australia, India, Indonesia, Malaysia, Kenya, South Africa, Thailand and Singapore has higher complementarity with other member countries. Economies like Bangladesh, Comoros, Madagascar, Iran, Mauritius, etc. have limited complementarity. Clearly, the emerging and larger economies are likely to play a vital role in shaping regional integration in IOR-ARC region.

The possible sectors of trade between countries of the region are also analysed using Intra-Industry Trade (IIT) index.[14] This index measures products and sectors in which intra-industry trade is happening in a country. The index was developed by by Herb Grubel and Peter Lloyd. If the index is 1 it means there is only intra-industry trade and no inter-industry trade. On the other hand, if

Table 7: Average of Trade Complementarity Index Among IOR-ARC Member Countries

Countries	*Exports*		*Importers*	
	2005	*2013*	*2005*	*2013*
Australia	0.32	0.23	0.26	0.29
Bangladesh	0.09	0.09	0.24	0.24
Comoros	0.08	0.06	0.22	0.19
India	0.42	0.50	0.24	0.29
Indonesia	0.35	0.33	0.27	0.28
Iran	0.17	0.20	0.24	0.24
Kenya	0.29	0.30	0.26	0.26
Madagascar	0.16	0.13	0.24	0.25
Malaysia	0.38	0.41	0.24	0.27
Mauritius	0.21	0.19	0.26	0.27
Mozambique	0.10	0.20	0.24	0.24
Oman	0.15	0.22	0.23	0.25
Seychelles	0.15	0.12	0.22	0.23
Singapore	0.42	0.42	0.25	0.25
South Africa	0.33	0.34	0.27	0.30
Sri Lanka	0.18	0.17	0.25	0.28
Thailand	0.45	0.46	0.26	0.27
UAE	0.36	0.38	0.26	0.27
Tanzania	0.20	0.23	0.25	0.24
Yemen	0.14	0.19	0.25	0.26

Source: UNCTAD

the index is 0 implying that there is only inter-industry trade but no intra-industry trade. Several sectors are identified where intra-industry trade in happening in these countries. Most of the countries have high intra-industry trade in sectors like iron and steel, textiles, automobiles, footwear, rail related technologies, organic chemicals, etc. The commodity-wise index is presented in Annexure III.

Conclusion and Way Ahead

Analysis of RCA and IIT indices, there are several sectors in which countries of IOR-ARC region may progress towards regional cooperation. Also, trade patterns and their respective complementarity are important in this regard. Each country has its own specific characteristics. The above discussions establish complementarity between countries for regional trade integration at greater levels. It is further supplemented by the fact that each country has different natural endowments and therefore different economic structure. Countries are also experiencing different stages of economic development. Thus, the following are the areas in which regional cooperation may be pursued:

- Trade integration: Trade is an important element of economic progress and economic cooperation. In the present scenario of negotiations on various multilateral tables, future of trade is likely to be shaped by comprehensive trade-related cooperation between countries. On the other hand, countries are also exploring trade and investment related cooperation with other regional organisations such as ASEAN and EU. With respect to emerging trend of economic regional cooperation and progress towards internationalisation of regional institutions, trade is likely to catalyse future economic and geopolitics in the world. The IOR-ARC region needs to explore such a process. The trend of trade pattern as well as relative competitive and comparative advantage suggests that member countries can expand trade in the areas of crude oil, petroleum products, pharmaceuticals, construction materials, textiles, vegetables, food-grains capital goods, electronic and electrical products and chemicals, etc. These sectors are important areas where IOR-ARC can increase its trade potential apart from various other traditional trade sectors like FMCG and machinery.
- Trade in services: Trade in services is not discussed in detail in our exercise. However, to complement trade in goods, it becomes essential to open services sector as well. The countries in the region have limited cooperation with each other in the services sectors. For example, India has high trade in services with UAE and Singapore but limited with other countries like Indonesia, Malaysia, Thailand and South Africa. Services sectors which requires close cooperation to boost trade between countries in IOR-ARC

region are the transportation sector, communication sector, banking and financial sector, etc. Close linkages between banking and financial institutions of member countries are essential to boost bilateral trade as well as regional trade.

- Trade Facilitation and Connectivity: Trade facilitation is one of the important agenda of World Trade Organisation and its member countries. Most of the IOR-ARC countries are developing countries. These countries need close cooperation on the aspect of modernisation and upgradation of trade-related procedures in their respective countries. Trade integration becomes easy on account of cooperation in the area of trade facilitation. Important aspect related to this is the adoption of the Kyoto Protocol on customs procedures and implementation of the simplification plan of the procedure. Sharing information with each other on account of customs modernisation is also an imperative step in this regard.

ANNEXURES

(Based on Authors' Calculations)

Annexure I

Code	Commodities	Australia	Bangla-desh	Comoros	India	Indonesia	Iran	Kenya	Mada-gascar	Malaysia	Mauritius
'01	Live animals	3.14	0.00	0.00	0.03	0.33	0.31	1.09	0.08	0.73	6.12
'02	Meat and edible meat offal	4.84	0.00	0.13	2.08	0.02	0.01	0.29	0.00	0.03	0.02
'03	Fish, crustaceans, molluscs, aquatic invertebrates nes	0.65	3.59	4.18	2.62	2.74	0.07	1.41	10.16	0.48	7.48
'04	Dairy products, eggs, honey, edible animal product nes	1.71	0.00	0.00	0.42	0.25	0.02	0.40	0.03	0.37	0.14
'05	Products of animal origin, nes	0.88	0.30	0.00	0.70	0.18	2.14	0.41	0.58	0.10	9.82
'06	Live trees, plants, bulbs, roots, cut flowers, etc	0.03	0.00	0.24	0.20	0.09	0.02	113.17	0.06	0.50	0.69
'07	Edible vegetables and certain roots and tubers	1.07	0.35	0.25	1.14	0.16	0.64	15.00	4.98	0.23	0.18
'08	Edible fruit, nuts, peel of citrus fruit, melons	0.74	0.65	0.01	0.93	0.43	2.48	2.91	1.63	0.10	0.50
'09	Coffee, tea, mate and spices	0.06	0.12	284.03	3.49	4.35	0.62	87.66	39.44	0.24	0.41
'10	Cereals	4.72	0.02	0.05	5.09	0.01	0.00	0.26	0.03	0.01	0.11
'11	Milling products, malt, starches, inulin, wheat gluten	2.82	0.03	0.02	0.92	0.48	0.03	0.90	0.05	0.37	4.50
'12	Oil seed, oleagic fruits, grain, seed, fruit, etc, nes	2.20	0.10	0.02	1.01	0.24	0.03	1.62	0.88	0.03	0.01

'13 Lac, gums, resins, vegetable saps and extracts nes	0.06	0.00	0.00	17.84	0.93	1.12	1.38	11.68	0.09	0.00
'14 Vegetable plaiting materials, vegetable products nes	0.02	0.55	0.00	4.49	4.90	1.32	0.63	50.60	5.13	0.01
'15 Animal,vegetable fats and oils, cleavage products, etc	0.52	0.08	0.06	0.53	19.19	0.01	2.08	0.11	12.68	0.30
'16 Meat, fish and seafood food preparations nes	0.18	0.27	0.00	0.13	1.98	0.01	1.36	10.08	0.35	58.69
'17 Sugars and sugar confectionery	0.34	0.26	0.00	1.24	0.46	0.05	2.25	6.76	0.43	47.63
'18 Cocoa and cocoa preparations	0.27	0.00	3.38	0.10	2.50	0.10	0.33	3.82	2.00	0.02
'19 Cereal, flour, starch, milk preparations and products	0.85	0.18	0.01	0.41	0.99	0.13	0.37	0.04	1.53	2.16
'20 Vegetable, fruit, nuts, food preparations, etc	0.21	0.12	0.00	0.41	0.33	0.30	8.10	3.32	0.21	0.13
'21 Miscellaneous edible preparations	0.56	0.01	0.01	0.49	1.05	0.05	2.71	0.28	1.55	0.25
'22 Beverages, spirits and vinegar	1.29	0.04	0.09	0.21	0.13	0.03	1.34	0.73	0.60	0.99
'23 Residues, wastes of food industry, animal fodder	0.54	0.07	0.00	2.46	0.90	0.01	0.16	0.05	0.55	2.84
'24 Tobacco and manufactured tobacco substitutes	0.09	1.29	0.00	1.42	2.25	0.00	7.66	0.42	0.74	2.18
'25 Salt, sulphur, earth, stone, plaster, lime and cement	0.49	0.27	0.04	2.37	0.37	3.24	8.43	3.22	0.63	0.28
'26 Ores, slag and ash	23.60	0.07	0.00	0.52	2.63	3.13	0.12	4.56	0.22	0.00
'27 Mineral fuels, oils, distillation products, etc	1.45	0.02	0.00	1.16	1.76	4.37	0.78	0.25	1.24	0.00

'28 Inorganic chemicals, precious metal compound, isotopes	3.46	0.07	0.07	0.63	0.39	0.80	2.90	0.04	0.39	0.22
'29 Organic chemicals	0.03	0.00	0.00	1.60	0.61	1.86	0.07	0.07	0.78	0.03
'30 Pharmaceutical products	0.49	0.05	0.03	1.29	0.09	0.04	0.51	0.00	0.03	0.46
'31 Fertilisers	0.22	0.00	0.00	0.06	1.00	3.52	1.00	1.99	0.74	0.92
'32 Tanning, dyeing extracts, tannins, derivs, pigments, etc	0.59	0.00	0.00	1.73	0.43	0.06	0.63	0.04	0.72	0.46
'33 Essential oils, perfumes, cosmetics, toileteries	0.36	0.00	17.63	0.79	0.55	0.01	0.44	3.05	0.23	0.79
'34 Soaps, lubricants, waxes, candles, modelling pastes	0.19	0.02	0.00	0.50	1.81	0.13	4.75	0.02	1.18	1.03
'35 Albuminoids, modified starches, glues, enzymes	0.74	0.02	0.00	0.68	0.16	0.05	0.34	0.04	0.38	0.11
'36 Explosives, pyrotechnics, matches, pyrophorics, etc	0.51	0.00	0.00	1.07	0.46	0.07	0.29	0.04	0.30	0.50
'37 Photographic or cinemato-graphic goods	0.06	0.00	0.00	0.08	0.02	0.00	0.08	0.00	0.74	0.53
'38 Miscellaneous chemical products	0.15	0.01	0.00	0.99	2.06	0.14	0.27	0.03	1.68	0.12
'39 Plastics and articles thereof	0.11	0.08	0.00	0.57	0.43	1.46	0.51	0.09	0.93	0.34
'40 Rubber and articles thereof	0.08	0.02	0.00	0.79	4.58	0.02	0.21	0.03	3.23	0.06
'41 Raw hides and skins (other than furskins) and leather	2.64	5.06	0.02	2.24	0.43	0.97	9.44	2.11	0.07	0.09
'42 Articles of leather, animal gut, harness, travel goods	0.07	0.77	0.13	1.96	0.49	0.00	0.14	1.93	0.06	2.69

'43 Furskins and artificial fur, manufactures thereof	0.04	0.00	0.00	0.00	0.02	0.00	0.02	0.00	0.09	0.06
'44 Wood and articles of wood, wood charcoal	0.55	0.01	0.06	0.14	2.72	0.01	0.36	0.49	2.61	0.11
'45 Cork and articles of cork	0.05	0.00	0.00	0.08	0.01	0.00	0.03	0.00	0.01	0.01
'46 Manufactures of plaiting material, basketwork, etc.	0.01	1.56	0.56	0.06	3.25	0.00	1.91	24.36	0.03	0.29
'47 Pulp of wood, fibrous cellulosic material, waste, etc	0.35	0.00	0.00	0.00	3.99	0.01	0.20	0.06	0.08	0.16
'48 Paper and paperboard, articles of pulp, paper and board	0.37	0.03	0.00	0.36	2.16	0.00	0.86	0.62	0.44	0.51
'49 Printed books, newspapers, pictures, etc	0.36	0.02	0.00	0.41	0.09	0.03	2.23	2.15	0.40	1.13
'50 Silk	0.08	0.02	0.00	2.90	0.02	0.01	0.01	0.17	0.01	0.05
'51 Wool, animal hair, horsehair yarn and fabric thereof	12.82	0.01	0.00	0.62	0.03	0.40	1.02	0.44	0.38	11.21
'52 Cotton	2.64	0.37	0.00	8.86	1.19	0.07	0.08	4.94	0.46	5.15
'53 Vegetable textile fibres nes, paper yarn, woven fabric	0.01	86.87	0.00	4.26	0.20	0.00	20.29	16.32	0.09	0.55
'54 Manmade filaments	0.03	0.06	0.00	3.01	2.60	0.09	0.06	0.14	1.06	0.38
'55 Manmade staple fibres	0.03	0.25	0.00	2.97	5.84	0.22	0.29	0.08	0.65	1.02
'56 Wadding, felt, non-wovens, yarns, twine, cordage, etc	0.09	0.60	0.19	0.79	0.61	0.05	0.28	4.13	0.64	0.26
'57 Carpets and other textile floor coverings	0.20	0.50	0.00	5.89	0.44	3.29	0.03	0.02	0.10	0.98

'58 Special woven or tufted fabric, lace, tapestry, etc	0.02	0.12	0.00	1.69	0.72	0.02	0.16	3.29	0.26	2.16
'59 Impregnated, coated or laminated textile fabrics	0.08	0.01	0.01	0.51	0.45	0.01	0.02	0.03	0.20	0.31
'60 Knitted or crocheted fabrics	0.02	0.12	0.04	0.44	0.38	0.02	0.03	0.32	0.27	8.02
'61 Articles of apparel, accessories, knit or crochet	0.03	34.17	0.34	1.66	1.53	0.00	2.64	8.33	0.27	14.50
'62 Articles of apparel, accessories, not knit or crochet	0.03	37.58	0.20	2.31	1.90	0.00	2.68	9.91	0.14	12.42
'63 Other made textile articles, sets, worn clothing, etc	0.13	9.79	0.13	4.06	0.53	0.04	0.72	0.80	0.25	0.65
'64 Footwear, gaiters and the like, parts thereof	0.03	2.39	0.29	1.11	3.03	0.01	0.63	0.01	0.09	0.16
'65 Headgear and parts thereof	0.11	12.05	2.48	0.27	0.40	0.00	0.09	2.57	0.21	0.38
'66 Umbrellas, walking-sticks, seat-sticks, whips, etc	0.04	0.63	0.00	0.03	0.04	0.00	0.27	0.09	0.01	0.21
'67 Bird skin, feathers, artificial flowers, human hair	0.00	1.55	0.14	2.61	3.97	0.00	2.66	0.01	0.02	0.00
'68 Stone, plaster, cement, asbestos, mica, etc articles	0.09	0.21	0.00	1.53	0.34	0.18	0.22	0.04	0.86	0.05
'69 Ceramic products	0.08	0.65	0.05	0.58	0.66	0.15	0.32	0.01	0.50	0.06
'70 Glass and glassware	0.14	0.02	0.00	0.51	0.54	0.24	0.49	0.01	0.96	0.54
'71 Pearls, precious stones, metals, coins, etc	1.75	0.00	0.00	3.84	0.44	0.00	0.04	0.41	0.40	1.90
'72 Iron and steel	0.24	0.05	0.78	1.39	0.16	0.29	0.79	0.00	0.24	0.20
'73 Articles of iron or steel	0.19	0.02	0.06	1.27	0.69	0.05	0.40	0.08	0.78	0.30

'74 Copper and articles thereof	1.59	0.21	0.00	1.00	1.05	0.44	0.78	0.00	1.62	0.01
'75 Nickel and articles thereof	2.01	0.01	0.00	1.00	3.44	0.00	0.00	135.49	0.20	0.00
'76 Aluminium and articles thereof	1.75	0.00	0.00	0.68	0.42	0.44	0.75	0.03	0.99	0.38
'78 Lead and articles thereof	8.59	0.15	0.00	1.51	0.10	1.06	0.55	0.05	3.26	0.00
'79 Zinc and articles thereof	4.63	0.15	0.00	2.05	0.07	2.18	0.40	0.00	1.35	0.11
'80 Tin and articles thereof	0.10	0.00	0.00	0.67	29.25	0.00	0.16	0.00	9.31	0.00
'81 Other base metals, cermets, articles thereof	0.61	0.01	0.00	0.23	0.07	0.01	0.15	31.67	0.42	0.00
'82 Tools, implements, cutlery, etc of base metal	0.24	0.01	0.01	0.77	0.15	0.03	0.26	0.03	0.39	0.07
'83 Miscellaneous articles of base metal	0.13	0.00	0.00	0.44	0.30	0.00	0.74	0.17	0.46	0.05
'84 Machinery, nuclear reactors, boilers, etc	0.21	0.01	0.05	0.35	0.29	0.01	0.16	0.09	0.95	0.12
'85 Electrical, electronic equipment	0.09	0.02	0.05	0.29	0.50	0.00	0.12	0.03	2.31	0.28
'86 Railway, tramway locomotives, rolling stock, equipment	0.21	0.01	0.05	0.26	0.05	0.01	0.07	0.36	0.25	0.00
'87 Vehicles other than railway, tramway	0.16	0.04	0.00	0.55	0.34	0.01	0.15	0.01	0.11	0.02
'88 Aircraft, spacecraft, and parts thereof	0.31	0.03	0.01	0.71	0.05	0.02	0.05	1.26	0.19	0.09
'89 Ships, boats and other floating structures	0.13	0.03	13.59	1.30	0.63	0.03	0.03	0.03	0.18	0.05
'90 Optical, photo, technical, medical, etc apparatus	0.35	0.04	0.01	0.22	0.13	0.01	0.13	0.08	0.97	0.58

'91 Clocks and watches and parts thereof	0.13	0.00	0.00	0.11	0.03	0.00	0.01	2.29	0.41	4.26
'92 Musical instruments, parts and accessories	0.13	0.00	0.00	0.15	8.41	0.00	0.03	0.06	0.75	0.01
'93 Arms and ammunition, parts and accessories thereof	0.47	0.00	0.00	0.19	0.01	0.00	0.21	0.00	0.01	0.00
'94 Furniture, lighting, signs, prefabricated buildings	0.08	0.10	0.00	0.28	0.81	0.01	0.21	0.01	0.98	0.15
'95 Toys, games, sports requisites	0.20	0.14	0.00	0.19	0.68	0.01	0.57	0.23	0.30	0.67
'96 Miscellaneous manufactured articles	0.10	0.04	0.00	0.60	0.73	0.01	0.75	0.43	0.61	2.02
'97 Works of art, collectors pieces and antiques	0.27	0.01	0.03	0.61	0.06	0.09	0.62	0.12	0.01	0.05
'99 Commodities not elsewhere specified	1.84	0.06	0.39	0.67	0.00	0.03	0.35	0.28	0.34	0.00

Annexure 1 Continued..

Code	Commodities	Mozambique	Oman	Seychelles	Singapore	South Africa	Sri Lanka	Tanzania	Thailand	UAE	Yemen
'01	Live animals	0.02	0.81	0.14	0.02	0.41	0.02	0.20	0.40	0.20	0.00
'02	Meat and edible meat offal	0.00	0.09	0.01	0.03	0.28	0.03	0.01	0.27	0.05	0.00
'03	Fish, crustaceans, molluscs, aquatic invertebrates nes	1.83	0.42	40.42	0.11	0.80	4.28	5.12	1.62	0.07	4.93
'04	Dairy products, eggs, honey, edible animal product nes	0.00	0.92	0.20	0.21	0.59	0.08	0.03	0.21	0.54	1.06
'05	Products of animal origin, nes	0.35	0.00	0.75	0.09	0.36	0.21	1.18	0.31	0.01	0.25
'06	Live trees, plants, bulbs, roots, cut flowers, etc	0.01	0.01	0.05	0.07	0.57	1.18	5.29	0.44	0.02	0.21
'07	Edible vegetables and certain roots and tubers	1.80	0.22	0.54	0.02	0.54	0.79	6.53	1.91	0.17	0.76
'08	Edible fruit, nuts, peel of citrus fruit, melons	2.60	0.09	0.06	0.07	5.19	2.17	8.23	0.89	0.13	1.18
'09	Coffee, tea, mate and spices	0.58	0.05	0.30	0.26	0.53	75.92	24.12	0.10	0.64	1.99
'10	Cereals	0.02	0.04	0.02	0.03	1.46	0.15	1.37	2.99	0.09	0.09
'11	Milling products, malt, starches, inulin, wheat gluten	1.10	3.33	0.16	0.09	2.55	3.59	11.57	5.63	0.34	3.34
'12	Oil seed, oleagic fruits, grain, seed, fruit, etc, nes	2.32	0.04	0.20	0.06	0.27	0.30	6.99	0.11	0.03	0.02
'13	Lac, gums, resins, vegetable saps and extracts, nes	0.00	0.02	0.00	0.17	0.17	0.31	0.26	0.41	0.19	0.00

'14	Vegetable plaiting materials, vegetable products nes	0.00	0.03	0.00	0.90	0.77	41.40	1.32	0.55	0.02	4.63
'15	Animal,vegetable fats and oils, cleavage products, etc	0.85	0.61	1.89	0.17	0.56	0.37	1.46	0.65	0.49	0.18
'16	Meat, fish and seafood food preparations nes	0.00	0.07	214.79	0.08	0.52	0.09	0.04	11.41	0.15	0.40
'17	Sugars and sugar confectionery	16.70	0.08	0.05	0.17	2.05	0.11	7.83	4.87	0.83	0.25
'18	Cocoa and cocoa preparations	0.01	0.01	0.02	0.68	0.24	0.21	1.49	0.11	0.60	0.01
'19	Cereal, flour, starch, milk preparations and products	0.06	0.67	0.06	0.99	0.67	0.69	0.25	1.37	0.38	0.60
'20	Vegetable, fruit, nuts, etc food preparations	0.02	0.19	0.00	0.10	1.95	1.76	0.90	2.57	0.35	0.63
'21	Miscellaneous edible preparations	0.08	0.38	0.25	0.98	1.30	1.39	0.14	2.38	0.24	0.03
'22	Beverages, spirits and vinegar	0.21	0.02	0.43	1.11	2.45	0.15	0.63	0.89	0.12	0.04
'23	Residues, wastes of food industry, animal fodder	0.64	0.02	2.50	0.12	0.47	1.43	2.42	1.40	0.12	0.25
'24	Tobacco and manufactured tobacco substitutes	28.15	1.33	0.05	0.96	1.32	4.26	12.88	0.19	0.50	0.75
'25	Salt, sulphur, earth, stone, plaster, lime and cement	0.47	1.54	23.26	0.07	1.90	0.67	5.05	1.48	2.69	0.02
'26	Ores, slag and ash	2.88	1.81	0.00	0.00	10.54	0.05	6.66	0.03	0.05	0.00
'27	Mineral fuels, oils, distillation products, etc	1.87	4.19	0.00	0.97	0.60	0.02	0.13	0.35	3.77	5.06
'28	Inorganic chemicals, precious metal compound, isotopes	0.08	0.09	0.02	0.18	1.39	0.14	0.11	0.41	0.08	0.01

'29	Organic chemicals	0.00	0.95	0.01	1.78	0.56	0.00	0.01	1.20	0.19	0.00
'30	Pharmaceutical products	0.00	0.03	0.05	0.61	0.17	0.01	0.02	0.07	0.08	0.03
'31	Fertilisers	0.28	4.39	0.81	0.01	1.35	0.02	1.78	0.15	0.77	0.00
'32	Tanning, dyeing extracts, tannins, derivs, pigments, etc	0.00	0.04	0.37	0.73	0.81	0.09	0.30	0.59	0.29	0.00
'33	Essential oils, perfumes, cosmetics, toileteries	0.02	0.05	0.03	1.81	1.05	0.48	0.35	1.44	0.41	0.01
'34	Soaps, lubricants, waxes, candles, modelling pastes	0.01	0.30	0.01	0.48	1.58	0.13	1.42	1.03	0.42	1.23
'35	Albuminoids, modified starches, glues, enzymes	0.00	0.00	0.04	0.48	0.47	0.34	0.04	2.24	0.08	0.00
'36	Explosives, pyrotechnics, matches, pyrophorics, etc	0.13	0.00	0.00	0.31	6.48	0.02	0.89	0.19	0.08	0.00
'37	Photographic or cinemato-graphic goods	0.00	0.01	0.04	0.48	0.21	0.00	0.02	0.09	0.09	0.00
'38	Miscellaneous chemical products	1.29	0.09	0.10	1.12	0.95	0.86	0.10	0.35	0.19	0.00
'39	Plastics and articles thereof	0.06	0.42	0.13	1.11	0.48	0.17	0.38	1.70	0.63	0.02
'40	Rubber and articles thereof	0.04	0.04	0.14	0.28	0.58	8.54	0.05	6.61	0.09	0.00
'41	Raw hides and skins (other than furskins) and leather	0.15	0.02	0.06	0.19	2.42	0.02	1.80	1.38	0.05	1.62
'42	Articles of leather, animal gut, harness, travel goods	0.00	0.00	0.01	0.40	0.17	0.56	0.02	0.54	0.05	0.00
'43	Furskins and artificial fur, manufactures thereof	0.00	0.00	0.00	0.01	0.08	0.00	0.89	0.01	0.11	0.00

'44	Wood and articles of wood, wood charcoal	1.72	0.02	0.09	0.04	0.65	0.68	1.01	1.30	0.09	0.00
'45	Cork and articles of cork	0.00	0.14	0.00	0.02	0.08	0.00	0.16	0.01	0.07	0.00
'46	Manufactures of plaiting material, basketwork, etc	0.01	0.20	0.00	0.03	0.22	1.02	0.04	0.33	0.18	0.01
'47	Pulp of wood, fibrous cellulosic material, waste, etc	0.00	0.01	0.02	0.38	2.93	1.04	0.08	0.24	0.17	0.09
'48	Paper and paperboard, articles of pulp, paper and board	0.10	0.06	0.08	0.42	0.81	0.41	1.11	0.60	0.16	0.02
'49	Printed books, newspapers, pictures, etc	0.19	0.03	0.18	4.33	0.49	1.42	0.21	0.16	0.33	0.01
'50	Silk	0.00	0.01	0.14	0.10	0.13	0.01	0.04	0.33	0.11	0.00
'51	Wool, animal hair, horsehair yarn and fabrics thereof	0.00	0.00	0.03	0.02	5.37	0.02	0.00	0.26	0.01	0.00
'52	Cotton	6.73	0.02	0.01	0.06	0.11	1.05	6.94	0.90	0.08	0.02
'53	Vegetable textile fibres nes, paper yarn, woven fabrics	1.21	0.00	0.01	0.01	0.12	51.24	22.57	0.35	0.01	0.00
'54	Manmade filaments	0.00	0.02	0.02	0.20	0.14	0.26	0.16	1.33	0.32	0.00
'55	Manmade staple fibres	0.00	0.05	0.01	0.18	0.15	1.41	0.53	2.72	0.10	0.00
'56	Wadding, felt, nonwovens, yarns, twine, cordage, etc	0.20	0.01	0.08	0.18	0.37	1.69	1.72	1.34	0.08	0.00
'57	Carpets and other textile floor coverings	0.01	0.01	0.02	0.07	0.43	0.67	0.03	0.93	0.62	0.00
'58	Special woven or tufted fabrics, lace, tapestry, etc	0.00	0.00	0.02	0.16	0.24	6.39	0.07	1.38	0.08	0.00

'59	Impregnated, coated or laminated textile fabrics	0.00	0.00	0.02	0.19	0.31	0.68	0.38	0.54	0.09	0.01
'60	Knitted or crocheted fabrics	0.00	0.00	0.01	0.11	0.14	1.57	0.14	0.81	0.01	0.01
'61	Articles of apparel, accessories, knit or crochet	0.01	0.02	0.03	0.14	0.19	19.04	0.28	0.66	0.08	0.00
'62	Articles of apparel, accessories, not knit or crochet	0.03	0.01	0.12	0.11	0.21	16.93	0.03	0.40	0.07	0.00
'63	Other made textile articles, sets, worn clothing, etc	0.06	0.05	0.06	0.12	0.50	1.48	4.71	0.46	0.21	0.01
'64	Footwear, gaiters and the like, parts thereof	0.00	0.03	0.01	0.12	0.29	0.42	0.08	0.45	0.05	0.03
'65	Headgear and parts thereof	0.00	0.00	0.09	0.06	0.55	5.40	0.02	0.60	0.07	0.00
'66	Umbrellas, walking-sticks, seat-sticks, whips, etc	0.00	0.02	0.00	0.07	0.39	0.33	0.00	0.06	0.07	0.00
'67	Bird skin, feathers, artificial flowers, human hair	9.72	0.00	0.00	0.01	0.48	0.65	0.22	0.42	0.02	0.00
'68	Stone, plaster, cement, asbestos, mica, etc articles	0.00	0.90	0.03	0.14	0.56	0.92	0.22	0.68	0.37	0.04
'69	Ceramic products	0.01	0.44	0.15	0.07	0.49	1.42	0.05	1.17	0.81	0.02
'70	Glass and glassware	0.01	0.18	0.04	0.16	0.54	0.75	1.80	0.66	0.55	0.00
'71	Pearls, precious stones, metals, coins, etc	0.01	0.01	0.05	0.58	5.40	1.37	10.77	1.29	3.98	0.07
'72	Iron and steel	0.22	0.62	0.12	0.24	3.09	0.01	0.35	0.43	0.46	0.30
'73	Articles of iron or steel	0.65	0.35	0.12	0.47	0.95	0.04	0.31	1.10	0.55	0.01
'74	Copper and articles thereof	0.01	0.11	0.93	0.26	0.77	0.18	0.31	0.67	1.46	0.02
'75	Nickel and articles thereof	0.00	0.00	0.00	1.29	3.30	0.00	0.00	0.03	0.06	0.00

'76	Aluminium and articles thereof	29.03	1.62	0.17	0.23	2.22	0.06	0.12	0.65	2.55	0.00
'78	Lead and articles thereof	1.28	0.02	0.00	0.50	0.86	3.69	0.07	0.39	1.79	0.03
'79	Zinc and articles thereof	0.01	0.00	0.00	0.14	0.32	0.03	0.52	0.37	0.39	0.00
'80	Tin and articles thereof	0.01	0.04	0.00	4.77	0.03	0.00	0.08	5.14	0.24	0.00
'81	Other base metals, cermets, articles thereof	0.01	0.00	0.00	0.24	1.86	0.00	0.01	0.34	0.02	0.00
'82	Tools, implements, cutlery, etc of base metal	0.30	0.03	1.44	0.98	0.66	0.19	0.83	0.48	0.10	0.14
'83	Miscellaneous articles of base metal	0.01	0.01	0.03	0.39	0.43	0.16	0.11	1.18	0.20	0.01
'84	Machinery, nuclear reactors, boilers, etc	0.21	0.05	0.12	1.23	0.63	0.10	0.24	1.46	0.13	0.04
'85	Electrical, electronic equipment	0.03	0.08	0.05	2.63	0.21	0.18	0.06	1.12	0.10	0.02
'86	Railway, tramway locomotives, rolling stock, equipment	1.32	0.01	0.01	0.07	1.65	0.02	0.11	0.06	0.07	0.01
'87	Vehicles other than railway, tramway	0.08	1.06	0.07	0.14	1.17	0.07	0.09	1.54	0.07	0.02
'88	Aircraft, spacecraft, and parts thereof	0.25	0.07	0.09	0.92	0.21	0.08	0.31	0.28	0.09	0.23
'89	Ships, boats and other floating structures	6.75	0.17	0.20	0.74	0.15	0.98	1.13	0.79	1.07	0.04
'90	Optical, photo, technical, medical, etc apparatus	0.52	0.02	0.57	1.24	0.20	0.12	0.13	0.65	0.05	0.01
'91	Clocks and watches and parts thereof	0.00	0.11	0.01	1.63	0.06	0.01	0.01	0.93	0.17	0.00

Code	Commodity										
'92	Musical instruments, parts and accessories	0.10	0.24	0.09	0.23	0.11	0.05	0.01	0.28	0.03	0.00
'93	Arms and ammunition, parts and accessories thereof	0.01	0.00	0.00	0.00	0.00	0.00	0.67	0.04	0.02	0.00
'94	Furniture, lighting, signs, prefabricated buildings	0.06	0.07	0.09	0.27	0.47	0.23	0.10	0.51	0.18	0.04
'95	Toys, games, sports requisites	0.00	0.00	0.25	0.35	0.15	1.42	0.01	0.86	0.06	0.00
'96	Miscellaneous manufactured articles	0.00	0.07	0.05	0.25	0.51	1.31	0.37	1.15	0.09	0.02
'97	Works of art, collectors' pieces and antiques	0.04	0.00	0.25	0.39	0.61	0.00	0.04	0.02	0.14	0.11
'99	Commodities not elsewhere specified	0.00	0.03	0.22	5.52	0.17	0.00	0.00	0.00	0.36	0.00

Source: Authors' calculations

Annexure II

Trade Complementarity Index

	2005 Exporter																			
Importers	*Australia*	*Bangladesh*	*Comoros*	*India*	*Indonesia*	*Iran*	*Kenya*	*Madagascar*	*Malaysia*	*Mauritius*	*Mozambique*	*Oman*	*Seychelles*	*Singapore*	*South Africa*	*Sri Lanka*	*Thailand*	*UAE*	*UR Tanzania*	*Yemen*
Australia	–	0.11	0.06	0.40	0.45	0.18	0.27	0.16	0.47	0.19	0.09	0.16	0.13	0.44	0.37	0.19	0.57	0.38	0.18	0.16
Bangladesh	0.28	–	0.09	0.46	0.33	0.15	0.31	0.16	0.34	0.19	0.13	0.12	0.18	0.39	0.29	0.15	0.38	0.35	0.23	0.12
Comoros	0.31	0.09	–	0.37	0.26	0.11	0.31	0.17	0.26	0.20	0.10	0.11	0.18	0.29	0.28	0.16	0.38	0.27	0.17	0.11
India	0.38	0.08	0.08	–	0.40	0.20	0.18	0.15	0.42	0.20	0.10	0.16	0.07	0.41	0.47	0.20	0.39	0.38	0.24	0.11
Indonesia	0.33	0.08	0.08	0.46	–	0.25	0.31	0.14	0.42	0.20	0.12	0.21	0.19	0.52	0.35	0.16	0.49	0.45	0.19	0.20
Iran	0.32	0.07	0.08	0.41	0.31	–	0.26	0.16	0.33	0.20	0.10	0.14	0.13	0.42	0.35	0.15	0.44	0.33	0.17	0.11
Kenya	0.32	0.10	0.09	0.47	0.40	0.21	–	0.15	0.36	0.18	0.11	0.18	0.19	0.41	0.33	0.19	0.44	0.42	0.19	0.18
Madagascar	0.25	0.11	0.05	0.46	0.31	0.12	0.39	–	0.29	0.22	0.10	0.11	0.23	0.39	0.29	0.18	0.42	0.32	0.19	0.11
Malaysia	0.31	0.07	0.07	0.37	0.37	0.18	0.22	0.13	–	0.16	0.11	0.14	0.10	0.71	0.33	0.16	0.53	0.32	0.18	0.12
Mauritius	0.32	0.11	0.09	0.48	0.34	0.12	0.40	0.18	0.34	–	0.12	0.10	0.25	0.43	0.33	0.20	0.45	0.40	0.25	0.13
Mozambique	0.33	0.09	0.08	0.39	0.30	0.12	0.33	0.18	0.30	0.24	–	0.15	0.15	0.37	0.31	0.17	0.41	0.31	0.18	0.12
Oman	0.34	0.07	0.07	0.37	0.31	0.14	0.25	0.16	0.32	0.19	0.10	–	0.10	0.36	0.37	0.19	0.46	0.30	0.18	0.08
Seychelles	0.27	0.07	0.16	0.36	0.23	0.11	0.36	0.19	0.25	0.19	0.09	0.14	–	0.34	0.25	0.16	0.32	0.28	0.24	0.12
Singapore	0.27	0.06	0.05	0.36	0.40	0.21	0.24	0.13	0.67	0.19	0.08	0.18	0.14	–	0.27	0.15	0.50	0.44	0.15	0.19
South Africa	0.40	0.09	0.06	0.38	0.45	0.23	0.22	0.19	0.44	0.26	0.09	0.24	0.09	0.45	–	0.20	0.52	0.41	0.16	0.17
Sri Lanka	0.33	0.10	0.06	0.42	0.43	0.20	0.26	0.16	0.36	0.21	0.12	0.18	0.11	0.31	0.33	–	0.42	0.38	0.23	0.17
Thailand	0.33	0.07	0.09	0.36	0.43	0.28	0.20	0.13	0.52	0.18	0.10	0.26	0.08	0.50	0.36	0.18	–	0.41	0.18	0.22
UAE	0.33	0.10	0.07	0.47	0.35	0.14	0.27	0.20	0.40	0.35	0.09	0.13	0.10	0.44	0.43	0.25	0.51	–	0.23	0.10
UR Tanzania	0.29	0.10	0.09	0.48	0.36	0.13	0.37	0.14	0.35	0.20	0.10	0.11	0.21	0.45	0.33	0.19	0.47	0.35	–	0.10
Yemen	0.34	0.07	0.07	0.43	0.28	0.12	0.40	0.16	0.29	0.22	0.12	0.13	0.27	0.39	0.30	0.17	0.39	0.34	0.19	–

	2013 Exporter																			
Importers	*Australia*	*Bangladesh*	*Comoros*	*India*	*Indonesia*	*Iran*	*Kenya*	*Madagascar*	*Malaysia*	*Mauritius*	*Mozambique*	*Oman*	*Seychelles*	*Singapore*	*South Africa*	*Sri Lanka*	*Thailand*	*UAE*	*UR Tanzania*	*Yemen*
Australia	_	0.10	0.06	0.46	0.40	0.22	0.33	0.14	0.50	0.21	0.23	0.27	0.12	0.45	0.38	0.19	0.55	0.41	0.20	0.24
Bangladesh	0.22	_	0.06	0.45	0.30	0.17	0.28	0.14	0.36	0.18	0.26	0.19	0.12	0.32	0.27	0.15	0.39	0.31	0.28	0.14
Comoros	0.19	0.08	_	0.32	0.24	0.09	0.31	0.12	0.27	0.16	0.14	0.10	0.11	0.24	0.27	0.15	0.38	0.22	0.20	0.08
India	0.33	0.07	0.08	_	0.36	0.50	0.21	0.11	0.37	0.17	0.21	0.47	0.08	0.33	0.39	0.16	0.34	0.67	0.25	0.42
Indonesia	0.26	0.09	0.05	0.55	_	0.26	0.27	0.13	0.48	0.18	0.26	0.27	0.12	0.53	0.34	0.16	0.51	0.42	0.23	0.21
Iran	0.21	0.08	0.06	0.44	0.34	_	0.29	0.12	0.36	0.18	0.15	0.12	0.10	0.37	0.34	0.18	0.54	0.29	0.24	0.08
Kenya	0.21	0.10	0.05	0.58	0.37	0.20	_	0.12	0.43	0.17	0.22	0.23	0.11	0.48	0.32	0.17	0.47	0.38	0.21	0.18
Madagascar	0.18	0.12	0.05	0.57	0.31	0.13	0.34	_	0.35	0.23	0.19	0.17	0.13	0.42	0.30	0.18	0.42	0.31	0.24	0.13
Malaysia	0.27	0.08	0.06	0.47	0.36	0.19	0.29	0.13	_	0.16	0.24	0.23	0.12	0.63	0.35	0.15	0.53	0.39	0.25	0.18
Mauritius	0.23	0.11	0.06	0.59	0.32	0.12	0.35	0.15	0.40	_	0.20	0.17	0.18	0.44	0.33	0.22	0.49	0.35	0.27	0.15
Mozambique	0.20	0.08	0.04	0.53	0.28	0.13	0.32	0.10	0.38	0.15	_	0.18	0.12	0.44	0.32	0.15	0.42	0.33	0.20	0.14
Oman	0.24	0.07	0.05	0.53	0.29	0.18	0.29	0.11	0.40	0.15	0.17	_	0.11	0.46	0.39	0.15	0.49	0.35	0.21	0.15
Seychelles	0.17	0.08	0.13	0.49	0.24	0.09	0.32	0.11	0.33	0.16	0.19	0.15	_	0.38	0.28	0.17	0.39	0.29	0.23	0.14
Singapore	0.22	0.06	0.04	0.49	0.31	0.22	0.22	0.11	0.64	0.16	0.22	0.28	0.11	_	0.27	0.13	0.44	0.42	0.15	0.24
South Africa	0.29	0.10	0.08	0.46	0.40	0.30	0.33	0.14	0.46	0.22	0.22	0.33	0.12	0.45	_	0.19	0.53	0.47	0.23	0.29
Sri Lanka	0.24	0.10	0.06	0.51	0.38	0.23	0.33	0.15	0.43	0.21	0.25	0.25	0.13	0.41	0.33	_	0.47	0.42	0.26	0.21
Thailand	0.30	0.08	0.08	0.37	0.37	0.30	0.27	0.11	0.49	0.16	0.20	0.30	0.10	0.43	0.35	0.16	_	0.48	0.27	0.26
UAE	0.28	0.11	0.09	0.54	0.34	0.17	0.34	0.17	0.40	0.26	0.15	0.17	0.12	0.42	0.43	0.24	0.53	_	0.29	0.14
UR Tanzania	0.18	0.08	0.07	0.56	0.29	0.13	0.31	0.11	0.37	0.16	0.19	0.18	0.11	0.45	0.30	0.16	0.43	0.32	_	0.12
Yemen	0.23	0.09	0.04	0.50	0.27	0.19	0.33	0.14	0.32	0.32	0.19	0.24	0.11	0.42	0.43	0.15	0.41	0.30	0.22	_

Source: Authors' calculations

Annexure III

Intra-Industry Trade (IIT) Index

Code	Commodities	Australia	Bangladesh	Comoros	India	Indonesia	Iran	Kenya	Madagascar	Malaysia	Mauritius
'01	Live animals	0.17	0.00	0.00	0.95	0.37	0.82	0.54	0.42	0.61	0.82
'02	Meat and edible meat offal	0.11	0.43	0.01	0.00	0.16	0.02	0.78	0.44	0.10	0.01
'03	Fish, crustaceans, molluscs, aquatic invertebrates nes	0.97	0.14	0.73	0.02	0.14	0.40	0.63	0.68	0.82	0.43
'04	Dairy products, eggs, honey, edible animal product nes	0.47	0.00	0.00	0.10	0.29	0.07	0.42	0.05	0.60	0.03
'05	Products of animal origin, nes	0.84	0.19	0.00	0.38	0.34	0.23	0.93	0.80	0.96	0.93
'06	Live trees, plants, bulbs, roots, cut flowers, etc	0.24	0.14	0.00	0.37	0.24	0.55	0.02	0.86	0.17	0.65
'07	Edible vegetables and certain roots and tubers	0.42	0.12	0.10	0.76	0.29	0.36	0.31	0.16	0.38	0.09
'08	Edible fruit, nuts, peel of citrus fruit, melons	0.85	0.59	0.03	0.87	0.77	0.15	0.46	0.14	0.40	0.37
'09	Coffee, tea, mate and spices	0.12	0.11	0.00	0.30	0.12	0.43	0.29	0.03	0.45	0.42
'10	Cereals	0.04	0.01	0.00	0.00	0.01	0.00	0.03	0.00	0.02	0.02
'11	Milling products, malt, starches, inulin, wheat gluten	0.24	0.06	0.00	0.27	0.47	0.31	0.18	0.00	0.28	0.88
'12	Oil seeds, oleagic fruits, grain, seeds, fruit, etc, nes	0.13	0.11	0.05	0.30	0.28	0.08	0.96	0.32	0.14	0.04
'13	Lac, gums, resins, vegetable saps and extracts nes	0.14	0.00	0.00	0.10	1.00	0.74	0.88	0.17	0.31	0.00
'14	Vegetable plaiting materials, vegetable products nes	0.05	0.28		0.33	0.03	0.27	0.74	0.04	0.23	0.00
'15	Animal,vegetable fats and oils, cleavage products, etc	0.87	0.02	0.01	0.18	0.03	0.00	0.39	0.03	0.16	0.13

'16	Meat, fish and seafood food preparations nes	0.27	0.15	0.00	0.06	0.07	0.84	0.69	0.05	0.78	0.19
'17	Sugars and sugar confectionery	0.84	0.06	0.00	0.71	0.21	0.04	0.27	0.66	0.41	0.21
'18	Cocoa and cocoa preparations	0.44	0.08	0.48	0.70	0.30	0.01	0.49	0.25	0.97	0.01
'19	Cereal, flour, starch, milk preparations and products	0.87	0.47	0.00	0.15	0.70	0.95	0.20	0.02	0.74	0.52
'20	Vegetable, fruit, nuts, etc food preparations	0.34	0.74	0.00	0.28	0.81	0.92	0.30	0.38	0.67	0.06
'21	Miscellaneous edible preparations	0.41	0.04	0.00	0.35	0.94	0.17	0.89	0.37	0.87	0.08
'22	Beverages, spirits and vinegar	0.97	0.84	0.02	0.95	0.82	0.60	0.76	0.60	0.96	0.52
'23	Residues, wastes of food industry, animal fodder	0.92	0.05	0.00	0.14	0.39	0.00	0.15	0.02	0.61	0.99
'24	Tobacco and manufactured tobacco substitutes	0.20	0.23	0.00	0.07	0.87	0.00	0.90	0.64	0.84	0.29
'25	Salt, sulphur, earth, stone, plaster, lime and cement	0.88	0.15	0.00	0.92	0.27	0.24	0.68	0.21	0.73	0.05
'26	Ores, slag and ash	0.01	0.86		0.44	0.14	0.04	0.39	0.00	0.78	0.14
'27	Mineral fuels, oils, distillation products, etc	0.77	0.09	0.00	0.55	0.88	0.02	0.39	0.20	0.79	0.00
'28	Inorganic chemicals, precious metal compound, isotopes	0.36	0.12	0.27	0.45	0.41	0.97	0.98	0.03	0.50	0.39
'29	Organic chemicals	0.15	0.01	0.00	0.88	0.56	0.46	0.11	0.37	0.95	0.23
'30	Pharmaceutical products	0.53	0.35	0.01	0.25	0.81	0.10	0.24	0.00	0.25	0.44
'31	Fertilisers	0.24	0.00	0.00	0.03	0.56	0.47	0.19	0.62	0.57	0.58
'32	Tanning, dyeing extracts, tannins, derivs, pigments, etc	0.96	0.00	0.00	0.73	0.41	0.10	0.31	0.06	0.97	0.27
'33	Essential oils, perfumes, cosmetics, toileteries	0.52	0.01	0.22	0.53	0.71	0.03	0.28	0.67	0.54	0.27

'34	Soaps, lubricants, waxes, candles, modelling pastes	0.35	0.03	0.00	0.99	0.69	0.33	0.96	0.02	0.83	0.40
'35	Albuminoids, modified starches, glues, enzymes	0.98	0.03	0.00	0.94	0.18	0.06	0.24	0.06	0.68	0.12
'36	Explosives, pyrotechnics, matches, pyrophorics, etc	0.37	0.00	0.00	0.26	0.29	0.60	0.09	0.07	0.83	0.21
'37	Photographic or cinemato-graphic goods	0.16	0.00	0.00	0.18	0.07	0.00	0.08	0.00	0.95	0.17
'38	Miscellaneous chemical products	0.35	0.02	0.01	0.94	0.71	0.29	0.11	0.02	0.76	0.14
'39	Plastics and articles thereof	0.27	0.10	0.00	0.77	0.50	0.77	0.20	0.11	0.96	0.31
'40	Rubber and articles thereof	0.11	0.06	0.00	0.92	0.38	0.04	0.10	0.03	0.69	0.07
'41	Raw hides and skins (other than furskins) and leather	0.13	0.43	0.02	0.58	0.49	0.07	0.10	0.78	0.34	0.05
'42	Articles of leather, animal gut, harness, travel goods	0.10	0.90	0.05	0.20	0.79	0.00	0.09	0.53	0.30	0.78
'43	Furskins and artificial fur, manufactures thereof	0.36	0.11		0.25	0.57	0.81	0.44	0.00	0.73	0.25
'44	Wood and articles of wood, wood charcoal	0.83	0.14	0.03	0.23	0.20	0.01	0.46	0.65	0.22	0.08
'45	Cork and articles of cork	0.10	0.00		0.64	0.07	0.00	0.65	0.00	0.35	0.05
'46	Manufactures of plaiting material, basketwork, etc.	0.03	0.03	0.67	0.93	0.02	0.01	0.75	0.02	0.36	0.30
'47	Pulp of wood, fibrous cellulosic material, waste, etc	0.87	0.00		0.00	0.97	0.05	0.64	0.60	0.49	0.72
'48	Paper and paperboard, articles of pulp, paper and board	0.54	0.04	0.00	0.65	0.54	0.00	0.22	0.36	0.67	0.29
'49	Printed books, newspapers, pictures, etc	0.41	0.08	0.00	0.75	0.69	0.23	0.70	0.50	0.94	0.57
'50	Silk	0.47	0.02		0.82	0.41	0.04	0.14	0.00	0.04	0.10

'51	Wool, animal hair, horsehair yarn and fabric thereof	0.05	0.00		0.60	0.07	0.72	0.23	0.01	0.93	0.85
'52	Cotton	0.06	0.02	0.00	0.13	0.49	0.32	0.03	0.51	0.87	0.40
'53	Vegetable textile fibres nes, paper yarn, woven fabric	0.07	0.28		0.91	0.41	0.02	0.31	0.48	0.98	0.25
'54	Manmade filaments	0.18	0.02	0.00	0.45	0.98	0.05	0.01	0.06	0.57	0.21
'55	Manmade staple fibres	0.26	0.03	0.00	0.45	0.73	0.11	0.04	0.03	0.67	0.22
'56	Wadding, felt, nonwovens, yarns, twine, cordage, etc	0.24	0.55	0.12	0.69	0.56	0.09	0.17	0.92	0.86	0.25
'57	Carpets and other textile floor coverings	0.18	0.86	0.00	0.08	0.71	0.33	0.02	0.13	0.55	0.68
'58	Special woven or tufted fabric, lace, tapestry, etc	0.15	0.02	0.00	0.57	0.48	0.01	0.08	0.54	0.84	0.33
'59	Impregnated, coated or laminated textile fabrics	0.27	0.00	0.33	0.48	0.31	0.01	0.01	0.03	0.59	0.21
'60	Knitted or crocheted fabric	0.23	0.02	0.53	0.81	0.16	0.03	0.01	0.07	0.79	0.66
'61	Articles of apparel, accessories, knit or crochet	0.06	0.03	0.29	0.04	0.11	0.01	0.92	0.10	0.56	0.11
'62	Articles of apparel, accessories, not knit or crochet	0.06	0.02	0.09	0.06	0.13	0.01	0.61	0.05	0.77	0.27
'63	Other made textile articles, sets, worn clothing, etc	0.17	0.11	0.02	0.15	0.34	0.15	0.10	0.17	0.80	0.50
'64	Footwear, gaiters and the like, parts thereof	0.07	0.28	0.14	0.27	0.20	0.03	0.26	0.08	0.70	0.14
'65	Headgear and parts thereof	0.13	0.22	0.94	0.46	0.52	0.00	0.05	0.39	0.76	0.36
'66	Umbrellas, walking-sticks, seat-sticks, whips, etc	0.11	0.34	0.00	0.18	0.19	0.00	0.06	0.09	0.19	0.16
'67	Bird skins, feathers, artificial flowers, human hair	0.01	0.72	0.33	0.07	0.16	0.00	0.56	0.02	0.49	0.01

'68	Stone, plaster, cement, asbestos, mica, etc articles	0.18	0.56	0.00	0.54	0.70	0.23	0.19	0.08	0.58	0.03
'69	Ceramic products	0.15	0.79	0.01	0.93	0.97	0.12	0.09	0.01	0.92	0.03
'70	Glass and glassware	0.33	0.03	0.00	0.96	0.99	0.28	0.18	0.00	0.98	0.33
'71	Pearls, precious stones, metals coins, etc	0.63	0.04	0.00	0.79	0.07	0.00	0.53	0.06	0.73	0.94
'72	Iron and steel	0.91	0.04	0.38	1.00	0.13	0.30	0.20	0.01	0.34	0.20
'73	Articles of iron or steel	0.22	0.04	0.03	0.68	0.62	0.07	0.18	0.11	0.82	0.23
'74	Copper and articles thereof	0.49	0.60	0.00	0.96	0.86	0.36	0.90	0.10	0.75	0.06
'75	Nickel and articles thereof	0.31	0.29		0.65	0.14	0.03	0.01	0.00	0.09	0.41
'76	Aluminium and articles thereof	0.51	0.00	0.00	0.79	0.56	0.91	0.43	0.10	0.98	0.30
'78	Lead and articles thereof	0.03	0.08	0.00	0.57	0.06	0.16	0.67	0.60	0.66	0.00
'79	Zinc and articles thereof	0.05	0.06		0.75	0.06	0.37	0.07	0.02	0.91	0.16
'80	Tin and articles thereof	0.60	0.00	0.00	0.54	0.02	0.00	0.83	0.11	0.60	0.00
'81	Other base metals, cermets, articles thereof	0.74	0.12		0.41	0.28	0.11	0.43	0.02	0.79	0.15
'82	Tools, implements, cutlery, etc of base metal	0.39	0.03	0.00	0.98	0.31	0.05	0.10	0.02	0.74	0.07
'83	Miscellaneous articles of base metal	0.21	0.01	0.00	0.88	0.43	0.00	0.29	0.17	0.96	0.03
'84	Machinery, nuclear reactors, boilers, etc	0.29	0.02	0.04	0.58	0.36	0.03	0.11	0.15	0.98	0.14
'85	Electrical, electronic equipment	0.21	0.06	0.04	0.55	0.73	0.02	0.12	0.11	0.92	0.36
'86	Railway, tramway locomotives, rolling stock, equipment	0.13	0.01	0.28	0.82	0.07	0.02	0.09	0.68	0.69	0.00
'87	Vehicles other than railway, tramway	0.19	0.15	0.00	0.50	0.73	0.06	0.08	0.03	0.41	0.03

'88	Aircraft, spacecraft, and parts thereof	0.28	0.23	0.01	0.76	0.19	0.92	0.02	0.22	0.24	0.55
'89	Ships, boats and other floating structures	0.41	0.11	0.41	0.68	0.91	0.10	0.33	0.31	0.56	0.03
'90	Optical, photo, technical, medical, etc apparatus	0.50	0.20	0.02	0.51	0.47	0.02	0.15	0.30	0.88	0.80
'91	Clocks and watches and parts thereof	0.29	0.00	0.00	0.45	0.39	0.01	0.03	0.62	0.55	0.97
'92	Musical instruments, parts and accessories	0.14	0.02	0.00	0.73	0.50	0.00	0.07	0.17	0.93	0.02
'93	Arms and ammunition, parts and accessories thereof	0.43	0.00	0.00	0.92	0.01	0.00	0.25	0.00	0.09	0.04
'94	Furniture, lighting, signs, prefabricated buildings	0.11	0.41	0.00	0.98	0.52	0.01	0.13	0.04	0.39	0.13
'95	Toys, games, sports requisites	0.17	0.67	0.00	0.70	0.60	0.02	0.73	0.62	0.87	0.50
'96	Miscellaneous manufactured articles	0.19	0.02	0.00	0.88	0.78	0.02	0.20	0.18	0.92	0.58
'97	Works of art, collectors' pieces and antiques	0.77	0.46	0.27	0.30	0.23	0.96	0.63	0.47	0.25	0.11
'99	Commodities not elsewhere specified	0.80	0.22	0.08	0.46	0.00	0.35	0.40	0.85	0.91	

Annexure III Continued...

Code	Commodities	*Mozambique*	*Oman*	*Seychelles*	*Singapore*	*South Africa*	*Sri Lanka*	*Tanzania*	*Thailand*	*UAE*	*Yemen*
'01	Live animals	0.04	0.54	0.73	0.08	0.57	0.08	0.71	0.72	0.46	0.00
'02	Meat and edible meat offal	0.00	0.19	0.01	0.20	0.45	0.83	0.08	0.47	0.10	0.00
'03	Fish, crustaceans, molluscs, aquatic invertebrates nes	0.64	0.41	1.00	0.51	0.70	0.65	0.13	0.84	0.37	0.04
'04	Dairy products, eggs, honey, edible animal product nes	0.00	0.61	0.18	0.49	0.63	0.03	0.09	0.52	0.63	0.22
'05	Products of animal origin, nes	0.37	0.06	0.80	0.75	0.38	0.38	0.05	0.85	0.43	0.04
'06	Live trees, plants, bulbs, roots, cut flowers, etc	0.07	0.20	0.57	0.60	0.41	0.09	0.08	0.31	0.20	0.87
'07	Edible vegetables and certain roots and tubers	0.87	0.57	0.35	0.13	0.78	0.18	0.06	0.41	0.28	0.58
'08	Edible fruit, nuts, peel of citrus fruit, melons	0.26	0.30	0.12	0.40	0.08	0.56	0.06	0.77	0.18	0.94
'09	Coffee, tea, mate and spices	0.98	0.19	0.45	0.82	0.77	0.10	0.01	0.51	0.77	0.72
'10	Cereals	0.00	0.07	0.02	0.31	0.91	0.06	0.18	0.25	0.18	0.01
'11	Milling products, malt, starches, inulin, wheat gluten	0.38	0.24	0.06	0.36	0.72	0.69	0.63	0.39	0.92	0.91
'12	Oil seeds, oleagic fruits, grain, seeds, fruit, etc, nes	0.26	0.55	0.70	0.70	0.97	0.96	0.10	0.21	0.05	0.05
'13	Lac, gums, resins, vegetable saps and extracts nes	0.00	0.19	0.04	0.86	0.35	0.47	0.83	0.63	0.68	0.00
'14	Vegetable plaiting materials, vegetable products nes	0.00	0.28	0.00	0.78	0.72	0.60	0.02	0.31	0.03	0.35
'15	Animal,vegetable fats and oils, cleavage products, etc	0.18	0.88	0.57	0.65	0.53	0.22	0.26	0.51	0.97	0.06
'16	Meat, fish and seafood food preparations nes	0.00	0.36	0.01	0.30	0.68	0.09	0.40	0.06	0.56	0.40
'17	Sugars and sugar confectionery	0.23	0.28	0.07	0.69	0.99	0.02	0.80	0.11	0.60	0.02

'18	Cocoa and cocoa preparations	0.02	0.02	0.04	0.84	0.54	0.34	0.29	0.48	0.90	0.01
'19	Cereal, flour, starch, milk preparations and products	0.06	0.97	0.05	0.50	0.79	0.61	0.38	0.71	0.59	0.18
'20	Vegetable, fruit, nuts, etc food preparations	0.02	0.34	0.00	0.58	0.55	0.40	0.76	0.26	0.74	0.15
'21	Miscellaneous edible preparations	0.06	0.93	0.13	0.73	0.84	0.95	0.23	0.69	0.46	0.02
'22	Beverages, spirits and vinegar	0.12	0.13	0.22	0.99	0.63	0.30	0.41	0.48	0.26	0.03
'23	Residues, wastes of food industry, animal fodder	0.83	0.10	0.78	0.64	0.51	0.64	0.26	0.77	0.61	0.11
'24	Tobacco and manufactured tobacco substitutes	0.22	0.99	0.03	0.95	0.69	0.80	0.42	0.73	0.38	0.30
'25	Salt, sulphur, earth, stone, plaster, lime and cement	0.06	0.76	0.18	0.14	0.69	0.06	0.60	0.50	0.36	0.01
'26	Ores, slag and ash	0.06	0.99	0.00	0.38	0.06	0.64	0.04	0.53	0.33	0.06
'27	Mineral fuels, oils, distillation products, etc	0.62	0.31	0.05	0.76	0.63	0.01	0.04	0.43	0.18	0.81
'28	Inorganic chemicals, precious metal compound, isotopes	0.08	0.25	0.06	0.62	0.84	0.14	0.06	0.56	0.25	0.03
'29	Organic chemicals	0.02	0.94	0.61	0.58	0.88	0.00	0.03	0.84	0.67	0.00
'30	Pharmaceutical products	0.00	0.21	0.21	0.49	0.32	0.02	0.01	0.38	0.31	0.03
'31	Fertilisers	0.15	0.07	0.21	0.82	0.90	0.00	0.28	0.09	0.18	0.00
'32	Tanning, dyeing extracts, tannins, derivs, pigmentsetc	0.00	0.19	0.18	0.87	0.83	0.06	0.25	0.58	0.60	0.00
'33	Essential oils, perfumes, cosmetics, toileteries	0.03	0.13	0.04	0.74	0.76	0.69	0.20	0.79	0.38	0.02
'34	Soaps, lubricants, waxes, candles, modelling pastes	0.00	0.50	0.01	0.99	0.82	0.16	0.60	0.98	0.63	0.61
'35	Albuminoids, modified starches, glues, enzymes	0.00	0.01	0.10	0.97	0.43	0.29	0.08	0.54	0.35	0.00
'36	Explosives, pyrotechnics, matches, pyrophorics, etc	0.11	0.00	0.00	0.83	0.51	0.05	0.13	0.31	0.29	0.00
'37	Photographic or cinematographic goods	0.00	0.07	0.12	0.63	0.32	0.00	0.02	0.22	0.28	0.00
'38	Miscellaneous chemical products	0.89	0.29	0.36	0.95	0.71	0.54	0.07	0.42	0.58	0.01

'39	Plastics and articles thereof	0.07	0.98	0.30	0.67	0.74	0.17	0.20	0.78	0.99	0.02
'40	Rubber and articles thereof	0.04	0.16	0.20	0.95	0.60	0.42	0.02	0.26	0.18	0.00
'41	Raw hides and skins (other than furskins) and leather	0.40	0.87	0.56	0.84	0.42	0.04	0.03	0.89	0.76	0.05
'42	Articles of leather, animal gut, harness, travel goods	0.00	0.03	0.06	0.68	0.36	0.64	0.06	0.97	0.08	0.01
'43	Furskins and artificial fur, manufactures thereof	0.00	0.00	0.00	0.61	0.25	0.00	0.14	0.65	0.15	0.00
'44	Wood and articles of wood, wood charcoal	0.90	0.07	0.08	0.34	0.93	0.79	0.99	0.48	0.25	0.00
'45	Cork and articles of cork	0.00	0.76	0.00	0.89	0.09	0.00	0.58	0.14	0.74	0.00
'46	Manufactures of plaiting material, basketwork, etc.	0.04	0.49	0.00	0.50	0.52	0.97	0.28	0.90	0.39	0.05
'47	Pulp of wood, fibrous cellulosic material, waste, etc	0.03	0.18	0.00	0.83	0.23	0.12	0.81	0.37	0.94	0.77
'48	Paper and paperboard, articles of pulp, paper and board	0.09	0.26	0.08	0.96	0.82	0.19	0.62	0.87	0.39	0.02
'49	Printed books, newspapers, pictures, etc	0.10	0.21	0.20	0.21	0.53	0.97	0.12	0.57	0.94	0.02
'50	Silk	0.00	0.04	0.60	0.89	0.69	0.01	0.54	0.91	0.07	0.00
'51	Wool, animal hair, horsehair yarn and fabric thereof	0.00	0.25	0.45	0.85	0.10	0.02	0.00	0.65	0.07	0.00
'52	Cotton	0.19	0.56	0.04	0.96	0.32	0.13	0.25	0.85	0.28	0.83
'53	Vegetable textile fibres nes, paper yarn, woven fabric	0.93	0.02	0.10	0.55	0.26	0.29	0.10	0.93	0.04	0.09
'54	Manmade filaments	0.00	0.22	0.30	0.55	0.27	0.10	0.23	0.97	0.20	0.00
'55	Manmade staple fibres	0.00	0.26	0.09	0.96	0.23	0.16	0.37	0.49	0.10	0.00
'56	Wadding, felt, non-wovens, yarns, twine, cordage, etc	0.19	0.08	0.01	0.86	0.55	0.84	0.83	0.80	0.23	0.00
'57	Carpets and other textile floor coverings	0.03	0.04	0.04	0.51	0.86	0.90	0.08	0.34	0.49	0.00

'58	Special woven or tufted fabrics, lace, tapestry etc	0.01	0.06	0.23	0.83	0.42	0.37	0.04	0.87	0.05	0.00
'59	Impregnated, coated or laminated textile fabrics	0.00	0.00	0.20	0.82	0.44	0.27	0.77	0.52	0.30	0.05
'60	Knitted or crocheted fabrics	0.00	0.09	0.07	0.91	0.28	0.08	0.22	0.86	0.01	0.62
'61	Articles of apparel, accessories, knit or crochet	0.04	0.23	0.20	0.59	0.41	0.04	0.75	0.27	0.09	0.08
'62	Articles of apparel, accessories, not knit or crochet	0.13	0.08	0.52	0.63	0.41	0.11	0.08	0.56	0.10	0.00
'63	Other made textile articles, sets, worn clothing, etc	0.02	0.35	0.09	0.76	0.75	0.32	0.87	0.92	0.24	0.02
'64	Footwear, gaiters and the like, parts thereof	0.00	0.26	0.08	0.65	0.32	0.91	0.12	0.54	0.08	0.05
'65	Headgear and parts thereof	0.01	0.00	0.20	0.58	0.59	0.24	0.02	0.45	0.18	0.00
'66	Umbrellas, walking-sticks, seat-sticks, whips, etc	0.00	0.52	0.00	0.70	0.79	0.41	0.00	0.22	0.19	0.00
'67	Bird skin, feathers, artificial flowers, human hair	0.11	0.05	0.00	0.26	0.44	0.58	0.29	0.52	0.03	0.03
'68	Stone, plaster, cement, asbestos, mica, etc articles	0.00	0.94	0.04	0.38	0.68	0.69	0.19	0.79	0.45	0.07
'69	Ceramic products	0.00	0.64	0.09	0.35	0.42	0.81	0.02	0.95	0.70	0.01
'70	Glass and glassware	0.00	0.57	0.04	0.47	0.87	0.79	0.91	0.90	0.71	0.00
'71	Pearls, precious stones, metals, coins, etc	0.61	0.08	0.65	0.96	0.10	0.99	0.00	0.71	0.83	0.52
'72	Iron and steel	0.18	0.84	0.15	0.70	0.39	0.01	0.13	0.27	0.71	0.19
'73	Articles of iron or steel	0.32	0.37	0.12	0.81	1.00	0.04	0.09	0.79	0.54	0.01
'74	Copper and articles thereof	0.29	0.17	0.41	0.98	0.78	0.30	0.75	0.57	0.49	0.16
'75	Nickel and articles thereof	0.00	0.02	0.00	0.80	0.17	0.00	0.00	0.17	0.22	0.00
'76	Aluminium and articles thereof	0.65	0.46	0.45	0.81	0.43	0.09	0.17	0.60	0.52	0.00
'78	Lead and articles thereof	0.24	0.03		0.37	0.77	0.84	0.70	0.23	0.43	0.28
'79	Zinc and articles thereof	0.02	0.01	0.00	0.65	0.35	0.04	0.15	0.52	0.80	0.00
'80	Tin and articles thereof	0.51	0.68	0.00	0.98	0.05	0.00	0.52	0.93	1.00	0.00

'81	Other base metals, cermets, articles thereof	0.84	0.03		0.64	0.51	0.01	0.40	0.76	0.07	0.00
'82	Tools, implements, cutlery, etc of base metal	0.20	0.14	0.75	0.97	0.64	0.25	0.45	0.48	0.18	0.27
'83	Miscellaneous articles of base metal	0.01	0.05	0.01	1.00	0.61	0.14	0.10	0.84	0.37	0.02
'84	Machinery, nuclear reactors, boilers, etc	0.19	0.17	0.13	0.93	0.62	0.14	0.24	0.92	0.22	0.11
'85	Electrical, electronic equipment	0.04	0.43	0.13	0.87	0.35	0.34	0.09	0.89	0.20	0.07
'86	Railway, tramway locomotives, rolling stock, equipment	0.30	0.14	0.04	0.64	0.86	0.01	0.15	0.46	0.39	0.02
'87	Vehicles other than railway, tramway	0.06	0.85	0.20	0.92	0.95	0.09	0.05	0.61	0.12	0.02
'88	Aircraft, spacecraft, and parts thereof	0.82	0.67	0.05	0.93	0.69	0.46	0.41	0.38	0.05	0.66
'89	Ships, boats and other floating structures	0.04	0.96	0.03	0.72	0.37	0.94	0.66	0.70	0.71	0.99
'90	Optical, photo, technical, medical, etc apparatus	0.11	0.12	0.99	0.83	0.39	0.31	0.24	0.87	0.20	0.07
'91	Clocks and watches and parts thereof	0.02	0.31	0.02	0.93	0.20	0.06	0.09	0.85	0.14	0.00
'92	Musical instruments, parts and accessories	0.82	0.91	0.80	0.61	0.28	0.07	0.09	0.59	0.10	0.00
'93	Arms and ammunition, parts and accessories thereof	0.18	0.00	0.00	0.66		0.00	0.73	0.08	0.01	0.00
'94	Furniture, lighting, signs, prefabricated buildings	0.05	0.26	0.09	0.98	0.82	0.40	0.12	0.73	0.25	0.16
'95	Toys, games, sports requisites	0.01	0.08	0.32	0.88	0.22	0.45	0.04	0.52	0.16	0.01
'96	Miscellaneous manufactured articles	0.00	0.21	0.09	0.93	0.57	0.62	0.23	0.75	0.15	0.01
'97	Works of art, collectors' pieces and antiques	0.96	0.12	0.95	0.92	0.73	0.54	0.32	0.36	0.35	0.03
'99	Commodities not elsewhere specified		0.82	0.15	0.30	0.07	0.00			0.77	

Source: Authors' calculations

NOTES

1. M. Kearney, *The Indian Ocean in World History* (New York: Routledge, 2004).
2. S. Bose, *A Hundred Horizons: The Indian Ocean in the Age of Global Empire* (Cambridge, MA: Harvard University Press, 2006).
3. G.R. Campbell, "The Indian Ocean Rim (IOR) Economic Association: Historical Perspective", in G. Campbell, ed., *The Indian Ocean Rim: Southern Africa and Regional Cooperation* (New York: Routledge, 2013).
4. S.C. Jain and P.N. Ghauri, "Indian ocean rim trade bloc: Prospects and problems, *The International Executive*, Vol. 38, No. 5, 1996, pp. 583-597; R. Shandand K.P. Kalirajan, "Yamazawa's Open Economic Association: An Indian Ocean Grouping for Economic Cooperation", *The Developing Economies*, Vol. 35, No. 1, 1997, pp. 3-27; Beelasingh Dabee and Mahinder Reddy, "Regional Agreements in the Indian Ocean", *The World Economy*, Vol. 23, No. 9, 2000, pp. 1149-1160; S. Seechurn, *The Rise of the Indian Ocean Economies: Why the Spotlight's Shifted", IOR-ARC Special Supplement* (Port Louis: LB Associates in association with IOR-ARC Secretariat, 2013).
5. IOR. <http://www.iora.net/projects/flagship-projects/preferential-trade-agreement.aspx> accessed 25 August 2015.
6. S. Kelegama,"Open Regionalism in the Indian Ocean: How Relevant is the APEC Model for IOR-ARC?", *Journal of the Asia-Pacific Economy*, Vol. 5, No. 3, 2000, pp. 255- 274.
7. B.M. Nowbutsing, "The Impact of Openness on Economic Growth: Case of Indian Ocean Rim Countries", *Journal of Economics and Development Studies*, Vol. 2, No. 2, 2014, pp. 407-427.
8. G.R. Campbell and M. Scern, "The Prospects for an Indian Ocean Rim (IOR) Economic Association", *South African Journal of International Affairs*, Vol. 2, Issue 2, 1994, pp. 11-37.
9. <http://www.ris.org.in/images/RIS_images/pdf/Final%20IOR-ARC%20Report.pdf> accessed 15 August 2015.
10. RCA index has been calculated using the following formula: RCAij = (Xij/Xwj)/(Xi/Xw); Where, Xij = ith country's export of commodity j; Xwj = world exports of commodity j; Xi = total exports of country i; and, Xw = total world exports. An RCA index value of more than one reveals that the country has a comparative advantage. The data for calculation of RCA has been taken from Trade Map database of International Trade Centre, Geneva.
11. B. Balassa, "Trade Liberalisation and 'Revealed' Comparative Advantage", *The Manchester School*, Vol. 33, 1965, pp. 99–123; B. Balassa, "'Revealed' Comparative Advantage Revisited: An Analysis of Relative Export Shares of the Industrial Countries, 1953-1971", *The Manchester School of Economic & Social Studies*, Vol. 45,

Issue 4, 1977, pp. 327-44.

12. T.L. Vollrath, "Revealed Competitive Advantage for Wheat", *Economic Research Service Staff Report No. AGES861030* (Washington DC: US Department of Agriculture, 1987); T.L. Vollrath, "Competitiveness and Protection in World Agriculture", *Agricultural Information Bulletin No. 567, Economic Research Service* (Washington DC: US Department of Agriculture, 1989); T.L. Vollrath and De Huu Vo, "Agricultural Competitiveness in an Independent World", in *Agriclture and Governments in an Independent World, International Association of Agricultural Economists Occasional Paper No. 5* (Gower: Hampshire, 1990); T.L. Vollrath, "A Theoretical Evaluation of Alternative Trade Intensity Measures of Revealed Comparative Advantage", *Weltwirtschaftliches Archiv*, Vol. 130, 1991, pp. 265–279; A.J. Yeats, "Does Mercosur's Trade Performance Raise Concerns About the Effects of Regional Trade Arrangements", *International Economics Department*, The World Bank, 1997. S. Bender and K.W. Li, (2002) "The Changing Trade and Revealed Comparative Advantages of Asian and Latin American Manufacture Exports", (Yale University: Economic Growth Centre Discussion Paper Series No. 843, 2002).
13. The trade complementarity (TC) index can provide useful information on prospects for intraregional trade in that it shows how well the structures of a country's imports and exports match. It also has the attraction that its values for countries considering the formation of a regional trade agreement can be compared with others that have formed or tried to form similar arrangements. It is one of the overlapping indices that enable a comparison of export and import profiles between two countries, i.e. how the export set of industries from the source country matches with the import set of industries from a destination country. In one conception of the determinants of trade, complementarity can be thought of as a proxy for relative resource endowments and can show how much scope there is for further trade

$$\mathrm{TCI} = \left(1 - \left(\Sigma\left|\frac{\Sigma_w m_{iwd}}{\Sigma_w M_{wd}} - \frac{\Sigma_w x_{isw}}{\Sigma_w X_{sw}}\right|\right) \div 2\right) \times 100$$

Where: d - importing country of interest; s - exporting country of interest; w - set of all countries in the world; i - set of industries; x - commodity export flow; X - total export flow; m - commodity import flow; M - the total import flow. The degree of TCI ranges between 0 and 100 per cent. Higher complementarity value indicates a better export/import match, while 0 (zero) indicates no complementarity at all.

14. Intra-industry trade attempts to ascertain how much trade between two economies occurs within the same industry. It is based on the premise that economies of scale provide an incentive to trade, even when factor endowments and consumer preferences are identical between partner economies. The IIT index ranges between zero and one, with larger values indicating a greater level of trade between firms in the same industry. Higher IIT ratios suggest that net gains from specialisation in different products are being exploited and that the participating country is increasing its integration into the world economy. IIT is calculated as: $IIT^{jk} = 1 - [\text{sumi} \mid X_{ijk} - M_{ijk} \mid / (X_{ijk} + M_{ijk})]$; Where, X_{ijk} and M_{ijk} represent exports and imports of products from industry i in country j to and from country k. The increase in intra-industry trade according to some studies influencing the success or failure of efforts to promote industrialisation and growth plays an important positive role. Intra-industry exchange produces extra gains from international trade over and above those associated with comparative advantage because it allows a country to take advantage of larger markets. By engaging in IIT, a country can simultaneously reduce the number of products it produces while increasing the variety of goods available to domestic consumers.

8

Governance in Federations: Agendas for Change in India and Australia

RFI Smith

ABSTRACT

This paper examines strategic issues in federal governance in India and Australia. Despite large differences in history, context and scale the two countries share overlapping agendas for change in federal arrangements. Both are about the hard task of promoting collaboration and managing intergovernmental competition in uncertain times. The paper focuses in particular on the path to economic liberalisation in both countries and the impacts of liberalisation on intergovernmental relations.

Introduction

This paper compares federal governance and agendas for change in India and Australia. Despite large differences in history, context and scale the two countries share overlapping proposals for change in federal arrangements. In both, changed agendas mix proposals for structural changes with questions about how to make more effective use of existing institutional frameworks. But change is rarely straightforward and a clean slate is not available.

A governance perspective looks beyond institutions and structural change: "Governance as theory prompts people to pay less attention to allegedly fixed institutions and more to shifting processes".[1] Governance is complex because federal constitutions, no matter how detailed, are "incomplete contracts".[2] Further, what appears to be promised in solemn documentation can be modified as participants pursue their self-interest and when reinterpretation takes place. Thus as Grewal and Sheehan propose, the incompleteness of federal compacts provides "an inherent rationale for intergovernmental competition for wider legislative competence".[3] In this circumstance how participants in a federation manage their relationships becomes a key question. Participants may compete and collaborate, look ahead and fail to look ahead, look for hazards and fail to look for hazards, and learn and fail to learn. For this reason also federal arrangements are always "in the making".[4]

Recent agendas for change in India and Australia flow from two linked sources. First is the continuing impact on public policy and management of initiatives in economic liberalisation in the 1980s and 1990s.[5] Second are the challenges of managing intergovernmental relations in view of consequent debates about the appropriate scope and capabilities of the different levels of government.[6] Comparison is encouraged by a mix of shared institutional and process characteristics. First, India and Australia are both constitutional federations with systems of responsible cabinet government. Second, in both the states have significant roles. Third, both share a preoccupation with fiscal relationships, including high levels of vertical fiscal imbalance.[7] Fourth, recent specific reform proposals in both countries have included a similar mix of "cooperative agreements, incentive payments, earmarked payments and centralising decisions".[8] Fifth, a recurring theme in common is the interaction between intergovernmental competition, strategies to promote cooperation, fiscal arrangements and wider political and social change, including the impacts of globalisation. Proposed remedies veer between strategies to improve collaboration, manage intergovernmental competition and implement root and branch change. Sixth, however change, when it occurs, takes place through existing federal processes.

Comparison is encouraged also by past associations and current trends towards closer relationships.[9]India's Finance Commissions, appointed every five years to make recommendations on federal/state financial relations, began after an official mission in 1946 to Australia. Since then Indian and Australian officials and scholars have continued to interact on fiscal federalism.[10] For example, members of the Twelfth Finance

Commission closely examined arrangements in Canada and Australia. Later work by the same authors also used Australian material.[11] Both India and Australia are also included in recent studies in comparative federalism.[12] Further, because of the significance of federal arrangements for public policy, the closer relationships currently pursued by governments in both countries may be facilitated by comparative studies.

The paper asks questions about trends in federal governance and about how some agendas are taken up and many others are not. Comparisons are drawn through 'process tracing' which focuses attention on possible causes and outcomes.[13]The paper examines in particular the paths to economic liberalisation in both countries and the chequeredhistory of post-liberalisation agendas of change. Throughout it is sensitive to the importance of strategic interactions between participants. Critical sets of interactions include those between ideas, advocates, interests, institutions, processes and events.[14] None of these factors provides convincing explanations on its own. However in conjunction they can suggest useful propositions. For example, ideas may lie fallow for years before an opportunity to apply them arises. Similarly, events may foster or foreclose opportunities to apply new ideas. Further, interaction between factors can lead to reciprocal change. Such a framework is used explicitly by recent studies of economic management in India.[15] Compatible frameworks are used also to explain economic liberalisation in Australia.[16]

The paper includes developments up to the end of the Australian Labour Party (ALP) federal government in 2013 in Australia and United Progressive Alliance (UPA) government in India in 2014. It is organised as follows: for each country a summary of key federal arrangements is followed by examination of its path to economic liberalisation and impacts on intergovernmental relations, followed by comparison of agendas for change. Of particular interest are the shared struggles to negotiate coordinated national policies (especially for economic management), maintain momentum for reform, and enlist the cooperation of state governments for national projects while managing the temptation to cut the policy space and resources that enable state governments to take valued local initiatives. These are very familiar themes. But recent Indian and Australian difficulties in securing significant federal reforms puts them into sharp relief. The paper proposes that the extent of shared themes encourages further comparative analysis.

Federal Arrangements and Agendas in India

Federal arrangements in India have evolved under strong forces that push in different directions. The Indian union began as a 'holding together' federation. Following the tragedy of partition the drafters of the constitution made extensive use of the colonial Government of India Act 1935, to establish a strong centre. The states have no separate constitutions, the centre can amend state boundaries and create new states, state Governors often act like agents of prime minister, under President's Rule governors can take direct control of state administrations, and amendments to the constitution, despite intentions to the contrary, can be made readily. Arrangements for fiscal transfers to the states, allocated in the constitution to successive Finance Commissions, expanded to include decisions of the Planning Commission, grants from central ministries, and the custom of providing top ups to states in fiscal difficulty. Creation of substantial networks of central state-owned enterprises and nationalisation of banks also added to central influence.

However unitary tendencies have jostled with forces for decentralisation.[17] Court decisions have discouraged imposition of President's Rule. An institutionalised system of national and state planning has battled with short-term political bargains. The dominance of the Congress Party at the centre and in most of the states gradually eroded. In Shalendra Sharma's terms, "inter-governmental cooperation between the centre and the states...has been transformed into a regime of inter-state cooperation and competition".[18] Related decentralising forces have included: internal social and economic diversity (29 states, 7 union territories, 26 scheduled languages), the prevalence until the election in 2014 of the Narendra Modi government of coalition governments at the centre, the emergence of parties representing regional interests and underprivileged groups many of which hold office at state level, the regular participation of some of these parties in central coalitions, and decentralisation of powers to layers of local government. Emboldened by the relaxation of central regulation in 1991 state governments often imposed their own restrictions. However the tasks of promoting an effective national market, managing international economic relations, coping with fiscal indiscipline at state level, and a tendency for the toughest electoral conflicts to be played out at state rather than federal level, gave new bite to central influence.

Contradictory forces have been managed through discussion, bargaining, and delay. Forums for interaction are both formal and informal. Formally constituted committees, for example of finance ministers, are often used to search for agreement on specific matters. However, much important business is conducted through informal and ad hoc arrangements. Two key questions have arisen: whether, in view of the range of matters demanding intergovernmental negotiation, such arrangements are sufficient; and how, in view of the range of contradictory interests, significant mistrust between the centre and the states[19], and blocking of many initiatives, more effective arrangements might be developed.

Paths to Economic Liberalisation

The transition to a more market based economy followed a history of smothered initiatives. The transition began at the centre, focused first on relaxing central restrictions and drew bipartisan support at the national level. Pragmatic, incremental initiatives, taken after assembling support from diverse stakeholders, slowly accumulated.[20] Higher and sustained economic growth took place. However, the sectoral coverage of initiatives left many gaps. Further, they were not supported by effective coordination with the states.

Critiques of India's planned economy began early. While in 1948 socialists split from the Congress Party because its policies were not socialist enough, others left Congress because it was building a *licence-quota-permit raj*. Balance of payments crises in 1957, 1966, 1973 and 1981 led to short-lived and "erratic spurts of liberalization".[21] In 1964 Nehru's successor Lal Bahadur Shastri took unexpected initiatives in deregulation. But his death in 1966 brought these to an end. It has been argued that, in any case, they would have received little continuing support.[22] More small steps took place at the start of Indira Gandhi's emergency in 1975, became more focused in the early 1980s and gathered pace under Rajiv Gandhi before faltering after election setbacks in 1987.[23] However developments under Rajiv Gandhi left important legacies: some industrial deregulation, corporatisation of parts of the telecommunications industry, a government-fostered and forward looking industry association (Confederation of Indian Industry), software sector exports, research in central agencies—Prime Minister's Office, Ministry of Commerce and Industry and Ministry of Finance—on economic liberalisation, and close study of economic growth in East and Southeast Asia, particularly Malaysia. Such legacies led to growing awareness of potential new directions.[24]

In 1991 these trends provided domestic support for a change. The need to seek International Monetary Fund (IMF) assistance to handle yet another balance of payments crisis provided an opportunity for reform. Political leadership, dramatisation of the problems, credible proposals for change, and support from or acquiescence by business, enabled the central government to take the opportunity. Prime Minister Narasimha Rao backed tough decisions proposed by the Minister of Finance Manmohan Singh and formulated by senior civil servants.[25] The process was highly interactive. Cumulative combinations of ideas, advocates, interests and events drove the dramatic change that the liberalisation decisions of 1991 came to represent.

However the "autonomous internal process"[26] on which continuing reform depended had notable limits. One of these was gradualism. Political support did not extend to effective implementation.[27] Further, gradualism and clarity in broad directions masked uncertainty about how to identify feasible institutional arrangements.[28] Closely linked to this limitation was institutional asymmetry of support for liberalisation. Within the civil service key agencies in the central government had much to lose. At state level political leaders and civil servants gathered support from disaffected interests by imposing state level restrictions. While the "quality of institutions" has been praised as "India's underrated strength"[29] the task of negotiating centrally desired reforms with the states proved to be a task for which even the most talented of leaders and most prestigious central institutions had no ready answers. Paradoxically, liberalisation led to a state that could more easily negotiate with international agencies like the World Bank than implement the new policies internally.[30]

Impacts on Intergovernmental Relations

Following 1991 competition between the states with each other and with the centre took place in plain view. As Sinha has argued, economic liberalisation led to a dual process: abolition of central controls made existing state level controls much more visible; and reregulation by state officials enhanced state roles in investment policy.[31] Different states adopted different strategies for economic development, including strategies for attracting foreign investment. International agencies such as the World Bank began dealing directly with specific states, with the centre facilitating loans after terms had been negotiated. Economic disparities between states increased. Control of necessary market supporting regulatory functions tended to drift to the states. This did not halt regulatory reform. However initiatives often involved protracted negotiations or reform by stealth.[32]

Where the central government had constitutional power, for example in telecommunications, negotiations took place within the governing coalition and the civil service. But where the central government shared power with the states, results varied. For example, recent top down attempts to control transfer of senior civil servants by states and to compel states to implement anti-corruption measures failed.[33] While negotiations with the states supported the Right to Information Act,[34] in the power sector, difficult negotiations for national regulatory arrangements needed an external stimulus from the World Bank.[35] Further, in the case of labour policy, as Jenkins has argued, low key attempts at reform tended to undermine the very institutions needed to manage the change.[36]

More generally the long lists of issues demanding reform depended also on the cooperation of the states. While many states undertook reform programmes which were emulated elsewhere the impacts were uneven. The proliferation of centrally-sponsored schemes under which the centre made funds available to the states for specific programmes drew criticism about unclear objectives, ineffective implementation and lack of transparency in financial administration.[37] Disparities between states continued to throw up problems, for example successful states resented revenue redistribution to poorer states. Further, many regional political interests not only opposed reform but saw winning office as an opportunity for rent seeking. Obstacles to systematic initiatives remained significant.

Agendas for Change in Intergovernmental Relations

For these reasons many ideas for new directions have focused on how to improve intergovernmental relations. Four broad categories of agendas have been identified.

The first is about relationships between the central and state governments. Instead of hierarchy, one-party dominance and insulation from external economic forces, central and state governments have become involved in burgeoning networks of consultation and negotiation with each other, with industry and with community groups. Jenkins has described this as "the thickening of the Indian polity's institutional structure".[38] However questions that remained unresolved went to the changed role of the state, the management of economic relations in which international and local interests collide, the building of market supporting regulatory institutions, and the equitable distribution of opportunities and rewards of economic growth. Further, questions also arose about the quality of arrangements for governance and public management; the distribution of capabilities between the centre and the states; and the distribution of capabilities between states. During the UPA government barely a week passed without the prime minister or other senior ministers fruitlessly beseeching the states to collaborate on matters of national importance. Demands for change linked further prospects for economic reform to improved governance and more effective public management.

The second category of agendas was thus about intergovernmental relations. The range and scope of inter-governmental forums have extended incrementally. The list includes: National Development Council (Prime Minister, Chief Ministers and selected central ministers), Inter-State Council (Prime Minister, Chief Ministers and selected central ministers) meetings of Chief Ministers, meetings of central and state ministers, "empowered" committees of ministers, and task groups of officials. But these bodies did not cover the whole range of government activities. The National Development Council was responsible for negotiating the recommendations of the Planning Commission. The Inter-State Council resulted from a constitutional review, was regarded as having unfulfilled potential and remained advisory. The bodies with the most engaged role on tough issues were "empowered" committees of ministers. However, the history of negotiations over the design and implementation of a Goods and Services Tax suggests that such committees had limited bite.[39] Agendas to improve capability to manage intergovernmental relations have been slow to crystallise.

The third category of agendas was about fiscal federalism. This category contains the most developed proposals. The chief problems were about the shrinking fiscal space for state governments, the intermixing roles of central and state governments, multiple channels for fiscal transfers to the states, and multiple ways in which states can arrange loans. Specific problems have included: single year budgets, difficulties in relating budget and plan expenditures, little commitment to budgets, structural deficits, parking of deficits with government owned banks, top ups and bail outs for state deficits, fudging of compliance with fiscal responsibility legislation, growing central expenditure in areas of joint or state responsibility, growing use of conditional grants, lack of market discipline on borrowing, and the overlapping responsibilities of the Planning Commission and Finance Commissions.

Many of these issues were included in the terms of reference of the Commission on Centre-State Relations which reported in April 2010. They were also addressed by the Thirteenth Finance Commission the report of which was adopted by the government in February 2010. For the first time this was asked to examine not only the distribution of finances but also fiscal management. This concern continued in the terms of reference for the Fourteenth

Finance Commission. However the impacts of these initiatives were slow to be seen. In the meantime analysis by scholars and local and international officials provided a menu of options ready to match with new opportunities for change. M. Govinda Rao and Nirvikar Singh set out the strategic significance of fiscal federalism and argued that change was feasible through a collaborative approach.[40] They nominated three chief areas for reform: a simpler, more transparent, incentive compatible and better targeted fiscal transfer system; tax reforms to improve efficiency of collection, reduce allocative distortions, and improve equity; and effective decentralisation of spending authority. A World Bank team argued that the states could increase their own revenues through reform of tax policies and administration.[41] They argued further that the centre could increase incentives for the states by strengthening market based discipline for state borrowings and replacing annual targets for deficit reduction by monitoring actual end of year stocks of debt and liabilities. M. Govinda Rao proposed a substantial list of measures including: increasing central revenues by a spectrum 3G auction and 'seriously initiating' a programme of divestment/ disinvestment; strengthening collection of direct taxes; and in collaboration with the states finalising arrangements to introduce a dual Goods and Services Tax (GST).[42] These proposals probed three areas of political and institutional sensitivity: the reluctance of governments, central and state, to privatise state owned enterprises (corporatisation and allowing private investors to take up a small proportion of equity were preferred); the difficulties of maintaining a balance between central and state abilities to raise revenue; and the capabilities of the civil service to enforce existing laws and implement new initiatives. However taking up of such suggestions was limited. The UPA government approached any disinvestment proposals with great caution. Further, proposals for a GST to be implemented in 2010 failed to meet this and subsequent target dates.

On fiscal administration generally a wide range of proposals have been canvassed. Rao argued that fiscal discipline required commitment by spending as well as finance agencies.[43] Singh and Srinivasan proposed strengthening the Finance Commission as a fiscal monitor; later they proposed that the Inter-State Commission constitute itself as a Fiscal Review Council to review the medium and long term fiscal policies of the states and the centre.[44] Amaresh Bagchi (2007) argued for a thorough review of relationships between the Planning Commission and the Ministry of Finance, the introduction of multi-year budgeting and a review of arrangements for fiscal transfers to the states.[45] A State Finance Commission Chairman also argued that state finance commissions needed to provide more positive assistance to local governments on economic development, social justice and provision of public services.[46] A substantial unfinished agenda remained.[47]

The fourth category of agendas was about minorities and their search for representation. Unlike the previous agendas they were agendas from below. They are illustrated by renewed claims for the reorganisation of states. In 1956 and against the wishes of Jawaharlal Nehru the states were reorganised on linguistic lines. More recently minorities sharing the language of existing states began arguing for separate states of their own. Their grounds included backwardness and deprivation. After popular agitations the National Democratic Alliance government (1998-2004) created three new states. In 2010 the UPA government faced sometimes violent agitations from the Telangana region for a separate state. The government temporised and eventually set up a commission of inquiry. But after the inquiry reported it continued to delay a decision. In the end, it granted the demand. But as deliberations ground messily to an end, proponents of other new states advanced their own demands. The government's pragmatic and changeable responses led to demands for the formulation of principles to apply to new state claims and for a second states reorganisation commission. However, it was argued also that the complexity of Indian society meant that "no reorganisation of states can produce an internally homogeneous and administratively and financially viable set of states in all cases".[48]

Perhaps the strongest message that came from the demands for new states was the extent to which significant numbers of people felt that the institutions of government, national, state and local were deaf to their needs. Representatives of both central and state governments have acknowledged regularly that they must do better. The long lists of proposed further economic reforms are similar acknowledgements. Existing governance arrangements and public sector capabilities have not come together to produce local level performance seen to create value for citizens. However, political leaders have yet to turn such acknowledgements into feasible agendas.[49] In the meantime they have faced the challenge of managing federal arrangements in which state asymmetry continued to grow.

The still developing range of issues suggests that the most significant agendas about the management of issues that involve both the centre and the states have yet to crystallise. Liberalisation took place in 1991 because astute central participants turned an external problem into a domestic opportunity for change. However in implementation it was more a "stroke of the pen" change than pursuit of an "agenda of integration and deregulation" that engaged state governments.[50] Two different critiques emerged. The first lamented the negative impacts of economic liberalisation on federalism.[51] The second argued that managing global economic interaction demanded further domestic institutional reform.[52] One critic proposed that the "the most difficult reforms are yet to be achieved".[53] In the meantime, strategies of gradualism grappled with crosscutting trends towards centralisation and decentralisation, neither of which provided much satisfaction. The most significant trend was the extension of the range of forums in which central and state governments could negotiate their roles. Building incentives to enrich the range and outcomes of such negotiations emerged as one of the most important reform proposals.[54]

Federal Arrangements and Agendas in Australia

Against the expectations of most of its founders the Australian federation has experienced relentless trends to centralisation. The Australian commonwealth began as a 'coming together' federation. Six small, self-governing settler colonies formed what they thought would be a limited federal government. Within existing boundaries the states maintained their own constitutions, parliaments, courts and public services. Powers not specifically assigned to the federal government remained with the states; surplus federal funds were to be returned to the states. Constitutional amendments could be made only by referendum requiring a majority of voters in a majority of states. However, the actual assignment of powers led to a high proportion of shared and contested functions; and precedence in the exercise of concurrent powers lay with the federal government.

Four factors are commonly identified as agents of federal pre-eminence: federal financial power, negotiated transfers of power by the states, favourable constitutional interpretations by the High Court and social and economic trends favouring national approaches to public policy.[55] The High Court ruled that an Inter-State Commission provided for in the constitution usurped judicial power. An agreement with the states, confirmed by a rare constitutional amendment, enabled the federal government to control state borrowing. During the 1939-45 war the federal government negotiated the transfer of state income taxation powers, a transfer made permanent by the High Court in 1959. In later cases the court upheld broad application in the federal government's favour of the external affairs power, removed important residual state-controlled taxing powers, and expanded the corporations' power to support federal government action wherever a corporation was involved. Federal dominance of taxation provided the federal government with substantial influence through its ability to make special purpose grants to the states. Invariably, revenue sharing with the states was arranged on federal terms. Although the Commonwealth Grants Commission provided a high degree of fiscal equalisation between states, vertical fiscal imbalance remains pronounced. A goods and services tax introduced by the federal government in 2000 with revenue assigned to the states provided limited relief. Ambiguities in the arrangements enabled the then federal government to claim that the states had not reduced regulatory burdens as agreed or provided efficient services for which they were well funded.[56] Running through these specific centralising threads was the sense, articulated in political debate and policy analysis, that common problems, whether social or economic, demanded common solutions.[57]

However federal pre-eminence is contingent.[58] First, a large number of government activities depend on joint action. For this reason, Australia has evolved a formal process for intergovernmental negotiation which, following the liberalisation reforms, became the Council of Australian Governments (COAG) which includes the prime minister, state premiers, territory chief ministers and a representative of local government. Second, the federal public service is stronger in policy skills than in operational management.[59] Third, state governments have become increasingly sensitive to the local impacts of international trends and begun to frame dissenting views in the language of national interest and international opportunities.[60] They have also upgraded the policy skills in their public services and their ability to subject central proposals for national schemes to critical analysis.[61] Further they have set up their own forum—the Council for the Australian Federation (CAF).[62]

In ways that the constitution did not fully envisage both the federal government and the states need each other. Skilful intergovernmental diplomacy provides ways to address issues formally within state responsibilities that now seem to demand a national approach.[63] However pathways between central compulsion and dogmatic opposition are rarely clear. While a concentrated central strategy is often attractive, many pathways to dissidence are open. For the federal government, too many successful but resisted interventions risk mobilising widening circles of opposition.[64] For the states, collaborating too readily in the development of national policy risks progressive marginalisation.[65]

Paths to Economic Liberalisation

As in India, economic liberalisation in Australia began with realisation that changes internationally made long settled policies of domestic protection and regulation insupportable. However, implementation had far-reaching effects on federal governance and national policy. Change took place through extensive negotiations between an inclusive mix of stakeholders. Key participants included a federal Labour government, a mixture of Labour and non-Labour state governments, business and trade unions. Economic analysis by public service and university economists underpinned negotiations. At the federal level the opposition broadly supported the changes. However consequential adjustments in industry and the community precipitated strong and continuing social and political impacts.

Change began in the 1980s. In the face of economic reverses and political opposition, earlier initiatives in the 1960s to cut import restrictions and in the 1970s to cut tariffs had petered out. However by the 1980s arguments for macro and micro economic reform had gained strength.[66] Key changes included:[67]

- Reforms to open up the public sector to competition (deregulation, outsourcing and privatisation)
- Measures to expose private markets to greater competition (freer international trade, fewer barriers across Australian state borders and deregulation)
- Workplace reform
- A shift to more market-based techniques of economic intervention, with less use of regulations, controls, protective barriers or cross-subsidisation of public services and more use of market incentives, such as subsidies or tax concessions, or at least market-neutral devices such as direct budgetary payments.

Significantly, the changes replaced labour market regulation with competition policy at the centre of the regulatory framework.[68]

Three forces drove the changes: ideas current among the policy elite, strong leadership by the Prime Minister Bob Hawke and Treasurer Paul Keating, and extensive strategies of consultation.[69] Brennan and Pincus take a more path dependent view. They argue that external changes demanded a policy shift and to which domestic changes responded.[70] However formulation and implementation of specific measures entailed the identification of many opportunities and the negotiation of just as many blocking points. Paths to change demanded skilled advocates, adaptable institutions and strategies for securing the acquiescence of well organised interests. Further, to promote a national market, redesign arrangements for regulation of business and promote competition the cooperation of the states, secured in part through a fiscal dividend for implementing agreed changes, was needed.[71]

The process of drawing in the states began after a more than usually acrimonious heads of government meeting in 1990.[72] To avoid another such meeting Prime Minister Hawke proposed a special Premier's Conference to discuss cooperative arrangements. He foreshadowed a broad agenda including reduction of duplication of functions between levels of government and a rebalancing of federal-state financial arrangements. The initiative had the support of the five Labour premiers and the one Liberal premier. The new forum, which became the Council of Australian Governments, made a good start. However the supportive state Liberal government lost ground at an election and a leadership challenge forced Hawke from office.

Problems of organising further meetings led to the state premiers holding discussions on their own at which they agreed on a statement of principles for managing the federal system. They agreed also on "mutual recognition of standards and the elimination of impediments to a national market of goods and services".[73] Although when Paul Keating succeeded Hawke as prime minister the agenda for discussion changed, the impetus for economic reform continued. Throughout the changes the federal government led the way and liberalisation confirmed its financial dominance. However, state participation and concurrence was essential.

Impacts on Intergovernmental Relations

Following liberalisation, the spirit in which it was negotiated, disappeared. While a conservative government elected in 1996 continued much of the reform agenda, Prime Minister Howard was ambivalent about negotiating through the Council of Australian Governments. The government straddled contradictory appeals to economic liberalism, conservative nationalism and those who felt disadvantaged by liberalisation. It sidelined the union movement, introduced the GST (Treasurer Keating had considered a similar reform before being over ruled), and passed legislation to deregulate the labour market (Work Choices). Further, near the end of its term the government initiated a flurry of largely ineffective interventions in fields of state responsibility. Despite High Court backing for Work Choices the political opposition mobilised by the policy played a significant role in the government's defeat.[74]

In the face of Howard's centralism the states experimented with their own reform agenda. Much of this was absorbed by the approach of the next federal Labour government elected in 2007.[75] Key elements included further competition and regulatory reforms together with human capital and natural resource management reforms. Strategies for change mixed demands for national consistency with financial incentives and performance agreements. An Intergovernmental Agreement on Federal Financial Relations negotiated in 2008 was intended to provide a framework for improved relationships with the states.[76] It had three main components: national agreements to consolidate over 90 specific purposes payments into five new payments; national partnership agreements for specific projects; and performance and assessment frameworks for public reporting and accountability. An independent COAG Reform Council, reporting direct to COAG, was set up to assess and report on performance. But, despite promising beginnings, consistent directions and momentum did not develop.[77] Intergovernmental relations continued to oscillate between centralism and collaboration.

Two different appreciations emerged. One explored modes of federal policy dominance and how they were or might be implemented. The other, while acknowledging the superior resources of the federal government, explored opportunities for further collaborative reform. Not infrequently commentators combined the two and differed mainly in where they struck a balance.

The first appreciation analysed dominance through a variety of overlapping lenses, including: programme federalism, conditional federalism, coercive federalism, opportunistic federalism, executive federalism, and managerial federalism. Three kinds of "creeping centralism" were identified. One was to reformulate relations with the states in terms of principal and agents, offers of funds in return for performance and threats of national takeovers in cases of poor performance. A second was to organise centrally sponsored services to citizens through competitive tendering between states, private providers or non-government organisations. A third was to bypass the states by providing funding direct to end users who could then choose their own providers.[78]

The second appreciation drew lessons from the process of economic reform, especially about the contributions of the states. It identified the potential of the states to contribute to the future development and implementation of national policies. Relationships between levels of government need not be a zero sum game. In this view, the route to reform was through existing federal arrangements;[79] referendums, judicial review and intergovernmental competition and collaboration could all be used.[80] It focused on how credible and feasible proposals could be formulated and support from both levels of government mobilised.

Agendas for Change in Intergovernmental Relations

Three agendas for improving intergovernmental relations stand out. The first is about improving the role of COAG by providing it with a stronger institutional basis. When it is used, COAG has provided a vehicle for developing shared approaches to national policy problems, managing intergovernmental competition, and providing the states with an arena in which to influence national agendas from below. Suggestions for strengthening it have included an intergovernmental agreement to underpin its proceedings and provide improved roles for the states in managing business. Doing so would moderate adversarial tactics, encourage mutual respect between jurisdictions, and support mechanisms of accountability that emphasised results rather than deals. Such suggestions for institutional thickening have emphasised that productive relationships between federal units are encouraged by the policy skills, flexibility and diplomacy of participants.[81] Such factors helped facilitate decisions on liberalisation. It is hoped that building up the role of COAG would make replication less elusive. However it could be expected that states, regardless of party allegiances, would continue to scrutinise federal proposals closely for cost shifting, and onerous requirements for matching funds, reporting requirements and operational controls and that the federal government would continue to deploy. its financial and constitutional power.

A second agenda is about addressing irritants in relationships. Two in particular stand out. The first is about how the federal government distributes GST proceeds to the states. Several states commissioned analysis to support claims that allocation by a formula for horizontal fiscal equalisation should be replaced by a per capita basis. These claims had no success but support did emerge for increased transparency in how funds were distributed.[82] A second is about sorting out which levels of government did what. External stakeholders hoped it would cut duplication and over regulation. States thought it might insulate them from at least some central initiatives. But some commentators with federal experience thought it might also allow the centre to set policies while the states delivered services. The contradictory perspectives did not dim the popularity of the suggestion. But regardless of the care with which agreements about functions were made, as "incomplete contracts" they would be vulnerable to intergovernmental competition for jurisdiction.[83] Possibly, a process for successive adjustments through COAG mediated intergovernmental agreements might offer a pragmatic way forward.

A third agenda is about analysis and assessment. As the states deployed proposals backed by policy analysis and the Productivity Commission was drawn into assessment of proposals, attention began to focus on program outcomes and accountability for performance. While this was regarded as a promising development[84] it was still at an early stage. Performance information was often elusive. Essential information was controlled by the states, ever mindful of the risks of too eager collaboration. And because of variations in local conditions, the state wishes to maximise flexibility and continued to make a comparison of performance difficult.

In these agendas a common theme was to limit tendencies for conflict and maximise opportunities that led to negotiations about shared benefits.

Conclusion

The common thread in this paper is about how two federal polities made significant changes in policy and institutional arrangements and the difficulties that they faced in maintaining momentum for change. Despite the many differences between India and Australia their paths to economic liberalisation touched at many points. Five stand out. First, external stimuli provided the opportunity for radical rethinking of economic management. Second, domestic forces led by coalitions of committed political and public service leaders with shared ideas drove significant change. Third, programs of change were tailored to enlist support from influential interests. Fourth, liberalisation focused attention on interactions between external and internal factors with continuing implications for federal arrangements. Fifth, processes of change were exceptional mainly in the degree to which they were mutually supportive.

Paths to liberalisation also diverged, especially with regard to the roles of the states. In Australia, despite its extensive legal and financial resources the federal government needed to enlist the concurrence of the states. The result was far reaching reforms, including a national regime of business regulation. However, in India lack of capability to engage the states placed limits on the scope of change and allowed state governments to capture regulatory space vacated by the centre.

Following liberalisation both countries struggled with strategies for further national economic reform. In Australia many agendas for more change focused on improving the institutional support for intergovernmental negotiation provided by COAG. In India a proliferation of intergovernmental forums and proposals for reform did not crystallise around a similar set of arrangements. But as Australian experience has shown, the existence of facilitating institutions is in itself an insufficient condition for reform. For both countries how best to identify and exploit opportunities for policy change is a continuing problem. The conjunction of forces that led to economic liberalisation has proved hard to replicate. Although in both countries the central level of government has greater resources than the states, in order to make major changes the centre often needs state support. Three reasons apply: first, where states have relevant constitutional powers; second, where states have access to greater information and skills in policy and management; and third, where, although the centre has the power to act alone, an imposed change risks political discontent.

If each country could learn one thing from the other, India could examine Australia's methods for handling intergovernmental relations and Australia could reflect on India's retreat from central dominance. Both could also reflect further on how to manage federal arrangements as incomplete contracts. As Oliver Williamson has argued:[85]

> [M]any economic agents have the capacities both to learn and to look ahead, perceive hazards and factor these back into the contractual relations, and thereafter to devise responsive institutions. In effect limited but intended rationality is translated into incomplete but farsighted contracting.

To do so would sharpen attention to capabilities for managing intergovernmental relations, searching for agreement about shared problems and negotiating solutions. However, learning about federal arrangements needs to be about more than economics. As Amaresh Bagchi has argued "a great merit of federalism lies in its promise of respecting plurality of identity of human beings".[86] Realising this promise in radically changing circumstances while also fostering capability to address shared problems, is a challenge that both India and Australia share.

NOTES

1. Mark Bevir, *Governance: A Very Short Introduction* (Oxford: Oxford University Press, 2012), p. 114.
2. Bhajan Grewal and Peter Sheehan, "Understanding the evolution of constitutional federalism: The case of Australia", *Public Finance and Management*, Vol. 4, No. 4, 2004, pp. 559-591; Oliver Williamson, *The Mechanisms of Governance* (New York: Oxford University Press, 1999), pp. 6-10.
3. Grewal and Sheehan, n. 2, p. 582.
4. Ian Copland and John Rickard, *Federalism: Comparative Perspectives from India and Australia* (New Delhi: Manohar, 2001), p. 18.
5. Stephen Howse and M. Govinda Rao, eds., *Federal Reform Strategies: Lessons from Asia and Australia* (New Delhi: Oxford University Press, 2013), p. ix.
6. See for example: M. Govinda Rao and Nirvikar Singh, *Political Economy of Federalism in India* (New Delhi: Oxford University Press, 2005); Amaresh Bagchi, "Role of Planning and the Planning Commission in the New Indian Economy: Case for Review", *Economic and Political Weekly*, 3 November 2007, pp. 92-100; J.N. Keddie and RFI Smith, "Leading from Below: How Sub-National Governments Influence Policy Agendas", *Australian Journal of Public Administration*, Vol. 68, No. 1, 2009, pp. 67-82; RFI Smith, "How do international pressures affect federal governance in India?" in Lance

Brennan and Auriol Weigold, eds., *Re-thinking India: Perceptions from Australia* (New Delhi: Readworthy, 2013), pp. 74-87; Howse and Rao, n. 5, p. ix.

7. See: Nirvikar Singh and Garima Vasishtha, "Patterns in Centre-State Fiscal Transfers: An Illustrative Analysis", *Economic and Political Weekly*, 6 November 2004, pp. 4897-4903; M. Govinda Rao and Nirvikar Singh, n. 6, pp. 26-44; Nirvikar Singh and T.N. Srinivasan, "Federalism and economic development in India: An Assessment", *Munich Personal RePEc Archive, MPRA Paper No. 12452*, 2008; Grewal and Sheehan, n. 2, p. 559; and Howse and Rao, n. 6.
8. Howse and Rao, n. 6, pp. 22-3.
9. RFI Smith, "India and Australia: Closer and Closer?" *Politico* (New Delhi), Vol. 2, No. 2, 2014, pp. 118-129.
10. Devesh Kapur, "Ideas and Economic Reforms in India: The Role of International Migration and the Indian Diaspora", *India Review*, Vol. 3, No. 4, 2004, pp. 364-384; B.K. Nehru, *Report of the Australian System of Federal Finance and its Applicability to Indian Conditions* (New Delhi: Ministry of Finance, Government of India, 1947), (not sighted); and Copland and Rickard, n. 4.
11. C. Rangarajan and D.K. Srivastava, "Fiscal Transfers in Canada: Drawing Comparisons and Lessons", *Economic and Political Weekly*, 8 May 2004, pp. 1897-1909; Rangarajan and Srivastava, "Fiscal Transfers in Australia: Review and Relevance to India", *Economic and Political Weekly*, 14 August 2004, pp. 3709-3722; Rangarajan and Srivastava, "Reforming India's Transfer System: Resolving Vertical and Horizontal Imbalances", *Economic and Political Weekly*, 7 June 2008, pp. 47-60.
12. Copland and Rickard, n. 4; Thomas O. Hueglin and Alan Fenna, *Comparative Federalism: A Systematic Inquiry* (Toronto: University of Toronto Press, 2006); Baogang He, Brian Galligan and Takashi Inoguchi, *Federalism in Asia* (Cheltenham UK: Edward Elgar, 2007); Howse and Rao, n. 6.
13. Alexander L. George and Andrew Bennett, *Case Studies and Theory Development in the Social Sciences* (Cambridge, Mass: MIT Press, 2004), p. 6.
14. John W. Kingdon, *Agendas, Alternatives, and Public Policies*, 2nd edn, (New York: Longman, 1995); Anthony Seldon, "Ideas are not enough", in David Marquand and Anthony Seldon, eds., *The Ideas That Shaped Britain Since 1945* (London: Fontana, 1996), pp. 257-280.
15. Rob Jenkins, "How Federalism Influences India's Domestic Politics of WTO Engagement (and is Itself Affected in the Process)", *Asian Survey*, Vol. 43, No. 4, 2003, pp. 598-621; Kapur, n. 10; Rahul Mukherji, "Managing Competition: Politics and the Building of Independent Regulatory Institutions", *India Review*, Vol. 3, No. 4,

2004, pp. 278-305.

16. Fred Argy, "Economic Governance and National Institutional Dynamics", in Stephen Bell, ed., *Economic Governance and Institutional Dynamics* (South Melbourne: Oxford University Press, 2002), pp. 34-52; Geoffrey Brennan and Jonathan Pincus, "Australia's Economic Institutions", in Geoffrey Brennan and Francis G. Castles, eds., *Australia Reshaped: 200 Years of Institutional Transformation* (Cambridge: Cambridge University Press, 2002), pp. 53-85; Paul Gretton, "National Economic Reform in a Federal System: The Case of the Australian Competition Policy and Related Reforms", in Howse and Rao, n. 6, pp. 33-63.
17. Lloyd Rudolph and Susanne Hoeber Rudolph, *In Pursuit of Lakshmi: The Political Economy of the Indian State* (Chicago: University of Chicago Press, 1987).
18. Shalendra D. Sharma, "A Political Economy of the Indian State in the Era of Globalisation: A Review", *South Asia*, Vol. 32, No. 3, 2009, p. 369.
19. M. Govinda Rao and Tapas K. Sen, "Federalism and Reforms in India", in Howse and Rao, n. 6, p. 149.
20. Rahul Mukherji, The State, Economic Growth and Development in India, *India Review*, Vol. 8, No. 1, 2009, pp. 81-106.
21. E. Sridharan, "The Growth and Sectoral Composition of India's Middle Class: Its Impact on the Politics of Economic Liberalisation", *India Review*, Vol. 3, No. 4, 2004, pp. 405-428.
22. Mukherji, n. 20; S. Kale, "Inside Out: India's Global Reorientation", *India Review*, Vol. 8, No. 1, 2009, pp. 43-62.
23. Kale, n. 22.
24. Mukherji, n. 20; Arvind Panagariya, *The Indian Growth Miracle: What Are the Lessons?* (Hyderabad: K.L.N. Prasad Lecture, January 2009). <http://www.columbia.edu/~ap2231/Policy%20Papers/Hyderabad%20KLN%20Lecture%20Final%20Final%20Jan%206%202009.pdf> accessed 18 December 2014.
25. Panagariya, n. 24.
26. Montek Singh Ahluwalia, "Understanding India's Reform Trajectory: Past Trends and Future Challenges", *India Review*, Vol. 3, No. 4, 2004, pp. 269–277.
27. Ibid.
28. Dani Rodrik, *One Economics, Many Recipes* (Princeton: Princeton University Press, 2007), p. 36.
29. Dani Rodrik and Arvind Subramaniam, "Why India Can Grow at 7 Per Cent a Year or More: Projections and Reflections", *Economic and Political Weekly*, 17 April, 2004, p. 1593.
30. Jason A. Kirk, "Banking on India's States: The Politics of World Bank Reform Programmes in Andhra Pradesh and Karnataka", *India*

Review, Vol. 4, No. 3, 2005, pp. 287-325.

31. Aseema Sinha, "The Changing Political Economy of Federalism in India: A Historical Institutionalist Approach", *India Review*, Vol. 3, No. 1, 2004, pp. 25-63.
32. Rob Jenkins, "Labour Policy and the Second Generation of Economic Reform in India", *India Review*, Vol. 3, No. 4, 2004, pp. 333-363.
33. Vikram K. Chand, "Governance Reforms in a Federal Polity", in Howse and Rao, n. 6, p. 164.
34. Ibid., p. 164.
35. Mukherji, n. 20.
36. Jenkins, n. 32.
37. Jay Chaudhuri, "Going to the Operating Room without a Diagnostic: Reforming Centrally Sponsored Schemes", *India Review*, Vol. 9, No. 2, 2010, pp. 169-203.
38. Jenkins, n. 15, p. 616; Balveer Arora, et al., "Indian Federalism", in K.C. Suri and Achin Vanaik, eds., *Indian Democracy* (New Delhi: Oxford University Press, 2013), pp. 101-160.
39. Rao and Sen, n. 19, p. 149.
40. Govinda Rao and Nirvikar Singh, n. 6, pp. 384-385.
41. V.J. Ravishankar, et al., "Indian States' Fiscal Correction: An Unfinished Agenda", *Economic and Political Weekly*, 20 September, 2008, pp. 57-62.
42. M. Govinda Rao, "The Fiscal Situation and a Reform Agenda for the New Government", *Economic and Political Weekly*, 20 June 2009, p. 84; M. Govinda Rao, "Goods and Services Tax: Some Progress towards Clarity", *Economic and Political Weekly*, 19 December 2009, pp. 8-11.
43. Rao, n. 42, p. 85.
44. Singh and Srinivasan, n. 7, p. 37.
45. Bagchi, n. 6.
46. M.A. Oommen, "Have the State Finance Commissions Fulfilled Their Constitutional Mandate?" *Economic and Political Weekly*, 24 July 2010, pp. 40-44.
47. Rao and Sen, n. 19, p. 159.
48. Mahendra Prasad Singh, "A Borderless Internal Federal Space? Reorganisation of States in India", *India Review*, Vol. 6, No. 4, 2007, pp. 247.
49. The Accountability Initiative. <http://www.accountabilityindia.in/ > accessed 19 December 2014, provides wide ranging insights on problems of official performance and accountability at local levels.
50. Howse and Rao, n. 6, pp. 1-2.
51. Amaresh Bagchi, "Globalisation and Federalism: Uneasy Partners?" *Economic and Political Weekly*, 20 September 2008, p. 47.

52. Smith, n. 6; Sharma, n. 18, p. 371.
53. Sharma, n. 18, p. 371.
54. Rao and Sen, n. 19, pp. 158-160.
55. J. Madden, *Australian Federalism Reforms and Global Integration: Working Paper 148* (Stanford: Centre for Research on Economic Development and Policy Reform, Stanford University, 2002); Grewal and Sheehan, n. 2; Brian Galligan, "Processes for Reforming Australian Federalism", *UNSW Law Journal,* Vol. 31, No. 2, 2008, pp. 617-642; Alan Fenna, "Centralising Dynamics in Australian Federalism" in Howse and Engele, n. 55; Howse and Rao, n. 6, p. 68.
56. Andrew Parkin and Geoff Anderson, "The Howard Government, Regulatory Federalism and the Transformation of Commonwealth-State Relations", *Australian Journal of Political Science,* Vol. 42, No. 2, 2007 pp. 295-314; R. Wilkins, "A New Era in Commonwealth-State Relations?", *Public Administration Today,* April 2006, pp. 8-13.
57. Andrew Podger, "Federalism Reform", *Public Administration Today,* January-March 2008, p. 36; Fenna, n. 55.
58. Cliff Walsh, "The Economics of Federalism and Federal Reform", *UNSW Law Journal,* Vol. 31, No. 2, 2008, pp. 553-582; Brian Galligan, n. 55, pp. 617-642.
59. For the views of a former senior federal and state public servant see: Terry Moran, *A New Federation.* <http://www.ipaa.org.au/documents/2014/11/ceda-perth.pdf> accessed 22 December 2014.
60. Helen Silver, "Getting the Best Out of Federalism: The Role of the Productivity Commission and the Limits of National Approaches", *Australian Journal of Public Administration,* Vol. 69, No. 3, 2010, pp. 326-332; Geoff Anderson, "The Council of Australian Governments: A New Institution of Governance for Australia's Conditional Federalism", *UNSW Law Journal,* Vol. 31, No. 2, 2008, pp. 493-508; Howse and Rao, n. 6.
61. Silver, n. 60; Anderson, n. 60.
62. Anne Tiernan, "The Council for the Australian Federation: A New Structure of Australian Federalism", *Australian Journal of Public Administration,* Vol. 67, No. 2, 2008, pp. 122–134.
63. Fenna, n. 55, p. 583.
64. Walsh, n. 58, pp. 562 and 582, states "there is an important difference between the *appearance* of dominance and the reality of the political consequences of trying to *exercise* it".
65. Robyn Hollander, "National Competition Policy, Regulatory Reform and Australian Federalism", *Australian Journal of Public Administration,* Vol. 65, No. 2, 2006, pp. 33-47.
66. Brennan and Pincus, n. 16, p. 81; Argy, n. 16, p. 44; Gretton, n. 16, pp. 39 and 43; Walsh, n. 58, pp. 553-554.

67. Argy, n. 16, p. 40.
68. John Braithwaite, "Globalization and Australian Institutions", in Brennan and Castles, n. 16, p. 102.
69. Argy, n. 16, p. 44.
70. Brennan and Pincus, n. 16, pp. 78 and 81.
71. Gretton, n. 16, pp. 33, 49 and 61.
72. J C Bannon, "From Confrontation to Cooperation: Australian Commonwealth-State Relations in the 1980s and 1990s", in Copland and Rickard, n. 4, pp. 240-248.
73. Bannon, n. 72, p. 245; Walsh, n. 58, p. 580.
74. Walsh, n. 58, p. 582.
75. Gretton, n. 16, p. 57; Howse and Engele, n. 55, p. 71; Walsh, n. 58, pp. 558-559; Anderson, n. 60, p. 500.
76. Mary Ann O'Loughlin, "Accountability and Reforms to Australia's Federal Financial Relations", *Australian Journal of Public Administration*, Vol. 72, No. 3, pp. 376–381.
77. Howse and Engele, n. 55, p. 80.
78. Hollander, n. 65, p. 44; Wilkins, n. 56, pp. 11-12; Anderson, n. 60, p. 497.
79. Howse and Rao, n. 6, p. 2.
80. Galligan, n. 55, p. 641.
81. Anne Twomey and Glenn Withers, *Federalist Paper 1 Australia's Federal Future: Delivering Growth and Prosperity, Federalist Paper 1, Prepared for the Council for the Australian Federation* (Melbourne: Government of Victoria, 2007). <http://www.caf.gov.au/documents/australiasfederalfuture.pdf> accessed 23 December 2014; John Wanna, et al., "Common Cause: Strengthening Australia's Cooperative Federalism", *Final Report to the Council for the Australian Federation*, May 2009. <http://www.caf.gov.au/documents/FP3%20-%20final.pdf>accessed 23 December 2014.
82. Walsh, n. 58, p. 573.
83. Walsh, n. 58, p. 567; Grewal and Sheehan, n. 52.
84. Gretton, n. 16, p. 61.
85. Williamson, n. 2, p. 9.
86. Bagchi, n. 51, p. 48.

9

Maritime Security in the Indo-Pacific Region: String of Pearls and Maritime Silk Road

Wang Dehua

ABSTRACT

As East Asia struggles to cope with the growing challenges to maritime security in the Indo-Pacific including changes in great power balance, the intensification of maritime disputes, and fundamental disagreements on the interpretation of the Law of the Seas, three new imperatives are redefining the geopolitics of the region. The author discusses the significance of maritime security and international cooperation as China surprised the world community recently once again with a new initiative—this time in the maritime domain with the idea of working together in the "maritime silk route" in the Indo-Pacific region.

Evolving Concept of "Indo-Pacific": A Chinese Scholarly Perspective

I am of the view that Chinese academia took cognisance of the term 'Indo-Pacific construct' only since former US Secretary of State Hillary Clinton coined the phrase in the course of her speech in Honolulu on 28 October 2010 underlining the importance of "the Indo-Pacific basin" to global trade and commerce.[1]

No doubt, the term Indo-Pacific reflects some reality: firstly, it relates to the "rise" of China and the emergence of India to some extent around the same time; secondly, it reflects the increasing strategic importance of the Indian Ocean; thirdly, it shows China and India are stretching their strategic space beyond their respective spheres of influence, accelerating thereby a strategic competition in Asia.

Besides, the term "Indo-Pacific" reflects some countries in the region wanting to raise their own international status by using this moment when the US announced its Asia-Pacific Rebalance strategy or "pivot to Asia" following the 'rise' of China and its increased activities to defend its maritime rights and overseas interests in the Indian Ocean.

In response, the US seeks to establish an alliance partnership comprising Japan, Australia and India to counter-balance the rise of China more effectively given its current domestic economic difficulties and financial pressure. In the Indo-Pacific, the US is actively engaged in setting up a formal macro-multilateral military cooperative system based on the foundations of several trilateral cooperative units such as US-India-Australia; US-India-Japan; US-Japan-Korea; and US-Australia, Japan; and Japan-India, and Australia-India bilateral strategic and security cooperation mechanisms.

The Debate Over Indo-Pacific Geo-Strategy: Illusion or Reality?

It is commonly believed that from geopolitical perspective, with the US pivot to Asia, most critical regions are the Northeast Asia and Southeast Asia, which involve China, the US and Japan in several ways. Australia and India are not stick-holders. The current geo-strategic structure is in accordance with geo-economic and geopolitical reality, but there are no positions for India and Australia. Although India has a "Look East" policy, its major concern is still the Indian Ocean. Booz Allen and Robert Kaplan fabricated a "string of pearls" strategy, but Emily Brunjes and her colleagues do not see China's activity as threatening to regional stability or Indian security.

"Indo-Pacific" is an illusion. This geo-strategic design is a hegemony-seeking strategy. It comes from Alfred Thayer Mahan and Nicholas John Spykman's geo-strategy: control of key sea-lanes and the rim-land is more important than the heartland of Asia. Indo-Pacific is a geo-strategic design based on geo-economics and geopolitics. But just as former US Assistant Secretary of State Kurt M. Campbell stated the next challenge to American strategic thinking is how to connect Indian and Pacific oceans at the operational level.[2]

From geo-economic perspective, industries in "Indo-Pacific" are not well-distributed. The center of gravity is in Northeast Asia. The centre of the Pan-Asia economic plate is China. China is the world's workshop, and the largest country for international trade. India is far behind. From this perspective, the importance of the concept of "Indo-Pacific" only lies in the commercial and energy sea-lanes.

Predictably in the next 5-10 years, India may become the next industrial hub under the leadership of Prime Minister Narendra Modi. East Asia struggles to cope up with the growing challenges to maritime security in the Indo- Pacific region including changes in great power balance, the intensification of maritime disputes, and fundamental disagreements on the interpretation of the Law of the Sea, all of which are redefining the geopolitics of the region. More to the immediate point, China's neighbours have become actively engaged with it in a remarkable range of fora, dialogues, and consultations on matters of mutual concerns or interests. Despite these frenetic diplomatic activities, it is reported that the US military presence and China's emergence as an immovable military object is of critical concerns to them. Those nations with active territorial disputes with China—a list that includes India, Japan, Korea, the Philippines and Vietnam—are particularly apprehensive.

In terms of maritime security, two events have drawn the attention of world media in recent years. One event is the International Maritime Security Conference that was held on 15 May 2013 at Changi Exhibition Centre (CEC) Singapore on the theme "Safe and Secure Seas: Strengthening Cooperation in Maritime Security".[3] Over 350 delegates drawn from respective governments and military establishments discussed the evolving transnational threats to maritime security and safety and new naval security challenges and examined in detail prevailing operating paradigms and suggested further collaboration towards a regional security framework and cooperative action across borders which in my considered judgement is beneficial to maritime security and international cooperation.

The second event is a naval fleet of the Chinese People's Liberation Army (PLA) in September 2013 passed through the Miyako Strait and entered the Western Pacific Ocean for a training mission. Noting that the PLA Navy has been conducting regular high-seas training missions, fleet commander Wang Dazhong said such high-intensity and frequent training carries great significance in China's plan to build a blue-water navy.[4]

Since the end of the Cold War, the Indo-Pacific region has emerged as the world's most dynamic geopolitical zone. Shifting balances of power in the larger Indo-Pacific region are reshaping international perceptions. They are also fuelling apprehensions about the economic, military and political trends; hardening territorial disputes; and driving changes in the US economic, political, and military roles in Asia. The uncertainties these shifts entail are causing Asian nations to seek reassurance in reaffirmations of civilisational, cultural, and historical identity. They are redefining relationships with the United States. The principal, but far from the only force at work in these complex interactions is the return of China to wealth and power.[5]

In *India and Australia: Maritime Partners in the Indo-Pacific*, C. Raja Mohan pointed out: "One is the growing recognition that the security problems in the East Asian waters must be addressed within the broader framework of the Indo-Pacific. The second is a weakening of the United States which has been the principal security provider in the Indian and Pacific Oceans for many decades. The third is a consequential change in India's maritime orientationfrom being a lone ranger to a partner eager to build maritime coalitions".[6] Washington has repeatedly reaffirmed that it will remain a 'resident power' in the Western Pacific and the Indian Ocean, and the Obama administration has matched the rhetoric with an intense diplomatic focus on Asia in the last two years. "To be sure, the United States[7] will remain the most powerful military force in Asia for a long time to come. Nevertheless, its forward presence in the Indo-Pacific is coming under stress amidst the proliferation of advanced military capabilities in the littoral and the adoption of asymmetric strategies by its competitors, most notably China and Iran."[8]

Traditionally, the Pacific and Indian oceans have been viewed as two different and self-contained worlds. A number of developments have begun to compel a more integrated view of the Pacific and Indian oceans. East Asia's high growth path has generated stronger economic links with resource rich West Asia and Africa. India is now looking beyond the Strait of Malacca to include the South China Sea in its national security calculus. As India became a trading nation, like China before it, it was inevitable that Delhi's national security policy would acquire a new maritime focus. The new reliance on the sea for importing ever-growing quantities of energy and mineral resources, and for exporting its products to widely dispersed global markets, meant India would naturally turn towards building a blue water navy.[9]

In order to make the Asian economic community (AEC) manageable, Asia would have to approach regional economic integration in a phased manner. This is the approach that has been adopted by the successful regional blocs of today, viz. European Union and North American Free Trade Agreement that started with an effective skeleton comprised of a core group of countries before expanding the membership later to others. In view of the attempts already made at regional economic integration, the Asian economic community in its initial phase, it is argued, be built of five strong blocs of Asia that might form a core group, viz. ASEAN, China, India, Japan, and Korea (ACIJK). Once the process of integration is consolidated and some gains of integration are visible, AEC could be thrown open to other economies of the region. Southeast Asian nations and India agreed to step up cooperation on maritime security, a move that comes amid tension with China in the potentially oil and gas-rich South China Sea.[10]

Recently in a vision statement agreed at a summit in New Delhi, India and the 10-member Association of Southeast Asian Nations (ASEAN) set their sights on a new "strategic partnership" that would bring closer political, security and economic cooperation. Significantly, they underlined the need for freedom of navigation, a contentious issue because of competing claims with Beijing over parts of the South China Sea, though there was no mention of China in their statement. In speeches, the Philippines and Vietnam referred to tensions in their region, but India's foreign minister sought to distance New Delhi from the wrangling over the South

China Sea.[11] Taken together new challenges to communication lines open the space for Delhi and China to consult more intensively on maritime issues and develop a comprehensive framework for security cooperation in the increasingly turbulent waters of Asia

The phrase 'String of Pearls' was first used in 2005, in a report entitled "Energy Futures in Asia" provided to US Defence Secretary Donald H. Rumsfeld by defense contractor Booz Allen Hamilton. It alleged that China was adopting a "string of pearls" strategy of bases stretching from the Middle East to southern China. These "pearls" were naval bases or electronic eavesdropping posts built by the Chinese in Myanmar, Bangladesh, Pakistan and Sri Lanka. The purpose was to project its power overseas and protect its oil shipments. Nearly ten years have since elapsed. The phrase, or theory, still sticks in the international media and in some think tank reports.

However, the so-called "bases" are found nowhere in the Indian Ocean. The most telling evidence is that the PLA Navy has been conducting counter-piracy operations in the Gulf of Aden for five years without any bases of their own. Jean-Paul Adam, the Seychelles foreign affairs minister, announced in December 2011 that his country had invited China to set up a military base in his country, but the Chinese Ministry of Defence only responded that the Chinese side would "consider" replenishment or port calls in the Seychelles and other countries.

Role Played by China in Asia and Indo-Pacific Oceans

China has only two objectives in Asia and Indo-Pacific Oceans: economic gains and the security of Sea Lines of Communication (SLOC). The first objective is achieved through commercial interactions with littoral states. For the second, the Chinese Navy has, since the end of 2008, joined international military efforts in combating piracy in the waters off the coast of Somalia. In fact, the only thing justifiable in the "string of pearls" theory is that it underlines the growing importance, even then, of the Indian Ocean for China's ever-expanding national interests, especially in terms of energy import. In the 21st century China is securing its energy needs from all parts of the world, but the Middle East still remains as the most important source. By the end of 2013, China had become the largest trader and the largest oil importer in the world. The Indian Ocean, and hence the security of SLOCs from Bab-el-Mandeb, Hormuz, to the Malacca Strait, is thus vitally important for China.

Two countries are most important for China's freedom of navigation in the Indian Ocean: the US and India. The US is the only country that has the full capabilities to control the chokepoints in the Indian Ocean and cut off the SLOCs all the way to China, but it is unlikely to exercise such capabilities, unless, perhaps, in an all-out war with China. Even during the Cold War neither the US nor the Soviet Union endeavoured to cut off any SLOCs in the world. Besides, the SLOCs are life-lines for all states. Cutting off China's SLOCs will also affect US allies such as Japan, Republic of Korea (ROK) and Australia. So long as Sino-American relations remain manageable, such a worst-case scenario is unlikely to occur.

For, China is dependent on these routes to trade with nations and increase its gross domestic product from $200 billion in 1978 to about $10 trillion by 2013. China's trade has increased from $620 billion in 2002 to $3.8 trillion in 2012. Significantly, a large section of the above trade figures are based on the maritime domain, with very less trade transiting through the land borders. This overwhelming dependence on the maritime has added new demands on the maritime areas. Given its continuing dependence on maritime, China's increasing profile is in the possession of world-class merchant fleet, production of containers and the expansion in port-handling capacity.

Maritime Silk Road and Energy Cooperation

Another driving factor behind the maritime silk route is China's energy consumption. In 2012 China became the largest energy consumer with nearly 22 per cent of global total energy demand. According to the estimates of British Petroleum, China is to overtake the United States as the largest oil consumer by 2025 and Russia by 2027 as second largest gas consumer. Most of this currently, over 80 per cent, passes through the Indian Ocean region with West Asia contributing to about 56 per cent of China's oil imports while Africa accounting for the rest. Even though China, Russia and Central Asia have expanded land routes in the energy sector, for the foreseeable future, China's "Malacca Dilemma" is not expected to be resolved without naval or diplomatic initiatives in the Indian Ocean. Naval and diplomatic efforts then are behind this idea of the silk route.

The rivalry between the Elephant and Dragon is often hyped, but India would not challenge China unnecessarily. There is no dispute between China and India in the Indian Ocean. The Line of Actual Control along the Sino-Indian border has by and large remained peaceful. Although there have been some standoffs, notwithstanding this, not a single bullet has been fired across the border in over fifty years. The queer idea of China encircling India from the sea with the help of Pakistan only exists in the wildest imagination of some Indian strategists.

Access, rather than bases, is what the Chinese Navy is really interested in the Indian Ocean. The unchartered waters of the Indian Ocean could be friendlier than the disputed waters in the Pacific. In the Pacific Ocean, China has territorial disputes with a number of countries, but this is not the case in the Indian Ocean. The security of SLOCs is thus in the interests of all other nations. The undergoing counter-piracy mission involves navies from over twenty countries. It could serve as a future mode of cooperation among stakeholders in the Indian Ocean to address common threats.

Interestingly the route of Chinese Task Forces departing from the southern Chinese coast for fighting piracy in the Indian Ocean is not dissimilar from the Maritime Silk Road that Admiral Zheng He and his fleet embarked upon in 1405. Currently, the Chinese leadership is reinvigorating the Maritime Silk Road. China tabled a 3 billion Yuan China-ASEAN Maritime Cooperation Fund for the maritime economy, environment, fishery and salvage, and communications in the sea. In October 2013, Chinese President Xi Jinping proposed to ASEAN to build the Maritime Silk Road of the 21st Century. This coincides with Chinese Premier Li Keqiang's pledge to upgrade the Gold Decade (2000-2010) of China-ASEAN cooperation into a Diamond Decade. In the Indian Ocean, China is cooperating with littoral states in building the China-Pakistan Economic Corridor and Bangladesh-China-India-Myanmar-Economic Corridor. These mega-projects, with heavy investment from China will fundamentally change the political and economic landscape of the Indian Ocean and benefit all countries in the region. They will also help to mitigate security concerns in the Maritime Silk Road, ranging from territorial disputes in the South China Sea to transnational threats such as piracy, armed robbery and terrorism.

In the 15th century, Admiral Zheng He went on his seven voyages to the West Pacific and the Indian Ocean with the largest naval fleet in the world. These voyages were not aimed for conquest of peoples or of territories. Instead, they were visits to swap Chinese silk and porcelain for exotic souvenirs such as zebras and giraffes. Zheng He did not venture to establish bases either. In doing so, he left a legacy that is intangible but invaluable for China today. It is an image of China that the Chinese people would like to project again in the 21st century as they did 600 years ago: a country standing tall in the center of world, strong yet benign, and friendly to all.[12] Cambodian experts have voiced their support for China's initiative of a "maritime silk road" in cooperation with the 10-country Association of Southeast Asian Nations (ASEAN), saying this ambitious plan would bring better connections and closer maritime cooperation if it became a reality. "This initiative is very good since China and ASEAN are neighbours and have good cooperation in all fields," Mao Thora, secretary of state at the Ministry of Commerce, told Xinhua. "This expresses China's strong commitment to build a region of peace, development and prosperity" and further emphasised that "If such project comes to a reality, it will further enhance the relations and cooperation between China and ASEAN in economy, trade, investment, tourism and so on". It will be easier to exchange goods between China and ASEAN and among ASEAN countries themselves".[13]

India's new interest in the Pacific has often been conflated with China's rising profile in the Indian Ocean. But India has no desire to neither confront China in the Western Pacific nor prevent it from establishing a presence in the Indian Ocean. At the beginning of the 21st century, India and China have the unique opportunity and resources to improve mutual relations as well as to promote peace in their neighbourhood as well as at the global level. Every Chinese leader, right from Chairman Mao to President Xi Jinping has acknowledged India to be a great civilisation and a great power, and a complementary economic force parallel to China's own growth. China has much to learn and benefit from Indian culture and philosophy: Indians' entrepreneurial spirit, the tradition of public debate and argument, and the fondness for logic and mathematical thinking are but a few of the attractive qualities that India has to offer. For lasting peace, both cultures and economies must continue to grow and prosper.

India-Australia and China Maritime Security Cooperation

There have been a number of 'false starts' in the Australian-Indian security cooperation efforts in the past. In 1998, Australia immediately suspended its defence cooperation with India after the nuclear weapons test. When the fledgling Quadrilateral Initiative in 2007 that envisaged the joint participation of Australia, India, Japan, Singapore and the US in a maritime exercise drew a strong hostile Chinese reaction, the newly elected Centre-left Labour government publically withdrew in 2008 in a move that annoyed many Indian officials who saw it as Australia bowing to Chinese pressure. Since their nadir in 2008-2009, Australian-Indian relations and defense ties have markedly improved. Indeed, defense and security engagement between the two countries have steadily increased to culminate in the signing of the New Framework for Security Cooperation (NFSC) on 18 November 2014 during Prime Minister Narendra Modi's bilateral visit to Australia. The NFSC combined and expanded several previous agreements and committed both countries to hold annual high-level summits, cooperate closely on counter-terrorism and international crime, hold regular bilateral maritime exercises and focus on the early operationalisation of the Civil Nuclear Energy Cooperation Agreement (CNECA) to assist India's quest for energy security. Most of the statements in the lead up to and after the signing of the NFSC have shown that both sides intend to make maritime security the key pillar in the defence cooperation.

Is there a China factor in Australian-India Relations? Providing an additional, if publicly unspoken, convergence in both countries' serious concerns about China's increasing presence in the Indian Ocean, which have been growing more massively and becoming bolder over the years while it is rumoured that of particular concern has been the emergence of Chinese submarines evidently practising long-range deployments in the Indian Ocean, with the latest incident occurring when a Chinese nuclear submarine surfaced just off Sri Lanka in September 2014. While China has legitimate interests in safeguarding its commercial routes that pass through the Indian Ocean, India is inherently concerned about the Chinese military potentially surrounding it by land and by sea as well as eroding its dominance in what it has long considered its backyard. Australia likewise has been concerned by China's new posturing in the South China Sea and is particularly interested in ensuring that no nation is able to establish a maritime advantage in its own neighbouring waters.

Heading into the future, Australian-Indian and Chinese defence ties are likely to deepen significantly, especially in the field of maritime security. The first formal bilateral maritime exercise between the three countries is scheduled to be conducted in the current year (2015), although the exact date is yet to be notified. While piracy in the Indian Ocean may be on the decline, nevertheless, there is plenty of room for bilateral cooperation over other illegal maritime activities such as smuggling of people and narcotics in the region. Australia also has several state-of-the-art defence training facilities such as the Submarine Escape Facility in Western Australia that would be of definite interest to the Indian defence forces, and 2015 could see arrangements for joint training courses to be run in the near future.

In short, Australia, China and India can enhance cooperation particularly in areas of maritime development and infrastructure, with undercurrents indicating that all three countries can simultaneously become maritime powers, without conflict of interest, as Chinese President Xi Jinping's initiative of the 21st Century Maritime Silk Road confirms the aspirations of each state to a large extent. Therefore, the need of the hour is to create a positive and constructive environment in which the development strategies of the three states could interact with each other, push forward cooperation in the fields of infrastructure building, agriculture, finance and nuclear power, and fully utilise related mechanisms to advance maritime and even aerospace cooperation.

(This Paper is a revised version of my address at Tirupati University, India, October 2014)

NOTES

1. According to *Asia Times*, recent developments signalling the United States' continued commitment to maintaining a presence in the Asia-Pacific have been seen as marking a turning point in the history of the region. The reasons for this are two-fold. First, references by US Secretary of State Hillary Clinton to an "Indo-Pacific" presence for the US are believed to reflect the recognition of India's importance in the region. Second, US President Barack Obama's announcement that American Marines would be stationed in Western Australia is perceived as a definite challenge to China's aggressive posturing on issues, maritime disputes in particular. On both these counts however, the optimism generated in some quarters requires tempering. While sketching the contours of an "Indo-Pacific" presence for the US, Clinton had re-emphasised Obama's assertion that the "relationship between India and America will be one of the defining partnerships of the 21st century, rooted in common values and interests". <http://www.atimes.com/atimes/South_Asia/ML08Df03.html> accessed 12 September 2015.
2. Kurt M. Campbell cited in Mark E. Manyin, Stephen Daggett, Ben Dolven, Susan V. Lawrence, Michael F. Martin, Ronald O'Rourke and Bruce Vaughan, "Pivot to the Pacific? The Obama Administration's 'Rebalancing' Towards Asia", *Congressional Research Service*, 28 March 2012. <https://www.fas.org/sgp/crs/natsec/R42448.pdf> accessed 13 September 2015.
3. For details see <http://www.acnnewswire.com/press-release/english/13001/imdex-asia:-government-and-military-leaders-to-discuss-new-naval-security-challenges-at-international-maritime-security-conference-2013> accessed 13 September 2015.
4. "PLA Navy fleet enters W Pacific for training", *Xinhuanet*, 27 May 2013. <http://news.xinhuanet.com/english/china/2013-05/27/c_132411936.htm> accessed 13 September 2015. There is also a report that a Chinese blue-water-training-fleet sailed to the Indian Ocean to conduct combat exercises. The South China Sea fleet of the People's Liberation Army of China (PLA) sent three warships: Changbai Mountain, Haikou and Wuhan to cross the Sunda Strait. The fleet sailed through narrow waterways, changed formation, carried out coordinated battles and reconnaissance against suspected subjects on their way. The South China Sea fleet headed south-beginning January 20 and has cruised Xisha and Nansha islands and their surrounding waters. In the exercise, the submarines broke through blocked areas; the marines conducted beach-landing operations; and the PLA air force, submarines and the garrison forces in Xisha and Nansha also conducted coordinated battles with the

fleet. <http://newscontent.cctv.com/NewJsp/news.jsp?fileId=226873\> accessed 12 September 2015.

5. Chas W. Freeman Jr, "Indo-Pacific Dynamics in Trans-Pacific Perspective". <http://chasfreeman.net/indo-pacific-dynamics-in-trans-pacific-perspective/> accessed 6 September 2015.
6. C. Raja Mohan, "India and Australia: Maritime Partners in the Indo-Pacific", *Asialink*, 2 November 2011. <http://asialink.unimelb.edu.au/asialink_diplomacy/commentary-and-research/the_asialink_essays/past/india_and_australia_maritime_partners_in_the_indo-pacific> accessed 6 September 2015.
7. China and US militaries held an annual meeting under the Sino-US military Maritime Consultative Agreement from 27 to 28 September in the northern port city of Qingdao.

   The two militaries agreed to enhance contacts and communication in order to increase mutual trust and cooperation with a respectful, equal, active and constructive attitude. They exchanged views on maritime security situations of the two countries since 2010 and discussed detailed measures to solve problems in this area. The two sides agreed to strengthen military-to-military cooperation in anti-piracy and humanitarian aid as well as disaster relief efforts
8. C. Raja Mohan, "India and Australia: Maritime Partners in the Indo-Pacific", *The Australian*, 2 November 2011; also see Mohan, n. 6.
9. "China, US militaries hold annual maritime security meeting", *Xinhua*, 29 September 2012. <http://news.xinhuanet.com/english/china/2012-09/28/c_131880287.htm> accessed 6 September 2015.
10. Ross Colvin, "In China's shadow, ASEAN leaders look to India for maritime security", *Reuters*, 20 December 2012. <http://mobile.reuters.com/article/idUSBRE8BJ0Q220121220?irpc=932> accessed 13 September 2015.
11. Ibid.
12. During his visits to Indonesia and Malaysia, the Chinese delegation, headed by President Xi Jinping, pledged to foster comprehensive strategic partnerships with both countries and inked a wide array of important agreements with the two ASEAN member states. Apart from agreeing on five-year trade plans with Jakarta and Kuala Lumpur, the high-level visits saw Chinese corporate players signing several memoranda of understanding (MOUs) with local companies for collaborations in the areas such as industrial parks, currency swaps, aviation, and tourism.

    What surprised observers, however, was his proposal of re-building of the so-called 'new maritime silk road' in Southeast Asia. In his speech delivered in the Indonesian parliament on 3 October, the Chinese president made no reservation in echoing the Chinese plan to turn the centuries-old maritime passageways (the Straits of Malacca and the South China Sea) into one that would spur maritime connectivity in the 21st century. In order to support his proposal, Xi reiterated the Chinese government's readiness to fund ASEAN's maritime-related projects through its new state investment arm, the China-ASEAN Maritime Cooperation Fund. While such an announcement was not new, it seemed China is now taking a much more proactive approach in this matter.

13. Wang Qibing and Nguon Sovan, "Interview: China's 'maritime silk road' initiative vital to further enhance ties with ASEAN: Cambodian experts", *English.news.cn*, 18 January 2014. <http://news.xinhuanet.com/english/indepth/2014-01/18/c_133055311.htm> accessed 6 September 2015.

10

India's Role in the Emerging Indo-Pacific Security Architecture

Arvind Kumar

ABSTRACT

The contemporary debates on the Indo-Pacific region have reflected a number of varying perspectives especially in the geopolitical context about the relevance and growing significance in the emerging international security environment. The discourse on the Indo-Pacific region as a geopolitical region is gaining momentum. Undoubtedly, the way things are unfolding in the current milieu, it seems that the Indo-Pacific region will be attracting more attention from a number of major powers including India in the foreseeable future. The Indo-Pacific region as a whole reflects changes in economics, strategic behavior and diplomatic maneuvering among major powers especially when the nations compete with each other to create their sphere of influence and then exploit the potential of the region as a whole. The creation of a single strategic system in the Indo-Pacific region by combining the accelerated economic and security connections becomes the fulcrum between the Western Pacific and the Indian Ocean. Will the concept of 'Indo-Pacific' region help in integrating and uniting the major powers into one single strategic system remains a major question for the debates and the discussions.

Introduction

The emergence of India as a responsible player in the international system has bestowed certain responsibilities especially in the context of dealing with world affairs. However, whether India will assume the responsibilities for leading the world affairs in the foreseeable future remains a major part of the discourse among the members of the strategic and academic community. There are some remarkable signs coming up, which mainly symbolise India's strategic aspirations in the emerging geopolitical environment. India has been exploring ways and means to work with all the multiple poles of power in the international system. In this context, India has reflected its ambitions to be the key player in the probable Indo-Pacific security architecture. Whether India will play an important role in the security architecture of the Indo-Pacific region calls for an objective assessment.

The contemporary debates on the Indo-Pacific region have reflected a number of varying perspectives especially in the geopolitical context about the relevance and growing significance in the emerging international security environment. Whether the Indo-Pacific region can be considered as a geopolitical region has formed a major part of discourse among the members of the academic and strategic community. The geopolitical regions are largely connected by geographical contiguity and constant political, cultural and military interactions among the countries. Hence, the discourse on the Indo-Pacific region as a geopolitical region becomes important and significant. Undoubtedly, the way things are unfolding in the current milieu, it seems that the Indo-Pacific region will be attracting more attention from a number of major powers including India in the foreseeable future.

Major Powers' Perspectives on the Indo-Pacific Region

It must be pointed out here that the Asian geopolitics largely is now characterised by the ongoing debates on the term 'Indo-Pacific'. So far, Asia-Pacific remained the standard geopolitical term to connote a region and now the word 'Indo-Pacific' is being inducted into the *lexicon* of the entire major powers' strategy document. The usage of the term 'Indo-Pacific' in the strategy document encompasses nothing but a combination of Asia-Pacific and the Indian Ocean Rim countries. There is a serious move by the United States in particular to re-balance its Asia strategy and create its sphere of influence across the Indo-Pacific region. Geographically, Indo-Pacific region connects two of the major oceans in the world—Pacific and Indian. The Indian Ocean dimensions of America's Pacific rebalance is critical to its pivot strategy. The US, however, has also attempted to use the word 'Indo-Asia-Pacific'.

The other major power, Japan wants to be the promoter of rules across two inseparable oceans. It identified the Indo-Pacific region as the confluence of two seas. Indonesia, the power in Southeast Asia has called for a region-wide treaty to safeguard an Indo-Pacific engine of global growth. The other power, Australia has gone to the extent of formalising the concept of Indo-Pacific in its official documents. India has called for cooperation from East Asian counterparts in making the Indo-Pacific region stable, secure and prosperous. Singapore seems to be comfortable with the term Asia-Pacific despite the fact that its interests span the two oceans.

China, so far, has not been able to define the concept of 'Indo-Pacific' formally. But at the same time, the use of the term 'Indo-Pacific' is being seen in most of the Chinese scholarly writings and analysis. To a greater extent, such usage of the term will pave the way for China to develop Indian Ocean strategy. China has been completely preoccupied with the disputes in its eastern maritime edge. Such preoccupations have led China to enhance its presence and reflect its strategic ambitions in the Indo-Pacific region. China's overwhelming capabilities and its larger aspirations to become unipolar in Asia in a multipolar world have created competition among major powers. China's signalling to the rest of the world about its aggressiveness in military posturing has created serious debates on the challenges to the task of building Indo-Pacific security architecture.

The Indo-Pacific region as a whole reflects changes in economic, strategic behavior and diplomatic maneuvering among major powers especially when the nations compete with each other to create their sphere of influence and then exploit the potential of the region as a whole. The creation of a single strategic system in the Indo-Pacific region by combining the accelerated economic and security connections becomes the fulcrum between the Western Pacific and the Indian Ocean. Will the concept of the 'Indo-Pacific' region help in integrating and uniting the major powers into one single strategic system remains a major question for the debates and the discussions.

Indo-Pacific as a Region of Competition and Greater Power Rivalry

There seems to be a dominant view that the Indo-Pacific region is going to be marred by lot of differences, competition and will become a region for greater power rivalry. Undoubtedly, conflict seems less likely in the current era of interdependence among major powers. The roots of the new Indo-Pacific undisputedly seem to be economic but the larger consequences are going to be deeply strategic. It is, therefore, very important to understand the complexities involved in the region. The great power rivalry in the region will have negative consequences for peace and stability and also question the major issues involved in the Indo-Pacific security architecture. It must be emphasised here that this Indo-Pacific region is not going to be an ordinary geographic region and hence the management of the complexities will be more challenging for the major powers.

China seems to be emerging as the quintessential Indo-Pacific power. It is only because of its evolving economic and strategic capabilities. Japan also would like to be an active part of the Indo-Pacific great game. It has many challenges mainly emanating from China in the region. The strategic differences do exist in China-Japan relations. These differences obviously have seen a downslide in the relationship all these years. The greater power projection and force posturing by China has certainly created fears in the minds of Japan. Hence, it may be argued that a meaningful and effective strategic system in the Indo-Pacific region will be too difficult to evolve. A number of contradictions exist in all the possible permutations and combinations.

The emerging trends in the interactions of entire great and rising powers in the Indo-Pacific region are not coherent. The critical needs of the major powers in the Indo-Pacific including India vary and generate competition. The competition among major powers in the region will be mostly centred on tapping the natural and energy resources. In an age of globalisation, Indian Ocean in particular contain massive half of the world's container traffic. Indian Ocean Rim land from West Asia to Pacific accounts for 70 per cent of the traffic of petroleum products for the entire world.

The US has been playing a critical strategic role and presence of the United States in the Indo-Pacific region is mostly seen as a balancer. It has also been attempting to build a number of bilateral and trilateral understandings so that China's overwhelming presence is not considered as pre-eminent. China's growing wealth, its strategic interests, reach and military capability is being considered as a threat by the other major powers in the Indo-Pacific region. India, on the other hand, is being perceived as a part of the solution and not the part of the problem. India's emergence and acceptance as a rising power in the Indo-Pacific region has been viewed by other major powers including the United States as a responsible power in the international system.

India's likely future role in the Indo-Pacific region can only be analysed in the context of understanding the convergence of security dynamics and geopolitical compulsions of both the Asia-Pacific and the Indian Ocean regions. It is being acknowledged by the members of policy and strategic community that India is emerging as a significant power in the geopolitical dynamics of Southeast Asia. India has also been actively engaging itself in the Northeast Asia and the South Pacific despite other major powers presence in these regions. In the current situation, with the Narendra Modi (Bharatiya Janata Party) government in power in India, it is being anticipated that India has a much greater role to play in South Asia. There will obviously be an opportunity for India if it engages with its neighbourhood with a consistent and proactive policy. The signs of such changes in India's policies are becoming visible. The probable trajectory of India-Japan relations with the Modi government in India is going to be at an all time high. India will certainly get its own strategic space in the probable Indo-Pacific security architecture.

There is no doubt in saying that the major powers in the Indo-Pacific region should consider collective security arrangements not only to address the common threats like piracy and terrorism but also provide a platform and common guidelines to address the inter-state conflicts. India, in particular, has argued and proposed the idea of a 'Concert of Powers' spanning the Pacific and Indian Ocean. Such concert of powers will help in building the inroads to engage China effectively as a responsible player of a new strategic system. It might reduce the risk of unintended conflicts in the Indo-

Pacific region. India will certainly be an active member of such a concert of Asian powers. There will, however, be always a debate whether India's greater economic influence in the Indo-Pacific region would automatically translate and culminate into the larger strategic role in the foreseeable future. The idea of a concert of powers needs to envisage the challenges accruing from the strategic dimension. There will always be significant limitations on strategic interaction among major powers of this concert.

India's Emerging Role in the Indo-Pacific Security Architecture

Does India have strategic options in the Indo-Pacific remains a question, mainly in the context of analysing the challenges to the Indo-Pacific security architecture? Over the years, the aspirations and ambitions of India have grown. It wants to be acknowledged as a predominant power in South Asia and a power in the making in the whole of Asia. It also wants to be a leading power in the Indian Ocean Rim. Ultimately, it will have to assume the responsibilities and play a positive role in the world affairs. India's strategic orientations need to be shifted from the Indian Ocean region to the Pacific Rim if it has a desire to lead the world affairs.

India's strategic thinking about the Indo-Pacific seems to have been emerging. India's economy combined with its growing military and strategic capabilities has helped it to elevate its status and transform its larger behavioural pattern in the international system. India's transformation in its overall approach and intentions got reflected in evolving a multipolar regional system and also balancing against China to deter emergence of uni-polarity in Asia.

Until recently or through much of the Cold War, Nehruvian principles or thinking formed the major intellectual foundation of much of the strategic analysis from India's point of view. The core of this principle was the concept of non-alignment.[1] The concept of nonalignment had allowed India to cooperate with both the poles of power in the international system during the Cold War era. However, Nehruvian strategic doctrine inhibited India from playing a significant role in the Asia-Pacific till the early part of the 1990s. India mostly considered all the major powers of the Asia-

Pacific such as Japan, South Korea, Taiwan and Australia as the most preferred allies of the United States and hence India had not reflected much interest except Japan as a potential source of capital and technology.

The end of the Cold War saw too many changes in the global geopolitical calculus where each of the major powers were busy in enhancing and asserting their identities mainly through the intensification of the world system to be the multipolar one. India took a more pragmatic stand and moved from its so called rigid Nehruvian framework. India's vision was to emerge as one of the important poles of power in a multipolar system and chart out an independent plan of action without recourse to any alliance. There were a number of debates on different permutation and combination including the concept of Strategic Triangle among India, China and Russia. However, the realistic assessments suggested keeping India away from such strategic triangle. The attempt to create a countervailing bloc against the United States had very little to offer in geopolitical terms.

The later part of 1990s saw India becoming overtly nuclear and to a larger extent this action of India became a central point in its discourses on strategic and the probable changes in the geopolitical thinking. There is no doubt in saying that India's ambiguous nuclear policies in the past had thrown open a number of challenges in improving its relationship with the major powers including the United States. India's successful transition to a nuclear weapon country also elevated its status and effectively ended the long standing dominance of idealism in its foreign policy discourse. India was no more guided by the larger thinking which prevailed all these decades greatly influenced by the Nehruvian ideology. India had culminated into 'Realist' and 'Pragmatic' power because of the geopolitical changes and compulsions. The foreign policy discourse largely centredaround the larger role India might play in the international system. India had gained a capability through which it could negotiate with any major power from a position of strength.

If one analyses India's likely future moves in the Indo-Pacific region in the emerging geopolitical milieu, one can say with firm conviction that despite India's strategic ambitions, it will have several challenges. So far, India has not shown much assertion in its policies. The strategic history and behaviour of India suggests that there seems to be a long standing gap between rhetoric and strategic action. There is a lack of consistency between India's rhetoric and strategic actions. India has evolved a culture of "strategic restraint".[2]

India needs to be proactive in all its diplomatic maneuvering especially when it aspires to enlarge its interests and broaden the scope of engagement with the other major powers. Can India afford to build an informal coalition with the United States and Japan to counterbalance China remains a question for debate and discussion. India may propose a series of bilateral, trilateral and multilateral security dialogues and may become a leading coordinator of such dialogues. Such important dialogues may help build up a consensus for a collective security arrangement on the basis of the concert of powers concept. It would also help in the economic integration of India with the rest of other powers in the Indo-Pacific region. It will, at least, limit the role of China. Such dialogues will also see how a multipolar regional order is attained. The larger interest for India would be to expand its strategic interests in the Indo-Pacific region and get its own strategic space. The strategic autonomy will remain an important element in India's decision making process.

India's potential role in the Indo-Pacific security architecture is emerging as an important theme in Indian strategic thinking. Will India be dictated by neorealist paradigm and evolve a balancing coalition against China in the foreseeable future remains a question to debate? However, the current posturing suggests that India would be inclined more towards creating a multi-polar regional balance. It is, however, generally believed that balancing China has been very much in the DNA of India's geopolitics since the early 1950s.[3]

India's strategic thinking has traditionally been led by 'continental' outlook. However, India has also been seen developing its maritime power ambitions. The seafaring dimension in India's strategic orientations has certainly been changing its overall outlook. India's national interest had been made coterminous with maritime security.[4] It is generally believed among maritime strategists that the Indian Ocean must remain 'truly

Indian' and it was advocated much before India became independent that it shall establish forward naval bases in Singapore, Mauritius, Yemen and Sri Lanka through the creation of a steel ring.[5] It must be pointed out here that India's area of maritime interest is primarily focused on the northern Indian Ocean where it has developed strong security relationships with smaller states located near to or at choke points of entry into the Ocean.[6] In the year 2001, The Ministry of Defence Annual Report described what it called India's security environment as extending from the Persian Gulf in the west to the Straits of Malacca in the east.[7] In the last one decade or so, the debates among the key policy community have ranged from India's 'sphere of influence' to India's strategic footprints in the Indo-Pacific region.[8]

There is also a dominant view that control of the Indian Ocean including the chokepoints into the Pacific Ocean could give India an ability to dominate the whole of maritime Asia. In this context, the understanding on the Indo-Pacific region, which emphasises the sea as the main source for commerce and competition and hence India would like to see its overall interests are protected. The idea that the entire Indo-Pacific is becoming one inter-connected region will have its own limits. The strategic dimension in the relationship among major powers in the Indo-Pacific region will impede the idea of inter-connectedness to grow and flourish. The inherent tensions among the major powers whether it is between China and Southeast Asian states on the South China Sea or between China and Japan on the East China Sea will be the stumbling blocks for an effective single strategic system and a robust Indo-Pacific security architecture. India needs to play a balanced and measured role in the Indo-Pacific by prioritising its interests and maintaining a balanced relationship with the other major powers of the region. The major powers would have to share a set of strategic perceptions that have rapidly converged since the end of the Cold War. There will obviously be an effort made on the part of India to collaborate and cooperate on a number of pertinent important themes impacting the Indo-Pacific security architecture.[9]

The scale of commerce and volume of trade among the nations will certainly be given the priority by the major powers but certainly not at the cost of the strategic dimensions of the relationships. No major power in the Indo-Pacific region can afford to initiate measures, which would be inimical to their overall interest. The responsibility of entire group of major powers including India would be to build a conducive environment in the interest of the Indo-Pacific region. The emerging Indo-Pacific order will be based on mainly finding ways to manage the intersecting and expanding interests of a number of countries. The region will be mostly dictated by a combination of both realist and neo-liberalist paradigm of international relations theory. India will have to play a much bigger role in the foreseeable future.

Conclusion

India would need to adapt to the emerging geopolitical imperatives. The centre of gravity has shifted to the Indo-Pacific region, where the competitions and contests have become visible among major powers. The power projections and force posturing in the region by major powers have thrown open complex challenges. The Indo-Pacific security architecture calls for India to play an important and significant role. India's strategic outlook is in transition from 'continentality' to 'maritimity'. India has been very slowly and gradually driving its maritime aspirations to become the predominant naval power in the Indian Ocean. India wants to assume the responsibilities to lead the maritime domain. It has reflected its ambitions to take a direct security role in the Malacca Strait, which has been primarily identified as an area of interest by the Indian Navy. The significance and importance of the Malacca Strait is well known. It has been the primary chokepoint for sea traffic between the Indian and Pacific Oceans and Indian control over the Strait will send a symbolic message to the rest of the world with regard to its emerging power status. India, in turn, will also limit the aggressive designs of China.

India will continue to emphasise naval diplomacy and regional cooperation in which it can play a leading role in the Indo-Pacific region, Over the years, India has exploited its strengths in maritime policing and anti-terrorism, including the interdiction of supply routes. The geopolitical impetus to India mostly comes from the asymmetric sources of threats in the maritime domain. India has a proven track record of not intimidating or becoming aggressive and hence working with India has always been easier and a complete win-win situation. There will be a number of areas of concern including the South China Sea where India's maritime security ambitions would be difficult to realise. The expansion of China's interests in the Indo-Pacific region will also augment India's overall ambitions in the region. The primary responsibility of India in the Indo-Pacific security architecture will be to find ways and means to evolve a working relationship with all the major poles of power in the Indo-Pacific region.

NOTES

1. For a detailed and in-depth understanding on Nehruvian Strategic Thinking, see M.S. Rajan, *Studies on Nonalignment and the Nonaligned Movement: Theory and Practice* (New Delhi: ABC Publishing House, 1986); also see, K. Subrahmanyam, *Indian Security Perspectives* (New Delhi: ABC Publishing House, 1982).
2. Stephen Cohen has argued in detail about India's behavioural patterns and how it has evolved a culture of strategic restraint. See Stephen Cohen and Sunil Dasgupta, *Arming without Aiming: India's Military Modernisation* (Washington, DC: Brookings Institution Press, 2010).
3. C. Raja Mohan, "The Evolution of Sino-Indian Relations: Implications for the United States", in Alyssa Ayres and C. Raja Mohan, eds., *Power Realignments in Asia: China, India and the United States* (New Delhi: Sage Publications, 2009), p. 288.
4. David Scott, "India's Grand Strategy for the Indian Ocean: Mahanian Visions", *Asia-Pacific Review*, Vol. 13, No. 2, 2006, p. 109.
5. Ibid., p. 99.
6. In the year 2000, the then Defence Minister of India, George Fernandes spoke of an extended India's area of interest from the north of the Arabian Sea to the South China Sea. See the media report, Atul Aneja, "India, Vietnam Partners in Safeguarding Sea Lanes", *The Hindu* (Chennai), 15 April 2000.
7. *Annual Report 2000-2001* (New Delhi: Ministry of Defence, Government of India, 2001).
8. India's former Foreign Minister Jaswant Singh called India's sphere of influence and the former Prime Minister Manmohan Singh used the term India's strategic footprint. There is a dominant view emerging which suggests that the Indian Navy now sees itself as destined to be the predominant maritime security provider in a region encompassing from the Red Sea to Singapore and having a significant security role in areas beyond the South China Sea.
9. For details see, Darvesh Gopal and Dalbir Ahlawat, "Australia-India Strategic Relations: From Estrangement to Engagement", *India Quarterly* (New Delhi), Vol. 7, No. 3, pp. 206-220.

11

Indonesia-Australia Relations and the Indo-Pacific Developments

Munmun Majumdar

ABSTRACT

Australia and Indonesia are a diverse pair of neighbours as is possible to find. Tracing the path of Australia-Indonesia relations over the years shows a define pattern that oscillates over peaks and troughs. Developments in the region have influenced relations between the two in a divisive way. Both countries want to preserve the sovereignty of national borders. They acknowledge that cooperation between them is essential for securing their mutual interests. Consequently, there's scope for a strong and genuine partnership unencumbered by fundamental conflicts of interest, despite the occasional friction generated by non-state actors, cross-border activities, economic competition, media criticism, terrorism, etc. The key challenge would be to identify the common interests and prioritise those areas of common interest so that a long-term partnership can be established.

Introduction

Indonesia and Australia share a few similarities and are a diverse pair of neighbours as is possible to find. Both have different standards of wealth, education, languages, customs and culture. The judicial systems of the two countries are different and often not understood by each other. At 244.5 million people, Indonesia is more populous than Australia. Indonesia has the status of being the *primus inter pares* in ASEAN and is on the rise to becoming a major power.[1] In short, Australia and Indonesia have little in common. This assessment embodies the complexities and difficulties faced by the two countries in maintaining and nurturing their bilateral relationships. Should differences between them then prevent from becoming good neighbours? The answer is an obvious no. After all geography matters and regional security is a team sport. The separation of Australia's mainland from Indonesia by only 240 kilometres of ocean means that the two countries share strong security interdependencies. The National Security Strategy and Asian Century White Paper[2] recognise that a positive relationship with Indonesia is an important facet of Australia's security. The 2006 Lombok Treaty (ratified in 2008) commits the two countries to support each other's unity and territorial integrity and refrain from the use of force. This was reinforced by the September 2012 Defence Cooperation Arrangement. The relationship was elevated to a strategic partnership in March 2010.[3] Apart from geographical proximity, historically Indonesia and Australia also shared links dating back to the 16th and 17th centuries.[4]

Unlike Indonesia, Australia has seen a frequently rotating political leadership. For example, Indonesia was ruled by Suharto from 1965-1998 while in the same period a string of Australian leaders succeeded to the prime ministerial office. The rotating political leadership has had a bearing on the shape of bilateral relations between the two.[5] Indonesia perceived its relations to be warm when the Australian Labour Party (ALP) governments have been in power in Australia (such as the Labour governments of Gough Whitlam, Bob Hawke and Paul Keating). Indonesian leaders and also the Indonesian media have consistently held perceptions that the ALP leaders genuinely wanted to engage Indonesia (and Asia more generally).[6] Therefore, it is not out of place for the Indonesian government to face particular challenges in their attempts to engage with Australia say, under Prime Minister John Howard during his 1996–2007 terms. The difficulties got amplified over the way in which John Howard conducted his policy on the East Timor issue. At the same time, there was an opinion in certain quarters that as simultaneously the bilateral relationship has matured,[7] with both sides showing willingness to learn and to be open with each other so that a strong foundation can be built regardless of which political party forms the government in Australia.[8]

Very often domestic politics have trumped bilateral

relationships. History explains why Australia has very often sided with the major Western naval powers of the day and post-colonial Indonesia on the other hand tried to refrain from taking sides and instead drew advantage from seeking "million friends and zero enemies". While Indonesia continues to place emphasis on *bebasdanaktif* (independent and active foreign policy), the geographic imperatives tie Indonesia's primary focus to the region while seeking a global role simultaneously.

A stable Indonesia is important for Australia's strategic interests. The destination of Australia's exports to Asia requires a passage through Indonesia's air and sea space. These realities necessitate that they cooperate in terms of defence and military and seek to forge a balanced relationship that would serve to strengthen bilateral relations in the long run. Ushering of democracy in Indonesia is a welcome step as it gives an opportunity to both countries to pursue their political and strategic interests on an equal footing.[9]

Overview of Australia-Indonesia Relations

Tracing the path of Australia-Indonesia relations over the years shows a defined pattern that oscillates between crests and dips. As 2015 brings the 70th anniversary of Australia's first attempt to recognise Indonesia, it is an appropriate moment to revisit the relations between the two. Canberra was the first foreign capital to send a mission to Jakarta. After the Sukarno-Hatta's Proclamation of Independence on 17 August 1945, a small Australian mission headed by William Macmahon Ball as designate High Commissioner, landed at Kemayoran airport with the intention of having Australia recognise the Republic of Indonesia. However, the High Commissioner's mission was cut short when the Commander-in-Chief of the Allied Forces, General Philip Christison, refused to acknowledge Ball's credentials and expelled him from Batavia (Djakarta).[10] This is sufficient to infer that the birth of Australia-Indonesia relations was characterised by solidarity. During Indonesia's independence struggle, Australian unions and others played a key role in preventing the Dutch from regaining control of the country. The Labour government, under Ben Chifley, took crucial and ultimately successful diplomatic steps to bring about Indonesia's independence. Indonesia chose Australia by virtue of Macmahon Ball's good relationship with the Republic's first Prime Minister, Sutan Syahrir, as one of three members of the Good Offices Committee that ultimately led to full sovereignty in 1950. The relationship continued with the first official visit of Prime Minister Robert Menzies to Indonesia which was followed by introduction of the Colombo Plan, a scheme that brought young Indonesian (and other Asian) students to study in Australian universities.[11] While that was a clear peak in the bilateral relationship, there have been low points too. In the 1960s, Australia supported Britain and the newly federated Malaysia in their conflict with Indonesia. Australia's actions were conditioned by the perception that Sukarno's provocative stance was threatening for Australia's national interests and complicating its alliance relationships. As a result, Australia came into direct confrontation with Sukarno's Indonesia during the *Konfrontasi*. Yet what paid off was that Australia demonstrated a skilful policy. It did not withdraw its ambassador, kept its aid and trade links open even while it was engaged in a military combat thereby sending a clear signal about the benefits of a long-term relationship.

Since Australia's strategic approach to Indonesia has been fundamentally shaped by its ANZUS alliance with the US there have been occasions where policy differences have emerged over Indonesia such as the one in West Irian when Australia initially rejected Indonesia's claims to the territory and instead supported continued Dutch rule. Later Australia extricated itself from its support of the Dutch control of West Irian when it realised that both the UK and US were keen to give greater weight to Jakarta's opinion rather than go along with Australia and Holland. Without the support of the US and UK, Australian strategic appreciation of the territory changed from the perception that it was vital to Australia's defence to a recognition that the stability and orientation of Indonesia was more important. Prime Minister Menzies acknowledged as much in justifying Canberra's volte face on Indonesia's sovereignty over West Irian when he conceded that the hard facts of international life compel Australia to act in concert with its alliance partners.

Relations resumed an upward trajectory till 1975, when

Indonesia's invasion of Portuguese East Timor and the killing of Australian journalists (the Balibo Five) strained relations. Subsequently bilateral relations began to improve till a series of *Sydney Morning Herald* articles revealed corruption cases against Suharto and his family, caused a major setback. Articles appearing in the *Sydney Morning Herald* in 1986 accusing the First Family of corruption that evoked an angry response from the then president General Suharto. A Garuda jumbo jet full of Australian tourists on its way from Sydney to Bali was ordered by Indonesian authorities to return to Sydney.[12] Ties were effectively severed, with no ministerial visits either way for over two years. Military exchanges, a central plank of the relationship, were suspended overnight, although civilian intelligence exchanges continued unimpaired.

Although the 1990s started badly, with the massacre of civilians in a Dili cemetery by the Indonesian military, the Paul Keating years saw relations raised to new heights only to plummet again in 1999 when John Howard deployed the Australian peacekeepers (Interfet) in East Timor. This was once again another critical moment in the relationship.

Following East Timor, rather than repairing ties with Indonesia (as the East Timorese themselves seem to have done), Prime Minister Howard went on to drive the relationship into deep freeze. Indonesian President Megawati Sukarnoputri refused to meet Howard or even return his phone calls. In 2004, well into Howard's time as prime minister, Australian National University expert on regional affairs Greg Fealy, stated, "the Howard government remains one of the most unpopular foreign governments in Indonesia".[13]

When Labour returned to power in 2007, there was an opportunity to recalibrate the relationship. Despite challenges in relation to live cattle exports, the relationship remained strong which allowed improved cooperation on asylum-seeker issues too. The fresh start was embraced whole heartedly and from 2007 to 2012 there were around 130 high-level government officials' visits between Australia and Indonesia. Australia elevated Indonesia to a top position in its strategic relationship and included it in the list of countries that were consulted prior to preparing defence policy statements. Jakarta also reciprocated enthusiastically: a recent example is its April 2013 initiation of the Australia–Indonesia High Level Committee.[14]

At the strategic level, there was the Indonesia-Australia Defence Strategic Dialogue, as well as annual leaders' meetings (since 2010), the Australia–Indonesia Dialogue (since 2011), the '2+2' foreign and defence ministers' meeting (since 2012), and the inaugural meeting between the two countries' defence force chiefs in 2013. Again Indonesian and Australian navies together with Singapore, Thailand, New Zealand and the US, concluded a third coordinated patrol of the joint maritime borders. Indonesia participated for the first time in the multi-nation Exercise Black,[15] the first bilateral peacekeeping exercise,[16] the strengthening of search and rescue coordination and continued officer and English language training through the Bilateral Defence Cooperation Program.

Following the devastating 2004 tsunami, Australia's military worked alongside Indonesia's military in the emergency relief effort and the Australian government responded through the provision of more than $1 billion in aid. More recently, Australia donated four C-130H Hercules transport aircraft to Indonesia and, in April 2013, Australia agreed to sell a further five of the aircrafts on a discount basis.[17]

The 2013 Coalition victory in Australia clearly prioritised the Anglo sphere at the expense of Asia despite the rhetoric that Australia would be more Jakarta and less Geneva centric. The Abbott government in many ways had inherited Howard's tendency to act unilaterally within the region. The Coalition's poor understanding of the values and culture of Indonesia compounded this. An instance of Canberra's Operation Sovereign Borders policy to turn back the asylum seekers highlights the cultural difference between Australia and Indonesia. Though both countries have a large maritime jurisdiction, Indonesians and Australians think differently about the sea. For the Indonesians the sea binds nations together through the concepts of *wawasannusantara* with the sea linking the islands of the Indonesian archipelago rather than separating them, and *tanah air* meaning land and sea, with an inseparable relationship between the two environments. On the other hand, Australians tend to regard the surrounding oceans and seas as a barrier separating them from their neighbours. Given that

Australia and Indonesia are so close and yet so different, there is an ongoing need to understand and appreciate the cultural gap.[18]

Besides, Australia's economic and strategic interests dictate that Australia's priorities remain in its own dynamic region. Indonesia is the 12th largest export market and is set to be the world's 10th largest economy by 2025. Consequently, there are obvious economic benefits. In addition, it has a close relation with both the US and China and these are crucial so much so that no government in Australia can ignore. Prime Minister Tony Abbott also recognised the opportunity provided by actively participating in Asia's multilateral groupings in order to increase Canberra's influence more broadly. In this case, Australia was fortunate that American commitment to these processes meant that the US reinforced Abbott's policies.

Revelations in late 2013 that Australia had spied on Indonesia's former President Susilo Bambang Yudhoyono, his wife, Kristiani Herawati and other senior government officials including current Vice President Jusuf Kalla, was a major blow to relations.[19] The spying scandal took the relationship to its lowest point in years with President Susilo Bambang Yudhoyono. Given the significant personal capital invested by President Yudhoyono in good relations with Australia over many years, Indonesia felt a strong sense of betrayal.

Australian Prime Minister Tony Abbott was sufficiently pressurised to seek publicly apologise over revelations that Australian naval and coast guard vessels had 'unintentionally' entered Indonesian waters.[20] However, given the advanced nature of modern global positioning systems calls into question whether it was actually unintentional. Together with the manner in which the Australian government responded to revelations about the nature of its intelligence intercepts from Indonesia, had failed to satisfy Jakarta. As a consequence of these developments, Indonesia's ambassador to Australia Nadjib Riphat Kesoema was recalled on 19 November 2013 and Jakarta formally suspended military and law enforcement cooperation a day later.[21] Australia and Indonesia have agreed to the bilateral intelligence Code of Conduct that commits both Australia and Indonesia not to use intelligence to harm the other. The Code of Conduct paved the way for the resumption of full defence cooperation. Widely held as the fig leaf it allowed Yudhoyono to declare the matter closed although trust deficit continued to persist.[22]

What can be inferred from these occurrences is that bilateral relations lack weight and therefore, when crisis emerge it takes great effort at the political level to bridge the difference between the two. This is particularly the case with issues that impinge on Indonesian sovereignty or dignity and capture the imagination of Indonesian nationalists in the legislature and foreign ministry such as the espionage scandal that damaged relations between the two.

The inherent fragility in the relationship was well described by President Yudhoyono when he made a remarkable speech to the Australian Parliament in March 2010. He spoke very frankly about the misunderstandings and mistrust between the two.[23] The fact that his warnings received little attention reinforces that Australia had to put in more effort to understand Indonesia's importance.

Joko Widodo (Jokowi) and Indonesia-Australia Relations

Australia's relationship with Indonesia took centre stage during the televised debate on 22 June 2014, with one point of agreement, between candidates on their shared opinion of Indonesia's future relationship with Australia. Probowo Subianto blamed the unstable relationship on Australia's phobia of Indonesia while Joko Widodo (Jokowi) attributed it to a lack of trust. Jokowi said that there was a "lack of trust" between Indonesia and Australia and that if the asylum seeker issue could not be solved through dialogue, "we can bring them to international courts if necessary". Although he voiced support for stronger bilateral ties through initiatives such as educational and cultural exchanges, there were uncertainties in Jokowi's views on Australia.[24]

Joko Widodo's election is symbolic of the new democratic trend in Indonesia. He does not have a military background, and is a member of the Indonesian Democratic Party-Struggle headed by former President Megawati Sukarnoputri. He does not have a status bigger than Megawati Sukarnoputri in the party. His election policy platform (*Visi Misi Programme Aksi*), for example, included strong commitments to corruption eradication, good governance, human rights, etc. He was elected on the policy platform of defending Indonesia's political sovereignty and territorial integrity, economic nationalism, a robust anti-drug campaign, arguing that 18,000 Indonesians die from illicit drugs each year. That policy platform now manifests itself in a range of policy areas. Prominently the sinking of foreign illegal fishing vessels in Indonesian waters and the execution of the Bali Nine drug smugglers have once again brought to focus the undulating state of Indonesia-Australia relations.

Jokowi's policy on the right to burn or sinking of vessels that fish illegally in Indonesian territorial waters is based on Article 69, Paragraph 4 of Law No. 45/2009 on Fisheries. Fishing in the Indonesian fishing management area is understood as comprising the internal waters, the territorial sea and the exclusive economic zone (EEZ) of Indonesia. The action taken by Indonesian authorities validates the serious intention to address the issue of trespassing and illegal fishing and ultimately seeking a pronounced enforcement of maritime borders. On the other hand, Paragraph 114 of Law No. 35/2009 on Narcotics stipulates that drug couriers trafficking up to one kilogram or more is seen as a serious offence and will be liable for death penalty by firing squad. The execution of two Australian narcotics offenders, Andrew Chan and Myuran Sukumaran, had attempted smuggling 8.3 kilograms of heroin which clearly exceeded the stipulated amount leaving little recourse for leniency.

Both incidences have resulted in strong reactions and debate in Australia. Not granting clemency for two of the Bali Nine drug convicts from Australia will certainly have domestic and foreign policy repercussions in Australia and impact on the bilateral relations at least in the short term. Prime Minister Tony Abbott condemned the execution as "cruel and unnecessary" and said "we respect Indonesia's sovereignty but we do deplore what's been done and this cannot be simply business as usual". Australia expressed its disapproval at the political level by taking the unprecedented step of withdrawing its ambassador Paul Grigson in response to the killings.[25] In a rare show of solidarity, the Labor Party and the Greens fully supported the action. Although it is unclear at present whether other actions might be taken by

Australia, it is unlikely that the diplomatic gesture would be extended indefinitely or that trade and defence training and aid will discontinue. Although the death of the two Australians will result in short to medium term frictions between Canberra and Jakarta at the highest levels, it will soon ease as the two countries have a number of common interests that neither side can afford to abandon.

As for Indonesia it has defended itself, saying the executions were unpleasant but a necessary part of the nation's war on drugs. Given the fact that that Jokowi campaigned on a strong anti-drug platform, including using the death penalty, it was unlikely that he would make any concession that would force him to back down from his election promise. On the other hand, Jokowi's early policy proposals aim for a more inclusive economic growth: expanding infrastructure development, deepening agricultural reforms, overhauling the education system, and improving transparency within the police force go down well for Canberra.

Undoubtedly, President Jokowi inherited a difficult state of affairs. Domestically Joko Widodo inherited an Indonesian state with large account deficit and will therefore have to carefully tread through the economic discrepancies including the controversial fuel subsidy scheme and social unrest from labour disputations. There are doubts as to whether he has the capacity to enact a difficult reform agenda while balancing competing interests within a coalition government. Edward Aspinall in *Strategic Review* highlighted the predicament about whether Joko Widodo will succeed in implementing the fundamental reforms needed.[26] Several notable security concerns also stand in the way of a post-President Yudhoyono government. Additionally the growing tensions in the South China Sea posit new challenges.

Indonesia-Australia relations will have to begin afresh to do away with baggage of the past. Those difficulties have been most visibly manifest over the issue of beef, drugs and spies. Then there is the matter of the Australian Government that began Operation Sovereign Borders in November 2013 to turn the boats back to Indonesia in a bid at fortifying Australia's borders. The case of people smuggling has been a risk for Indonesia-Australia relations. Some of the memories of Indonesia-Australia relations will be positive too. These include effective cooperation between the two countries in their joint promotion of regional initiatives in areas like disaster preparedness, counter-terrorism and sustainable fisheries; long-standing defence and development relationships; and extensive assistance to Indonesian agencies dealing with issues including transport safety and security, immigration and finance. Indonesia is a like-minded partner in many regional and global affairs including environmental activism (e.g. climate change), transnational crime and irregular migration (e.g. the Bali Process), the promotion of democracy and human rights (e.g. the Bali Democracy Forum), and its active and constructive diplomacy over highly volatile issues such as Iran.[27]

Presently Australia's interests in the region largely coincide with that of Indonesia. Both are looking to take advantage of China's economic growth and prosperity without having China use force or the threat of force—physical or non-physical—to dictate inter-state relations or the terms of trade.[28] For Australia, the rise of the Indo-Pacific reality has obliged it to look further afield. A rising China is getting more explicit in contesting the regional security system, while America continues to invest considerable attention and resources to its Asian 'pivot'. Other regional powers, such as India and Japan, are looking more to the Southeast Asian region (and beyond) to further their foreign policy interests. The future of this order is in a flux due to the continuation of various disputes such as the South China Sea.[29] Indonesia's ascent and its heightened collaboration with the US have been rendered all the more important due to the shifting strategic order of Southeast Asia and the broader Indo-Pacific. Both Australia and Indonesia use the term Indo-Pacific to highlight the importance of the confluence between the Indian and Pacific oceans. Australia's 2013 Defence White Paper noted that the Indo-Pacific concept "adjusts Australia's priority strategic focus to the arc extending from India through Southeast Asia to Northeast Asia, including the sea lines of communications on which the region depends".[30] Engaging Asia is therefore, not a matter of choice for Australia, it's a necessity. Consequently developing a deeper understanding of Indonesia's foreign policy fundamentals in the context of Indo-Pacific developments is essential for Australian policy-makers.

Much like Australia, Indonesia's expansive economic engagement with China belies persistent ambiguity about Beijing's longer-term strategic intentions. Both Indonesia and Australia want to preserve the sovereignty of national borders while acknowledging that cooperation across them is essential for their preservation and mutual security in the broadest sense.

The strategic move to locate Indonesia as the global maritime nexus through the concept of global maritime axis (*porosmaritimdunia)* will enable the positioning of Indonesia as the pivotal country promoting stability in the Indo-Pacific region as well as promote connectivity between the Pacific Ocean and Indian Ocean. Jokowi's concept of a global maritime axis rests on five pillars: rebuilding maritime culture, enhancing maritime economy, improving maritime infrastructure and connectivity, engaging in maritime diplomacy and strengthening maritime defence.[31] Australia can assist Indonesia to support some of those pillars.

The strategy is very close to the one that had been adopted by the Srivijaya Kingdom in the 7th century, that had positioned itself at the centre of the trade between Western Asia and Eastern Asia passed through the ports that were under the domination of the empire. Their ability to protect the sea-lanes from pirates also legitimised Srivijaya's position as the maritime axis of the world. While the concept reinforces the geo-strategic significance of Australia's immediate neighbourhood it also sets the pace for a greater momentum for Australia and Indonesia to enhance maritime security cooperation. The importance of cooperation is enshrined in Articles 13 and 14 of the Australia-Indonesia 2006 Agreement on the Framework for Security Cooperation.

Australia and Indonesia face common security threats in the maritime domain such as people smuggling and illegal fishing, territorial disputes and threats to the security of sea lines of communication (SLOCs) which compel them to agree on the best approach to resolve the problems. Indonesia's strategic importance astride vital sea lanes connecting the Indian Ocean with the South China Sea, translates to increasing attention from major powers vying for influence in Southeast Asia.

So far Jowoki has done well in foreign policy emerging as pragmatic and economically focused. Many of Jowoki's projects are contingent on maintaining economic growth and investment.

Many of his projects will also depend on what role China and Japan can play in extending monetary aid. Indonesia will be an attractive destination for many regional and global suitors who will be eager to take advantage of the potential economic opportunities in Indonesia. In the past on many occasions Australia's shortsighted approach to relations with Indonesia has set a poor tone for bilateral relations. Australia realises that Canberra must avoid being sidelined by regional competitors such as China, Japan and Singapore and truly seize the opportunities with Indonesia. To do that, Australia will have to move beyond a relationship that has been dominated by issues relating to either asylum seekers or execution of the two Australians. An important requirement for Australia would be to rethink its long-term strategic interests in the light of Indonesia's emergence as a key player in the region. Engaging with Indonesia will require Australia to evolve a creative diplomatic solutions and an understanding of Indonesian concerns regarding sovereignty, intervention and security.

Australia can enter in areas that will be to the advantage of both. For example, Jokowi has already expressed interest in making use of maritime endowment for transport and resource exploitation as well as stopping unauthorised exploitation by domestic and foreign actors. That will require improved surveillance and reconnaissance, the capacity to intercept suspected interlopers as much as research about the nature of resources found in the maritime domain. Addressing maritime safety and marine environmental pollution is another common task. Because Indonesia is an archipelago, inter-island communication is vital for social and economic purposes. But Indonesia's maritime connectivity is poor and is subject to accidents and disasters. Australia has skill and expertise in those areas and could be engaged in building Indonesia's maritime capabilities to the advantage of both.

Similarly, partnering with and facilitating Indonesia's shaping of inclusive regional mechanisms, investing in and expanding Australia's Defence Cooperation programme with the Indonesian Armed Forces (TNI), are vital areas for bilateral cooperation. Personal links between military personnel, such as those facilitated by the Ikatan Alumni Pertahanan Indonesia-Australia (the defence alumni association, IKAHAN) will go a long way in developing trust and cooperation between ADF (Australian Defence Force) and the TNI.[32]

The interplay of domestic politics and sovereignty in Indonesia's current political climate since Joko Widodo assumed office as Indonesia's seventh president, there is every indication that Australia-Indonesia relations will shift to a new and more mature plane. Sabam Siagian and Endy Bayuni argue that Australia's own efforts have not been reciprocated by Jakarta, and this is demonstrated by the absence of a comprehensive policy on its relationship with Canberra together with its tendency to take Australia for granted until intermittent incidents when flashpoints occur.[33] There are several common security interests where Australia and Indonesia could cooperate. Hence, it is crucial to identify and prioritise those areas of common interest to secure a long-term partnership and Australia cannot afford to allow anger and disappointment to cloud its decisions and actions.[34] Undoubtedly both Australia as well as Indonesia will insist on minimising their maximum losses. Whether any future cooperation between the two countries would mean lessening the trust deficits is a wait and see game.

Conclusion

From the above discussion it can be concluded that although Australia and Indonesia are prone to occasional crises yet they have been reluctant to allow adversarial relations to develop. Disputes have been amicably resolved without escalating to threats of war. Solutions to Indonesia's drug problem, or Australia's illegal people movement problem, or any other, the shared challenges can be resolved only when the two countries work towards developing a clear narrative that is mutually rewarding. Until then Jakarta-Canberra relations will continue to be embroiled in periods of crises and cooperation akin to a game of snakes and ladders.

NOTES

1. Donald K. Emmerson, "Is Indonesia Rising? It Depends", in Anthony Reid, ed., *Indonesia Rising: The Repositioning of Asia's Third Giant* (Singapore: ISEAS, 2012), pp. 77–92.

2. *Australia's National Security Strategy* (Canberra: Department of the Prime Minister and Cabinet, 2013), p. 12. *Australia in the Asian Century: White Paper* (Canberra: Commonwealth of Australia, 2012), p. 25. See also: Hugh White, "What the Rise of Indonesia Means for Australia: Northern Exposure", *Monthly*, June 2013. <https://www.themonthly.com.au/issue/2013/june/1370181600/hugh-white/what-indonesia-s-rise-means-australia> accessed 5 September 2015.
3. *Indonesia Country Brief* (Canberra: Department of Foreign Affairs and Trade). <http://dfat.gov.au/geo/indonesia/pages/indonesia-country-brief.aspx> accessed 25 July 2015.
4. See A. Lucas, ed., *Half a Century of Indonesia–Australia Interaction, Monograph No. 6.* (Adelaide: Department of Asian Studies and Languages, Flinders University, 1996). H.A. Wolfsohn, *Australia Papers: Implications for Australia of Recent Developments in the Far East* (Sydney: Australian Institute of International Affairs, 1950).
5. *Near Neighbours- Good Neighbours: An Inquiry into Australia's Relationship with Indonesia* (Canberra: The Parliament of the Commonwealth of Australia, 2004).
6. See C. Brown, *Indonesia: Dealing with a Neighbour* (Sydney: Allen and Unwin, 1996); P. Kitley, R. Chauvel and D. Reeve, eds., *Australia di Mata Indonesia* (Jakarta: Gramedia, 1989).
7. See J. Monfries, ed., *Different Societies, Shared Futures: Australia, Indonesia and the Region* (Singapore: Institute of Southeast Asian Studies, 2006); M. Wesley, *The Howard Paradox, Australian Diplomacy in Asia, 1996–2006* (Sydney: ABC Books, 2007).
8. Pak Kevin, "Selamat Datang", *Jakarta Post*, (Editorial), 12 June 2008. <http://www.thejakartapost.com/news/2008/06/12/editorial-selamat-datang039-pak-kevin.html> accessed 21 October 2009.
9. M. Cook, *Australia and Indonesia: Partners in a New Era* (Sydney: Lowy Institute for International Policy Outcomes Report, 2009). < http://www.lowyinstitute.org/Publication.asp?pid¼10014> accessed 12 January 2010; H Dick, "Indonesia: The Past is Past", *The Asialink*, 2 May 2009, pp. 1–7.
10. Francis Palmos, "Journey to Jakarta: Australia's Forgotten First Attempt to Recognise Indonesia", *Australian Outlook*, 17 January 2015.
11. Many recipients of the Colombo Plan scheme in the 1960s now occupy important positions in Indonesia. One among them is Boediono, who was the Vice-President during Susilo Bambang Yudhoyono's presidency from 2009 to 2014.
12. Cited in Damien Kingsbury, *Power Politics and the Indonesian Military* (New York: Routledge, 2003), p. 150; David Jenkin, "After Marcos,

now for the Suharto billions", *Sydney Morning Herald*, 10 April 1986; Barbara Crossette, "Improving Australian Ties with Indonesia Turn Sour", *New York Times*, 28 April 1986. <http://www.nytimes.com/1986/04/28/world/improving-australian-ties-with-indonesia-turn-sour.html> accessed 4 May 2015.

13. Quoted in David Fickling, "Australia seen as America's deputy sherrif: Indonesia wary of Howard's government", *The Guardian*, 10 September 2004. <http://www.theguardian.com/world/2004/sep/10/indonesia.australia> accessed 4 May 2015.
14. Alan Dupont, "Indonesian Ties Much Tighter", *The Australian*, 8 April 2013.
15. *Exercise Pitch Black 12 Begins* (Canberra: Australian Department of Defence, 2012). <http://www.defence.gov.au/defencenews/stories/2012/jul/0727.htm> accessed 25 July 2015.
16. *Australia and Indonesia: Militaries Participate in the Inaugural Bilateral Peacekeeping Exercise, Garuda Kookaburra* (Canberra: Australian Department of Defence, 2013). <http://news.defence.gov.au/2013/05/17/australia-and-indonesia-militaries-participate-in-the-inaugural-bilateral-peacekeeping-exercise-garuda-kookaburra/> accessed 15 July 2015.
17. "Jakarta to Buy More Hercules", *Flight International*, 6 August 2013.
18. Sam Bateman, "Australia's Operation Sovereign Borders: Risks for Australia-Indonesia Relations", *RSIS Commentaries*, No. 179/2013, 1 October 2013.
19. Michael Brissenden, "Australia Spied on Indonesian President Susilo Bambang Yudhoyono: Leaked Edward Snowden Documents Revealed", *ABC News*, 18 November 2013.
20. Brendan Nicholson and Peter Alford, "Back Off, Jakarta Tells Australia" *The Australian*, 18 January 2014.
21. "Jakarta in No Hurry to Fix Ties with Australia: Indonesian Ambassador Will Not Return to Australia until Relations Have Improved", *Today* (Singapore), 20 February 2014; "'Biweekly Update: Indonesia': Southeast Asia from the Corner of 18th and K Streets", *CSIS*, Vol. 4, No. 24, 26 November 2013, p. 7.
22. "Australia and Indonesia sign spying code of conduct", *The Guardian*, 28 August 2014.
23. Susilo Bambang Yudhoyono, "Address by the President of the Republic of Indonesia" (Canberra: Commonwealth of Australia Parliamentary Debates, 2010). At an earlier conference, a former Indonesian ambassador to Australia, S. Wiryono, also highlighted the problem of public ignorance on both sides, but added that this was in contrast to a relatively better understanding between officials. S. Wiryono, "An Indonesian View: Indonesia, Australia and the

Region", in John Montries, ed., *Different Societies, Shared Futures: Australia, Indonesia and the Region* (Singapore: ISEAS, 2006).

24. Patricia Dias, "Australia-Indonesia Relations and a new Indonesian Leader", *Australian Institute of International Affairs,* 10 July 2014. <http://www.internationalaffairs.org.au/australian_outlook/australia-indonesia-relations-and-a-new-indonesian-leader/> accessed 20 July 2015; Bob Lowry, "Jowoki and Australia-Indonesia relations: There's scope for a strong and genuine partnership unencumbered by fundamental conflicts of interest", *The Diplomat,* 19 October 2014. <http://thediplomat.com/2014/10/jokowi-and-australia-indonesia-relations/> accessed 30 April 2015.
25. Jonathan Pearlman, "Executions mark a dangerous new phase for Australia-Indonesia relations", *The Telegraph,* 29 April 2015.
26. Edward Aspinall, "Democratic deepening in Indonesia: Challenges for the new administration", *Strategic Review,* 9 October 2014.
27. For example, Indonesia offered to mediate on the deadlock between Iran, the United States and the European Union concerning the alleged development of nuclear weapons. Ellen Nakashima, "Indonesia Offers to Mediate Talks with Iran", *The Washington Post,* 11 May 2006.
28. See Hugh White, "Power Shift: Rethinking Australia's Place in the Asian Century", *Australian Journal of International Affairs,* Vol. 65, No. 1, 2011, pp. 81-93.
29. Christopher Roberts, "The Future of East and Southeast Asian Regionalism", in Andrew Tan, ed., *East and Southeast Asia: International Relations and Security Perspectives* (London: Routledge, 2013).
30. *Defence White Paper 2013: Defending Australia and its National Interests* (Canberra: Department of Defence, 2013) p. 7. <http://www.defence.gov.au/whitepaper/2013/> accessed 20 August 2015.
31. Joko Widodo, "The seas should unite, not separate us", *The Jakarta Post,* 14 November 2014.
32. Stephen Smith, "Grading Australia-Indonesia defence relations: Good, but could do better", *The Interpreter,* 5 April 2013.
33. Sabam Siagian and Endy Bayuni, "RI-Australia ties: It's more important to be nice", *Jakarta Post,* 14 November 2012.
34. Bruno Hellendorff and Tanguy Struye de Swielande, "Australia in Asia: Time for a Dolphin Strategy", *Australian Outlook,* 19 February 2015.

12

Australia's Uranium Deal with India: Strategic, Economic or Simply *Ad Hoc*?

Aakash Tolani

ABSTRACT

In 2014, Australia's Abbott Government managed to secure a deal for uranium sale to economic giant India. This was a historic moment, as past Australian governments had juggled with the issue for over a decade given India's non-signatory status for the Nuclear Non-proliferation Treaty (NPT). For many, this radical shift in policy towards India was not so radical, rather a move already in the pipeline, given the US pivot towards India in the Indo-Pacific. For others, it was economic pragmatism. Despite being a NPT non-signatory, India maintains a relatively good record of non-proliferation. This paper however contends that none of these positions serve as an unambiguous demonstration of Australia's position on the subject. I put forward the proposition that it was an ad hoc decision which saw its turn coming due to the change of government in Australia more so than any strategic or economic interests in the Indo-Pacific. Longevity and sustenance of the deal remains a question and dependent on future Australian governments who in the past have been circumspect if not disinclined to supply uranium to India.

Introduction

For the most part, Australia-India relations have been tumultuous in the century gone by. Although that neither implies that relations have never seen better days nor that they cannot see better days. Yet the precedents indicate a phenomenon that is difficult to rule out today despite the relations at present enjoying relative strength, particularly vis-à-vis uranium trade.

The phenomenon in consideration is marked not by mere strategic or economic interests but by the nature of domestic politics within Australia, which plays a decisive role in defining the nature of the relationship between the two Indian Ocean democracies. India's stance on the use of uranium for its own nuclear power generation, for civilian and non-civilian purposes, has never fluctuated a great deal with different political parties coming into power. Not so at Australia's end, as the stance on uranium sale to India has vacillated across and within the two major political parties, Labour and Liberal.

There are no guarantees whether Australia's current uranium trade policy would be continued by the next government, while India's energy needs, regardless of what political party comes into power down under, would remain unchanged. Should any change occur with change in the government vis-a-vis the uranium sale, a domino effect would be felt across the Indian investments in Australia and the energy sector in India.

In the first instance, this paper seeks to shed light on the tumultuous nature of Australia-India relations. In the second instance, it delves into why the decision to sell uranium at present is not as much a normative strategic or an economic decision as opposed to being a political party's manoeuvre over the other. Holding on to this premise, the implications are outlined questioning the longevity and sustenance of the deal and its impact on Indian investment in Australia with relation to uranium trade.

The Nature of Australia-India Relations and the Uranium Deal

Since Independence, India's relations with the West, the US and its allies, had neither been cordial nor hostile. Jawaharlal Nehru's non-alignment stance in the wake of the world divided into two Cold War brackets saw India take a rather neutral, peaceful and an independent approach. In the words of Devdutt:"The government of India was opposed to military alliances, political pacts and economic aid with strings. It stood for coexistence, and preferred diplomacy of accommodation to the diplomacy of threats and balance of power".[1] In this regard, Weigold describes Nehru's role as a "broker between great and emerging powers" in promoting his "one world" ideals.[2] Nehru himself is known to have said, "we should not align ourselves with other power blocks. We can be of far more service without doing so...".[3] On occasions such as the recognition of the Communist China, Korean and Indo-Chinese wars, interaction with Russia, the Suez Canal crisis and South Africa's apartheid policies that led to its withdrawal from the Commonwealth, India is known to have exhibited its non-aligned stance.

Australia, on the other hand, has always been a participant in collective measures to "prevent and remove threats to the peace".[4] As Weigold notes: "As a nation with a small population in the post-war years, it relied for its defence and security agreements, as it still does, primarily on the United States as demonstrated in its 1950's determination to secure ANZUS and the now defunct SEATO".[5] It goes without saying that Pakistan being a founding member of the SEATO and Australia's participation in it, had at the time, clearly defined the course of relations between India and Australia. For India, as Lyon remarks, SEATO was an unwelcome intrusion bringing and settling Cold War rivalries into South Asia.[6]

Moreover, the point of contention was almost clearly set in stone when Australian leader Robert Menzies' suggestion came in 1957 that Australia might send forces to Kashmir along with the Australian statement on this matter to the United Nations Security Council.[7] This and many incidents alike—in the words of Meg Gurry—"alienated Nehru considerably" and led to the observation that Australia had no opinion of its own on international issues, that it was a "copy of the United States in foreign affairs", perhaps, at the same time "an American stooge".[8]

One such sore point has also been the selling of uranium to India, where bi-partisan and intra-party differences have changed the verdict many times. To briefly put the scenario in place with regard to the uranium sale to India in August 2007, Prime Minister John Howard started efforts with India and visited twice during his tenure, to strengthen bilateral ties. This included agreeing to sell Australian uranium to India for its civilian nuclear power needs, subject to abiding by the appropriate International Atomic Energy Agency safeguards, and entering into a security arrangement, the Quadrilateral Initiative with India, the United States and Japan.[9] This decision, however, was reversed by Australia's next Prime

Minister, Kevin Rudd, in January 2008 on grounds that India was not a signatory to the Nuclear Non-proliferation Treaty.[10] As Grare states, the decision was perceived in New Delhi as a sign of mistrust, even though in reality it had more to do with domestic politics.[11]

In the 2010 federal election the Julia Gillard-led Australian Labour Party suffered significant loss but remained in power by entering into coalition with the Greens and several independent members of Parliament. Notwithstanding this, in November 2011, Gillard announced that she would support a policy shift to allow Canberra to negotiate the export of uranium to India for civilian use.[12] To give further credence to her announcement, the Labour Party at its national conference in December 2011 approved her proposal. However, this was widely opposed by the Greens owing to their concerns overpotential proliferation risks and dangers of a consequent nuclear conflict; public health and environmental hazards posed by the risks of radiation pollution that are integral to any use of nuclear energy; and the unresolved and really long-term problem of nuclear waste disposal. Even after approval at the national conference, there was considerable opposition within the ranks of the Labour Party to this proposal and it was passed on the conference floor merely by a slim majority of 208 in favour with 185 against the sale. This inadvertently implies that the proposal was unpopular even within the Labour Party. Most notably, three senior ministers Anthony Albanese, Stephen Conroy, Peter Garrett opposed Gillard on this move.[13] However, the deal was finally sealed by Tony Abbott, the current Liberal Party prime minister on 5 September 2014[14] after Labour lost in the national election.

Key elements of the uranium sale agreement include:[15]

- India's assurance that it would use nuclear resources to reinforce energy security, separating military and civilian nuclear facilities.
- Mutual recognition that nuclear energy should be developed for peaceful purposes, consistent with the objective of supporting the non-proliferation of nuclear weapons.
- Confirmation that Australian supply of uranium to India is not inconsistent with peaceful purposes.

- Wide scope to provide and share technology, resources and personnel for the management of nuclear facilities.
- Australia's permission for India to reprocess and enrich nuclear materials exported between both nations; and
- A restriction on either Australia or India retransferring any nuclear material traded between each other to another nation.

Although Howard's legacy and Abbott's positive move both signal that the Liberal Party leadershipenvisages consistency and stability of the nuclear deal, in real terms, this may not be true in real sense. Mainly because of visibility of factions or rather a lobby group that is opposed to the deal, most notably the comments by Senator Back, a Western Australian Liberal party senator, in February 2015 during the Joint Standing Committee on Treaties (tabled on 28 October 2014).[16]

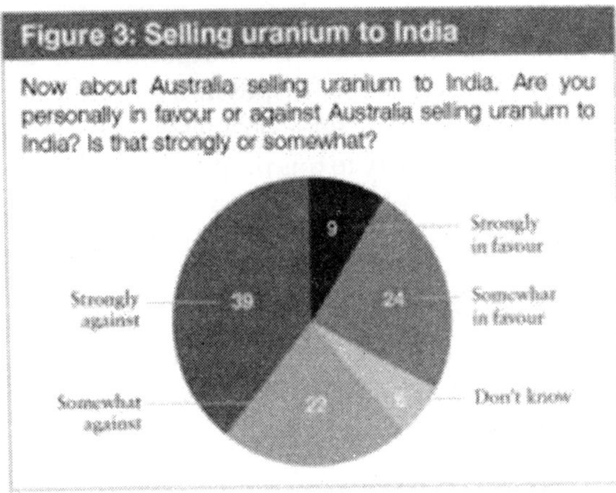

Figure 1: Uranium Sale to India, a Lowy Institute Poll (2012)

In addition to faction ridden political parties, public opinion poll suggests that the majority of the people in Australia are against the sale of uranium to India mainly because of its non-signatory status to the NPT. A 2012 Lowy Institute poll indicates that 61 per cent of Australians expressed their opinion against "Australia selling uranium to India", with 39% saying they are 'strongly against'. Women are more against it than men (71% compared with 51%) and among those saying they 'always vote Labour' two-thirds

(65%) are against it (54% of those who 'always vote Coalition' are also against)".[17]

Nonetheless, Julie Bishop, the current Australian Foreign Minister, is positive that the agreement to supply uranium to India is likely to be given clearance by the end of 2015 after the parliamentary process of examining the deal is completed. She said, the Comprehensive Economic Cooperation Agreement (CECA) not only provides an opportunity to enhance energy supply in coal, LNG and Uranium, but also gives Australia an opportunity to be a 'partner of choice' for India.[18]

With multiple conflicting factors at play in here, it certainly becomes crucial to determine as to what would sustain the deal in the long run. In other words, does Australia see its uranium deal with India economically and strategically above and beyond any domestic political differences, or is it still irrevocably a subject to it?

The following sections focus on the economic and strategic aspects of the deal, arguing that both these factors are less at play as opposed to the domestic politics in Australia, where even international obligations have arguably been circumvented due to the prevalent political climate.

Economic Aspects of the Deal

As far as India is concerned, New Delhi has certainly voiced its proposed plan for the nuclear energy expansion. The nuclear power capacity is expected to reach 10,080 MW by 2017. India also plans to start work on 19 new nuclear power reactors by 2017.[19] If this plan materialises it may have a total capacity of 17400 MW more in its energy basket. In the long term, India plans to install about 20 GWe nuclear power by 2020[20] and 274.56 GWe by 2052.[21]

The current nuclear expansion plan needs uranium. Though India has relatively large reserves of thorium oxide,[22] its uranium reserves are relatively low. As of May 2014, India was estimated to have 211,473 tonnes in situ U3O8 (179,329 tonnes of uranium) reserves.[23] It regularly assesses the "techno-economic viability" of extraction and development of uranium resources. Not all uranium deposits explored are yet mined and processed. Occasionally, mining and exploration of uranium reserves have been discontinued because of the low economic feasibility.[24]

The Department of Atomic Energy (DAE) has previously admitted that shortage of uranium has had an effect on functioning of the plants. Responding to a question in the Indian Parliament, the Indian government has stated: "The country's uranium requirement in the 12th Five Year Plan [2012-2017] period is estimated to be 5,057 tonnes. This includes 318 tonnes of low enriched uranium for Tarapur Atomic Power Station (TAPS) -1&2 and Kudankulam (KK) -1&2".[25] The Indian nuclear establishment maintains that the known uranium deposits can feed nuclear power plants with a capacity of about 10,000 MWe only.[26]

After the 2008 Nuclear Suppliers Group (NSG) exemptions, India signed agreements and contracts with several countries such as Namibia and Canada for uranium supply. However, so far, it has signed contractual agreements with the companies of only four countries—M/s. AREVA, France (during 2008), M/s. JSC TVEL Corporation, Russia (during 2009), M/s. NAC Kazatomprom, Kazakhstan (during 2009) and M/s. NMMC, Uzbekistan (2013). Regarding the uranium supply the Department of Atomic Energy informed the Indian Parliament that:

"(i) M/s. AREVA, France – one time supply of 300 MT of Natural Uranium Ore Concentrate during 2008-09 and 2009-10.

(ii) M/s. JSC TVEL Corporation, Russia – 2000 MT of Natural Uranium Oxide Pellets to be supplied in quantities of 200-400 MT annually; and Supply of 58 MT (one-time) Enriched Uranium Di-oxide Pellets received during 2009-10.

(iii) M/s. NAC Kazatom Prom, Kazakhstan – 2100 MT of Natural Uranium Ore Concentrate to be supplied in quantities of 300-400 MT annually during 2009-14.

(iv) M/s. NMMC Uzbekistan - 2000 MT of Uranium in the form of Uranium Ore Concentrate during 2014-18."[27]

For India, its energy requirements are not diminishable. This certainly makes India a reliable market for energy supply, with uranium being an essential ingredient. For Australia however, the reliability of it being a long-term supplier appears to be questionable. One key reason for this is perhaps the deal not being so economically attractive for Australia.

No doubt, Australia is certainly uranium rich, with over 40 per cent of the world's recoverable uranium, whilst only 19 per cent of this is being exported. However, this is no indication of Australia unambiguously recognising the sale of uranium to India as economically incentivising. As Thakur asserts, the economic merits to Australia are rather 'modest' when it comes to the uranium sale to India. Further he states: "Compared to the $63 billion iron ore export industry, for instance, Australia's uranium exports are worth only $1 billion and the most optimistic projections would see the rise restricted to under $2 billion."[28] That is to say, as compared to other resource-based export commodities, thus the sale of uranium is not recognised as incentivising.

On a corollary note, John Carlson, former Director General of Australian Safeguards and Non-Proliferation Office, also argued that Australia must be realistic about the size of the Indian market to speculate the offset of the deal in the future. In his submission to the Joint Senate on Treaties, he stated that the 'realistic target' for 2032, 27.5 GWe of installed nuclear capacity, represents a uranium requirement of around 5,500 tonnes a year. Assuming Australia secured for instance one quarter of this, on current uranium prices this would bring export revenue of around $140 million a year – "quite modest in terms of overall trade". Moreover, he questions whether uranium would be as important as India claims for its future when in the long-term having regard to India's plans for reprocessing and for developing the thorium fuel cycle, one can only speculate about long-term uranium requirements.

Moreover, some experts have even suggested that the deal would inadvertently affect the Australian coal industry, of which India is one of the key buyers. Uranium is an immensely concentrated source of energy—one tonne of uranium oxide generates the same amount of energy as 20,000 tonnes of black coal. Thus, between the two, the former gets the preference. Countering the popular assertion that the uranium deal with India is symbolic of betterment of bilateral trade relations between the two countries, Jim Green, from Friends of Earth Australia argues that such is not the case. If facts are indicative, then bilateral trade grew from $3.3 billion at the turn of the century to more than $20 billion in 2011, despite Australia's ban on uranium exports to India and other countries that have not signed the NPT. Since the uranium policy was overturned in 2011, bilateral trade has gone backwards and now stands at $15 billion.[29] That is to say the potential loss Australia may incur by back tracking on the deal in the future may not really have a huge impact on its bilateral trade with India. Therefore, although on an economic spectrum the supply of uranium remains to be crucial for India, for Australia it appears that the incentive from the deal is relatively not so substantial to anchor down for the long term.

Strategic Aspects of the Deal

The reasons behind Australia's decision to lift the ban are subject to debate. Economics alone cannot explain it, especially because the potential economic impact of the decision is debatable, as discussed in the previous section. However, Grare opines that the decision is partly triggered by a sense of relative strategic urgency, with the warming of India's nuclear ties with the United States, France and Canada, Australia may have feared being marginalised in India's diplomatic agenda.[30]

A recent country strategy document on India published by the Australian government reinforced this concern, underlining that Australia "must be mindful of competing demands. The relatively small Indian bureaucracy is actively courted by a large number of international partners". The document went on to stress that New Delhi is "focused mostly on tackling domestic poverty and ensuring sustainable development"; suggesting Canberra to address these aspects in order to get India's attention.[31]

In the recent past, Australia certainly has made vital moves to enhance its relations with India, of which the Uranium trade is the latest most significant development so far. However, this indeed is not the first case where Australia has struck such a deal with another country to strengthen its bilateral ties. Previously Australia has sold uranium to Russia and China. Neither of them share a neat proliferation record.

Prime Minister Howard's 2007 choice to sell uranium to Russia in order to give substance to the Australia-Russia relationship was part of such a larger partnership move. A 2006 decision to engage in uranium trade with China also had diplomatic connotations.

According to Rory Medcalf from the Lowy Institute, the Australian government took into account Chinese needs for nuclear energy "to help fuel its economic development, which in turn would aid social stability within China and reinforce China's reliability as a destination for other, more lucrative, Australian exports".[32]

To better define and place this gesture into a larger context, the deal with India appears to be in the wake of power shifts in the Indo-Pacific region. Prior to 2008, the nuclear issue presented a major impediment to any significant rapprochement between the two countries. However, Prime Minister Gillard made this argument explicitly when she declared in November 2011 that it was time for Australia to "modernise ... [its] platform" in an attempt to bolster its "connection with dynamic, democratic India".[33] Days later, then Foreign Minister Kevin Rudd echoed this sentiment, remarking that "the strategic relationship with India for the decades ahead is of great importance to ... [Australia's] national interest".[34] When the Labour Party made the uranium export policy official, Gillard stated that it was not rational to sell uranium to China but not to India.[35] At least symbolically, as Grare observes, the nuclear trade deal addressed all these issues and, in India's mind, constituted an additional concrete step towards ending the perceived nuclear apartheid.[36]

However, although lifting of the ban appears to be a key strategic move, it cannot be ruled out that the move has come too late and after heavy contestation, despite the US having agreed to sell the uranium in 2008. Under Rudd, the issue of uranium sale was riddled with the question of whether the new Labour government would support an agreement at the Nuclear Suppliers Group (NSG) to allow international nuclear trade with India.

The US and India wanted the NSG to exempt New Delhi from its requirement that transfers of nuclear technology be made only to countries which have a comprehensive safeguards agreement with the International Atomic Energy Commission. Failure to secure this exemption would have given a huge setback to the US-India civil nuclear agreement and the US attempts to establish a strategic alliance with India—a rather balancing act in the Indo-Pacific. To this end, the US and India undertook a three-year campaign to win the support of NSG countries, including Australia, before the NSG decision in August 2008.

The US Embassy in Canberra regarded Rudd as a strong supporter of the US alliance. But there was concern over whether Labour's nuclear policy would restrain Australia from supporting the US position at the NSG. Now it is somewhat clear that the pressure on the Rudd government to back the exemption came from the Australian High Commission in India as well as from the US as per the leaked Wiki Leaks cables. The cables reveal how Labour's official position on nuclear matters differed from the private views of individuals in the government.[37] In other words, the US pressure did little to change Labour's verdict on the issue back then. The US designs and shift of power motivations for the Indo-Pacific were overridden by domestic political concerns of the Labour Party. It would verily not be incorrect to assert that although supporting the US in its strategic decision making in the region and internationally has largely been held iconic of Australia's strategic policy making; the delay in this deal is emblematic of the domestic politics acting as a speed breaker, if not a complete road blocker.

An *Ad Hoc* Decision

As has been already discussed, this deal does not have many economic or strategic incentives, as the definition of incentives itself varies across the board in Australia. This paper thus asserts that the decision taken to lift the ban was rather an ad hoc decision, which saw its turn coming due to domestic politics, rendering the decision as a fragile one in the long run.

To expound upon it further, three case studies can be undertaken—the Vietnam War, putting a price over carbon emissions and the asylum seeker crisis. It must be noted that even though the sale of uranium to India cannot be compared entirely with all of these cases, they nevertheless highlight a feature of the Australian domestic politics, where differences in opinion between and within the political parties have blurred the definition of a singular concept of a national interest, above and beyond domestic politics.

If the first case of the Vietnam War is considered, during 1966, the Labour Party opposed Australian involvement in Vietnam, despite the US being Australia's most important ally. This has parallels with the sale of Uranium to India, as in this case as well the Rudd government did not lift the ban despite US green signal to do so, post NSG exemption to India in 2008. In November 1966 federal election, the Labour Party suffered an electoral setback due to the strong anti-war position of its leader, Arthur Calwell. Following the election, Calwell was replaced as Labour leader by Gough Whitlam, who in 1967 led a right-wing attack on the Labour Party's anti-war policy. The Labour Party's previous policy of calling for the withdrawal of Australian troops from Vietnam was hence narrowed down to a position of "withdraw to holding areas", which implied accepting continued US and Australian occupation of Vietnamese territory.

This out-manoeuvring of Labour's anti-war policy due to domestic political pressure demonstrates similarities with the sale of uranium to India. In both the cases the indecisiveness in identifying a singular national interest objective is clear. The swing from a decision to withdraw troops to retaining them or as in the current case, not selling uranium to India to recently agreeing on selling it; rather appears to be a substantial swing. This certainly varies with the nature of Indian politics, as regardless of the political party in power, Ogden asserts that the concept of national security has remained relatively constant.[38] For instance, regarding acquisition of nuclear technology the Congress Party laid down the necessary ground work but the 1998 nuclear tests were conducted by the BJP government when it came into power.

The second case study, putting price over carbon emissions also displays this contested nature of the decision-making process in Australia. In December 2006 the Howard government established the Prime Ministerial Task Group on Emissions Trading, chaired by Peter Shergold, to advise on implementation of an emissions trading scheme (ETS).[39] Upon release of the final report, the Howard government committed to introduce an ETS. Although the Howard government then was keen on introducing the ETS, it still did not sign the Kyoto Protocol, despite having a faction led by Malcolm Turnbull, the then Minister for the Environment and Water Resources, urging the cabinet to do so.[40]

With the Labour government led by Kevin Rudd coming to power in 2007, the Kyoto Protocol was ratified later that year. In

2008 Rudd commissioned 'Garnaut Climate Change Review' was released. A key recommendation of this review was to levy a price between $20 and $30 per tonne of carbon dioxide (CO2) equivalent with a rise of 4 per cent each year.[41] Following this, the Rudd Government released a green paper for its Carbon Pollution Reduction Scheme (CPRS), outlining the intended design of the scheme as well as a detailed white paper on 15 December 2008.[42] The Malcolm Turnbull led Liberal opposition supported the scheme in principle, although at times in 2009 indicated disagreement with various details including the timing of implementation of the scheme, timing of the vote on the relevant legislation and on the level of assistance to be provided to polluting industries. In the process, negotiated greater compensation for polluters affected by the scheme in November 2009.[43]

However, in December 2009, Tony Abbott defeated Malcolm Turnbull in a leadership challenge. Abbot immediately called a secret ballot on support for the ETS among coalition MPs that was ultimately rejected.[44] The Coalition then withdrew its support on the carbon pricing policy and joined the Greens and Independents in voting against the relevant legislation in the Parliament in December 2009.[45] As the Rudd government required the support of either the Coalition or the Greens to secure passage of the bill, it was defeated in the Senate. In April 2010, the Government deferred the scheme to the post-2012 timeframe. Again with the change of prime minister, the Gillard-led Labour Party, introduced a carbon pricing scheme- popularly termed as the 'Carbon Tax', in July 2012. This tax was eventually repealed in 2014, when the Abbott-led Liberal government came to power.[46]

This case is not only another classic example of the back-and-forth peddling of decisions within the Australian polity but also particularly sheds light on the internal party politics, within both the Labour and the Liberal Party ranks. Disagreement and frequent debate on policies can be stated as a cornerstone of a robust democracy, however from an Indian investor's point of view, this is critical and perhaps detrimental. The case of uranium sale to India has experienced almost the same wavelength pattern as this case, the internal party politics, resentment from the environmental groups and the Greens; and most importantly an unclear and uncertain support from the Australian public, very much like the reception given to the 'Carbon Tax'.

The third case study of the asylum seekers also shares traits like the aforementioned two cases. In August 2001, a Norwegian tanker, the *Tampa*, picked up 438 people whose vessel was sinking off the coast of Indonesia. The Howard government refused to allow the boat to land, saying it was a matter for Norway and Indonesia to work out between themselves. Neither made a move, creating a three way diplomatic standoff which became known as the Tampa Affair.[47]

Howard hereafter initiated the 'Pacific Solution' whereby, refugees were prevented from landing on Christmas Island or Ashmore Reef and those seeking asylum were redirected to nearby island nations such as Papua New Guinea and Nauru. Just like the Vietnam War, the minority Labour Party in this case opposed the policy. In 2003, Julia Gillard promised that the Labour Party would end the Pacific Solution "because it is costly, unsustainable and wrong as a matter of principle".[48]

Indeed, when the Labour Party did come to power in 2007, Rudd abandoned the Pacific solution, installing a more liberal policy of settling asylum claims within three months. Over the next few years the number of asylum seekers arriving in the country increased substantially. In 2008, there were 161 immigrants under asylum laws; in 2009, claims jumped to 2,800.[49] In May 2011, with the Labour's leadership reshuffle to Julia Gillard, the government announced plans to address the issue by swapping new asylum seekers for long-standing genuine refugees in Malaysia. The so-called Malaysian Solution was eventually ruled unconstitutional. In June 2012, Gillard government effectively reinstated the Pacific Solution, and re-introduced offshore processing for asylum seekers.

In July 2013, Rudd, returning to power as Prime Minister, went a step further, perhaps to rectify his image, announced that anyone who arrived in Australia by boat without a visa would not be eligible for asylum. In cooperation with Papua New Guinean Prime Minister Peter O'Neill, the Regional Settlement Agreement was drafted. Under the agreement, new asylum seekers would be sent to Papua New Guinea where legitimate cases would be granted asylum, but would lose any right to seek asylum in Australia.This case not only adds to the already discussed notion of back-and-forth decision making process in the Australian polity, but also raises concerns over the fact that Australia despite having international obligations, has somehow circumvented the issue by depriving the refugees, who come by boat, of their right to seek asylum in Australia.

Australia is a signatory to the United Nations' Convention relating to the Status of Refugees. However, the prolonged detention of refugees is contrary to the Convention. Detention is viewed by the United Nations Human Rights Committee (UNHRC) as a measure of last resort to be used only when national interests are threatened. The UNHRC findings have particularly concluded that Australia has violated Section 14 of the International Covenant on Civil and Political Rights which recognises and protects right to justice and a fair trial.[50]

From an Indian perspective, this certainly should be concerning, as Australia has demonstrated means of circumventing an international obligation. Challenging or revoking the bilateral deal in the near future remains to be a reality that cannot be wished away under the garb of bilateral ties and strategic partnership. The Prime Ministers of India and Australia although have instructed their respective negotiators to work out 'the administrative arrangement' as soon as possible, only after signing the contractual agreements, the Australian supply of uranium would come to India.

Implications for India

In light of the above discussed case studies as well as the strategic and economic attributes of the deal, it can be said that if the deal is not substantially disadvantageous to back out from, it is also not substantially an advantageous one to hold on to. From the very outset this should act as a caution to India to not lay too many eggs into the Australian basket. For India to have confidence in this deal, it should realistically secure support from both the political parties. This certainly is not a feasible solution any time soon. However, this does imply that should the government change, the deal itself would more than likely be up for amendment or rather a complete repeal.

This should be critical for the Indian government, as like any other nation, India can choose its friends, but not its neighbours. Sharing borders with two nuclear powers, China and Pakistan, with whom the record has particularly been of border disputes and hostility; it goes without saying that India would not take directions from third parties to defend itself or by that measure restrain itself from enhancing its non-civilian nuclear arsenal, should the circumstances be so.

In 1974 India tested its first nuclear device under 'Operation Smiling Buddha', where plutonium produced in the Canadian-supplied CIRUS reactor was used, that raised international concerns. In 1998 again India performed nuclear tests, against international pressure under 'Operation Shakti'. It is evident from both these cases that nuclear power for non-civilian purposes in India is a reality which cannot be wished away. In other words, to sustain the deal in the long run, there ought to be an implicit, if not explicit, understanding on the Australian end that it would indirectly be contributing to India's nuclear arsenal by freeing up its local resource for non-civilian utility; which certainly is unlikely to be a disposition at the Australian end.

Moreover, even the deal itself stipulates that it can be revoked at any time, should either party terminates the proposed agreement at one year's written notice to the other party. The party seeking termination on one year's notice would be required to provide reasons for doing so, but the proposed Agreement would not place any limit on the reasons.[51] That is to say, even with little reasoning and non-mutually agreeable solution, either party can nullify the deal.

An already complex relation, the Australia-India bilateral tie would only have another sore point should this deal be repealed. The bilateral trade as such may not be significantly hit, as India still maintains trade relations with a country like China with whom it shares border-dispute. However, it could affirm a long held view within certain ranks in New Delhi that perhaps trade with Australia, essentially the uranium trade, is rather a slippery ground and rather another exhibit of 'Nuclear Apartheid', just like the NPT.

Conclusion

The India-Australia uranium deal is certainly a deal between the two un-equals. For India, there is no compromise on what constitutes an over-arching security interest for the nation. However, for Australia, there is still room to fluctuate and accommodate different narratives of security under varied circumstances. From the very beginning, Australia and India were never on the same side of strategic policy making. Where Australia is popularly held as following in US footsteps in the region, India has more or less held its 'non-alignment' ground. Today, when India has started to show signs of posturing towards the US initiated tilt or balance of power in the Indo-Pacific, one would have expected Australia to be in conformity with the US position from the very outset.

This certainly has not been the case necessarily. Australia, despite being a close US ally, did have its fair share of domestic political hurdles, before it actually came on board to allow uranium sale to India. On a strategic plane, this translates into an indecisive or rather ambiguous position by the nation. On the one hand, the deal itself shows Australia's accommodation of US interests in the region and also strengthening its own ties with India, on the other hand, the delayed and contested nature of the deal paints a completely different picture of scepticism and hesitation towards India. That is to say, what constitutes Australia's strategic interest in the real sense is either blurred or not relatively stable at all.

On an economic paradigm as well, it is hard to ascertain conclusively whether it is significantly advantageous or disadvantageous to uphold the deal. That is, the deal itself is not incentivising enough for Australia to be significantly hurt in the future, should it decide to pull out or amend it. Moreover, given India's pragmatism in trade, which it has extended to even hostile neighbouring countries such as China, there is little substance in asserting that bilateral trade would be significantly reduced due to a possible withdrawal of the uranium deal.

Given the above two factors vis-à-vis the deal being not so strategically and economically meritorious, it is hereby asserted that the deal is rather an ad hoc decision, largely in part due to the nature of domestic politics in Australia. Examples such as the

Vietnam War, putting price over carbon emissions and the asylum seeker crisis are robust enough to depict similar traits of a divided and indecisive Australian polity.

The third example of the asylum seeker crisis particularly sheds light on the fact that international obligations have also been circumvented or rather reversed due to changing domestic political consensus on international subjects within Australia. This is concerning for the Indian investors, as with the change of the government or intra-party differences, the verdict on the deal also has the potential to be altered or reversed in the future.

Furthermore, if the deal is to last across the board, both parties must implicitly if not explicitly, acknowledge the fact that supply of uranium to India would free up its own to be used in non-civilian activities. Neither of the parties would be completely party to this proposition, either implicitly or explicitly. For the Indian investors this could imply that should a nuclear test or a possible stand-off within the subcontinent emerges, the Australian decision to sell uranium, albeit for civilian usage, could be changed depending on the domestic political pressure at the time.

It is thus recommended that the Indian investor carefully considers Australia as its ideal uranium supplier. Although Australia has the largest deposits of uranium, the domestic politics within the country, renders any deal uncertain or rather unsustainable. India is better placed to deal with other nations like Kazakhstan, Mongolia and other African nations, where although the uranium deposits may be lower than Australia, the reliability of the deal is relatively stable.

NOTES

1. Devdutt, "Non-Alignment and India", *The Indian Journal of Political Science*, Vol. 23, No. 1/4, January-December, 1962, pp. 380-397.
2. Auriol Weigold, "Menzies and Nehru: A long foreign policy shadow?", *Asian Studies Association of Australia*, 2010. <http://asaa.asn.au/ASAA2010/reviewed_papers/Weigold-Auriol.pdf> accessed 31 May 2015.
3. Jawaharlal Nehru, *India's Foreign Policy: Selected Speeches, September 1946-April 1961* (Bombay: The Publication Division, Ministry of Information and Broadcasting, Government of India, 1961), p. 47.
4. Richard Gardiner Casey, *Friends and Neighbours* (East Lansing, MI:

Michigan State University Press, 1968), p. 16.

5. Weigold, n. 2.
6. Peter Lyon, "Conflict between India and Pakistan", *ABC-CLIO*, 2008, p. 154.
7. Talk with Australian High Commissioner, 12 April 1957, pp. 103 and 435-36 cited in Weigold, n. 2.
8. Meg Gurry, Leadership and Bilateral Relations, pp. 518-19 in Weigold, n. 2.
9. "Australia to Allow Uranium Exports to India", *World Nuclear News*, 5 December 2011. <www.world-nuclear-news.org/NP-Australia_to_ allow_uranium_exports_to_India-0512115.html> accessed 31 May 2015.
10. "Australia Bans India Uranium Sale", *BBC News*, 15 January 2008.
11. Frederic Grare, *The India-Australia Strategic Relationship: Defining Realistic Expectation* (Washington, DC: Carnegie Endowment for International Peace, 18 March 2014). <http://carnegieendowment.org/2014/03/18/india-australia-strategic-relationship-defining-realistic-expectations/h4k3#> accessed 31 May 2015.
12. David Fickling and Ray Brindal, "Australia Seeks End of India Uranium Ban", *Wall Street Journal*, 15 November 2011. <http://online.wsj.com/news/articles/SB10001424052970204323904577038803821819984> accessed 31 May 2015.
13. Rohit Revo, "Can Kevin Rudd be trusted?",*The Indian Herald*, 12 August 2013. <http://indianherald.com.au/blogs/rohit_revo/can-kevin-rudd-be-trusted/6688/> accessed 31 May 2015.
14. *Joint Statement with PM Modi on the State Visit of the Australian PM to India*, 5 September 2014. <https://www.pm.gov.au/media/2014-09-05/joint-statement-prime-minister-modi-new-delhi-india> accessed 31 May 2015.
15. *Agreement between the Government of Australia and the Government of India on Cooperation in the Peaceful Uses of Nuclear Energy*, New Delhi, 5 September 2014. <http://www5.austlii.edu.au/au/other/dfat/treaties/ATNIF/2014/26.html> accessed 31 May 2015.
16. *Joint Standing Committee on Treaties - 12/02/2015 - Treaty tabled on 28 October 2014*. <http://parlinfo.aph.gov.au/parlInfo/search/display/display.w3p;query=Id%3A%22committees%2Fcommjnt%2F4e154c16-3030-400c-893f-28c3701bdd90%2F0001%22> accessed 31 May 2015.
17. Fergus Hanson, "The Lowy Institute Poll 2012: Public Opinion and Foreign Policy" (Sydney: *The Lowy Institute)*, 5 June 2012. <http://www.lowyinstitute.org/publications/lowy-institute-poll-2012-public-opinion-and-foreign-policy> accessed 31 May 2015.
18. Surojit Gupta, "Australia hopeful of finalising economic cooperation

agreement by year-end", *The Times of India*, 29 May 2015. <http://timesofindia.indiatimes.com/business/india-business/Australia-hopeful-of-finalizing-economic-cooperation-agreement-by-year-end/articleshow/47464745.cms> accessed 31 May 2015.

19. *Unstarred Question No. 643, 'Nuclear Power Generation'* (New Delhi: Department of Atomic Energy, Lok Sabha, Government of India, 27 February 2013).
20. *Meeting Demand Projection* (New Delhi: Department of Atomic Energy, Government of India)
21. *Tables* (New Delhi: Department of Atomic Energy, Government of India).
22. 8.56 lakh tonnes of thorium Oxide as per Government of India, Department of Atomic Energy, Lok Sabha, starred Question No. 379, 'Untapped Uranium/Thorium Reserves', 19 December 2012/
23. *Unstarred Question No. 5033, 'Atomic Minerals Deposits'* (New Delhi: Department of Atomic Energy, Lok Sabha, Government of India, 13 August 2014).
24. Rajiv Nayan, "Strategic Significance of the India-Australia Civil Nuclear Cooperation Agreement", *IDSA*, 15 September 2014. <http://www.idsa.in/idsacomments/StrategicSignificanceoftheIndia Australia_rnayan_150914.html> accessed 31 May 2015.
25. *Unstarred Question No. 396, 'Requirement of Uranium'* (New Delhi: Department of Atomic Energy, Lok Sabha, Government of India, 21 December 2012).
26. *Unstarred Question No. 3278, 'Uranium Reserves'* (New Delhi: Department of Atomic Energy, Lok Sabha, Government of India, 14 December 2011).
27. *Unstarred Question No. 4894, 'Agreement for Supply of Uranium'* (New Delhi: Department of Atomic Energy, Lok Sabha, Government of India, 13 August 2014).
28. Ramesh Thakur, "Selling Australian Uranium to India", *Australian Institute of International Affairs*, 4 September 2014. <http://www.internationalaffairs.org.au/australian_outlook/selling-australian-uranium-to-india/> accessed 31 May 2015.
29. Jim Green, "Australia's uranium agreement with India under attack", *On Line Opinion*, 8 October 2014. <http://www.onlineopinion.com.au/view.asp?article=16752&page=2> accessed 31 May 2015.
30. Grare, n. 11.
31. David Brewster, "The India-Australia Security Engagement: Opportunities and Challenges", *Gateway House, Research Paper No. 9*, October 2013, pp. 34–35. <www.gatewayhouse.in/wp-content/uploads/2013/11/The-India-Australia-Security-

Engagement-Opportunities-and-Challenges.pdf> accessed 31 May 2015.

32. Rory Medcalf, "Australia's Uranium Puzzle: Why China and Russia, But Not India?", *Fearless Nadia Occasional Papers on India-Australia Relations, Australia India Institute,* Vol. 1, Spring 2011, p. 4. <http://www.aii.unimelb.edu.au/sites/default/files/Fearless%20Nadia%20paper%201.pdf> accessed 31 May 2015.
33. Fickling and Brindal, n. 12.
34. "Reversal of Ban Won't Automatically Translate into Uranium Sales to India: Aus FM", *Indian Express,* 28 November 2011. <http://indianexpress.com/article/news-archive/print/reversal-of-ban-wont-automatically-translate-into-uranium-sales-to-india-aus-fm> accessed 31 May 2015.
35. "Australia's Labour Clears Uranium Sale to India", *Indian Express,* 5 December 2011. <http://expressindia.indianexpress.com/karnatakapoll08/story_page.php?id=884139> accessed 31 May 2015.
36. Grare, n. 11.
37. *Cable 07 New Delhi 3728, Indian Parliament Adjourns Again Over Nuclear,* 16 August 2007. <https://wikileaks.org/cable/2007/08/07NEWDELHI3728.html> accessed 31 May 2015.
38. Chris Ogden, *Hindu Nationalism and the Evolution of Contemporary Indian Security* (New Delhi: Oxford University Press, 2014), p. 127.
39. *Australian Climate Change Policy: A Chronology* (Canberra: The Parliament of Australia, 2 December 2013). <http://www.aph.gov.au/About_Parliament/Parliamentary_Departments/Parliamentary_Library/pubs/rp/rp1314/Climate Change Timeline> accessed 31 May 2015.
40. Ibid.
41. "Key points: Update Paper 6: Carbon pricing and reducing Australia's emissions", *Garnaut Climate Change Review,* 17 March 2011. <http://garnautreview.org.au/update-2011/update-papers/up6-key-points.html> accessed 31 May 2015.
42. *Australian Climate Change Policy: A Chronology,* n. 39.
43. Chris Aulich and Mark Evans, eds., *The Rudd Government: Australian Commonwealth Administration 2007- 2010* (Acton, ACT: ANU ePress, 2010).
44. Phillip Coorey, "Shock result as Abbott wins Liberal leadership by one vote ... ETS dead", *Sydney Morning Herald,* 1 December 2009. <http://www.smh.com.au/national/shock-result-as-abbott-wins-liberal-leadership-by-one-vote—ets-dead-20091130-k1uz> accessed 31 May 2015.
45. *Carbon Pricing* (Canberra: Department of the Environment, Australian Government). <http://www.environment.gov.au/

climate-change> accessed 31 May 2015.

46. *Repealing of the Carbon Tax* (Canberra: Department of the Environment, Australian Government). <http://www.environment.gov.au/climate-change/repealing-carbon-tax> accessed 31 May 2015.
47. R. Manne, "How Tampa sailed into 2002", *The Age*, 30 December 2002. <http://www.theage.com.au/articles/2002/12/29/1040511254630.html> accessed 31 May 2015.
48. Phil Mercer, "Is Australia asylum U-turn a 'better option'?", *BBC*, 15 August 2012. <http://www.bbc.com/news/world-asia-19267489> accessed 31 May 2015.
49. Matt Siegel, "Australia adopts tough measures to curb Asylum seekers", *The New York Times*, 19 July 2013. <http://www.nytimes.com/2013/07/20/world/asia/australia-adopts-tough-measures-to-curb-asylum-seekers.html?pagewanted=all&_r=0> accessed 31 May 2015.
50. Marian Sawer, Norman Abjorensen and Philip Larkin, *The State of Democracy* (Annandale: Federation Press, 2009), p. 27.
51. *Agreement between the Government of Australia and the Government of India on Cooperation in the Peaceful Uses of Nuclear Energy* (New Delhi), 5 September 2014. <http://www5.austlii.edu.au/au/other/dfat/treaties/ATNIF/2014/26.html> accessed 22 July 2015.

Bibliography

Books

Archer, Clive, Alison J.K. Bailes and Anders Wivel, eds., *Small States and International Security: Europe and Beyond* (Oxon: Routledge, 2014).

Amitav, Acharya and Barry Buzan, eds., *Non-Western International Relations Theory: Perspectives on and Beyond Asia* (London: Routledge, 2010).

Batra, A., *Regional Economic Integration in South Asia: Trapped in Conflict?* (New York: Routledge, 2013).

Batra, Ravi, *Proutist Economy and India's Brilliant Future* (Bombay: Jaico Publishing House, 1990).

Batra, Ravi, *The New Golden Age: A Revolution Against Political Corruption and Economic Chaos* (New York: Palgrave Macmillan, 2008).

Bateman, Sam and Joshua Ho, eds., *Southeast Asia and the Rise of Chinese and Indian Naval Power: Between Rising Naval Powers* (Oxon and New York: Routledge, 2010).

Bernstein, Richard and Munro Ross, *The Coming Conflict with China* (London: First Vintage Press, 1997).

Bhatia, Rajiv K. and Vijay Sakhuja, eds., *Indo-Pacific Region: Political and Strategic Prospects* (Delhi: Vij Books India Pvt Ltd, 2014).

Blank, Steven, *Natural Allies: Regional Security in Asia and Prospects for Indo-American Strategic Cooperation* (Carlisle: Strategic Studies Institute, 2005).

Bose, S., *States, Nations, Sovereignty: Sri Lanka, India and the Tamil Ealm Movement* (Delhi: Sage, 1994).

Bose, S., *A Hundred Horizons: The Indian Ocean in the Age of Global Empire* (Cambridge, MA: Harvard University Press, 2006).

Brands, H., *The Promise and Pitfalls of Grand Strategy* (Carlisle: US Army War College Strategic Studies Institute, 2012).

Brewstar, David, *India's Ocean: The Story of India's Bid for Regional Leadership* (Oxon and New York: Routledge, 2014).

Burchill, Scott, et al., eds., *Theories of International Relations*, 4th edn. (Basingstoke: Palgrave Macmillan, 2009).

Buzan, B. and O. Waever, *Regions and Powers: The Structure of International Security* (Cambridge: Cambridge University Press, 2003).

Campbell, G., ed., *The Indian Ocean Rim: Southern Africa and Regional Cooperation* (New York: Routledge, 2011).

Chau, D. and T. Kane, eds. (2014). *China and International Security: History, Strategy, and 21st Century Policy* (New York: Praeger, 2014).

Cole, Bernard D., *Asian Maritime Strategies: Navigating Troubled Waters* (Annapolis: Naval Institute Press, 2013).

Crocker, Chester A., Fen Osler Hampson and Pamela Aall, eds., *Rewiring Regional Security in a Fragmented World* (Washington, DC: United States Institute of Peace Process, 2011).

De Silva, K.M., *Regional Powers and Small State Security: India and Sri-Lanka 1977-1990* (Washington DC: Woodrow Wilson Center Press, 1995).

Devare, Sudhir T., ed., *A New Energy Frontier: The Bay of Bengal* (Singapore: Institute of Southeast Asian Studies, 2008).

Goldstein, Avery, *Rising to the Challenge: China's Grand Strategy and International Security*, (Stanford: Stanford University Press, 2005).

Goldstein, Avery and Edward Mansfield, eds.,*The Nexus of Economics, Security and International Relations in East Asia* (Stanford: Stanford University Press, 2012).

Ghosh, Anjali, Tridib Chakraborti, Anindyo Jyoti Majumdar and Shibashish Chatterjee, eds., *India's Foreign Policy* (New Delhi: Dorling Kindersley (India) Pvt Ltd, 2009).

Gordon, Sandy, *India's Rise as an Asian Power: Nation, Neighbourhood, and Region* (Washington DC: Georgetown University Press, 2014).

Hackett, Conrad and Brian J. Grim, *Global Christianity: A Report on the Size and Distribution of the World's Christian Population* (Washington, DC: Pew Research Centre's Forum on Religion and Public Life, 2011).

Hall, Ian, ed., *The Engagement of India: Strategies and Response*, (Washington: Georgetown University Press, 2014).

Haushofer, Ernst, *Geopolitics of the Pacific Ocean*, English translation by Tambs, Lewis and Brehm, Ernst (Lampeter: Edwin Mellor, 2002).

Kaplan, Robert D., *China's Two Ocean Strategy, China's Arrival: A Strategic Framework for Global Cooperation* (Washington DC: Centre for a New American Security, September 2009).

Kaplan, Robert D., *Monsoon: The Indian Ocean and the Future of American Power* (New York: Random House, 2010).

Kavalski, Emilian, ed., *China and Global Politics of Regionalisation* (Farnham and Burlington: Ashgate Publishing Limited, 2009).

Kavalski, Emilian, ed., *The Ashgate Research Companion to Chinese Foreign Policy* (Surrey: Ashgate Publishing Company, 2012).

Kearney, M., *The Indian Ocean in World History* (New York: Routledge, 2004).

Keohane, Robert O., *After Hegemony: Cooperation and Discord in the World Political Economy* (Princeton: Princeton University Press, 1984).

Khalid, N., *The Tides that Bind: Maritime Trade in the Indian Ocean and its Growth Prospectus* (Kuala Lumpur: Maritime Institute of Malaysia, 2007).

Lenze, Nele and Charlotte Schriwer, eds., *Converging Regions: Global Perspectives on Asia and the Middle East* (Farnham and Burlington: Ashgate Publishing Limited, 2014).

Li, Rex, *A Rising China and Security in East Asia: Identity Construction and Security Discourse* (Oxon and New York: Routledge, 2009).

Malik, Mohan, ed., *Maritime Security in the Indo-Pacific: Perspectives from China, India, and the United States* (Lanham: Rowman & Littlefield, 2014).

Maslow, Sebastian, Ra Mason and Paul O'Shea, eds., *Risk State: Japan's Foreign Policy in an Age of Uncertainty* (Farnham and Burlington: Ashgate Publishing Company, 2015).

Mazumdar, Arijit, *Indian Foreign Policy in Transition: Relations with South Asia* (Oxon and New York: Routledge, 2015).

McKercher, B.J.C., ed., *Routledge Handbook of Diplomacy and Statecraft* (New York: Routledge, 2012).

Michael, Arndt, *India's Foreign Policy and Regional Multilateralism* (New York: Palgrave McMillan, 2013).

Middlebrooks, William C., *Beyond Pacifism: Why Japan must become a Normal Nation* (Santa Barbara, CA: Praeger, 2008).

Mohan, C. Raja, *Crossing the Rubicon: The Shaping of India's New Foreign Policy* (New York: Palgrave McMillan, 2003).

Mohan, C. Raja, *Samudra Manthan: Sino-Indian Rivalry in the Indo-Pacific* (Washington, DC: Carnegie Endowment for International Peace, 2012).

Moller, J. Ostrom, *How Asia Can Shape the World: From the Era of Plenty to the Era of Scarcities* (Singapore: Institute of South East Asian Studies, 2011).

Naqvi, Z.F. and P. Schuler, eds., *The Challenges and Potential of Pakistan-India Trade* (Washington DC: The World Bank, 2007).

Nau, Henry and Deepa Ollapally, eds., *Worldviews of Aspiring Powers: The Domestic Foreign Policy Debates in China, India, Iran, Japan and Russia* (Oxford and New York: Oxford University Press, 2012).

Ogden, Chris, *Hindu Nationalism and the Evolution of Contemporary Indian Security: Portents of Power* (New Delhi: Oxford University Press, 2014).

Pant, Harsh, *China's Rising Global Profile: The Great Power Tradition* (Eastbourne, Oregon and Ontario: Sussex University Press, 2012).

Ross, Robert, *Chinese Security Policy: Structure, Power and Politics* (Oxon and New York: Routledge, 2009).

Rumley, Dennis and Timothy Doyle, eds., *Indian Ocean Regionalism* (London: Taylor & Francis, 2014).

Sakhuja, Vijay, *Asian Maritime Power in the 21st Century: Strategic Transactions: China, India and Southeast Asia* (Singapore: Southeast Asian Studies, 2011).

Saunders, Phillip C., Christopher Yung, Michael Swaine and Andrew Nien-Dzu Yang, eds., *The Chinese Navy: Expanding Capabilities, Evolving Roles* (Washington DC: Institute for National Strategic Studies, 2011).

Shambaugh, David L., ed., *Power Shift: China and Asia's Dynamics* (Berkeley, Los Angeles and London: University of California Press, 2005).

Sharma, G.D., *Indo-US Defence Coopeartion* (New Delhi: Vij Books India Pvt Ltd, 2013).

Sharma, Reetika, Ramvir Goria and Vivek Mishra, *India and the Dynamics of World Politics: A Book on Indian Foreign Policy* (New Delhi: Dorling Kindersley (India) Pvt Ltd, 2011).

Singh, Jasjit, *India's Security in a Turbulent World* (New Delhi: National Book Trust, 2013).

Snetkov, Aglaya and Stephen Aris, eds., *The Regional Dimensions to Security: the Other Sides of Afghanistan* (New York: Palgrave McMillan, 2013).

Spykman, Nicholas, *The Geography of the Peace* (New York: Harcourt Brace and Company, 1944).

Stewart-Ingersoll, Robert and Derick Frazier, *Regional Powers and Security Orders: A Theoretical Framework* (Oxon and New York: Routledge, 2012).

Thomas, Raju G., *Indian Security Policy* (Princeton: Princeton University Press, 1986).

Till, Geoffrey, and Patrick Bratton, eds., *Sea Power and the Asia-Pacific: The Triumph of Neptune?*(Oxon and New York: Routledge, 2012).

Tow, William T., ed.,*The New US Strategy Towards Asia: Adapting to the American Pivot* (Oxon and New York: Routledge, 2015).

Tow, William T. and Douglas Stuart, eds., *The New US Strategy Towards Asia: Adapting to the American Pivot* (Oxon and New York: Routledge, 2015).

Wang, Rong and Cuiping Zhu, eds., *Annual Report on the Development of International Relations in the Indian Ocean Region 2014* (New York: Springer, 2015).

Ward, Richard Edmund, *India's Pro-Arab Policy: A Study in Continuity* (New York: Praeger Publishers, 1992).

Wesley-Smith, Terence and Edgar A. Porter, *China in Oceania: Reshaping the Pacific?* (Oxford: Berghahn Books, 2010).

Williams, Paul D., ed., *Security Studies: An Introduction*, 2nd edn. (London and New York: Routledge, 2013).

Yang, Fengang, *Why Christianity is Thriving in China Today* (Georgetown, Georgetown University: Berkeley Centre for Religion, Peace and World Affairs, 2011).

Yoshihara, Toshi and James R. Holmes, *Asia Looks Seaward: Power and Maritime Strategy* (Westport: Praeger Security International, 2008).

Journal Articles

Acharya, Amitav, "Will Asia be Past its Future?", *International Security*, Vol. 28, No. 3, pp. 149-164.

Ahlawat, Dalbir, "India's Strategic Perceptions: Continuity and Change", *Journal of International Affairs*, Vol. 17, No. 1 & 2, 2013, pp. 59-80.

Anand, Dibyesh, "Remembering 1962 Sino-Indian Border War: Politics of Memory", *Journal of Defence Studies*, Vol. 6, No. 4, 2012, pp. 177-196.

Anderson, Walter and Shrey Verma, "Washington's India Pivot", *India Quarterly*, Vol. 71, No. 2, 2015, pp. 95-109.

Arif, Mohd, "A History of Sino-Indian Relations: From Conflict to Cooperation", *International Journal of Political Science and Development*, Vol. 1, No. 4, 2013, pp. 129-37.

Auslin, Michael, "Tipping Point in the Indo-Pacific", *The American Interest*, Spring 2010, pp. 17-34.

Ayoob, Mohamed, "India in South Asia: The Quest for Regional Predominance", *World Policy Journal*, Vol. 7, No. 1, 1989, pp. 107-133.

Bajwa, J.S., "Defining Elements of Comprehensive National Power", *Centre for Land Warfare Studies*, Summer 2008, pp. 151-62. <http://www.claws.in/images/journals_doc/1302263399_JSBajwa.pdf>

Banerjee, Dipankar, "India's Defence and Security in the 21st Century: Hard Choices", *CLAWS Journal*, Winter 2014, pp. 1-16.

Barry, Tom, "The US Power Complex: What's New", *Foreign Policy in Focus*, November 2002, pp. 1-11.

Bergsten, C.F., "Open Regionalism", *World Economy*, Vol. 20, Issue 5, 1997, pp. 545-565.

Bhaskar, Uday C., "Tsunami Reveals Indian Military's Humanitarian Response Capability", *Institute of Defence Studies and Analyses*, 8 January 2005.

Bert, W., "Burma, China and the USA", *Pacific Affairs*, Vol. 77, No. 2, 2004, pp. 263-282.

Bhattachariya, Biswa Nath, "Prospects and Challenges of Integrating South and Southeast Asia", *International Journal of Development and Conflict*, Vol. 4, 2014, pp. 40-66.

Blair, David, "The Clash of Historical Memory: The 'Century of Humiliation' vs. the 'Post-WWII Liberal World Order"', *China Currents*, Vol. 12, No. 2, 2013. <http://www.chinacenter.net/2014/china_currents/12-2/the-clash-of-historical-memory-the-century-of-humiliation-vs-the-post-wwii-liberal-world-order>

Blazevic, Jason J., "Defensive Realism in the Indian Ocean: Oil, Sea Lanes and the Security Dilemma", *China Security,* Vol. 5, No. 3, 2009, pp. 59-71.

Bouchard, Christian, "Indo-Pacific region: Political and strategic prospects", *Journal of the Indian Ocean Region,* Vol. 10, No. 2, 2014, pp. 250-252.

Bradford, John F., "The Maritime Strategy of the United States: Implications for Indo-Pacific Sea Lanes", *Contemporary Southeast Asia,* Vol. 33, No. 2, 2011, pp. 183–208.

Breslin, Shaun, "China's Emerging Global Role: Dissatisfied Responsible Great Power", *Politics,* Vol. 30, Supp. 1, 2010, pp. 52-62.

Brewster, David, "India's Defence Strategy and India-ASEAN Relationship", *India Review,* Vol. 12, No. 3, 2013, pp. 151-164.

Brewster, David, "The Bay of Bengal: India's Growing Role as a Regional Security Provider", *The Strategist,* 11 December 2014. <http://www.aspistrategist.org.au/the-bay-of-bengal-indias-growing-role-as-a-regional-security-provider/>

Brewster, David, "Beyond the 'String of Pearls': Is there really a Sino-Indian security dilemma in the Indian Ocean?", *Journal of the Indian Ocean Region,* Vol. 10, No. 2, 2014, pp. 133-149.

Campbell, G.R. and M. Scern, "The Prospects for an Indian Ocean Rim (IOR) Economic Association", *South African Journal of International Affairs,* Vol. 2, Issue 2, 1994, pp. 11-37.

Campbell, Kurt M. and Ely Ratner, "Far Eastern Promises-Why Washington Should Focus on Asia?",*Foreign Affairs,* May/June 2014. <http://www.foreignaffairs.com/articles/141241/kurt-m-campbell-and-ely-ratner/far-eastern-promises>.

Chacko, Priya, "A New 'Special Relationship?': Power Transitions, Ontological Security, and India-US Relations", *International Studies Perspectives,* Vol. 15, 2014, pp. 329-46.

Chandramohan, Balaji, "Modi's rise: The far flank implications", *New Zealand International Review,* Vol. 39, No. 4, July/August 2014, pp. 6-9.

Clinton, Hillary, "America's Pacific Century", *Foreign Policy,* Issue 189, November 2011, pp. 56-63.

Cohen, Florette and Sheldon Solomon, "The Politics of Mortal Terror", *Current Directions in Psychological Science,* Vol. 20, No. 5, 2011, pp. 316-320.

Dabee, Beela Singh and Mahinder Reddy, "Regional Agreements in the Indian Ocean", *The World Economy,* Vol. 23, No. 9, 2000, pp. 1149-1160.

Devdutt, I, "Non-Alignment and India", *The Indian Journal of Political Science,* Vol. 23, No. 1/4, January/December, 1962, pp. 380-397.

Doyle, Timothy, "India and the Allure of the 'Indo-Pacific'", *International Studies*, Vol. 49, No. 3-4, 2012, pp. 165-188.

Dwivedi, S.S., "Exploring Strategies and Implications of an Opportunistic Alliance: A Case Study of Pakistan and China", *Asian Journal of Political Science*, Vol. 21, No. 3, 2013, pp. 306-327.

Egreteau, Renaud, "The China–India Rivalry Reconceptualised", *Asian Journal of Political Science*, Vol. 20, No. 1, pp. 1-22.

Fickling, D. and R. Brindal, "Australia Seeks End of Uranium Ban", *Wall Street Journal*, 15 November 2011. <http://online.wsj.com/news/articles/SB10001424052970204323904577038803821819984>

Friedberg, Aaron, "The Future of US-China Relations: Is Conflict Inevitable?", *International Security*, Vol. 30, No. 2, 2005, pp. 7-45.

Garver, J., "Asymmetrical Indian and Chinese threat perceptions", *Journal of Strategic Studies*, Vol. 25, No. 4, 2002, pp. 109-134.

Gilboy, George J., and Eric Heginbotham, "Double Trouble: A Realist View of Chinese and Indian Power", *The Washington Quarterly*, Vol. 36, No. 3, 2013, pp. 125-142.

Gopal, Darvesh, and Dalbir Ahlawat, "Australia–India Strategic Relations: From Estrangement to Engagement", *India Quarterly*, Vol. 71, No. 3, 2015, pp. 206-220.

Gurry, Meg, "Leadership and Bilateral Relations: Menzies and Nehru, Australia and India, 1949-1964", *Pacific Affairs*, Vol. 65, No. 4, 1993, pp. 501-526.

Ho, Joshua H, "The Security of Sea Lanes in Southeast Asia", *Asian Survey*, Vol. 46, No. 4, 2006, pp. 558-574.

Hoffman, Jeanne, "China's Search for the Futures: A Genealogical Approach", *Futures*, Vol. 54, 2013, pp. 53-67.

Hoffman, Jeanne, "Unpacking Images of China Using Causal Layered Analysis", *Journal of Futures Studies*, Vol. 16, No. 3, 2012, pp. 1-24.

Holmes, James and Toshi Yoshihara, "History Rhymes: The German Precedent for Chinese Seapower", *Orbis*, Vol. 54, No. 1, 2010, pp. 14-34.

Huntington, Samuel P., "The Clash of Civilisations?",*Foreign Affairs*, 1993. <https://www.foreignaffairs.com/articles/united-states/1993-06-01/clash-civilizations>

Inayatullah, Sohail, "World Futures and the Global Financial Crisis: Narratives that Define and Scenarios that Create", *Ekonomiaz*, Vol. 76, No. 1, pp. 64-86.

Iskander, Rehman, "Keeping the Dragon at Bay: India's Counter-Containment of China in Asia", *Asian Security*, Vol. 5, No. 2, 2009, pp. 114-143.

Jain, S.C. and P.N. Ghauri, "Indian Ocean rim trade bloc: Prospects and problems", *The International Executive*, Vol. 38, No. 5, 1996, pp. 583-597.

Jain, Pankaj, "Dharmic Ecology: Perspectives from the Swadhyaya Practitioners", *Worldviews*, Vol. 13, 2009, pp. 305-20.

Johnston, Alastair Iain, "Is China a Status Quo Power?",*International Security*, Vol. 27, No. 4, 2003, pp. 5-56.

Johnston, Alastair Iain, "Thinking about Strategic Culture", *International Security*, Vol. 19, No. 4, 1995, pp. 32-64.

Joshi, Shashank, "Why India is Becoming Warier of China", *Current History*, April 2011, pp. 156-161.

Kapoor, Rakesh, "Plural Dreams: India in the 21st Century", *Futures*, Vol. 36, 2004, pp. 637-653.

Katz, Richard, "Mutually Assured Production: Why Trade will Limit Conflict between China and Japan", *Foreign Affairs*, July/August 2013, pp. 201-206.

Kelegama, S., "Open Regionalism in the Indian Ocean: How Relevant is the APEC Model for IOR-ARC?",*Journal of the Asia Pacific Economy*, Vol. 5, No. 3, 2000, pp. 255- 274.

Kelly, Patricia, "Engineering, A Civilising Influence?", *Futures*, Vol. 42, No. 10, 2010, pp. 1110-18.

Kennedy, Andrew B., "China's New Energy Security Debate", *Survival: Global Politics and Strategy*, Vol. 52, No. 3, 2010, pp. 137-158.

Khurana, Gurpreet S., "China's 'String of Pearls' in the Indian Ocean and its Security Implications", *Strategic Analysis*, Vol. 32, No. 1, 2008, pp. 1-39.

Khurana, Gurpreet S., "China-India Maritime Rivalry", *Indian Defense Review*, Vol. 23, No. 4, October-December 2008, pp. 1-8.

Kostecka, Daniel, "Hambantota, Chittagong and the Maldives", *China Brief*, Vol. 10, No. 23, 19 November 2010.

Ladwig, Walter C., "Delhi's Pacific Ambition: Naval Power, 'Look East' and India's Emerging Influence in the Asia-Pacific", *Asian Security*, Vol. 5, No. 2, 2009, pp. 87-113.

Ladwig III, Walter C, "Indian Military Modernization and Conventional Deterrence in South Asia", *The Journal of Strategic Studies*, Vol. 38, No. 5, pp. 729 – 772.

Li, Xin, "India through Chinese Eyes", *World Policy*,Winter 2013/2014. <http://www.worldpolicy.org/journal/winter2013/india-through-chinese-eyes>

Majeed, Akhtar, "Indian Security Perspectives in the 1990s", *Asian Survey*, Vol. 30, No. 11, 1990, pp. 1084-1098.

Malik, Hasan Yaser, "The Strategic Importance of Gwadar Port", *Journal of Political Studies*, Vol. 19, No. 2, 2012, pp. 57-69.

Malone, D. and R. Mukherjee, "India and China: Conflict and Cooperation", *Survival*, Vol. 52, No. 1, February/March 2010, pp. 137-158).

Mazumdar, Arijit, "India's South Asia Policy in the Twenty-First Century: New Approach, Old Strategy", *Contemporary Politics*, Vol. 18, No. 3, 2012, pp. 286-302.

Mearsheimer, John J., "China's Unpeaceful Rise", *Current History*, Vol. 105, No. 690, 2006, pp. 160-162.

Mearsheimer, John J., "The Gathering Storm: China's Challenge to US Power in Asia", *The Chinese Journal of International Politics*, Vol. 3, No. 4, 2010, p. 381-396.

Medcalf, Rory, "Indo-Pacific: What's in a Name?",*The American Interest*, Vol. 2, No. 2, 2013, pp. 58-66.

Medcalf, Rory, "In defence of the Indo-Pacific: Australia's new strategic map", *Australian Journal of International Affairs*, Vol. 68, No. 4, 2014, pp. 470-483

Mitra, Subrata K., "Nuclear, Engaged and Non-Aligned: Contradiction and Coherence in India's Foreign Policy", *India Quarterly: A Journal of International Affairs*, Vol. 65, No. 1, pp. 15-35.

Mohan, C. Raja, "Balancing Interests and Values: India's Struggle with Democracy Promotion", *The Washington Quarterly*, Vol. 30, No. 3, Summer 2007, pp. 99-115.

Mohan, Malik, "India Balances China", *Asian Politics and Policy*, Vol. 4, No. 3, 2012, pp. 345-376.

Muni, S.D., "Problem Areas in India's Neighbourhood Policy", *South Asian Survey*, Vol. 10, No. 2, 2003, pp. 185-196.

Naidu, G.V.C., "Prospects for IOR-ARC Regionalism: An Indian Perspective", *Journal of the Indian Ocean Region*, Vol. 8, No. 1, 2012, pp. 21-36.

Namrata Goswami, "Power Shifts in East Asia: Balance of Power vs. Liberal Institutionalism", *Perceptions*, Vol. 18, No. 1, 2013, pp. 3-31.

Neil, De Votta, "Is India Over Extended? When Domestic Disorder Precludes Regional Intervention", *Contemporary South Asia*, Vol. 12, 2003, pp. 365-380.

Nowbutsing, B.M., "The Impact of Openness on Economic Growth: Case of Indian Ocean Rim Countries", *Journal of Economics and Development Studies*, Vol. 2, No. 2, 2014, pp. 407-427.

Nye, Joseph S., "Get Smart: Combining Hard and Soft Power", *Foreign Affairs*, July/August 2009, pp. 160-163.

Ollapally, Deepa and Rajesh Rajagopalan, "The Pragmatic Challenge to Indian Foreign Policy", *The Washington Quarterly*, Vol. 32, No. 4, Spring 2011, pp. 145-162.

Pant, Harsh, "India in the Indian Ocean: Growing Mismatch between Ambitions and Capabilities", *Pacific Affairs*, Vol. 82, No. 2, Summer 2009, pp. 279-297.

Pashakhanlou, Arash Heydarian, "Waltz, Mearsheimer and the post-Cold

War world: The rise of America and the fall of structural realism", *International Politics*, Vol. 51, No. 3, 2014, pp. 295-315.

Phillips, Andrew, "A Dangerous Synergy: Energy Securitization, Great Power Rivalry and Strategic Stability in the Asian Century", *The Pacific Review*, Vol. 26, No. 1, 2013, pp. 17-38.

Raman, B., "China's Strategic Influence in South Asia", *Maritime Affairs: Journal of National Maritime Foundation of India*, Vol. 7, No. 2, 2011, pp. 134-141.

Rogers, James, "European (British and French) Geostrategy in the Indo–Pacific", *Journal of the Indian Ocean Region*, Vol. 9, No. 1, 2013, pp. 69-89.

Roy, Denny, "Southeast Asia and China: Balancing or Bandwagoning?", *Contemporary Southeast Asia*, Vol. 27, No. 2, 2005, pp. 305-322.

Rich, T., "Integrating Microstates into Cross-National Research: An Explanatory Analysis", *Journal of International and Global Studies*, Vol. 6, No. 1, November 2014, pp. 1-13.

Rumley, Dennis, T. Doyle and S. Chaturvedi, "Securing' the Indian Ocean? Competing regional security constructions", *Journal of the Indian Ocean Region*, Vol. 8, No. 1, 2012, pp. 1-20.

Sakhuja, Vijay, "Chinese Submarines in Sri Lanka Unnerve India: Next Stop Pakistan?", *China Brief*, Vol. 15, No. 11, May 2015, pp. 15-18.

Sakhuja, Vijay, "From Malabar to Malacca: Post-Cold War Indo-US Naval Relations", *Indian Defence Review*, Vol. 27, No. 4, December 2012, pp. 25-29.

Sardar, Ziaudin, "Coming Home: Sex, Lies and all the 'I's in India", *Futures*, Vol. 29, No. 10, 1997, pp. 891-908.

Scott, David, "The 'Indo-Pacific'-New Regional Formulations and New Maritime Frameworks for US-India Strategic Convergence", *Asia-Pacific Review*, Vol. 19, No. 2, 2012, pp. 85-109.

Scott, David, "Australia's embrace of the 'Indo-Pacific': New term, new region, new strategy?", *International Relations of the Asia-Pacific*, Vol. 13, No. 3, 2013, pp. 425-448.

Shambaugh, David, "China Engages Asia: Reshaping the Regional Order", *International Security*, Vol. 29, No. 3, Winter 2004/05, pp. 64-99.

Shambaugh, David, "Coping with a Conflicted China", *The Washington Quarterly*, Vol. 34, No. 1, 2011, pp. 7-27.

Shand, R. and K.P. Kalirajan, "Yamazawa's Open Economic Association: An Indian Ocean Grouping for Economic Cooperation", *The Developing Economies*, Vol. 35, No. 1, 1997, pp. 3-27.

Shen, Simon, "Exploring the Neglected Constraints on Chindia: Analysing the Online Chinese Perception of India and its Interaction with China's Indian Policy", *The China Quarterly*, Vol. 207, 2011, pp. 541-60.

Snyder, Glenn H., "The Security Dilemma in Alliance Politics", *World Politics*, Vol. 36, No. 4, July 1984, pp. 461-495.

Stets, J.E. and P.J. Burke, "Identity Theory and Social Identity Theory", *Social Psychology Quarterly*, Vol. 63, 2000, pp. 224-237.

Terrill, Ross, "What Does China Want?",*Wilson Quarterly*, Vol. 29, No. 4, 2005, pp. 50-61.

Wahi, Gautam, "The Common Futures of India and Pakistan: A New Approach", *Journal of Futures Studies*, Vol. 18, No. 2, 2013, pp. 83-102.

Walt, Stephen M., "Rigor or Rigor Mortis?: Rational Choice and Security Studies", *International Security*, Vol. 23, No. 4, 1999, pp. 5-48.

Wang, Vincent Wei-cheng, '"Chindia' or Rivalry? Rising China, Rising India, and Contending Perspectives on India-China Relations", *Asian Perspectives*, Vol. 35, 2011, pp. 437-69.

Xiao, Gongqin, "Superficial, Arrogant Nationalism", *China Security*, Vol. 5, 2009, pp. 53-58.

Yan, Xuetong, "The Rise of China in Chinese Eyes", *Journal of Contemporary China*, Vol. 10, No. 26, 2001, pp. 33-39.

Yi, S., "Endogenous Formation of Customs Unions under Imperfect Competition: Open Regionalism is Good", *Journal of International Economics*, Vol. 41, 1996, pp. 153-177.

Yoshihara, Toshi, "The US Navy's Indo–Pacific Challenge", *Journal of the Indian Ocean Region*, Vol. 9, No. 1, 2013, pp. 90-103.

Yoshimatsu, H., "Collective Action Problems and Regional Integration in ASEAN", *Contemporary Southeast Asia*, Vol. 28, No. 1, 2006, pp. 115-140.

Zhong Xiang, Zhang, "China's Energy Security, the Malacca Dilemma and Responses", *Energy Policy*, Vol. 39, No. 12, 2011, pp. 7612-7615.

Contributors

Prof. D. Gopal is Director, School of Social Sciences, Professor of Political Science and Head, Centre for Gandhi and Peace Studies, Indira Gandhi National Open University (IGNOU), New Delhi. Prof. Gopal has received accolades for outstanding contribution in setting up the Centre for Gandhi and Peace Studies in IGNOU. Prof. Gopal is a leading International Studies and Australian Studies scholar. He is recipient of the prestigious Government of Australia (Australia-India Council) Special Award, 2009 for Education in recognition and appreciation for his outstanding contribution towards strengthening of academic/institutional relations between India and Australia. He has extensive experience in the development of Australian Studies Programme in IGNOU; organised several international conferences on Australian Studies and has participated in Track II India-Australia Dialogues. His recent publications include *Australia in the Emerging Global Order; India-Australia: Issues and Opportunities; Politics of Globalisation; Australia and India Relations: Convergences and Divergences; Cultural Diversity: Governance and Policy; Globalisation and Regional Security: India and Australia;* and *Governance, Development and Conflict and World Peace and Global Order: Gandhian Perspectives.*

Dr. Dalbir Ahlawat is Senior Lecturer at the Department of Policing, Intelligence and Counter Terrorism, Macquarie University, NSW, Australia. Dr. Ahlawat has over 15 years' experience in conducting research on topics related to strategic and security perspectives. He has broad experience of working with government agencies and academic institutions. In addition, he has worked in collaboration with the United Nations High Commissioner for Refugees and International Organisation for Migration. Based on the research outcomes he has published three books and around 20 research papers in journals and edited books. His research interests include: Indo-Pacific strategic and security issues; Australia's security challenges; India-China strategic perceptions; US security challenges in the Indo-Pacific region.

Capt. (R) Fred C. Smith is Lecturer at the Department of Policing, Intelligence and Counter Terrorism, Macquarie University, NSW, Australia. Fred is a retired United States Navy Captain with 30 years military intelligence experience in the Pacific and Middle East, as well as assignments in Europe and the Mediterranean, with the North Atlantic Treaty Organisation (NATO), and in both Australia and Japan. He has extensive experience in all-source intelligence fusion analysis, intelligence preparation of the operational environment, operational intelligence and intelligence watch operations.

Dr. Pankaj K. Jha is Director (Research), Indian Council of World Affairs (ICWA), New Delhi. Dr. Jha has previously worked as Deputy Director with National Security Council Secretariat, Prime Minister's Office. He has also worked as Research Fellow with ICWA as Associate Fellow with Institute for Defence Studies and Analyses (IDSA). Dr Jha's areas of interests include Southeast Asia, Indo-Pacific, Indian Ocean, terrorism, and economic issues. He has widely published his research findings in reputed journals like *Strategic Analysis, Indian Defence Review, Indian Ocean Digest, World Focus, India Quarterly* and *South Asian Politics.* In addition to delivering lectures on several academic and policy platforms, he has participated in Track II India-Australia Dialogues, India-Malaysia Bilateral Strategic Dialogue and Track II dialogue with New Zealand. Recently he published a book on *India and China in Southeast Asia: Competition or Cooperation*.

Dr. Jeanne Hoffman is Assistant Professor at Tamkang University, Taiwan. Dr. Hoffman is a leading scholar on futurology and has published several research papers on the futures of China using a six pillars analysis by using the futures field (mapping, anticipating, timing, deepening, creating alternatives and transforming). She has published highly valued research papers such as '*Alternative Images of China in 2035*' in the *Journal of Futures Studies*. Previously Dr. Hoffman worked with University of the Sunshine Coast and Macquarie University.

Dr. Glenn Diesen is Associate Lecturer at the Department of Policing, Intelligence and Counter Terrorism, Macquarie University, NSW, Australia. Dr. Diesen is a specialist on Inter-democratic security institutions, security dilemma in EU and NATO relations, and Russia after the Cold War. His research focus includes ideational and institutional influence on the rationality of EU and NATO decision-makers from a neo-classical realist perspective. Academically, Dr. Diesen teaches courses having bearing on Weapons of Mass Destruction: Proliferation and Control, Contemporary Security Challenges, Security in an Age of Risk, Global Politics, and the European Union in the International System. Dr. Diesen's current research interests include European and Eurasian integration, Russian foreign policy and democratisation, global energy politics, ethno-federalism, and conflict management in the former Soviet Union and former Yugoslavia.

Prof. Chintamani Mahapatra teaches at the Centre for Canadian, US and Latin American Studies, School of International Studies, Jawaharlal Nehru University. Prof. Mahapatra's teaching and researching experience include US foreign and national security policy, international security, Asian security and globalisation. He has provided valuable inputs in assessment and evaluation of policy making at different levels including participation in Track II diplomacy. He has been awarded multi-awards, fellowships and associations both in India and Overseas. He has widely published in reputed international journals on US foreign and security policy, security dynamics and paradigms in Southeast Asia and India in the global context.

Vivek Mishra is a Research Intern with the Southeast Asia Research Programme at the Institute of Peace and Conflict Studies. His primary area of research concerns probing the US role in the Indian Ocean, Indo-Pacific and the Asia-Pacific region. Currently he is working on his doctoral research *American Maritime Strategy in the Indian Ocean in the Post-Cold War Era, 1990-2012*. Previously, he has worked as a Research Fellow with the Centre for Joint Warfare Studies, Integrated Defence Staff and Ministry of Defence. He has also been an intern with Indicia Research & Advisory, a New Delhi based think tank specialising in consultancy in the Indian defence sector and internal security.

Prof. Faisal Ahmed is Area Chairman of International Business at FORE School of Management, New Delhi. His research and consulting areas include economic integration (FTA/CECA), least developed countries (LDC) issues, South-South Cooperation, and trade & geopolitics. He has also worked as Associate Director with CUTS International, a leading think tank on international trade and WTO issues; and as faculty member in business schools in India and abroad. He has been consultant to the United Nations Economic and Social Commission for Western Asia (UNESCWA), the Associated Chambers of Commerce and Industry of India (ASSOCHAM) and other institutions. He has also led projects supported by the Ministry of Commerce & Industry and Ministry of External Affairs, Government of India. Prof Ahmed has written several research papers, chapters in edited books, monographs and articles on various aspects of international trade. His recent book is a textbook entitled *Business Environment: Indian and Global Perspective* (August, 2014) published by Prentice-Hall of India (PHI).

M. Absar Alam is a Senior Fellow at the Asian Institute of Transport Development, a New Delhi based think tank with special consultative status in the United Nations. He has been a consultant to the Asian Development Bank (ADB) and other organisations on regional integration and trade facilitation. He is co-author of the book *Business Environment: Indian and Global Perspective* published by Prentice-Hall of India (PHI).

Dr. RFI Smith:Adjunct Senior Research Fellow, Monash University, Melbourne, Australia Adjunct Professor, School of Management, RMIT University, Melbourne, Australia. Dr. Smith has very wide experience of public sector and has held several high profile public service positions, including Deputy Director General, Office of the Cabinet, Member-Public Service Board of Victoria. His current research interest include agendas for reform of federal arrangements in India and Australia.

Prof. Wang Dehua is Director of the Centre for South Asian and Central Asian Studies, Shanghai Municipal Centre for International Studies and Centre for South Asia Studies, Tongji University. He is also Professor at the Centre for National Strategic Studies, Shanghai Jiao Tong University, advisor to the China Association for South Asia Studies. He has served as Vice President of the Shanghai Association for Ecological Economic Studies. Prof. Dehua is author of more than ten books: *Dragon and Elephant: A Comparative Study of Rising China and India in the 21st Century, The Big Power's Rivalry and Securities in the Asia-Pacific Region, On Harmonious Indian Ocean, Power Game in Indian Ocean, Rising China in the Age of Oil-Price Peak,* and *The Sovereignty Dispute Over Islands and Waters of the South China Sea.*

Prof. Arvind Kumar heads the Department of Geopolitics & International Relations at Manipal University. His research interests include strategic capabilities of China and Pakistan, nuclear doctrines and strategy, nuclear weapons and delivery systems, India's internal as well as external security. He has worked as Research Faculty at the National Institute of Advanced Studies, Bangalore and the Institute for Defence Studies and Analyses (IDSA) at New Delhi. He was a Visiting Fellow at the Henry L. Stimson Centre, Washington, DC, Post-Doctoral Fellow at the Sandia National Laboratories, USA and Visiting Research Scholar at the Institute of International Studies at Stanford University. He was appointed as the Visiting Fellow at the University of New South Wales, Sydney for a three-year period. He has widely published, that include as co-editor of a volume titled *Science & Technology to Counter Terrorism* published by National Academies Press, Washington, DC.

Prof. Munmun Majumdar is faculty member of the Department of Political Science, Northeastern Hill University, Shillong, Meghalaya. Prof. Majumdar has published three books and several research papers. She has been a UGC fellow to pursue post-doctoral studies, visiting faculty to the Centre for South and Southeast Asian Studies, Calcutta University and Visiting Professor to ASEAN Centre, Chulalongkorn University, Bangkok, and Visiting Fellow, IDSA, New Delhi.

Aakash Tolani was a postgraduate scholar at the Centre for Policing, Intelligence and Counter Terrorism, Macquarie University-Australia. Currently he is pursuing advanced language studies at Charles Darwin University, Darwin. Previously he has worked as Research Fellow with The Observer Research Foundation, New Delhi-India and with the Centre for Muslim States and Societies at the University of Western Australia. Mr. Tolani has travelled widely in different conflict zones in South Asian countries. Mr Tolani's research interests include: Australia's foreign policy, Afghanistan-Pakistan affairs, China and its neighbourhood policy, rise of Islamist radicalisation in Southeast Asia and Hindu right-wing movements in India.

Index

Abbott, Tony 261, 263, 276
Abe, Shinzo 48
Adam, Jean-Paul 235
Afghanistan 15, 41, 43
    policy 40
    wars in 16
Africa 234
African nations 289
Air Defence Identification Zone (ADIZ) 37
Aksai Chin 76
Albanese, Anthony 275
American politics 145
Ansari 100, 102
anti-terrorism 253
ANZUS alliance 258
APEC 156
    Forum 154
Arab Spring 15
Arabian peninsula 159
Argentina 127
Arjuna, mythic narrative of 87
Armenia 122
Arunachal Pradesh 25, 42, 76, 90
ASEAN 144, 151, 156, 172, 234
    countries 22, 26, 162
    nations 45, 49
    states 84
Asia 28, 44, 91, 122, 129, 249
Asia-Pacific 34, 52, 245
    nations 35, 146
    Rebalance strategy 235
    region 16, 41, 64
    security 61
    strategy 145
Asia-Pacific Economic Cooperation (APEC) Forum 67-8, 153-4
Asian century 29
Asian economic community (AEC) 234
Asian Infrastructure Investment Bank (AIIB) 18, 94
Asian powers 249
Asian values 92
Aspinall, Edward 264
Assam province 90
Association of Southeast Asian Nations (ASEAN) 238
asylum 285
Atlantic Ocean 129
Auslin, Michael 62
Australia 26, 37, 43-4, 50, 61, 66-7, 71, 85, 91, 145, 155, 159, 166, 168-70, 206, 212, 215-6, 222-4, 235-6, 239, 246, 250, 256-8, 260, 263, 265-6, 274, 281-2, 286, 289
Australia-India 236
    bilateral tie 287
    relations 272-3
Australia-Indonesia relations 257, 268
Australia-Russia relationship 280

Australian domestic politics 282
Australian-Indian and Chinese defence ties 240
Australian-Indian relations 239
Australian-Indian security cooperation 239
Australian Labour Party (ALP) 206, 256
Australian polity 284, 286
Australian state 218
Australian tourists 259
Australian uranium 274
Australia's current uranium trade policy 273
Australia's Defence Cooperation programme 267
Australia's economic and strategic interests 261
Australia's illegal people movement problem 268
Australia's relationship with Indonesia 262
Australia's uranium exports 279

Bahrain 150
Bajpai, Kanti 100
Ball, William Macmahon 257-8
Bangladesh 162, 166, 170, 235
Bangladesh-China-India-Myanmar (BCIM) Economic Corridor 100
Bayuni, Endy 268
Beijing's power 118
Belarus 120, 122
Bhagavad Gita 87
Bharatiya Janata Party (BJP) 84, 248
    government 283
Biden, John 145-6
BIMSTEC 161
Bishop, Julie 277
Bisley, Nick 35
Booz Allen 236
Brazil 101
BRICS (Brazil, Russia, India, China and South Africa 18, 134
    Bank 38
    countries 128
    Development Bank 48, 94, 127
    nations 63
British imperialism 91
Brunei 50
Brzezinski, Zbigniew 21-2, 121
Buddhism 88, 97
Burma 84

Calwell, Arthur 283
Cambodia 50
Campbell, Kurt M. 145, 236
Canada 206, 278
Canberra 267, 275, 282
capitalism, modern 61
Carbon Pollution Reduction Scheme (CPRS) 284
Carlson, John 279
Central Asia 118, 120, 148, 151
Chan, Andrew 263
Changlong, Fan 22
Chifley, Ben 257
China 16-7, 20-21, 23, 49, 66, 75, 78, 83, 89, 92, 102, 120, 121, 125-6, 128-31, 134, 144, 149, 154-5, 233-4, 238-9, 250, 252-4, 266-7, 280-1, 287
    'big power' ambition 24
    economic and political success 93
    economic development 36
    economic diplomacy 44
    energy consumption 236
    influence in South and Southeast Asia 26
    international trade 127
    long-term strategy 95
    military modernisation 42, 62
    new assertiveness 52
    oil imports 236
    one-on-one relations 35
    possession of nuclear weapons 83

rising power 25
Silk Road initiative 68
supremacy 52
China and India,
civil society of 92
dispute between 237
militaries 100
China-centric Asia 43
China-India border dispute 83
China-India futures 103
China International Payment System (CIPS) 128
China-Japan 77
relations 247
China Maritime Security Cooperation 239
China-Mongolia-Russia-Belarus-Poland-Germany 129
China National Petroleum Corporation (CNPC) 128
China-Pakistan 77
Economic Corridor 237
China Seas, East and South 84
China Threat 82, 87
theory 91
Chindia 95, 101
myth 94
Chinese 235
academia 230
Academy of Social Sciences 89, 102
Bridgehead 125
forces 44
hegemony 130
incursion in Indian soil 24
incursions 86
influence 42, 123
leadership 19, 21
legacy, ancient 20
naval capability 150
Navy 237
nuclear submarine 240
power 136
primacy 26
society 97
supremacy in Asia 83
Task Forces 237
Union Pay cards 128
-led Asian Infrastructure Investment Bank (128
-Russian border 125
Chinese People's Liberation Army (PLA) 233
Christianity 97
Christians 97
Civil Nuclear Cooperation Agreement 27
Classical Chinese statecraft 89
Clinton, Bill 85
Clinton, Hillary 43, 61, 145, 235
Cold War 36, 49, 77, 249
end of the 15, 233, 250, 252
legacy 42
rivalries 274
Colombo 84
Colonel Huang Shuofeng 89
Commonwealth Grants Commission 216
Communist Party of China 35, 84, 101
Comoros 166, 170
Confucian approach 21
Confucianism 97
Congress Party 207-8, 283
Conroy, Stephen 275
corruption 88
Council for the Australian Federation (CAF) 217
Council of Australian Governments (COAG) 217, 221-3
Reform Council 220
Council on Foreign Relations (CFR) 67
counter-terrorism 265
Cuba 126

Dai Bing 26
Dalai Lama 76, 90

democracy and globalisation 82
democracy and human rights 265
Dempsey, Martin 40
Direct Communications Link (DCL) 66
Disparities 211
domestic social issues 88
Doval, Ajit 101

East Asia 232
  Economic Community 63
  Summit (EAS) 63, 153
  powers 24
  security 71
East China Sea (ECS) 37, 252
East Siberia-Pacific Ocean (ESPO) 128
Eastern Asia 266
Eastern Indian Ocean (EIO) 66
Eastern Siberian 128
economic liberalism 219
economic reforms 211, 214
Eisenhower administration 153
Enlai, Zhou 76, 91
environmental pollution 88, 267
Eurasian strategy 122
Eurasian Union 122
Europe 122, 129
European identity 117
European powers 128
European Russia 118
European Union (EU) 15-6, 119, 130, 172, 234
Exclusive Economic Zones (EEZs) 45

Fealy, Greg 259
federalism 220
Finance Commission 212-3
fiscal federalism 212
Five Principles of Peaceful Co-existence 100
France 128
Free-Trade Agreement 135
Fukushima accident 133

G20 128
Gandhi, Indira 209
Gandhi, Mahatma 85
Gandhi, Rajiv 101, 209
Garrett, Peter 275
Gartzke 82
General Bikram Singh 100
Germany 21, 83, 120, 128
Gillard, Julia 275, 281, 285
Goods and Services Tax (GST) 213
Gorbachev 119
Grare 281
Grubel, Herb 170
Guen-hye, Park 130
Gujarat 98
Gwadar 84

Hagel, Chuck 47-8
Hailing, Ye 89
Harrison, Selig 67
Hawke, Bob 218-9, 256
Herawati, Kristiani 261
Howard, John 219, 256, 259, 280
Huntington, Samuel P. 24

income gap 88
India 26, 37, 44, 50-1, 66, 75, 78, 85, 89, 98, 102, 118, 127, 135, 145, 149-50, 166-8, 170, 204, 212, 222-4, 234, 250, 281, 283, 286-7
India and China 97-8, 101
  economic and political rise of 93
India and Pakistan 28
India-ASEAN Commemorative Summit 62
India-China 77
  border negotiations 101
  relations 100
  relationship 86
  solidarity 95
  strategic challenges 23

strategic relationship 79, 102
India-Japan relations 248
India-Pakistan 77
dispute over Kashmir 25
India-US 28
strategic dialogue 28
Indian and Chinese independence 76
Indian and Chinese leaders, world-views of 101
Indian bureaucracy 280
Indian Kashmir 24
Indian middle classes 91
Indian Ocean 77, 158-9, 165, 233, 236, 238, 240, 246, 252
democracies 273
Indian Ocean Region (IOR) 144, 150, 248
Indian Ocean Rim 245
land 247
Indian Ocean Rim Association 63
for Regional Cooperation 65
IOR-ARC (Indian Ocean Rim Association for Regional 159
IOR-ARC countries 161, 173
IOR-ARC region 172
Indian society 214
Indian subcontinent 159
India's Act East policy 68
India's decision making process 251
India's geopolitics 251
India's pragmatism in trade 288
India's problems 98
India's strategic balancing role 27
Indo-Chinese wars 274
Indo-Pacific 41, 148, 265, 282
concept 68
futures 79
multilateralism in the 63
oceans 235
order 253
power 247
region 16, 19, 27, 34, 51-2, 117-8, 123-4, 134, 146-7, 150-2, 155, 233, 245, 248-9, 251-4, 281
security architecture 246, 249, 252
security environment 53
strategic 33
Indo-Pacific Economic Corridor (IPEC) 144, 148, 151
Indo-Russo partnership 134
Indo-US naval cooperation 150
Indo-US relationship 146
Indonesia 37, 50,-1, 61, 91, 154, 162, 166-8, 170, 172, 255-6, 258, 260, 265-7
Indonesia-Australia relations 262-4
Indonesian Democratic Party-Struggle 262
Inter-State Commission 213
Inter-State Council 212
International Atomic Energy Agency safeguards 274
International Monetary Fund (IMF) 17, 209
international terrorism 40
Iran 40-1, 165-6, 170, 233
Iraq 15-6, 43
Islamic fundamentalism 125
Italy 128

Jakarta-Canberra relations 268
Japan 18, 21, 26, 28, 35, 37, 43-6, 48, 50, 52, 66, 71, 84-5, 91, 118, 130, 133, 150, 154, 232, 234-6, 246, 250-2, 267, 274
Japan-India 77, 236
Japanese aircraft 46
Japanese investments 133
Japanese Senkaku Islands 37
Japan's anti-China overtures 22
Jenkins 210-11
Jinping, Xi 38, 49, 93, 99, 101-2, 237, 238, 240
Chinese President 19

Jokowi 263, 266-7

Kalla, Jusuf 261
Kant, Immanuel 82
Kantian peace ethic 101
Kaplan, Robert 236
Kauravas 87
Kazakhstan 120, 122, 289
Keating, Paul 218-9, 256, 259
Kennedy, Paul 67
Kenya 162, 166-7, 170
Keqiang, Li 237
Kerry, John 145-6
Kim Jong Il 132
Korea 43, 71, 232, 234
Korean Peninsula 153
Krishna 87
Kudankulam 278
Kyrgyzstan 122

Labour Party 281-3, 285
Laos 50
Liberal Party 284
liberalisation 215
Ling, Wang 91
Lloyd, Peter 170
Locklear, Samuel J. 145-6
Lombok Treaty 256
Longyu, Yu 88
Lower Mekong Initiative (LMI) 144
Lyon 274

Madagascar 166, 170
Mahan, Alfred Thayer 236
Maharashtra 98
Malaysia 37, 50-1, 127, 162, 166-8, 170, 172, 285
Malik, Mohan 95
Mattis, James 34
Mauritius 162, 166, 170, 252
McMahon Line 84
Medcalf, Rory 281
Medvedev, Dimitri 127
Menon, Shivshankar 102
Menzies, Robert 258, 274
Modi, Narendra 42, 70, 84, 99, 101, 135, 232, 239, 248
  government 207
  view 102
Mongolia 289
Mozambique 162, 166-7
Mughal Empire 92
multi-polar world system 21
Multi-Sectoral Technical and Economic Cooperation 66
Multilateralism 63
Muslim-majority country by 2050 98
Myanmar 50, 84, 154, 235

Namibia 278
National Democratic Alliance government 214
National Development Council 212
Nehru, Jawaharlal 76, 208, 214, 273
Nehruvian ideology 250
Nehruvian principles 249
New Zealand 37, 50, 66, 154, 155
North American Free Trade Agreement 234
North Atlantic Treaty Organisation (NATO) 15, 94, 118-9, 123, 153
  alliance partners 22
  member states 128
North Korea 38, 130, 132
  border 131
Northeast Asia 133, 248, 265
Norway 133
nuclear powers 278, 287
Nuclear Suppliers Group (NSG) 281-3
nuclear tests 28, 283

Obama, Barack 27-8, 39-41, 68
  administration, 67, 145-6, 150, 153-4, 233
Oman 162

Pacific Ocean 237
Pakistan 24-5, 38, 40-2, 84, 92, 98, 100, 152, 235, 274, 287
Pakistan Occupied Kashmir 24
Pakistan's nuclear programme 27
Pakistan's strategic programme 86
Panchsheel Treaty 100
People's Liberation Army (PLA) 19-20
People's Liberation Army Navy (PLAN) 41
Persian Gulf 149
Philippines 37, 43, 45, 50, 52, 232, 234
Phillips, Andrew 35
piracy and terrorism 248
Planning Commission 212, 214
Poland 120
Portuguese East Timor 259
post-Cold War security 118
Protocol, Kyoto 283
Purchasing Power Parity (PPP) 76
Putin 124, 133

radiation pollution 275
Raja Mohan, C. 233
Rao, M. Govinda 213
Rao, Narasimha 209
Regional Comprehensive Economic Partnership (RCEP) 160
Regional Economic Zones 63
Regional Settlement Agreement 285
Regional Trade Agreements (RTAs) 63
Republic of Korea (ROK) 236
Reserve Bank of India 77
Ricardian hypothesis 169
Right to Information Act 210
Rudd, Kevin 281, 284
Rumsfeld, Donald H. 235
Russia 21, 38, 85, 118, 120-2, 124-6, 128-31, 133, 135, 250, 274, 280
  China-India alliance 91
Russian energy supplies 16
Russian Federation 66
Russian power 118
Russian-Japanese relations 133
Russian-led Customs Union 137
Russia's relationship with India 136

SAARC 161
Sakhalin–Khabarovsk–Vladivostok (SKV) 124
Sea Lines of Communication (SLOC) 147, 235-6
Seychelles 167
Shanghai Cooperation Organisation 18, 38
Shastri, Lal Bahadur 208
Shergold, Peter 283
Shinohara, Naoyuki 128
Siagian, Sabam 268
Sikkim 90
Singapore 50, 85, 91, 127, 133, 154, 162, 166-8, 170, 172, 252, 267
Singh, Manmohan 61, 209
Singh, Nirvikar 213
Sino-Indian border 237
  war of 1962 84
Sino-Indian relations 78
Sino-Indian War of 1962 85
Sino-Japanese tension 154
Sino-Russian strategic partnership 128
social inclusion 98
social injustice 88
Sood, Vikram 83
South Africa 166-8, 170, 172
  apartheid policies 274
South Asia 89, 148, 249, 274
South Asian countries 42
South China Sea 22, 43, 152, 234, 252, 264-6
South China Sea islands 19
South China Sea strategy 155
South Korea 44, 48, 50, 66, 84-5, 91, 118, 127, 130-3, 250

South Pacific islands 70
Southeast Asia 26, 144-5, 148, 159, 209, 246, 248
Southeast Asia Treaty Organisation (SEATO) 153, 274
Southeast Asian nations 49
Southeast Asian region 265
Southern and Eastern Africa 159
Soviet Republics 122
Soviet Union 90, 133, 236
spiritual awakening 99
spirituality 98
Spykman, Nicholas John 236
Sri Lanka 25, 84, 166-7, 235, 240, 252
Srivijaya Kingdom 266
Suez Canal crisis 274
Suharto, General 256, 259
Sukarnoputri, Megawati 259, 262
Sukumaran, Myuran 263
Sumerian prominence 158
Sun Tzu, Chinese strategist 19
Swadhyaya movement 97-8
Swaraj , Sushma 99
SWIFT system 126, 128
Switzerland 127
Syahrir, Sutan 258

Taiwan 44, 50, 84, 133, 250
Talwar, Puneet 151
Tanzania 162, 166-8
Taoism 97
Tarapur Atomic Power Station (TAPS) 278
Tawang-Arunachal Pradesh 24
Telangana region 214
Terrill, Ross 95
Thailand 50-1, 91, 162, 166-8, 170, 172
Trans-Korean-Railway (TKR) 131
Trans-Pacific Partnership (TPP) 63, 154, 160
Turnbull, Malcolm 283-4

UAE 166-8, 172
UK 127, 258
Ukraine 120, 134
UN Security Council 90, 94
    membership 17
unclear 284
United Arab Emirates (UAE) 159
United Kingdom 18
United Nations Human Rights Committee (UNHRC) 286
United Progressive Alliance (UPA) 206
United States (US) 15-8, 20, 23, 26, 28, 37-9, 49-50, 62, 66-7, 69, 76, 78, 81, 84, 92, 97, 102, 133-4, 145, 148-50, 154, 233, 236, 248, 250-1, 258, 265, 274, 281, 288
    alliance partners 44
    alliance system 19, 44
    and China 118
    forces in Australia 40
    forces in Japan 40
    forces in South Korea 40
    forces in the Philippines 40
    foreign policy 144
    hegemony 16, 119, 121
    Indo-Pacific strategy 146
    military alliance relationship 45
    Unipolar World with a Multi-polar Asia 39
UPA government 211, 213
uranium 281, 286
US-Australia 236
US-China: Counterbalance through Strategic Engagem 42
US-Chinese bipolar 118, 137
US-India civil nuclear agreement 281
US-India relationship 28, 41
US-India-Australia 236
US-India-Japan 236
US-Japan Security Treaty 46
US-Japan-Korea 236
US-led TPP 155

US Pacific Command (PACOM) 146
US-Philippines Mutual Defence Treaty 47
Uzbekistan 120

Vajpayee, Atal Bihari 85, 87
Verma, Bharat 83
Vietnam 26, 28, 37, 45, 47, 50, 84-5, 118, 130, 154, 232, 234, 283
    War 282, 285, 289
Vladivostok 131

Weiwei, Zhang 87
Wendt, Alexander 84
West Asia 247
West Irian 258
West Pacific Naval Symposium (WPNS) 71
Western anti-China forces 88
Western Asia 266
Western countries 15
Western European states 15
Western naval powers 257
Western Pacific 233, 238, 246
Western values 21
Western Xinjiang province 125
Whitlam, Gough 256, 283
Widodo, Joko 262, 264, 268
Wiki Leaks cables 282
Williamson, Oliver 224
World Bank 17, 94, 210
World Trade Organisation 173
World War, Second 16, 18, 35, 125, 133
world's largest economy 92
world's most populous nation 92

Xiangsham Forum 48
Xiaoping, Deng 19
Xinhua 238
Xuetong, Yan 91, 97

Yamen 166
Yeltsin administration 119
Yemen 162, 252
Yi, Wang 99
Yuan, Luo 40
Yuanchao, Li 100
Yudhoyono, Susilo Bambang 261-2
    government 264
Yujun, Yang 48

Zedong, Mao 90-1, 238
Zheng 237-8